D1532195

THE BASTILLE

A book in the series

Bicentennial Reflections on the French Revolution

General Editors: *Keith Michael Baker,* Stanford University
Steven Laurence Kaplan, Cornell University

The Cultural Origins of the French Revolution,
Roger Chartier

Soldiers of the French Revolution,
Alan Forrest

Revolutionary News: The Press in France, 1789–1799,
Jeremy Popkin

A Rhetoric of Bourgeois Revolution:
The Abbe Sieyes and What Is the Third Estate?
William H. Sewell Jr.

THE BASTILLE

A HISTORY OF A SYMBOL OF DESPOTISM
AND FREEDOM

Hans-Jürgen Lüsebrink and Rolf Reichardt

Translated by Norbert Schürer

DUKE UNIVERSITY PRESS

Durham and London

1997

© 1997 Duke University Press
All rights reserved
Printed in the United States of America
on acid-free paper ∞
Originally published as *Die "Bastille":
Zur Symbolgeschichte von Herrschaft und Freiheit*
by Fischer Taschenbuch Verlag, 1990.
Library of Congress Cataloging-in-Publication
Data appear on the last printed page of this book.
Publication of this work was made possible by a grant from
Inter Nationes program for the promotion of translations
of German books into universal languages.

CONTENTS

Editors' Introduction   vii

Preface   xvii

Translator's Note   xix

Introduction   1

1. Genesis of a Political Symbol: The Bastille, 1715–1789   6

   Anti-Bastille Journalism: Scandalous Stories of Prisoners   6

   The Reality-Forming Power of the Symbolic:
   Prison Practice versus Social Consciousness   26

2. The Storming of the Bastille: The Historical Event
   as Collective Symbolic Action   38

   The Storming of the Bastille: Causes and Process   38

   How a Decisive Event in World History
   Is "Made": The Symbolic Exaggeration of 14 July 1789   47

3. Revolutionary Symbolism under the Sign of the Bastille,
   1789–1799: A Prime Example of the Self-Mystification of the
   French Revolution   79

   Radicalization and Diversification of a Collective Symbol   79

The New Heroes: The Role-Model Function and Self-Staging
of the Victors of the Bastille   86

Martyrs of Freedom, Victims of Despotism:
The Triumph of the Prisoners of the Bastille   106

"The Patriot" Palloy:
Conqueror of the Bastille and Vulgarizer   118

The Patriotic Cult of Relics: The Staging of the Bastille Stones
in Paris and in the French Provinces   131

The Symbolic Foundation of National Identity: Festivals,
Speeches, and Monuments Commemorating 14 July 1789   147

Revolutionary Activism under the Sign of the Bastille   169

Echo and Export of Bastille Symbolism Abroad: Germany as a
Significant Example   181

Appendix A   200
Appendix B   202
Appendix C   203

4. Bastille Symbolism in Modern France: The Republican Legacy
of the French Revolution   205

Heroic Martyrs of Freedom in History and Literature   205

The Storming of the Bastille: A National Act of Faith   212

Utilizations in Domestic Politics: From the July Revolution
to the Resistance   220

Appendix A   239
Appendix B   239

Final Remarks: On the Origin and Function
of a Historical Symbol   241

Appendix: Reports on the Storming of the Bastille, 1789   247

Notes   251

Works Cited   287

Index   297

I N PARIS, IN THIS SYMBOLIC NIGHT OF 14 JULY, NIGHT OF fervor and of joy, at the foot of the timeless obelisk, in this Place de la Concorde that has never been more worthy of the name, [a] great and immense voice . . . will cast to the four winds of history the song expressing the ideal of the five hundred Marseillais of 1792." The words, so redolent in language and tone of the instructions for the great public festivals of the French Revolution, are those of Jack Lang, French Minister of Culture, Communications, Great Public Works, and the Bicentennial. The text is that of the program for the grandiose opera-parade presenting "a Marseillaise for the World," the internationally televised spectacle from Paris crowning the official celebration of the bicentennial of the French Revolution.

The minister's language was aptly fashioned to the occasion. It was well chosen to celebrate Paris as world-historical city—joyous birthplace of the modern principles of democracy and human rights—and the Revolution of 1789 as the momentous assertion of those universal human aspirations to freedom and dignity that have transformed, and are still transforming, an entire world. It was no less well chosen to leap over the events of the Revolution from its beginning to its end, affirming that the political passions engendered by its momentous struggles had finally ceased to divide the French one from another.

The spectacle on the Place de la Concorde exemplified the unavowed motto of the official bicentennial celebration: "The Revolution is over." Opting for a celebration consonant with the predominantly centrist, consensualist mood of the French in the late 1980s, the presidential mission charged with the organization of the bicentennial celebrations focused on the values which the vast majority of French citizens of all political persuasions underwrite—the ideals exalted in the Declaration of the Rights of Man. It offered the nation—and the world—the image of a France finally at peace with itself: a people secure in the tranquil enjoyment of the human rights that constitute France's true revolutionary patrimony, confident in the maturity of French institutions and their readiness to meet the challenges and opportunities of a new European order, firm in the country's dedication to securing universal respect for the democratic creed it claims as its most fundamental contribution to the world of nations. No hint of subsequent radicalization, no echo of social conflict, no shadow of the Terror could mar this season of commemoration. It followed that the traditional protagonists and proxies in the great debate over the Revolution's character and purposes, Danton and Robespierre, were to be set aside. The hero for 1989 was Condorcet: savant, philosopher, reformer, "moderate" revolutionary, victim of the Revolution he failed to perfect and control.

But the Revolution—ambiguous, complex, subversive as it remains, even after two hundred years—still proved refractory to domestication. Not even the solemn bicentennial spectacle on the night of 14 July was sheltered from certain treacherous counterpoints. Spectators watching the stirring parade unfold down the Champs-Élysées toward the Place de la Concorde already knew that this same route would shortly be followed by participants in a counterrevolutionary commemoration returning a simulacrum of the guillotine to its most notorious revolutionary site. These spectators were moved by the poignant march of Chinese youths pushing their bicycles in evocation of the recent massacre in Tienanmen Square, even as this brutal silencing of demands for human rights was being justified in Beijing as reluctant defense of the Revolution against dangerous counterrevolutionary elements. The spectators were stirred by Jessye Norman's heroic rendition of the *Marseillaise,* even as it reminded all who cared to attend to its words that this now universal chant of liberation was also a ferocious war song calling for the letting of the "impure blood" of the enemy. On the very day of the parade a politely exasperated Margaret Thatcher, publicly contesting the French claim to the paternity of the Rights of Man and insisting on the identity of Revolution with Terror, reminded the world of the jolting equation, 1789 = 1793. For their part, the performers sent by the USSR to march in the parade, garbed in dress more Russian than Soviet, raised questions about the socialist axiom that the Russian Revolution was the necessary conclusion to the French. As men and women throughout the communist world rallied for human rights, was it any longer possible to see 1917 as the authentic future of 1789?

The tensions and contradictions of commemoration have their own political and cultural dynamic, but they are nourished by the tensions and contradictions of historical interpretation. If the Revolution has been declared over in France, its history is far from terminated — either there or elsewhere. Indeed, the bicentennial of the French Revolution has reopened passionate historiographical debates over its meaning that began with the Revolution itself. As early as September 1789, readers of the *Révolutions de Paris* — one of the earliest and most widely read of the newspapers that were to play so powerful a role in shaping the revolutionary consciousness — were demanding "a historical and political picture of everything that has happened in France since the first Assembly of Notables," to be offered as a means of explaining the nature of "the astonishing revolution that has just taken place." Observers and participants alike sought from the outset to grasp the causes, nature, and effects of these remarkable events. And if they concurred on the momentous character of the Revolution, they differed vehemently on its necessity, its means, its fundamental mission. Burke and Paine, Barnave and de Maistre, Condorcet and Hegel were only among the first in a dazzling succession of thinkers who have responded to the need to plumb the historical identity and significance of a phenomenon that has seemed from its very beginning to demand, yet defy, historical comprehension.

This rich tradition of political-philosophical history of the Revolution, which resounded throughout the nineteenth century, was muted and profoundly modified in the wake of the centennial celebrations. In France, 1889 inaugurated a new age in revolutionary historiography dedicated to that marriage between republicanism and positivism that underlay the very creation of the Third Republic. This marriage gave birth, within the university, to the new Chair in the History of the French Revolution at the Sorbonne to which Alphonse Aulard was elected in 1891. From this position, occupied for more than thirty years, Aulard directed the first scholarly journal devoted to the study of the Revolution, presided over the preparation and publication of the great official collections of revolutionary documents, and formed students to spread the republican-positivist gospel. He established and institutionalized within the university system an official, putatively scientific history: a history dedicated to discovering and justifying, in the history of the Revolution, the creation of those republican, parliamentary institutions whose promise was now finally being secured in more felicitous circumstances. Danton, the patriot determined in 1793 to institute the emergency government of the Terror to save the Republic in danger, but opposed in 1794 to continuing it once that danger had eased, became the hero of Aulard's French Revolution.

Given his institutional authority, his posture as scientific historian, and his engaged republicanism, Aulard was able to marginalize conservative interpretations of the Revolution, ridiculing the amateurism of Hippolyte Taine's frightened account of its origins in the philosophic spirit and culmination in the horrors of mass violence, and dismissing, as little more than reactionary ideology, Augustin Cochin's analysis of the genesis and implications of Jacobin sociability. Within the university, the revolutionary heritage became a patrimony to be managed, rather than merely a creed to be inculcated. But this did not preclude bitter divisions over the manner in which that patrimony was to be managed, or its now sacred resources deployed. Aulard's most talented student, Albert Mathiez, became his most virulent critic. The rift was more than an oedipal conflict over the republican mother, Marianne. Mathiez questioned Aulard's scientific methods; but above all, he detested his mentor's Dantonist moderation. As an alternative to an opportunistic, demagogic, and traitorous Danton, he offered an Incorruptible, Robespierre, around whom he crafted a popular, socialist, and Leninist reading of the Revolution. The Bolshevik experience reinforced his Robespierrism, investing it with a millennial hue, and stimulated him to undertake his most original work on the "social movement" of the Terror. Thereafter the relationship between the Russian Revolution and the French Revolution, between 1917 and 1793, haunted the Marxianized republican interpretation to which Mathiez devoted his career.

Although Mathiez was denied Aulard's coveted chair, he taught in the same university until his early death. His exact contemporary, Georges Lefebvre, shared much of his political sensibility and his interest in history from below, and succeeded him as president of the Society for Robespierrist Studies. Lefebvre's election to the Sorbonne chair in 1937 proved decisive for the consolidation, and indeed the triumph, of a social interpretation of the French Revolution based on the principles of historical materialism. More sociological than Mathiez in his approach, and more nuanced in his judgments, he broke fresh ground with his monumental work on the peasants (whose autonomy and individuality he restituted) and his subsequent studies of social structure; and he rescued important issues from vain polemics. His rigor, his pedagogical talent, and the muted quality of his Marxism—most effectively embodied in the celebrated study of 1789 he published for the sesquicentennial of the French Revolution in 1939—earned him, his chair, and the interpretation he promoted worldwide prestige. After 1945, and until his death in 1959, he presided over international research in the field as director of his Institute for the History of the French Revolution at the Sorbonne. Under Lefebvre's aegis, the Marxianized republican interpretation of the French Revolution became the dominant paradigm of revolutionary historiography in France following the Second World War; and it was largely adopted, from the French leaders in the field, by the growing number of historians specializing in the subject who became so striking a feature of postwar academic expansion, particularly in English-speaking countries.

Lefebvre conveyed his mantle of leadership to his student, Albert Soboul, who succeeded to the Sorbonne chair in 1967. Soboul owed his scholarly fame above all to his pioneering thesis on the Parisian sansculottes, a work recently subjected to severe criticism of its sociological and ideological analyses, its understanding of the world of work, and its often teleological and tautological methods. But his influence far transcended this acclaimed monograph. A highly placed member of the French Communist party as well as director of the Institute for the History of the French Revolution, Soboul saw himself as both a "scientific" and a "communist-revolutionary" historian. Tireless, ubiquitous, and prolific, he tenaciously rehearsed the Marxist account of the French Revolution as a bourgeois revolution inscribed in the logic of the necessary transition from feudalism to capitalism. But his relish for confrontation, and his assertive defense of an increasingly rigid orthodoxy, eventually invited—and made him the chief target of—the revisionist assault on the dominant interpretation of the Revolution as mechanistic, reductive, and erroneous.

Challenges to the hegemony of the Sorbonne version of the history of the French Revolution were offered in the late 1950s and early

1960s by Robert Palmer's attempt to shift attention toward the democratic politics of an Atlantic Revolution and, more fundamentally, by Alfred Cobban's frontal assault on the methodological and political assumptions of the Marxist interpretation. But such was the power of the scholarly consensus that, condemned more or less blithely in Paris, these works drew relatively little immediate support. Not until the late 1960s and early 1970s did the revisionist current acquire an indigenous French base, both intellectual and institutional. The charge was led by François Furet, who left the Communist party in 1956 and has subsequently gravitated toward the liberal political center. One of the first French historians to become intimately familiar with Anglo-American scholarship (and with American life more generally), Furet served as the third president of the École des Hautes Études en Sciences Sociales, accelerating its development into one of Europe's leading centers for research in the social sciences and humanities—and a formidable institutional rival to the Sorbonne. Disenchanted with Marxism, he also turned away from the *Annales* tradition of quantitative social and cultural history vigorously espoused in his earlier work. For the past fifteen years he has sustained a devastating critique of the Jacobin-Leninist "catechism," redirecting scholarly attention to the dynamics of the Revolution as an essentially political and cultural phenomenon; to the logic, contradictions, and pathos of its invention of democratic sociability; to its fecundity as a problem for the political and philosophical inquiries of the nineteenth century upon whose inspiration he insists historians must draw.

It is one of the great ironies of revolutionary historiography, then, that whereas the centennial of the Revolution inaugurated the consolidation of the official republican exegesis, so the bicentennial has marked the disintegration of its Marxist descendant. The field of inquiry is now more open, more fluid, more exciting than it has been for many decades. By the same token, it is also shaped by concerns and sensibilities deriving from recent changes and experiences. These latter are many and varied. Any comprehensive list would have to include the eclipse of Marxism as an intellectual and political force; the dramatic decline in the fortunes of communism, especially in France; the resurgence of liberalism in the West, with its rehabilitation of the market as model and morality, asserting the intrinsic connection between political liberty and laissez-faire; the dramatic shifts in the East from Gulag to glasnost and perestroika, from Maoism to Westernization, with their oblique and overt avowals of communist failure and ignominy extending from Warsaw to Moscow to Beijing. But such a list could not omit the memory of the Holocaust and the traumas of decolonization among colonized and colonizers alike, from the Algerian War to the sanguinary horrors of Polpotism. It would have to include the stunning triumph and the subsequent exhaustion of the *Annales* paradigm, with its metaphor of levels of determination privileging a long-run perspective and quantitative techniques; the emergence of a new cultural history, pluralistic and aggressive, fueled by diverse disciplinary and counterdisciplinary energies; the striking development of the École des Hautes Études en Sciences Sociales as counterweight to the traditional French university; and the efflorescence of a tradition of French historical studies outside France whose challenge to Parisian hegemony in the field can no longer be ignored. Neither could it neglect the dramatic eruption of the revolutionary imagination in the events of 1968, and the new radical politics of race, sex, and gender that have become so profound a preoccupation in subsequent decades.

The implications of this new situation for the study of the French Revolution are profound. Many fundamental assumptions, not only about the Revolution itself but about how to study it, have been called into question. Though the Revolution is better known today than ever before, the collapse of the hegemonic structure of learning and interpretation has revealed egregious blind spots in what has hitherto counted for knowledge and understanding. While the republican-Marxist view innovated in certain areas, it sterilized research in many others. Today it is no longer possible to evoke complaisantly the bourgeois character of the Revolution, either in terms of causes or effects; the roles, indeed the very definition, of other social actors need to be reexamined. A rehabilitated political approach is avidly reoccupying the ground of a social interpretation in serious need of reformulation. Questions of ideology, discourse, gender, and cultural practices have surged to the forefront in fresh ways. Fewer and fewer historians are willing to accept or reject the Revolution "en bloc," while more and more are concerned with the need to fathom and connect its multiple and contradictory components. The Terror has lost the benefit of its relative immunity and isolation. And despite extravagant and often pathetic hyperbole, the Right has won its point that the Vendée in particular—and the counterrevolutionary experience in general—require more probing and balanced treatment, as do the post-Thermidorian terrors. Finally, there is a widespread sense that the narrow periodization of Revolutionary studies must be substantially broadened.

When the bicentennial dust settles, there will therefore be much for historians of the French Revolution to do. Many questions will require genuinely critical research and discussion, searching reassessment, vigorous and original synthesis. Our ambition in editing these Bicentennial Reflections on the French Revolution is to contribute to this endeavor. In organizing the series, which will comprise twelve volumes, we have sought to identify fundamental issues and problems—problems that have hitherto been treated in fragmentary fashion; issues around which conventional wisdom has disintegrated in the course of current debates—which will be crucial to any new account of the French Revolution. And we have turned to some of the finest historians in what has become an increasingly international field of study, asking them to reassess their own understanding of these matters in the light of their personal research and that of others, and to present the results of their reflections to a wider audience in relatively short, synthetic works that will also offer a critical point of departure for further work in the field. The authors share with us the belief that the time is ripe for a fundamental rethinking. They will of course proceed with this rethinking in their own particular fashion.

The events that began to unfold in France in 1789 have, for two hundred years, occupied a privileged historical site. The bicentennial has served as a dramatic reminder that not only our modern notions of revolution and human rights, but the entire range of our political discourse derives from them. The French Revolution has been to the modern world what Greece and Rome were to the Renaissance and its heirs: a condensed world of acts and events, passions and struggles, meanings and symbols, constantly reconsidered and reimagined in the attempt to frame—and implement—an understanding of the nature, conditions, and possibilities of human action in their relation to politics, culture, and social process. To those who would change the world, the Revolution still offers a script continuously elaborated and extended—in parliaments and prisons; in newspapers and manifestoes; in revolutions and repressions; in families, armies, and encounter groups. . . . To those who would interpret the world, it still presents the inexhaustible challenge of comprehending the nature of the extraordinary mutation that gave birth to the modern world.

"Great year! You will be the *regenerating year,* and you will be known by that name. History will extol your great deeds," wrote Louis-Sébastien Mercier, literary anatomist of eighteenth-century Paris, in a rhapsodic *Farewell to the Year 1789.* "You have changed *my Paris,* it is true. It is completely different today. . . . For thirty years I have had a secret presentiment that I would not die without witnessing a great political event. I nourished my spirit on it: there is *something new* for my pen. If *my Tableau* must be *redone,* at least it will be said one day: In this year Parisians . . . stirred, and this impulse has been communicated to France and the rest of Europe." Historians of the French Revolution may not bid farewell to the bicentennial year in Mercier's rapturous tones. But they will echo at least one of his sentiments. Our tableau must be redone; there is something new for our pens.

Keith Michael Baker and Steven Laurence Kaplan
26 August 1989

PREFACE

T HE FOLLOWING CASE STUDY IN THE HISTORY OF A SYM-
bol emerged from a research project that was generously
supported by the Volkswagen-Stiftung over several years.
It constitutes a distilled version of a much broader investigation of
sources that cannot be provided here. This explains the density of presentation, which in places may go too far; nevertheless we hope that
readers will be rewarded for their concentrated reading. While the
iconography forms an integral part of our presentation, only a small
selection of it could be drawn on here. The world of prints is more
extensively explored in the exhibition catalog *Die Bastille: Symbolik und
Mythos in der Revolutionsgraphik* (The Bastille: Symbolism and myth in
the prints of the revolution).

That the Bastille is a collective symbol in the widest sense is apparent in the fact that the search for material can never be concluded,
since traces of a symbol can appear almost anywhere. In our investigation, we have therefore had to rely on the references of others
and would especially like to thank Christian Amalvi, Birgit Barufke,
Philippe Bordes, Robert Darnton, Martin Dinges, Claudia Fink,
Gudrun Gersmann, Thomas Grosser, Jacques Guilhaumou, Klaus
Herding, Gerd van den Heuvel, Werner Jost, Michael Meinzer, Pierre
Rétat, Alain Ruiz, Wolfgang Schmale, Herbert Schneider, Winfried
Schulze, Hans-Ulrich Seifert, Jürgen Voss, and Michael Wagner for
their valuable help.

H.-J.L. and R.R.

TRANSLATOR'S NOTE

A T THE END OF THE PREFACE IN THE GERMAN ORIGINAL, THE authors point out that "all quotations from French sources have been translated." While in this English edition all quotations have of course been translated into English, the authors in the German version also supply "the original [French] text for especially important quotations, and . . . ones that are hard to locate — provided they are not too long — in the footnotes." This practice is not followed in the present translation.

The only other major change in this translation concerns the arrangement of notes. While the German original relies exclusively on footnotes and then appends a bibliography, I have here chosen a three-part structure. First, extensive lists of sources that Lüsebrink and Reichardt provide in several of their footnotes — corpuses for specific investigations — are placed at the end of the relevant chapters or at the back of the volume as appendixes, which the tables and the quotations in the text then refer to by numbers. Second, the notes themselves contain complete bibliographical information either when they are references rather than sources of quotations, or when they concern quotations from manuscripts and anonymous newspaper articles. Third, the notes otherwise give short titles that refer to the list of works cited. This list in turn is divided into a section of primary sources and one of secondary works and studies.

Finally, I would like to thank Julie Harkness, Professor Cary Nathenson, Anjali Prabhu, Professor James Thompson, and Professor Jennifer Thorn for their friendship and support throughout the work on this translation.

N.S.

INTRODUCTION

RECENTLY, A YOUNG GERMAN STUDENT TOLD THE STORY of her first trip to Paris. At the earliest opportunity, she got out at the metro stop "Bastille" in order to visit the famous prison of which there had been so much talk in her history lessons, a place that was the first thing she thought of whenever the French Revolution was mentioned. To her surprise, however, she found a square busy with traffic surrounding the July Column with its Genius of Liberty instead of the ruins of the fortress conquered by the people of Paris on 14 July 1789 and was ashamed of her ignorance.

This anecdote is not as banal and insignificant as it may sound at first. For it seems to be symptomatic of the continuing presence of a phenomenon that long ago materially disappeared with the immediate demolition of the Paris Bastille (1789–90) but that still exists in people's imagination. Primarily, this is of course true in France. The Bastille is not invoked only on the national holiday every year. The opening volume of a new series of juvenile historical fiction,[1] a competition of modern painters and graphic designers,[2] and the project of a monumental glass picture mural for the bicentennial of the French Revolution[3] are dedicated to the Bastille as a matter of course. Asked what symbolizes the republican ideal, almost all French name "relics" of the French Revolution, not the least of which are the celebration of 14 July (19 percent) and the Place de la Bastille (9 percent).[4] And even in a philosophical work such as Jean-Paul Sartre's *Critique of Dialectical Reason* (1960), the Bastille is present. Here, 14 July 1789 serves as a historical paradigm for the theoretical reflection on how freedom becomes possible, and how social action comes into being from isolated actions of individuals under the pressure of a common threat.[5]

French domestic politics especially makes use of the tradition of this symbol, and in the process contributes to its consolidation. President Mitterrand, for example, celebrated his first election victory on 10 May 1981 with a rally on the Place de la Bastille,[6] and on 24 March 1988 the communist presidential candidate André Lajoinie marched to the July Column with eighty thousand mostly young supporters. The demonstrators, who were joined by a Franco-German peace brigade, carried banners and buttons with a slogan that alluded to the destination of the march as well as to the presidential elections and the political program of the French Communist Party (PCF): "I take the Bastille with Lajoinie!" Some wearing Phrygian caps, they chanted: "End the inequalities, the Bastilles must fall." And in his speech on the Place de la Bastille, Lajoinie referred to "this memorable site" of the Revolution and of the French people in order to call for a battle against the betrayal of the ideals of 1789, against unemployment and the nouveaux riches:

> Today we must fight a new French Revolution, found a new republic, storm new Bastilles. They have high walls and malicious defenders. . . . Yes, together we can make Bastilles fall, we can win rights for young people, we can open new perspectives for the people of France. I count on you. Forward!

And finally, a thunderclap at the end of the rally was supposed to suggest that this rhetorical storming of the Bastille would turn into concrete political conquests.[7]

But even beyond France — not least in Germany — the Bastille today is still an international symbol of faith. When on 24 November 1950, for instance, young Germans enthused about a united Europe demonstrated for international understanding and "broke through" the tollgates at the border with their column of cars, they were carrying the banner "Storm the Bastille Nation-State" (figure 1).

To the philosophy of Ernst Bloch, which became so important for the generation of 1968, the storming of the Bastille and the following "dance on the ruins of the Bastille" represented one of the remaining promising "archetypes of the situation of freedom," an "emblem of the future," an "archetype of highest utopian order."[8] And even more recently, Robert Jungk effectively summed up the fears and the unconditional rejection of the opponents of nuclear power by calling the new atomic power plant Cattenom a "new Bastille." The silhouette of

Figure 1. Young people from the Federal Republic of Germany demonstrate for a unified Europe without frontiers and customs barriers at the border crossing of Hirschtal near Pirmasens on 24 November 1950 (Bilderdienst Süddeutscher Verlag).

the cooling tower of this monster on the banks of the Mosel was in fact reminiscent of the former Paris fortress,[9] but its actual storming would be ridiculous.

As to the question how such symbolism, which is almost completely unrelated to the actual prison practice of the historical Paris Bastille of the eighteenth century, came into being, could spread and remain operative, there is no satisfactory answer in the overabundance of relevant literature. In France and elsewhere, this material does nothing but either more or less critically rehash the well-known history of events at the Paris Bastille, a history interspersed with myth,[10] or demystify the story of the old state prison and its conquest.[11] Apparently symbols of national history, and particularly of the French Revolution, have become so prominent in France that the actual historical issue is hardly perceived. In general, the political symbolism of more recent history has been examined much less than, say, symbols of rule in the Middle Ages.[12] The following investigation into the history of a mentality starts from this self-evident truth, the unfailing sign of social validity. Assuming that collective perceptions, attitudes, and opinions, "false" or "correct," are at least as "real" and influence actions in society as much as quantifiable material facts,[13] we intend first of all not to retell and demystify the history of an institution—the Bastille—but to trace and explain how that institution became such a general symbol, and what the function of this symbol has been in social history. We use the term "symbol" in the sense of the concept of "collective symbolism" developed by Jürgen Link,[14] namely, to refer to the culturally specific system of stereotypical, superlinguistic, nonarbitrary signs that integrates the discourses and practices of a society, the practical and theoretical realms of a culture. As the examples above suggest, and as further investigation will confirm, all the important characteristics of a symbol apply to the Bastille:

Semantic Secondarity. Originally restricted to a particular fortress in Paris, the word "Bastille" developed from a proper name into a symbol because the immediate designation of an edifice became a metaphor for "prison," and even for the political regime that kept such prisons.

Iconicity. The symbolic character of the Bastille further consists in that it is not just a signifier, a term, but also a concrete fortress, typical in its form and outline, that is still recognizable in its emblematic simplification. By thus practically "materializing" a political regime, the Bastille catered to a strong desire of preindustrial society for self-evidence and the illustration of basic political and social terms. As a generally known emblem, it belonged to a social world of pictures ("imaginaire social").[15]

Motivatedness. In the end, the symbolic meaning of the Bastille is based not on arbitrary linguistic convention but—from the perspective of the individual speaker—on common features of the historical function of the Bastille and the situation the name is applied to.

Ambiguity. The symbol Bastille has several meanings. It stands not only for prisons, abuse, and a despotic reign of injustice but since 14 July 1789 also for freedom and a revolutionary struggle. Therefore, it signifies opposites.

Associative Extension. Beyond its polar basic meaning "despotism/freedom," the symbol Bastille simultaneously evokes a whole series of further notions, notions we can separate into a kind of semantic field of vision. On the one hand, there are torture chambers, balls and chains, and famous captives, and on the other hand, the storming of the Bastille, the liberation of prisoners, the tribute to the conquerors, and the dance on the ruins of the razed prison.

Emotional Appeal. As a political symbol that is shared in its meaning and evaluation by various groups in society, the Bastille provoked and still provokes collective emotional responses that motivate, direct, and influence sociopolitical action.[16]

Thus equipped with all the characteristics of a collective symbol, the Bastille is also a model case of the history of a symbol in modern times, because it has inspired a profusion of more than two thousand symbolic textual and visual documents in France and Germany alone,[17] documents that have never been systematically examined. Since interest was hitherto restricted to the "real" history of the Bastille, the immense number of contemporary pamphlets and leaflets were dismissed as worthless propaganda.[18] These very stereotypical and fanciful sources, which by their mass alone make the social range of the symbol Bastille appreciable, form the basis of our investigation. In order to interpret them in detail with utmost efficiency, we apply a number of serial and sometimes quantifying methods, some of which had to be developed for this purpose.[19] We regard these methods neither as fashionable ends in themselves, nor as means of impressing the academic community, but as instruments for achieving results that hermeneutic interpretation cannot attain or can attain only with great difficulty. These results can then be illustrated by the representative analysis of truly exemplary individual cases.

Finally, the history of the symbol "Bastille" elucidates the recently discovered cultural and mental dimension of the French Revolution.[20] This key event of modernity is the pivotal period for the full formation of the Bastille as a symbol, one in turn that characterizes the French Revolution as a revolution of consciousness. We will examine its preparation through underground publications during the ancien régime, the self-mystification that occurred mostly during the years 1789–94, the cultural transmission of the symbol to foreign countries, and its constitutive importance for the political culture of modern France.

1. GENESIS OF A POLITICAL SYMBOL

The Bastille, 1715–1789

Anti-Bastille Journalism: Scandalous Stories of Prisoners

ORIGINALLY, "BASTILLES" WAS NOTHING MORE THAN A technical term for the municipal peel towers of the late Middle Ages built during the Hundred Years' War in Southern France. In the singular, the term also described the royal fortress with eight towers built between 1356 and 1382 at the gate to the Northwestern part of Paris, the later Faubourg Saint-Antoine. In the end, the use of the word was restricted to this edifice alone.[1] The technical term–turned–proper name only started attaining a figurative meaning, and thus the character of a symbol, as the Bastille was increasingly refashioned from a fortress protecting Paris into a state prison. This remodeling had already begun during the reign of Louis XI (1461–83), but it occurred primarily during the time of Cardinal Richelieu.[2] Finally, under the personal rule of the Sun King, not only rebellious aristocrats and spies but also loyal subjects were imprisoned in the Bastille if they had, like the superintendent of finance Fouquet, provoked the king[3] or had, like many Protestants, refused to swear to the exclusive legitimacy of the Catholic religion.[4] Because it was centrally located, beyond the rules of proper justice, and employed in a spectacular fashion, the Paris Bastille became the embodiment of terrifying absolutist domination and despotism in underground literature at the turn of the eighteenth century. In 1688, for instance, the satirist Claude Le Petit, who was later burned at the stake for writings offending the sovereign, published a successful *Chronique* *scandaleuse, ou Paris ridicule* (Scandalous chronicle, or ridiculous Paris; at least eight editions by 1714) with a passage on the Bastille, calling it a place that makes "everyone tremble." [5] And a famous anonymous treatise from the opposition that was forming against Louis XIV around 1690 criticized "the despotic power of the court in France. . . . Since the richest and the most powerful are exposed to view most of all, they are also most in danger; if it pleases the despotic government, they are sent to the Bastille." This criticism was radical enough to warrant republishing in 1788.[6] When the Sun King was carried to his grave in 1715 and his coffin had to be protected from the angry attacks of the destitute populace, the Bastille, at least among the upper classes, was considered a "trademark" of absolutism in France, and of its misuse of power.[7] Motivated by the contemporary situation, the name of the fortress had gained semantic secondarity.

But the Bastille did not become the prominent institutionalized state symbol of the old France throughout society until later in the eighteenth century. This enhancement in significance and emotional appeal, registered in numerous scattered sources,[8] was supported by journalism, which was increasing and intensifying its activity with the Enlightenment. Mostly, former prisoners of the Bastille breached the oath they were usually forced to take—to maintain complete silence concerning their imprisonment—by publishing their narratives. These form a series of scandalous stories that refer to each other and become more intense and radical from one to the next, conforming to a repeated basic pattern (table 1): The victim of the Bastille tends to stress his noble (in the cases of Latude and the imaginary Count de Lorges, invented) origin and his economic and social ascent, which was interrupted.[9] He places the blame for the arrest not on himself but on the base motives of other captives, mistresses, ministers, and police officers, on their fear of legitimate criticism and their envy of (sexual) rivals. The authors denounce the arrest warrants made out in the name of the king (lettres de cachet) as well as their assault-like arrest, often made possible only by deception and falsehood, and their subsequent secret commitment to the state prison. They further complain about bodily searches, the removal and confiscation of personal items, insidious interrogation by the governor of the Bastille, and imprisonment in badly furnished, barely lit and ventilated, either too cold or too hot cells secured by thick walls and heavy doors and locks. They particularly stress not only the physical suffering they are

Texts, Years, and Page Numbers

	Renneville 1715	Bucquoy 1719	Regné 1760	Remarques 1774	Linguet 1783	Latude 1787	Comte de Lorges 1789
1 Noble (legitimate) birth	lxviii, 10	8				6–7	[3]
2 His social and professional rise brings him in contact with court	10–12	30			7–9		[5–6]
3 He criticizes court	xlvii–xlix, 13–18	Foreword, 32					6
4 Envy of a superior or his subalterns	19–21	28, 36–38			29–31, 36, 49	17, 49, 65	
5 Enemies obtain a *lettre de cachet*	32–33	36–38, 172–78			10–12, 16–22	6–7	
6 Arrest warrant	27–33	38	6–7		12–13	10	7
7 Incarceration in a repulsive cell	35–42, 107–9	106–16, 146	7–8	13–14	62–70	10–11	7–8
8 Deceptive interrogations	62–67		17, 25–28, 62, 122			101–8	8–9, 14–15
9 Physical sufferings, sicknesses	liv–lvi, 2–4	181	20–24, 52, 57–58, 137		80–83, 100–103	120	9, 15
10 Humiliating despotism of the governor:							
Ban on walks				24, 26	85–90	9	
Isolation		181–82	9, 79	27–28	51, 76, 98		
Letters opened	46				61	21	9–10
Ban on reading and writing			80	22	51–52		
Insufficient clothes	xxv, 2						
Murder of pets	3, 164					120	
11 Escape attempts		72–88, 122–70				11–14, 29–41, 78	10–11
12 Incarceration in underground dungeons	xxii	92	48, 104–9, 117, 129	8–10	108	17, 66, 75, 86, 97	14
13 End of imprisonment by death				33			
secret release	xlviii		147	33		93, 112	
rebels on 14 July							11–13

Narrative Sequences

Table 1. The Fate of Prisoners of the Bastille
in Scandal Histories, 1715–1789 (French editions)

subjected to—from hunger and thirst to illness and supposed poisoning (Linguet) to chaining in underground dungeons (*cachots*) on bread and water—but at least as much the humiliations and mental agonies, which are arbitrary acts of revenge by the governor. If a prison break is successful, it is staged as an adventure story and serves as a vehicle in which the martyr of the Bastille is presented as a hero of the oppressed people. Since the most spectacular of these scandalous stories were immediately translated into other Western European languages, we can here quote most of them from contemporary translations. In this respect, the following "collection of cases" documents not only the development of the symbol "Bastille" in France but also its dissemination into the German and English cultural spheres.

Constantin de Renneville provides the first tale of woe. Renneville was a middle-class tax official from Normandy, who as a Protestant went to the Netherlands at the end of the seventeenth century and worked for the French secret service there. At the same time, however, he also spied for the Dutch government and for that reason was imprisoned in the Bastille from 1702 until 1713. Supported by a pension from George I in his London exile after his release,[10] he took revenge by way of a sensational indictment that presented his sufferings as representative of those of all prisoners of the Bastille. In the title, he likened the function and the inner defects of the state prison to those of the Catholic Inquisition as it could be observed in Spain and its South American colonies. In the engraving for the first chapter of the work, the fortress, which had not been remodeled since the fifteenth century, proves its suitability as a dark image of threat and terror (figure 2). The caption supporting that image holds the governor of that time, Bernaville, responsible for the similarity between the Bastille and the Inquisition in Peru. In a free translation, the caption in the German version of Renneville's account reads:

> The castle where cruelty, misery, and persecution howl,
> Which should make the bottom of hell shudder in amazement,
> Which would make the devil feel dread if he lived here,
> Is now subject to the wild Bernaville.

Another stanza of four lines later adds:

> Mortals, be frightened by this image of hell,
> A tyrant rules here, the devil is his slave,

Figure 2. Anonymous copperplate engraving, 136 by 76 mm, in Constantin de Renneville, *Entlarvte und jedermann zur Schau dargestellte Französische Inquisition, oder Geschichte der Bastille* . . . (n.p., 1715), vol. 1, before p. 1.

For Satan punishes only the guilty,
But Bernaville may cut down Innocence herself.[11]

In great detail and in a tone of passionate indignation, Renneville tells the story of how he was persecuted and arrested through lower-level ministerial vindictiveness, neither formally charged nor sentenced, of how the prison guards stole his valuables, the commanding officer embezzled his daily allowance, and the doctor aggravated his illnesses rather than healed them. The common prison cells in themselves were torture enough:

The walls were dirty and soiled with filth; only the ceiling was still fairly clean and white. The furniture consisted of a small broken feeding table, a small collapsed chair of straw on which one could no longer safely sit; and the entire room was swarming with fleas; in a minute I was covered with them. The names of the prisoners were written on the unclean walls. Here, a camp bed, a thin mattress, a feather pillow, a vile torn cover eaten by moths were laid down for me. I had never seen so much vermin, and I only kept myself free of it through constant effort to exterminate it. . . . I ate poorly, and slept even worse. In addition, the room was filled with rotten and unhealthy fumes, and every quarter of an hour, the sentry tolled a bell that was so close to my room that it seemed it was hanging from my ears.[12]

But the greatest sufferings were caused by the dark, unheated underground dungeons into which captives were thrown for refractoriness, after attempts to escape, or merely on the inclination to make them suffer. He, too, had languished in such a *cachot:*

Under an opening in the wall, I saw human bones; it was like a cemetery, and since I found the cellar in parts without paving, I dug, and found a corpse wrapped in rags. I stood still with disgust and horror, and it hardly reassured me that the warder said that they had kept the sorry remains of a captive there for a while who had hanged himself in his cell; two other men and one woman had suffered the same fate. A strong chain was attached to the middle of the cellar; a countless number of rats settled down around me, and slept with me. Whoever had been imprisoned here before me had made them so tame that they ate and slept with him; he had even given them names, and when he called them one after the other, they came running; if he wanted to be rid of them, he lightly struck their tails, and they ran back to their holes. What was a pastime for him became a terrible nuisance for me, and I had difficulties freeing myself of it. . . . I stayed in this wretched prison for twenty-two days, lying naked, only in a shirt and sleeping pants on straw that had rotted from the dampness, and received only bread and water as nourishment. My hands and feet were beset by such trembling that I feared a paralysis of my whole body. The cold nights brought about such a discharge that my entire face was swollen.[13]

Renneville followed up this eyewitness account of his suffering with three further volumes in 1724 that imaginatively transformed the love

and prison stories of three dozen supposed additional victims of the
Bastille into a veritable series of novels in the fashion of the time.[14]

Renneville's fantastic story of suffering came to serve as a model.
Most of the subsequent anti-Bastille pamphlets used it to confirm their
accusations. It is related to the following captive's report, for example,
in at least two respects. Renneville himself mentions the successful
prison break of Bucquoy de Manican on 5 May 1709, which took place
during his imprisonment; the prologue to the German translation of
Bucquoy's story in turn quotes Renneville at length and likens the two
works: "Anyway, the count and abbot Bucquoy and Mr. Renneville
agree in calling the Bastille the hell of the living."[15] The adventures of
both were a common topic of conversation among educated people.
Leibniz (in Vienna) and the Prussian electress Sophie (in Hannover),
for instance, exchanged pertinent information in early 1714 and wrote
that it was "a recommendation to have been in the Bastille" and that
it seemed as if Bucquoy had "left it more gloriously than other" prisoners.[16] That Bucquoy was reported on in the form of letters written
in 1711 from a lady in Paris to a lady in The Hague conforms with the
kind of communication typical of the early baroque era.

The adventure story of the self-proclaimed "Count" Bucquoy, an
escaped cleric who was arrested in Burgundy on 9 June 1707 for espionage and salt smuggling, hardly reads like the ordeal of innocence
persecuted. Rather, Bucquoy, who is presented as "a very quick person" and a "sworn enemy of despotism in France,"[17] deftly manages
to secure all desired privileges in the Bastille by feigning illnesses. He
suffers no torture and is well provided for. "For in the Bastille the
prisoners are not kept on water and bread, but the King wants to do
well by them, for which He pays well enough." Nevertheless, the governor is accused of not having a "compassionate heart," because he
had some windows bricked up after an escape attempt. Rumors concerning secret murdering devices and death cells in the La Chapelle
tower are circulated without challenge: "From this latter, hardly anyone usually comes out, unless he also at the same time leaves his life;
and it is said that the same place houses the drawbridges described
earlier, which many say that people whom one wants to transport
to the next world secretly are forced to jump across." In short, the
Bastille appears as the instrument of an inquisitory state of injustice.
"And actually the whole world speaks of the Bastille as a place even

the innocent must be afraid of."[18] This demonization is additionally supported in a "rather racy engraving" that

> presents hell and the devil—to be more precise, under the names Beelzebub and Astaroth—[as synonymous with] the names of the president of that Bastille, Mr. d'Argençon, and the governor of the same, Mr. Bernaville, [and presents them] so ambiguously that the words *ou d'Argençon le President* can be understood to mean either "The hell of the living, where d'Argençon is president" or "Beelzebub, or d'Argençon the president." The same equivocation was also used with Bernaville's name.[19]

Even though the accompanying prologue doubts that "a temporal prison" such as the Bastille can be likened to eternal hell or a human being to Satan,[20] this is exactly what the title page suggests (figure 3) by caricaturing the Paris police chief and the governor of the Bastille as tormenting, vindictive devils. In contrast to the earlier picture in Renneville, the iconic and hence symbolic quality of the Bastille has been enhanced. Abbé Bucquoy also becomes a stock figure of anti-Bastille journalism; when Latude's escape story caused an uproar on the eve of the Revolution, that of his predecessor was rewritten as a continuous narrative and republished.[21]

No other printed reports joined these early, exemplary histories of prisoners until the middle of the eighteenth century, when several were published after a long interruption. Although they are not comprehensive enough to be included in table 1, they contributed to the evolution of the image of the Bastille and were again and again used in journalistic accounts to prove the arbitrariness and sufferings to which the prisoners were defenselessly subjected. The greatest sensation was caused, however, by news, spread earlier by word of mouth, of the so-called man in the iron mask. This prisoner was committed in 1698, died after a short illness in 1703 at the age of about forty-five, and was pseudonymously buried in the cemetery adjacent to the prison, which was a common procedure.[22] Encoded as an anecdote of "Asian despotism" as late as 1745,[23] the story was put in circulation after 1751, mainly through Voltaire's successful *The Age of Louis XIV*. Introducing his chapter 24, Voltaire speaks of "an affair the parallel of which is not to be met with in history," one surrounded by the "utmost secrecy." His "news" is limited to the following:

Figure 3. Anonymous copperplate engraving, 148 by 94 mm. Frontispiece for *Die so genannte Hölle der Lebendigen, das ist die Welt-beruffene Bastille zu Paris . . .* (n.p., printed at the expense of good friends in the month of May 1719).

This prisoner wore . . . a masque, of which the lower part had steel springs, contriv'd so that he could eat without taking it off. Orders were given, that if he shewed any inclination to discover himself, he should be immediately killed. . . . This stranger being carried to the Bastile [*sic*], had the best accommodations which that castle could afford: nothing which he desired was refused him. His strongest passion was for linnen [*sic*] of extraordinary fineness, and for lace. His table was always served in the most elegant manner; and the Governor seldom sat down in his presence. . . . This unknown person died in 1703, and was buried in the night, in the parish of St. Paul. What increases the wonder is, that at the time . . . no considerable person disappeared in Europe.

When minister Michel de Chamillard, one of the few initiated into the mystery, was begged by his son-in-law on his knees to confide the secret to him, he "answered him, it was a secret of State, and he had sworn never to reveal it."[24]

This "report," which contains more allusions and ambiguous embellishments than verifiable facts, set off endless speculations as to whether the "murder victim" had been an illegitimate brother of Louis XIV or some other rival of the king[25] and even supplied the subject and title for an adventure novel.[26] No matter how much these speculations varied, they all contributed to the "man in the iron mask" becoming something like an embodiment of the principle of secrecy that shielded the Bastille and to the formation in the developing public sphere of the impression that this secrecy must be covering up political assassinations attributable to state "despotism." Hence, Louis-Sébastien Mercier was able to claim in 1786 that the man in the iron mask had been deliberately forgotten behind the walls of the Bastille and that "it would have been less barbaric and much more sure . . . to kill him than to thus cruelly let him live."[27]

Similar notions were encouraged by the posthumously published memoirs of two other prisoners of the Bastille. That of Pierre de La Porte, a favorite of Anna of Austria arrested in 1637 on orders from Richelieu because of involvement in court intrigues, told on the one hand of a torture chamber and on the other hand of the freedom of movement and contact that the prisoners at the Bastille enjoyed.[28] In contrast, the memoirs of the baroness Mme de Staël, who was in the Bastille from 1718 until 1720 as an accessory to the Cellamare conspiracy, appealed to the sensibility of the audience by describing how her affair with another prisoner was interrupted by the prison directors:[29] "state despotism," it seemed, did violence even to innocent human sentiments.

The next scandal had a more political quality. It was related to the sectlike Jansenist cult that had evolved after 1727 from miracle cures performed at the grave of Deacon François de Pâris in the cemetery of the Paris parish of Saint-Médard in the craftsmen's district Saint-Marcel. This cult had caused a great public sensation and had withdrawn to secret conventicles in order to avoid political persecution. Its approximately six hundred followers, mostly ordinary people, were called *convulsionnaires,* because they fell into ecstasy and performed bodily self-punishment when they were "visited by the spirit" during their spiritistic assemblies.[30] Since they violated state ideas of order as well as the orthodoxy of the Catholic Church, so many of them were arrested, interrogated, and imprisoned, especially in the Bastille under the reign of Cardinal Fleury, that deriding songs and pictures (figure 4) on the subject circulated and the Jansenist underground newspaper *Nouvelles ecclésiastiques* depicted the Bastille on its title vignette.[31] One of the mostly female *convulsionnaires,* a woman called Denyse Regné, had been arrested and brought to the Bastille on 17 March 1733. She put up a clever defense through the memoranda of sympathetic lawyers and was transferred to Vincennes in 1737 and finally to the Conciergerie. The story of her confinement, entrusted to her notary in August of that year, one that she as an illiterate person must have dictated, was published in 1760.[32] It describes the futile efforts of the governor and the Jesuits he was working with to force Regné into a confession that her ecstasies were artificial and blasphemous. She was spared nothing, from endless interrogations and torments of hunger to "injuries" inflicted by doctors to torturous treatment at the hands of a nun lodged with her and her confessor to the threatened use of a dismembering machine and her enchainment in an underground dungeon, where her shackles miraculously fell off overnight. On top of all that, she was supposed to swear an oath of silence: state and church did indeed seem to practice "tyrannical," "barbaric" justice in the Bastille.[33]

The tortures suffered in the Bastille by people ranging from Renneville to Denyse Regné could perhaps still be understood as the extreme misfortunes of individual wretches. Yet a pamphlet published in 1774

1. Carosse qui conduit les convulsionaires à la Bastille.
2. Grande porte de la Bastille.
3. Petite porte de la Bastille.
4. Cour de la Bastille.
5. Premier corps de garde.
6. M.r Herault Lieutenant de Police.
7. Medecins examinants les convulsionaires.
8. Maison du Gouverneur.
9. Gouverneur de la Bastille.
10. Fenestre ou le Gouverneur regarde ceux qui arrivent.
11. M.r Pierre la Porte.
12. Pierre Labir.
13. M.lle Girout.
14. M.r Maupoint.
15. Jesuite qui fait jetter un sceau d'eau sur le corps de M.r Maupoint.
16. Second corps de garde.
17. Tour de la Bastille.
18. Fossé de la Bastille.

Figure 4. Taking Jansenist *convulsionnaires* to the Bastille. Anonymous etching, around 1730 (Bibliothèque Nationale, Estampes, Qb1, M 96201).

made them seem typical and authentic by describing imprisonment at the Bastille in seemingly objective terms, systematically and with exact figures (including a ground plan), and presenting individual cases only in an appendix. Initially, it was presumed that the author of the pamphlet was a news bureau close to the underground that based its findings partly on the experiences of a prisoner, partly on Renneville.[34] Later, the brochure gained credibility when the British criminologist and reformer of the penal system John Howard used it in his standard book on European prisons and penitentiaries.[35] Even during the Old Regime, this pamphlet on the Bastille was praised for its "very comprehensive and correct description of the interior and exterior equipment of this hellish place" and for its preface, which denounced the Bastille as a symbol of the absolutist reign of injustice:

> Since the mortal wound was given to French liberty, Despotism, that scourge of human nature, which debases and dishonours, has acquired strength by striking at all ranks, and spreading a general terror. Nothing is heard of but banishments, proscriptions, and prisons; of which last the Bastille is undoubtedly the most formidable.[36]

This terror could be seen in the

> dungeons under the towers [which] are filled with a mud which exhales the most offensive scent. They are the resort of toads, newts, rats, and spiders. In a corner of each is a camp bed, formed of iron bars, soldered into the wall, with some planks laid upon them. In these are put prisoners whom they wish to intimidate, and a little straw is given them for their bed. Two doors, each seven inches thick, one over the other, close these dark dens: each has two great bolts, and as many locks. . . . There are five ranks of chambers. The most dreadful next to the dungeons, are those in which are *iron cages* or *dungeons*. Of these there are three. These cages are formed of beams lined with strong iron plates. They are six feet by eight.[37]

Worse still, even though their existence had not been proven, there were probably oubliettes at the Bastille, secret shafts of death in which prisoners were tormented between beams set with knives and barbs or simply left to die of hunger.[38] A secret desire for revenge and an absence of justice were common features of such abominations and chicanery, and of the customary state of affairs at the Bastille; for "in the Bastille nothing [happens] according to rules and laws, but everything according to the commands of the directors or according to the despotism of the superiors." [39]

With the 1774 pamphlet, anti-Bastille journalism became increasingly fundamental and radical on the subject of changing the system. While a movement to reform justice propagated the principle of habeas corpus and questioned the traditional judicial sovereignty of the king, [40] the stories of prisoners proliferated, ranging from complaints over injustices suffered and the deplorable state of affairs in the prison to general indictments of royal and state absolutism, which seemed to have materialized in the form of the Bastille. Increasingly politicized, Bastille journalism went from covering sensationalistic scandals to making a fundamental critique of the system and finally reached its prerevolutionary sharpness, achieving a growing social resonance, in the 1780s. None less than Count Mirabeau, the future tribune of the Revolution, opened the series of pamphlets appearing in increasingly rapid succession. Mirabeau transformed the experiences of his numerous imprisonments of many years, all of which had been arranged by his father in order to protect the family's honor, into a passionate denunciation of lettres de cachet and of state prisons. The pamphlet, fifteen thousand copies of which were printed anonymously by Mirabeau's publisher in Neuchâtel, decried as "illegal" and as "acts of tyranny" the royal "prerogative of arbitrary, and indefinite imprisonment," because of which they "bury in dreary dungeons whole generations." [41] For Mirabeau, the outrageous illegality of state prisons was manifested in the ubiquitous principle of underground imprisonment (he refers to "this place, where all is dungeon"); [42] in the tyranny of the prison director, "an absolute despot"; [43] and in the "state secret" veil spread over the entire affair. [44] This despotism of the dungeon became possible, however, only through corresponding ministerial and state "despotism, which disfigures, devours, and destroys everything"—a despotism from which ultimately the only escape was suicide. [45] Even though Mirabeau wrote this during his confinement at the prison tower in Vincennes between 1777 and 1778, he mentioned the Bastille so often and so emphatically, especially in his fundamental accusations, [46] that it was later assumed that he had actually been a prisoner at the Bastille. [47] After 1789, he was able to present himself as a martyr of the Bastille and politically legitimized himself by answering one of his critics: "I was writing for liberty in the dungeon while you were plotting against her in your antechambers."[48]

The well-known journalist Simon-Nicolas-Henri Linguet made a more immediate and sensational contribution to the symbolic charging of the Bastille. Linguet was held prisoner in the Bastille from 27 September 1780 until 11 May 1782 for reporting rather too openly on a civil suit in Paris. Even as a prisoner, he was the talk of town.[49] His *Mémoires sur la Bastille,* which he composed in his London exile, were published in 1783, not only in his political monthly.[50] There were also at least six French editions as a book, and the *Mémoires* were translated into all Western European languages at once, four times into German alone. Without being able to report torture he actually endured himself, much less the murder of prisoners in the oubliettes, Linguet complained of "tortures . . . of the mind" caused by uncertainty and isolation; of an utterly "void existence more cruel than death, since it does not exclude grief"; and of a "plan . . . formed to embitter the rest of my days," which led to an attempt to poison him and finally led him to make his will in prison.[51] In the Bastille, "where existence is but a repetition of tortures worse than death," even walks were "rendered rather an additional mortification, than a comfort," particularly since in the courtyard the captive had to bear the sight of a clock with a surface relief of two prisoners in chains.[52] The stories of Renneville, La Beaumelle, Lally, and Mirabeau provided confirmation:[53] "The regimen of the Bastille is purposely instituted to torment! And whom? Persons of acknowledged innocence."[54] For the "secrets of state" that surrounded the Bastille were supposed to hide people "whom they not only never intend to prosecute, but whom they have not the wherewithal to arraign."[55] Worse still, the Bastille afflicted not only innocence but virtue. Linguet called "patriotic enthusiasm" the driving force of his actions.[56] Moreover, he claimed to have noticed an "increase of rigour," because more and more regular criminals were held in the Bastille next to state prisoners—an "increase of barbarities" that contradicted the humanitarian efforts of the Enlightenment.[57] In the language of despotism, a "Prisoner of State" was nothing but "a man who has displeased a Minister, a Clerk in office, or a Valet."[58] Thus the Bastille almost acquires the features of a murderous monster: "The *Bastilles* of *France* have devoured, they are daily devouring, men of all ranks, and of all nations. At the avenues of these abysses might well be engraven that memento which is sometimes seen inscribed to transitory readers on church-yard gates: *Hodie mihi, cras tibi!*" [59] Linguet consciously speaks of the "*Bastilles* of *France*," for the lettres de cachet are a "peculiar" evil and can only perhaps be compared to "the plague in Egypt [or] the small-pox in Arabia." [60] In addition, nothing equals the Bastille either in the past or in the present of Asia, Africa, America, or Europe: "We can find no nation blighted by the shame and inhumanity of a permanent Bastille; of a pit always gaping to receive men, not for *punishment*—let this be fully borne in mind—but for *torture:* a political purgatory, where the most trivial faults, and often innocence itself, may be subjected arbitrarily to the torments of hell." [61]

Linguet protests his "homage to the virtuous King" Louis XVI,[62] whose name is misused by his ministers and the governor of the Bastille.[63] But this begs the question: "Whence then does it arrive, that the humanity of Louis XVI connives at the continuance of an institution invented by the tyranny of Louis XI?" [64] With the advance publication of excerpts from Linguet's *Mémoires,* one of the leading newspapers had answered this question with the suggestion to finally open the doors of this despicable place, let the prisoners out, and hand them over to regular courts, to raze the walls of the Bastille and, in their place, erect a statue of the reigning king with the inscription "Louis XVI on the grounds of the Bastille." [65] This appeal in turn prompted Linguet to have a frontispiece engraved that imagined the razing of the Bastille (figure 5)—six years before the fact—and that attracted attention as especially "remarkable and piquant":

> The statue of Louis XVI with the attributes of monarchy arises in the middle of the ruins of a demolished fortress, which represents the Bastille. —Benevolently, the king offers his hand to the prisoners whom he has just liberated, first of all Maître Linguet as the indirect author of their liberation. Linguet kneels and distinguishes himself by special gratitude. —The majestic yet charitable gesture of the king corresponds to the hemistich from *Alzire* at the bottom of the engraving: Live, and be free. —The very noble motto suggested by the *Courrier du Bas-Rhin* is inscribed on the base of the statue: "Louis XVI on the grounds of the Bastille." —In the upper background of the engraving, one notices a clock decorated with figures, like the one at the Bastille. The face is carried by a man and a woman who have chains on their neck, hands, and feet and around their body. These chains form

Figure 5. Spilbury after Wortman and Mutlow, Live, and be free!
Etching, 172 by 114 mm. Frontispiece for Linguet, *Mémoires*.

a kind of frame ornament and run together in an enormous knot: this is smashed by lightning. . . . This event corresponds to the words engraved below from the edict of 30 August 1780: "These inconceivable torments, these secret agonies are useless for our system of justice if their publicity and their deterring example does not contribute to the maintenance of law and order." [66]

What Linguet tries to pass off as a loyal appeal to royal justice is actually an attempt at pictorial compulsion. Like a puppet, Louis XVI acts not only as a captive of his own laws and a higher force coming down through lightning (God, perhaps also journalism) but finally as a captive of the symbolism of the Bastille itself.

By combining the pictorial conjuration of the future with an emphatic vocabulary that before had not been applied to the Bastille with such profusion and vehemence,[67] Linguet, the eloquent former lawyer and founding father of political journalism of opinion in France,[68] altogether demonized the Bastille as a stigma in the age of the Enlightenment, a symbol of "ministerial despotism." The success of Linguet's pamphlet is attested to by the small battle of leaflets it set off, which was reported in the underground press.[69] Conservative rebuttals dismissed Linguet's chronicle of scandals as slanderous lies, as wild fancies caused by a diseased persecution complex. Instead, they referred to the gentle practices of imprisonment at the Bastille and defended them as the proper institutions of royal power.[70] A reforming lawyer from an upper court in Grenoble, by contrast, mocked the idea that the Bastille was "divine" and that it corresponded to the "nature of monarchy to have one or several Bastilles, the more the better." [71] In the end, both sides strengthened the appeal of the Bastille and hence its importance as a central state symbol of the ancien régime.

The increased strategic importance of this symbol in the formation of public opinion became apparent in the affair of the necklace, which speeded up the French monarchy's loss of reputation. It was discovered that a diamond necklace worth 1,600,000 francs, offered to the queen by the jewelers Böhmer and Bassenge in 1784, had not been accepted by her but had been turned into cash by Countess Lamothe-Valois by way of forged signatures and scenes of disguise, and with the help of her connections to the Versailles court. The countess and a number of other suspects were taken into custody and finally sentenced by due process of law.[72] The affair, which discredited mainly Marie-Antoinette, caused all the more of a sensation because the suspects were held in custody at the Bastille: "All of Europe is looking toward France and these miserable walls, which in several centuries have confined many great men and which for some time now have surrounded Monseigneur le Cardinal de Rohan."[73] Rohan himself was so deeply entangled with the fraud that he avoided noisy complaints about his place of imprisonment. The miracle healer and mesmerist Cagliostro,[74] however, who was arrested only because he was acquainted with Countess Lamothe, and his lawyer Thilorier to a large extent based their defense on a terrifying vision of the Bastille:

> I am subjugated, accused, and denounced. What have I done to deserve this fate? . . . I thought I had found a new home [in France]: a peal of thunder has destroyed this dream; I am thrown into the dungeons of the Bastille. . . . An arrest warrant is issued against me. What crime have I committed? What am I accused of? Who has denounced me? Are there witnesses that give evidence against me? I know nothing of all of this. . . . I am carried . . . to the Bastille. . . . The terrible drawbridge is lowered, and I am led . . . [!] my wife suffers the same fate. Here I pause, trembling. I will conceal what I suffered. I want to save the sensitive reader a painful and outrageous account. I will allow myself only one word and call the heaven as a witness that it is the truth: If I could choose between the death penalty and six months in the Bastille, I would say without hesitation, "Take me to the place of execution."[75]

Significantly, anti-Bastille polemic here enters one of the pathetic, verbally radical memoranda that pugnacious lawyers composed more and more for their clients in scandal lawsuits toward the end of the ancien régime, and had printed in large editions in order to influence the public.[76] Earlier reports of the "terror of the Bastille" had obviously permeated social consciousness so far that the mere name of the "state dungeon" and a few vague allusions to the "sufferings" of the captives were enough to prejudice the audience in favor of the accused and against the law: the symbol "Bastille" was proving its emotional appeal.

This emotional appeal was what Cagliostro also made use of after his acquittal and his expulsion from the country in an open letter from

London of 20 June 1786, which was reprinted by the press, in order
to take revenge for his confinement and the forced separation from
his wife:

> So they drove me out of France; they deceived the King. Kings
> are indeed to be pitied who have such ministers; I am speaking of
> Baron de Breteuil, of my persecutor. . . . He cannot swallow the
> unpalatable fact that a man in irons, a foreigner under lock and
> key in the Bastille, should have raised his voice as I have done to
> unmask him. . . . Are all prisons like the Bastille? You can have
> no idea of the sheer horrors of that place; the cynical impudence
> there, the hateful lies, the false pity, the bitter irony, the unre-
> strained cruelty, the injustice and death that hold sway there. . . .
> Someone asked me if I would return to France. . . . Assuredly,
> I replied, *provided that the Bastille has become a public promenade.* May
> God grant it! . . . Yes, my friend, let me tell you this: a prince
> will reign over you who *will be famous for abolishing* lettres de cachet
> *at the convocation of the States General.* . . . This prince, beloved of
> Heaven, will realize that abuse of power is, in the long run, de-
> struction of power.[77]

As in Linguet, the story of a scandal leads to an appeal to Louis XVI
to no longer let his name be misused by "despotic ministers" and to
abolish, along with the misuse of power, its symbol—the Bastille. But
what if the king were to flinch from this symbolic action, in essence
admitting his guilt? The answer, left open by Cagliostro, would be
given three years later.

In addition to the series of histories of martyrs composed by former
prisoners of the Bastille examined here, which become more and more
political and radical, further notices of scandals such as the supposed
murder of prisoners[78] were published after 1787. Especially the sensational reports by Latude, whom Parisian high society celebrated as a
hero after his release, make it clear how commonly the Bastille had become an emblem of despotism on the eve of the Revolution. Among
intellectuals in particular, its symbolic power motivated almost hys-
terical solidarizations similar to those which could be observed in the
Federal Republic of Germany during the trials of terrorists Andreas
Baader and Ulrike Meinhof, when the philosopher Sartre visited the
terrorists, who were suffering "torture through isolation," in deten-
tion.[79]

*The Reality-Forming Power of the Symbolic: Prison Practice
versus Social Consciousness*

Voltaire did not write a prison story, yet the name of this Enlightenment figure par excellence is connected with the Bastille in a specific
fashion, and not without reason.[80] The aspiring writer, who was then
still calling himself Arouet, had composed an unusually fierce satirical
poem, which circulated in transcripts, on the reign of Louis XIV. One
part reads: "I have seen the Bastille and Vincennes / . . . and a thousand prisons / full of honorable citizens and faithful subjects."[81] Not
because of this poem, however, but because of pornographic verses
on the royal regent and his daughter, Arouet himself was actually imprisoned at the Bastille from 16 May 1717 until 10 April 1718 for the first
time. He assimilated this experience in the poem "La Bastille," which
also circulated secretly, ironically thanked the king for the gracious
granting of "shelter" and "safety," and hinted at shortcomings in heat-
ing, food, and freedom of movement.[82] In 1767 he converted his poem
into a philosophical story, in which an innocent Aborigine is thrown
into the Bastille because of a lettre de cachet—"like a dead corpse
going to the grave."[83] For all that, Arouet had eaten at the table of the
governor of the Bastille and had been released with a royal yearly pension of four hundred ecus. Voltaire was in the Bastille a second time
from 14 to 29 April 1726, because he had sent bullies to avenge an in-
sult delivered by the Cardinal de Rohan. Recognized by the minister as
a "genius" who needed "consideration" and every possible "liberty,"[84]
Voltaire received so many visitors that they had to be limited to five or
six a day. He stayed a day longer than necessary of his own free will in
order to settle some business. Nevertheless, he told his English friend
George Berkeley around 1721 that he had received neither writing material nor books at the Bastille and that he had been obliged to make
"paper" from his sheets in order to write his epos on Henri IV.[85] This
work, printed at least twenty-nine times between 1730 and 1781, which
repeated similar claims in the preface, contained the couplet that was
to become proverbial and a cliché of literature on the Bastille:

Dans cet affreux château, palais de la vengeance
Qui renferme souvent le crime et l'innocence.

[Those dreary towers
Where vengeance, *undistinguishing in blood,*
Too often confounds the guilty and the good.][86]

Although according to contemporary criteria it was rather the former adjective that applied to him, Voltaire cultivated the art of subliminal reproaches to despotism, and of tendentious ambiguity. On the one hand, he said that the opinion of the English that "half of the French nation are thrown into the Bastille [was] not quite correct," and he did not have much pity for his competitor as an author, La Beaumelle, who was imprisoned there. On the other hand, he was dismayed at the incarceration of men of letters such as Nicolas Fréret, Claude-Prosper Jolyot de Crébillon (Crébillon fils), and Denis Diderot: "There is nothing left for me to do but finish out life in my place of refuge [in Ferney], which I have removed from the reach of my persecutors."[87] And thus the typical gesture of "persecuted innocence" corresponds to the fact that Voltaire counted as *the* Bastille martyr of the Enlightenment, especially during the Revolution, even though he had been celebrated publicly in Paris and had lived undisturbed as late as 1778.

The case of Voltaire seems symptomatic of the widening gap between the treatment of prisoners at the Bastille in the eighteenth century and the perception of the Bastille in society. Measured by the standard of what was common in the judicial and penal system of the ancien régime, the Bastille did not stand out for unusual brutality and mismanagement, rather to the contrary. The letters bearing the king's official seal (lettres de cachet), which caused arrests, were justified from the principle of divine right, the principle that the king was the highest source of justice on earth. They served not only the prosecution of crimes against the state (espionage, conspiracies) but also—in the majority—the social desire for discipline: Without damaging "family honor" through a public police action and court trial, a father could call his son to order, a wife could chastise her intemperate husband, or a grown-up daughter could hand her crazed mother over to "royal custody."[88] None other than Voltaire himself signed the communal petition of several inhabitants of the Rue Vaugirard in Paris to have a lettre de cachet made out against a tripe seller who was supposedly disturbing the peace when she was drunk.[89] The Marquis de Mirabeau, the famous physiocrat who liked to be called "l'ami des hommes," obtained no fewer than thirty-eight lettres de cachet against members of his family, most of them against his son Honoré, Count Mirabeau.[90] Yet, as we have seen, the count publicly blamed for his numerous confinements not his father but the "despotic system"—

	1661–1715	1715–1743	1743–1774	1774–1789
For religious reasons				
Altogether	327	383	95	—
Annual average	6	14	3	—
Protestants	254	16	2	—
Jansenists	73	242	46	—
Convulsionnaires	—	125	47	—
For production and distribution of banned writings				
Altogether	176	212	286	9
Annual average	3	8	9	1
Jansenist writers	40	178	15	—
Total	2,320	1,459	1,184	306
Annual average	43	52	3	20

Source: Quétel, *Essai*, 33, 69, 78.

Table 2. Detentions in the Bastille, 1661–1789

even though since 1775 the government had been trying to curb the misuse of lettres de cachet by many families.[91]

Concerning the Bastille, the prison statistics[92] contradict the impression of overflowing dungeons and increasing despotic arbitrariness created by the scandal reports of everyone from Renneville to Latude. Between the reign of Louis XIV and that of Louis XVI, the number of captives was halved (table 2), while the average period of confinement dropped from three years to between one and two months.[93] So the approximately fifty cells of the Bastille were hardly filled in the first half of the eighteenth century; toward the end of the ancien régime most of them were usually empty. Apart from confinements for religious reasons—which were imposed at the discretion of the Catholic Church and reached a peak in the 1730s—arrests were usually based on valid laws and in the last forty-five years before the Revolution concerned economic and moral rather than clearly political infractions of laws (figure 6). Most imprisonments were due to the bread riots of 1775 (31 prisoners),[94] the affair of the diamond necklace of 1786 (11 cases), and the revolt of the upper judges in Rennes against a royal edict of 1788 (12 captives). To be sure, between 1774 and 1789 almost every third prisoner was in the Bastille for composing, printing, or selling unlawful writings. But more often than not, "obscene,

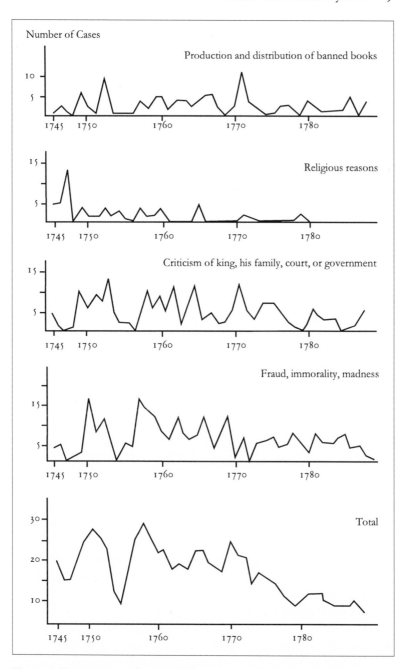

Figure 6. Detentions in the Bastille by reason of captivity, 1749–1789

Figure 7. Detentions of 133 authors in the Bastille
toward the end of the ancien régime

forbidden books" are named as the corpus delicti, and most of the
imprisoned writers (figure 7) were not political Enlightenment figures and later revolutionaries such as Jacques-Pierre Brissot[95] (in the
Bastille from 12 July until 10 September 1784) or Louis-Pierre Manuel
(3 February through 7 April 1786) but obscure hack writers and dubi-
ous fellow travelers who were trying to turn sensationalistic and lewd
side effects of the Enlightenment into material profit.[96] The store of
impounded books that the rebels discovered when they took the Bastille on 14 July 1789 did contain some radical Enlightenment tracts
such as Holbach's *Système de la nature* of 1770 (two copies) or Rabaut
Saint-Etienne's novel *Le Vieux Cévenol,* which concerned the emancipation of the Protestants of 1784 (240 copies). But mostly, it consisted
of political pornography such as Mirabeau's *Libertin de qualité* of 1784
(30 copies) or the *Vie privée d'un Prince célèbre* . . . of the same year (400
copies).[97] So Michelet's vision of the Bastille as a place where the spirit
of freedom was imprisoned was only a very limited reflection of historical facts.

The divergence between legend and fact becomes even starker
when one considers the fact that the conditions of imprisonment at
the Bastille had nothing in common with the horrifying reports of the
journalists but instead contrasted favorably with those found in provincial state prisons.[98] Around the middle of the eighteenth century,
the infamous underground dungeons (*cachots*) were used only for extraordinary disciplinary measures—when Latude was rearrested, for
instance, after his prison break in 1756. Under Louis XVI, not a single
prisoner was held in such a *cachot,* the inspector general Necker having
explicitly forbidden the practice in 1776. As the torture of captives in

the Bastille had already been abandoned in the seventeenth century, the "death cells," or oubliettes, existed only in the collective imagination.[99] Fatalities at the Bastille were very rare and had natural causes. Since the king paid a daily rate of ten livres per capita, state prisoners were so plentifully and luxuriously supplied with food that some of them drew on only half of the daily ration and had the rest paid out when they were released.[100] Needy prisoners were clothed at the state's expense and were allowed, for example, to select the material according to their own taste. What Latude called "half-rotted rags" was in reality a new fur-lined coat, which he sold after his second escape.[101] Warm baths, medicine cabinets, and renowned specialist doctors were all features of hygenic and medical care that was exemplary for the standard of the time. Medical historians have gone so far as to say that the Bastille was a pathbreaking psychiatric institution.[102] The furnishing of the cells, most of which were spacious tower rooms, was arranged according to the wishes of the prisoners, who were also able to bring their own furniture (as did the Count de Belle-Isle in 1759), or who had bookcases built specifically for their private library (as did La Beaumelle in 1753 for more than six hundred volumes).[103] Since in the later eighteenth century prisoners of the Bastille were given permission to receive visitors and to write, since they were allowed to bring their servants, since they could take out books from the prison library, and since there were opportunities for communal games of chess, bowling, and billiards, even their entertainment was more or less taken care of.[104]

All in all, one gets the impression that the government greatly liberalized conditions and generally tried to avoid imprisonments at the Bastille in the last decades of the ancien régime in an attempt to refute the scandals surrounding that prison, and to avoid creating martyrs. But since its self-chosen tenet of secrecy, which was supposed to protect state and family interests, made an informative public relations strategy impossible, the policy of liberalization—which was interpreted as weakness and admission of guilt—seems to have intensified the creation of legends rather than lessened it.

In the early eighteenth century, Voltaire had still uttered his malicious remarks on the Bastille in a spirit of tongue-in-cheek irony. A prisoner such as the Marquis de Sade, however, who had been confined at the wish of his family for abnormal sexual behavior, turned his malice into deadly seriousness at the end of the ancien régime. Moved to the Bastille in 1784 because of the closing of the prison tower in Vincennes, he enjoyed all possible liberality, from rooms redecorated especially for him to choice meals and red wine ordered for him personally from Burgundy and kept cool in the cellar to frequent hours unobserved with his wife. Nonetheless, he spread macabre rumors when he was forbidden to take his usual walks on the towers of the fortress because he had abused the guards: the Marquis "yesterday at midday . . . went to his window and at the top of his voice, so that he could be heard in the whole neighbourhood and by passers-by, yelled that he was being slaughtered, that the Bastille prisoners were being murdered, and would people come to their aid."[105] Had this incident of 1 July 1789 been the banal act of revenge of an eccentric person, the governor of the Bastille could have gone back to business as usual. But since Sade's cries effectively appealed to collective compulsive ideas, a dangerous situation arose for the prison administration, which it tried to defuse by immediately transferring the Marquis to Charenton. But what became established in the collective memory was the idea of Sade as a martyr of the Bastille. As late as 1938, the originally American, elective French citizen Man Ray, a surrealist photographer and graphic artist, painted an imaginary portrait (figure 8) in which Sade is composed of broad stone. Immured in the wall, he has, so to speak, become the Bastille. Cracks in the masonry allude to the consequences depicted in the background: the conquest and burning down of the dungeon enclosing a free spirit—a "storming of the Bastille" that still seemed necessary considering the continuing taboo on Sade's writings even in 1938.[106] With Sade, it becomes even clearer than with Voltaire: the symbol creates its own symbolic figure.

The growing discrepancy between prison practice at the Bastille and the image of the fortress in the public sphere toward the end of the ancien régime clearly exemplifies how the power of this collective symbol fashioned social consciousness—in a manner independent of any material reality. This discrepancy, however, which only grew wider during the course of the eighteenth century, did not signify a weakening of the motivatedness of the symbol, which was already securely established. Because the new horror stories coincided with actual detentions, they seemed credible. The silence of the state and the secrecy surrounding the Bastille promoted the formation of legends. The

Figure 8. Man Ray, Imaginary portrait of the Marquis de Sade, 1938. Oil on canvas, 549 by 451 mm (New York, collection of William N. Copley).

Bastille owed its place as a central symbol of antiabsolutism before the Revolution first of all to the sensational character of such legends and their iconicity, which a mere term such as "despotisme" lacked.[107] But also, as a negative symbol of the state, the Bastille embodied its tyranny and anonymous "ministerial despotism" without either attacking the king (who seemed to have no idea of what was going on) or questioning the privileges of individual groups in society.

So the consciousness-forming power of the symbol "Bastille" toward the end of the ancien régime proves to be a symptom of political crisis. Its broad effect confirms a number of indicators external to the prison. A successful, only moderately enlightened writer close to the people such as Louis-Sébastien Mercier, who had no firsthand knowledge of the Bastille whatsoever, was nevertheless fascinated by it. Already in his utopia of 1770, he imagines "The new Paris" (chapter 8) without the Bastille: "They tell me, that the Bastille has been demolished by a prince who did not think himself a god among men. . . . They say, moreover, that on the ruins of that hideous castle (so properly called the Palace of Vengeance, and of royal vengeance) they have erected a temple to Clemency."[108] The fourth act of Mercier's melodrama of national history concerning the religious wars takes place in an underground dungeon of the Bastille and invokes its horrors.[109] And in his portrayals of customs in prerevolutionary Paris, which were immediately translated throughout Europe, Mercier conceded that the state prisons had become deserted in comparison with earlier times. But he was not able to mention the Bastille without commemorating the "moaning of so many victims," Renneville's story of suffering, the secret surrounding the man in the iron mask, and other martyrs of the Bastille: "The famous Linguet still languishes there or no longer does. What is his offense? Nobody knows."[110] Even a city guidebook repeats Voltaire's familiar couplet in its section on the Bastille and disguises allusions to supposed horrors in a harmless aesthetic judgment: "The exterior of this old fortress is very characteristic; it could serve as a model for an artist painting the architecture of a beautiful horror."[111]

A further indication of the dissemination of the myth of the Bastille in prerevolutionary France is provided by the literary underground, the popularizing undercurrent of the Enlightenment. One creator of such "political pornography," whose ilk was referred to by Voltaire as "Rousseau of the gutter," Charles Théveneau de Morande, also never a prisoner of the Bastille himself, liked to open his anonymous accounts of scandals and all sorts of contemporary sensations with indignant and allusive references to the Bastille. Obviously, this was a good means of attracting the attention of the reader and simultaneously demonstrating his "oppositional" stance. In 1771, for instance, Morande claimed that strangling in Turkey and banishment to Siberia in Russia were equivalent to the Bastille in France. According to this author, the Bastille was so overfull with prisoners that the guards had to spend the night under canvases on the terraces.[112] Later, he called France the country of the Bastille (while England was the country of liberty), where police inquisition ruled; six months in the Bastille were worse than fifty years of forced labor in quarries.[113] In addition to these chronicles of scandals, the more radical anti-Bastille pamphlets were among the most sought-after forbidden literature sold under the counter—not only in Paris but also in the provinces. In 1784–85, the bookseller Mauvelain in Troyes, for instance, who specialized in illegal writings, ordered eighteen copies of *Remarques historiques sur la Bastille,* twenty-one copies of Mirabeau's *Lettres de cachet,* and thirty copies of Linguet's *Mémoires sur la Bastille* from the Société Typographique in Neuchâtel, which subsisted by marketing the French Enlightenment.[114]

Prevalent among the bourgeoisie as well as in the literary underground, the dreadful image of the Bastille finally pressed on government circles and directly on the Versailles court. First, it came disguised in the comic figure of Beaumarchais's Figaro, whose renowned monologue in the third scene of the fifth act of *The Marriage of Figaro* tells of the failed attempt to make money by writing: "My book was not sold, but confiscated; while my publishing venture was closed, I was ushered through the gate of the Bastille, where I was well received on account of the recommendation that put me there. I was housed and fed free of charge for six months, saved a lot of money on clothes, and truly, this economic retreat provided me the highest profit [le produit le plus net] I ever got from literature."[115] When in 1781 Madame Campan read this passage to Louis XVI, who wanted to review *The Marriage of Figaro* before giving permission to mount it, the king is said to have got up and exclaimed in agitation: "That's detestable; that shall never be played: the Bastille must be destroyed before the license to act this play can be any other than an act of most dangerous folly."[116] Nevertheless, Beaumarchais's scandalous piece was released for public performance because of general pressure in 1784 and played with great success. The passage on the Bastille was reduced, however, to the following: "I write on the value of money and interest. Soon I find myself inside a coach looking at the drawbridge of a prison, entering which, I left hope and freedom behind."[117]

Tearing down the Bastille, the "stigma of the Age of Enlightenment," an action suggested by Mercier, illustrated in Linguet's pamphlet, but still rejected by Louis XVI, was increasingly recommended even in circles close to the government before 1789. The municipal inspector of Paris, Corbet, put forward a plan in 1784 to create a generous "Louis XVI Square" on the site of the Bastille. The liberal Duc d'Orléans, nephew of the king, urged his uncle to abolish lettres de cachet and the Bastille in order to consolidate his popularity.[118] No less a figure than the deputy of the governor of the Bastille, the royal lieutenant Pierre-François de Rivierre Du Puget, prepared a memorandum for the Paris police lieutenant Louis Thiroux de Crosne in August 1788 in which he suggested saving the annual expenses of 120,000–140,000 livres for the Bastille by transferring the few prisoners to Vincennes, razing the fortress, and using the space for city redevelopment. The Bastille, he wrote, could be useful only as a military instrument against the nearby residents of Faubourg Saint-Antoine; but as such it could hardly be employed: "If it were put to use, the residents would be incited to take part in a rebellion in which they would play a major role."[119] As can be seen, prerevolutionary administrative deliberations were not motivated only by city-redevelopment concerns, reform policies, and finances. In the end, a subliminal fear of the mobilizing, subversive effect of the symbol "Bastille" can be discerned behind them. The social reality of the symbol was noted, whether it was liked or not. It seems as if this knowledge did not penetrate the government itself, however, for otherwise it would not have been so surprised by the storming of the Bastille.

On the eve of the Revolution in 1789, the demonized Bastille had as a matter of fact become a general collective symbol. Its emblematic status is illustrated, for example, by the leaflet containing a satiric dialog between the Bastille and the prison tower of Vincennes, which had been closed in 1784. The Bastille fancies itself to be above the other: "It is I, yes I, who rule in the center of the most enormous city of the world and openly unfurl the horrible armament of my power. . . . Within my walls, I have locked up the most excellent heroes, famous authors, and people, so to speak, of divine lineage. . . . The terrible and secret equipment of our cells constitutes a remarkable period in history, and we can pride ourselves in having carried out deadly tortures that would be the envy even of cannibals." But the prison tower warns: "Come on! It is quite possible that you will soon be forced to bury your colossus's presumptuous conceit in the dust."[120] The Bastille had become the incarnation of the defects of the old France to such an extent that in the crisis of the turn of the year 1789, the later Jacobin journalist Jean-Louis Carra expressed fear that the assembly of the States General would be restricted to submissive counseling, and then "be nothing but a confirmation of the perpetual slavery of the nation, a perpetual confusion of the finances of the state, a perpetual corruption of the court, and a perpetual Bastille for the decent citizen."[121] Moreover, the demand for the "abolition of the Bastille and of lettres de cachet"[122] in March and April 1789 proved to be a widespread concern of the grievance registers ("cahiers de doléances"), of the Third Estate in particular, for the approaching States General. This was the case not only in Paris,[123] where even the election meeting of the aristocracy joined the chorus,[124] but also in the provinces. The three estates of the constituency Montfort-l'Amaury and Dreux, for instance, demanded that "the Bastille and other fortresses called state prisons be razed, their property sold or immediately used for the general good, and that where the Bastille now stands a monument to liberty be erected for Louis XVI's glory."[125]

With the strong and widespread collective feelings of hate, fear, and suspicion that the Bastille evoked on the eve of the Revolution — and in this, the symbol also established its emotional appeal — a small incident was enough to unleash the mass uprising against this "fortress of terror." The symbol justified, even provoked the symbolic act.

2. THE STORMING OF THE BASTILLE

The Historical Event as Collective Symbolic Action

The Storming of the Bastille: Causes and Process

THE UNPRECEDENTED EVENT OF THE CONQUEST AND destruction of the notorious state prison on 14 July 1789 was a highly symbolic act.[1] The patriotic and festive ecstasy that took hold of the French capital expressed collective enthusiasm over the annihilation of the "bastion of despotism." Not so much its current significance as a state prison—which was minor—but its past role, deeply anchored in the collective consciousness, as an instrument of arbitrary rule was decisive in making the Bastille, situated on the eastern outskirts of Paris, of all places the goal of the rebels.

The long-term causes of the events of 14 July 1789 lie in the myth of the Bastille, which had become a central part of the political and social world of ideas during the eighteenth century. The short-term causes that set off the event itself lie in the extraordinarily tense political atmosphere of the first days of July 1789. On 5 May 1789, the States General (Etats généraux) had convened in Versailles in order to solve the financial crisis of the kingdom of France. As soon as deliberations opened, it became clear that the delegates of the Third Estate—the representatives of the middle classes, the crafts, and the farmers, i.e., of 95 percent of the French population—disagreed with the political preconditions that governed the assembly as well as the established mode of voting. They saw their real political mission as entailing a comprehensive reform of the kingdom—not just a solution of the financial crisis—and primarily demanded that the traditional mode of representation be abandoned. Following the principle of the equality of all citizens of the state, votes should be taken on a "one man, one vote" basis rather than according to each estate, as had been done before. The deliberations of the three estates—aristocracy, clergy, and Third Estate—were to take place in plenary sessions, not separately. In the face of the political resistance of the aristocracy, clergy, and the king to these radical suggestions for reform, which would have meant a dissolution of the traditional feudal representation of the estates, the representatives of the Third Estate unilaterally declared themselves to be the National Assembly on 17 June 1789 and called on the representatives of the other two estates to join them. Louis XVI had first declared this step illegal and had tried to put pressure on the representatives by concentrating troops around the assembly hall of the Third Estate in the Hôtel des Menus in Versailles. But because of the unreliability of the troops and more and more liberal defectors from within the aristocratic and clerical estates, he was forced to give in. On 27 June Louis XVI acknowledged the fait accompli and recognized parliament as a Constituent Assembly. According to the fundamental principles of the political philosophy of the Enlightenment, which formed the basis for the aims of the representatives of the Third Estate, political legitimacy and rule had by this act de facto passed on to the elected representatives of the people. The concept of the sovereignty of a people had become the philosophical fundament of the state.

Fascinated, the representatives of the National Assembly in Versailles as well as the Paris public attempted to determine during the following weeks whether this concession of the king and his advisers was the expression of a newfound political conviction or a tactical maneuver. Events seemed to speak in favor of the latter conclusion. After all, a series of marching orders went out to numerous regiments in the provinces after 22 June to move into position in and around the capital. The Parisian Champ de Mars—today the site of the Eiffel Tower—came to resemble an army camp; the deployment of forces was to be completed around 13 July. In vain, the National Assembly in a petition drafted by Mirabeau (8 July) called on the king to at least withdraw those regiments which consisted of foreign soldiers (Swiss, German). Instead, Louis XVI dismissed the popular prime minister Necker and appointed the conservative Baron de Breteuil as his successor (11 July) —news that hit Paris like a bombshell the next morning and provoked a wave of protest. Rumors of an impending occupation of the capital by the royal troops that had been gathered and of a violent dissolution of the National Assembly made the rounds. Even though neither Louis XVI nor Baron de Breteuil was following a fixed plan, the rumor that fifteen thousand soldiers would march toward Paris, level the city, and kill its rebellious citizens spread like a wildfire.[2] Journalists such as the subsequent deputy Camille Desmoulins told the crowd in the garden of the Palais-Royal—then a center of pamphleteers and political agitators, because it was free of police—that the governor of the Bastille, de Launay, had received orders from the Versailles court to point the cannons of the fortified state prison at the district of Saint-Antoine and to blow away any people gathered there.[3] Another rumor that went around in the lower-class districts of Saint-Marcel and Saint-Antoine claimed that the representatives of the National Assembly were already being held by the governor of the Bastille and had been locked up in the underground dungeons of the prison.[4] A letter from the later social-revolutionary conspirator François-Noël Babeuf, who traveled from the northern French provincial city of Saint-Quentin to Paris in July 1789, describes the atmosphere of collective fear and panic that permeated the life of the capital in these days in a letter to his wife:

On my arrival in Paris, there was talk everywhere of a conspiracy instigated by the Count d'Artois [the brother of Louis XVI] and other high aristocrats. It was a matter of nothing less than having a large part of the population of Paris killed, and only excepting those from the massacre who submitted to the aristocrats in Paris and in all of France, and who would accept the fate of slavery by offering their hands to the iron chains of the tyrants without complaint. If the Parisians had not discovered this plot in time, a terrible, unprecedented crime would have been committed. But as it is, it was possible to come up in time with an idea to take vengeance for this perfidious plan, which is unparalleled in all of history.[5]

Political news, rumors, and collective anxieties led to demonstrations, panicky reactions, and acts of violence. When citizens who had gathered at the Palais-Royal removed the bust of Necker and of the Duc d'Orléans, the reputedly liberal nephew of the king, from Curtius's waxworks and staged a protest march of five thousand people, they were bloodily dispersed in the garden of the Tuileries by the troopers of Prince Lambesc. On 12 July an excited crowd stormed the La Force and Conciergerie prisons and liberated the prisoners. In the night of 12 July forty of the fifty-four existing customhouses — tollgates that had surrounded Paris since the Middle Ages and at which customs duties and taxes had to be paid before entering the capital — were burned down, their records destroyed, their iron gates torn away.[6] At the same time, one of Paris's richest monasteries, the Monastère Saint-Lazare, was searched for weapons and pillaged, the furniture thrown through the windows onto the street, the archives destroyed, the stockpiles of grain and flour brought to the corn market. All stores of gunsmiths and saddlers were plundered in the search for weapons.

In order to restore public safety, the electors of Paris, who had been chosen in elections to the States General, formed a provisional city government (Comité permanent) at city hall on the morning of 13 July led by the head of the merchants, Jacques de Flesselles. They deployed a militia of about thirteen thousand in the city districts. Nevertheless, the crowd remained assembled in front of city hall on the Place de la Grève, where all transports, wagons, and letters coming into or leaving the city were publicly controlled. When the call for rifles and ammunition grew louder and louder, Flesselles let the gunpowder stocked at city hall — three barrels of it — be given out "to take the Bastille," as Abbé Lefevre wrote in the issue book.[7] But a delegation of electors dispatched to the barracks of the "invalides," retired soldiers who guarded the Bastille, for weapons came back in the afternoon without having accomplished their objective, while Flesselles sent the citizens to the Carthusian cloister and to the municipal arsenal in a futile search for guns. This increased their indignation and suspicion even more.

In the morning of 14 July about seven thousand citizens gathered on the Esplanade des Invalides in front of the barracks of the invalides and broke into their weapons depot. Since some of his own veterans as well as the regiments that had newly entered the city sympathized with the citizens, the governor, the Marquis de Sombreuil, did not put up any resistance. The citizens captured several cannons and forty thousand rifles — though no gunpowder or the necessary ammunition. The password "Marchons à la Bastille" had already been issued sporadically because of the rumors circulating concerning the Bastille. But it turned into a stirring slogan when it became known that in the past night a large part of the gunpowder, which earlier had been kept in the arsenal and the other weapons depots, had been moved to the state prison, which was considered impregnable, and which also served as a fortress. The revolutionary city committee, which was meeting in the city hall in the meantime and observed this development with alarm, tried to prevent any further escalation. As early as ten o'clock, it sent a first delegation to call on the governor of the Bastille to peacefully surrender the fortress—a demand de Launay categorically rejected. Then the initiative passed on to the citizens. Especially in Saint-Louis-de-la-Culture, the district bordering on the Bastille, the citizens felt threatened by de Launay's defense measures, above all by the cannons on the battlements. Around eleven-thirty this district in turn sent a delegation under Thuriot de La Rozière, a lawyer known at the Bastille. De Launay let him in to inspect the battlements, and he made a report, first to his district and then around noon at city hall, that the cannons had been withdrawn from the crenels and were not loaded but that de Launay refused the surrender of gunpowder. While Thuriot was reporting to the provisional government in the city hall and was entrusted by them with a new delegation, angry citizens gathered around the Bastille in larger and larger groups to demand weapons. When they succeeded at penetrating the outer courtyard of the fortress over the drawbridge, which had been pulled up but not secured, and when they did not take notice of the warnings of the garrison, de Launay grew fearful of a frontal attack and ordered the soldiers to fire on the intruders at one-thirty. At the same time, the invalides in the Bastille fired a cannon shot, their only one for the duration of the siege.

This impulsive act of the governor of the Bastille,[8] who was completely out of his depth, was misinterpreted as insidious treason and suddenly created a new situation by turning citizens looking for weapons into a revolutionary crowd with a distinct target. Announced by the cannon shot, delivered by eyewitnesses, and confirmed by the wounded who were being brought in, the news of de Launay's treason mobilized the crowd that was waiting on the square in front of the city hall. Even more furious because of an intercepted letter in which Flesselles exhorted the governor to hold out, they now demanded revenge. Only now, around two in the afternoon, did the cry "To the Bastille" (A la Bastille) become a slogan. The previously diffuse search for weapons now turned into a purposive expedition of conquest against the symbolically important fortress, and its significance, which the crowd had formerly been only potentially aware of, was suddenly obvious. Without waiting for two further delegations of the city committee, which vainly called on de Launay to hand the Bastille over to the militia, the citizens—mostly craftsmen from the Paris suburbs, small merchants, and former soldiers—streamed from city hall to the Bastille by the thousands, armed with pikes, knives, axes, and a few solitary rifles. The growing crowd around the Bastille began a chaotic and desperate "siege" of the fortress and its garrison of one hundred invalides and Swiss guards. Crowd members posed no danger to the defenders until soldiers fraternized with them. Groups of the royal regiments that had been transferred to Paris had refused to obey orders and rebelled, and they had been liberated from prisons and entertained at the Palais-Royal by citizens several times since the end of June.[9] Now, not only did they refuse to be deployed against the population, a situation that made the growing agitation possible in the first place, but some of them defected to the rebels and gave them military support. In particular, there was a group of seventy men from the French Guard that Hulin, the owner of a laundry and a burly former officer of the French Guard, mobilized at city hall and led from the Hôtel des Invalides to the Bastille with five cannons around three o'clock. Hulin and an officer who had defected from the French Guard named Elie took over command and employed the cannons. After several cannonballs had glanced off the walls of the Bastille, some daring cannon shots at the raised drawbridge leading to the inner courtyard of the fortress convinced its commander that a real battle was imminent. De Launay first threatened to blow up the entire fortress and a large part of the surrounding district with the gunpowder stockpiled in the Bastille. His soldiers, fearing the lynch-mob mentality of the indignant crowd, pressured him into capitulating, however, at around five o'clock. About one hundred of the attackers had been killed in the past hours and more than seventy wounded, while there was merely one victim among the defenders.

The intruders entering the Bastille seized the governor and the garrison, who greeted them as fellow citizens. Only later did they remember the Bastille prisoners, and then found a mere seven, all of them in tower rooms, none in the notorious underground dungeons. In triumph, these liberated captives were led from the Bastille to city hall. Further captives, among them the Marquis de Sade, had already been brought to other prisons such as Charenton during the first days of July. So on 14 July the only prisoners in the Bastille were four counterfeiters, the Count de Solages, who had been confined by his family for moral offenses, and two mentally disturbed men called Whyte and Tavernier.

The plundering of the arms supplies kept in the Bastille and the disarming of the defenders were followed by scenes of lynch law and violent revenge. Governor de Launay, whom Hulin and Elie had at first protected from the outraged mob, was torn from his guards shortly before his arrival at city hall, lynched, and killed with a kitchen knife by an unemployed cook named Dénot. Cheered on by the crowd,[10] Dénot, who boasted of his deed as late as 1792 and called it an "act of patriotism,"[11] also cut off de Launay's head. This was then carried through the streets on a pike as a trophy—a scene that was to be repeated in the following years as a sign of popular justice. Along with de Launay, who was mocked as the "monstre de la Bastille,"[12] three officers and three soldiers of the Bastille garrison as well as the head of the city committee, Flesselles, who was accused of insidious treason, were massacred by the crowd in the late afternoon of 14 July in spite of the guarantee of free withdrawal. Especially in the perspective of foreign observers, these scenes marred the "glorious events" of the day.[13]

The course of the attack on the Bastille, which was immediately felt to be an "unheard-of event," a far-reaching historical upheaval, even a "day of miracles,"[14] is characterized by an intimate combination of archaic and modern social ideas. It strikes one as archaic that rumors circulating only orally were able to have such explosive effects, and that they were believed to such an extent. The collective anxieties that prevailed among the population of Paris on 12, 13, and 14 July are reminiscent of the panic erupting into acts of violence that was typical of the bread riots of the seventeenth and early eighteenth centuries. These were continued by the rebellion of the Grande Peur in rural France after the storming of the Bastille and erupted again at the beginning of August 1789 in provincial cities such as Rouen in acts of revenge against tax collectors and inspectors.[15] The lynch law put into practice on 14 July 1789 for the first time also seems archaic: while it simultaneously observed the rules of a regular trial by appointing an improvised court and pronouncing a sentence, in its form of punishment it fell back on the practices of execution of the ancien régime, practices condemned as "cruel" and "barbaric" by such authors as Voltaire since the Enlightenment. In the eyes of the populist judges, it was a matter not only of executing a death sentence but of making the guilty person suffer publicly and bodily according to the seriousness of his crime. Like de Launay, the governor of the Bastille, who was viciously tortured to death, the criminals had to undergo torments and corporal punishment. In the minds of the self-styled judges and executioners of the years 1789–94, crimes "against the people" or the "nation"—like crimes against the sovereign in the ancien régime— could be compensated for only by the complete physical destruction of the guilty party. This explains the obsessiveness with which the angry crowd of 14 July 1789 in similar fashion dismembered the limbs of its victims, scattered them to the four winds, and carried de Launay's head through the streets in a triumphal procession only to heedlessly throw it into the gutter at nightfall and forget it there.

On close observation, the archaism of lynch law and the exaggerated effect of rumors in a society still dominated by oral communication media stand in contrast to some elements that make 14 July 1789 seem an event of surprising modernity. The gatherings of people on 12, 13, and 14 July resulted not only from collective fear and panic but also from direct political agitation centered on the Palais-Royal. Political agitators such as the Marquis de Saint-Huruge, who tried to mobilize public opinion in favor of the interests of the house of Orléans, a lateral branch of the reigning Bourbon dynasty, and the journalist Camille Desmoulins called for a storming of the Bastille in order to protect the achievements of the constitutional revolution from the intervention of reactionary forces. Even Hulin, a former officer and the well-paid owner of the royal laundry, had publicly and excitedly called on the crowd—before playing a decisive role himself in the storming of the Bastille—several times during the previous days to act and start an insurrection. On 13 July Hulin is supposed to have cried out in extreme agitation to Madame de Staël, Necker's daughter and later a writer, whom he knew through his occupation at court: "I want . . . to take revenge for your father on these bastards [the tyrants] who want to butcher us."[16]

The event of the storming of the Bastille also seems modern because it was here that the principle of the sovereignty of the people, which the National Assembly had elevated to the fundamental precept of its constitution on 17 June 1789, served to legitimize revolutionary violence for the first time. Legally, the events of 14 July were high treason of the first order ("crime de lèze-majesté au premier chef"), whose author according to established law should have been sentenced to the heaviest punishment: execution on the wheel. This stance was taken and energetically supported by the majority of the royal court, but also by some conservative citizens, among them the Paris bookseller Siméon-Prosper Hardy.[17] But in this matter too—as in June 1789—Louis XVI was forced to give way in the face of the tremendous mobilization of the public. After two days of indecisiveness and vacillation that were followed by a fascinated domestic and foreign press,[18] on 16 July he announced to the National Assembly that the troops would be withdrawn, accepted the invitation of the newly elected mayor of Paris Jean Sylvain Bailly, and had himself celebrated in the capital as "restaurateur de la liberté françoise," a title that the National Assembly would bestow on him officially on 8 August. The Count d'Artois, brother of the king, who was hated by the people of Paris, fled beyond the Rhine along a secret route during these days with the first wave of emigrants. King Louis XVI, by contrast, met with Mayor Bailly at the Paris border in Chaillot on 17 July 1789. Bailly received him with the words—which on closer inspection are extremely ambiguous—"Henri IV won back his people, here the people won back their king."[19] Under the eyes of citizens and the National Guard (the former militia), which was now officially under La Fayette's command, three hundred delegates from the National Assembly then accompanied the king to the Paris city hall. Here, Bailly pinned a tricolored cockade, the new symbol of liberty, on the king's hat in a commemoration ceremony for the victims of the attack on the Bastille. Contemporary observers noted some hecklers hostile to the king but also many cheers for the king ("Vive le Roi") and even more often the enthusiastic "Vive la Nation."[20]

This ceremony of 17 July, which strikes one as paradoxical from a twentieth-century perspective, celebrated the far-reaching symbolic significance of the storming of the Bastille in public, in the presence of the king and of many representatives of the Constituent Assembly. When the storming of the Bastille was officially legitimized as an act of liberation from despotic rule, the principle of the sovereignty of the people as the basis of a new political order was sanctioned. The solemnity of 17 July had already assigned the king a limited sphere of power, one laid down by the nation and its representatives. In contrast to the members of the detested court of Versailles, Louis XVI *received* the cockade as a symbol of his affiliation with the nation from the hand of the elected deputy of the people—whereas two days earlier de Launay and Flesselles had been expelled from society and executed as "criminals" by the rebels for their treason against the nation. The power of the people in the street was officially recognized as a means of reestablishing lost freedom by the ceremony of 17 July, which began with a thanksgiving service in Notre-Dame Cathedral. The magnitude of this development became clear only in the months and years that followed. The storming of the Bastille and its official celebration on 17 July revealed the basic elements of a revolutionary self-understanding that would further develop in the following years and only gradually manifest its full consequences. Along with the new political principles —above all the sovereignty of the people and the legitimation of violence—which soon came together in a kind of "revolutionary catechism" in the innumerable speeches and pamphlets on the storming of the Bastille, the "Vainqueurs de la Bastille" (a formal title of honor accorded to the victors of the Bastille by the National Assembly) appeared for the first time as a new type of national identification figure.

How a Decisive Event in World History Is "Made":
The Symbolic Exaggeration of 14 July 1789

The symbolic significance of the storming of the Bastille is not exclusively located in the historical event itself, the actual course of which has just been outlined; it lies also, indeed mainly, in the exaggerated, collective perception of contemporaries. If one understands the "great event" sociohistorically as social knowledge constituted through news media and through processes of communication,[21] one could say even that the storming of the Bastille and its individual aspects "exist" for those contemporaries only because the media reported on them repeatedly and emphatically. In order to go back behind the historical events constituting the "storming of the Bastille" as we know it today to the image people had of it then, we must uncover the multiplicitous and opinion-fashioning early news accounts of those events. In view of the fifty or so general reports on the storming of the Bastille published in France during 1789,[22] which were supplemented by dozens of leaflets and newspaper items on details, a differentiated serial analysis is necessary. Contemporary patterns of collective perception and opinion formation become visible only when source materials are listed chronologically and divided into repeated narrative sequences, and when differing versions of the story are compared with one another in terms of content and style (tables 3 and 4).

Where possible, the reports and accounts of the storming of the Bastille that our tabular interpretation is based on constitute all relevant printed prose texts of the first years of the Revolution, and especially of the summer of 1789, regardless of textual genre.[23] At first glance, the small share of newspaper items is striking. Only seven press organs ran articles worth mentioning in July 1789 concerning the events of 14 July in Paris: most important among them Gorsas's *Courrier* (no. 1), Béranger's *Point du Jour* (no. 8), the *Journal général de l'Europe* (no. 14), which appeared simultaneously in Liège and The Hague as well as in Paris, Mirabeau's *Courrier de Provence* (no. 19), and finally Rivarol's conservative *Journal politique national* (no. 22). The established daily newspaper *Journal de Paris* (no. 5) limited itself to repeating what the Vicomte de Noailles had said in the National Assembly at Versailles, while the official organ of the government, the *Gazette de France,* was silent, as if nothing had happened. Prudhomme's *Révolutions de Paris* (no. 15), a current occasional periodical that developed into a weekly solely because of the tremendous success of this report, published the most passionate prorevolutionary account.[24]

Since the "press revolution" of 1789 occurred only after 14 July,[25] the social image of the storming of the Bastille was mainly shaped by leaflets. This journalism, produced in haste for sale in the streets, consists on the one hand of—usually anonymous—accounts ranging from the printed letter (nos. 13, 18) to the sermonlike thanksgiving and memorial speech (nos. 7, 29) and on the other hand of eyewitness reports of defenders of the Bastille (nos. 24, 36). Mainly, however, we find statements made by people involved in the siege and seizure (nos. 3, 4, 24, 26, 28, 30, 31, 34, 35, 37, 38). These authors like to give even greater authenticity to their depictions by adding the signatures of other witnesses and often so drastically limit their narratives to personal experiences that many other occurrences go unmentioned. The first popular description, written down by Beffroy under dictation from the victors of the Bastille and published in fifty-six thousand copies (no. 9), attained something like official recognition. Similarly, the balanced account that the victor of the Bastille and man of letters Dusaulx presented on the first anniversary of the fourteenth of July (no. 45); the revolutionary almanac of the Protestant representative

Rabaut Saint-Etienne from the following year, which was also translated into German (no. 49); as well as the exhaustive chapters in a joint
work by Breton lawyers and writers, the most comprehensive and
earliest history of the French Revolution (no. 47), were all generally
accepted. Popular almanacs (nos. 38–40, no. 50) and a radical revolutionary commemorative text also demonstrate what had become common knowledge from the earlier accounts, as do depictions combined
with oral popular culture in the media of image and song—from the
repeatedly copied pictorial broadsheet of the Parisian publisher Gautier (no. 20, figure 9) to the illustrated "patchwork" on the history of
the Revolution by the engraver Janinet, which devoted no fewer than
eight series of plates to the storming of the Bastille in the spring of
1790 (no. 42), to the musical history of the Revolution by the popular
playwright Pitou, which retold the events of the time in songs, each
of which was accompanied by an introductory prose text (no. 51).

Textual relations that we cannot investigate in detail here indicate
which might have been the leading accounts. Beffroy de Reigny's *Précis
exact* (no. 9), for instance, was excerpted in the anonymous leaflet *Le
Grenadier patriote* (no. 16), which in turn found its way into the pamphlet *La Bastille au Diable* (no. 46). The descriptions of the *Révolutions de
Paris* (no. 15) and of victor of the Bastille Thuriot de la Rozière (no. 31)
were assimilated in Janinet's *Gravures historiques* and other publications.
The basic tenets of the leaflet *Les Lauriers du fauxbourg Saint-Antoine*
(no. 11) made their way not only into Gautier's pictorial broadsheet but
also into a popular woodcut by the provincial publisher Letourmi in
Orléans.[26]

If one now, on the basis of tables 3 and 4, looks at what and how
these texts report, one is not surprised to find that the storming of the
Bastille itself is by far the event mentioned most often (sequence 18).
But it is usually reported as a matter of fact, merely as an event that
occurred. The reporting of certain preparatory events, accompanying circumstances, and immediate consequences is quite different—
from the defection of the French Guard to the side of the citizens (sequence 10) to the supposed "treason" and execution of the governor
of the Bastille (sequences 17 and 20) to the liberation of the prisoners
and the celebration of the victors of the Bastille (sequences 22 and 23).
Concentrated in these narrative sequences are not only emphatically
revolutionary expressions of opinion but also critical or conservative
counterdescriptions. These sequences make up the strategic points at

Narrative Sequences

		Date	No.	Introduction (1)	Despotism (2)	Conspiracy (3)	Necker (4)	People awaken (5)	Palais-Royal (6)	Cockades (7)	Demonstration (8)	Repression (9)	Guards (10)	Citizens' Militia (11)	Patrols (12)	Search for weapons (13)	Invalides' (14)	To the Bastille! (15)	Delegations (16)	Treason (17)	Storming of B. (18)	To city hall (19)	Popular justice (20)	Justification (21)	Prisoners free (22)	Victors of B. (23)	Razing of B. (24)	B. Monument (25)	Vive le Roi! (26)	Retrospec. apprec. (27)	Tour (28)	Conspiracy conf. (29)	B. Archive (30)	Terror of Dungeons (31)

Table 3 continued

Note: The following numbered list gives abbreviated titles of the sources in which the reports appeared. Full bibliographic documentation can be found in the appendix of reports at the back of the book.

1. *Courrier*
2. *Journée du 14*
3. *Relation exacte*
4. Boucheron; *Récit*
5. *Journal de Paris*
6. *Il étoit temps*
7. *Semaine Mémorable*
8. [Bérenger], *Point du Jour*
9. Beffroy de Reigny, *Précis*
10. [Caraccioli] *Capitale délivrée*
11. *Lauriers du Fauxbourg*
12. *Relation*
13. *Ouvrage des six jours*
14. *Journal gén. de l'Europe*
15. *Révolutions de Paris*
16. *Grenadier patriote*
17. *Révolutions . . . ou Récit*
18. *Extrait d'une lettre*
19. *Dix-neuvième lettre*
20. *Siège de la Bastille*
21. [Ducray-Duminil], *Semaine*
22. *Journal polit. national*
23. *Victoire des Parisiens*
24. Flue, *Relation*
25. *Attaque . . . et reddition*
26. Ridet, *Récit*
27. *Les Fers brisés*
28. *Journée . . . Humbert*
29. *Le Parisien fêté*
30. La Reynie, *A mes . . . camarades*
31. Thuriot, *Récit*
32. Beffroy de Reigny, *Histoire*
33. *Remarques et Anecdotes*
34. *Journal de la Compagnie*
35. Fournier-L'Héritier, *Extrait*
36. *La Bastille dévoilée*
37. Cholat, *Service fait*
38. *Etrennes mignonnes*
39. *Etrennes nationales*
40. *Petit Théâtre de l'Univers*
41. *Relation véritable*
42. *Gravures historiques*
43. *Précis des événemens*
44. Pitra, *Mémoires*
45. Dusaulx, *L'Insurrection*
46. *La Bastille au Diable*
47. [Kerverseau et al.], *Histoire*
48. [Montjoye], *Histoire*
49. Rabaut Saint-Etienne, *Almanach*
50. André, *Almanach*
51. [Pitou], *Vaudevilles*
52. *Journées mémorables*

	Narrative Sequences	Type of Representation			Total
		x	■	o	
1.	Introduction	10	12		22
2.	Critique of despotism	2	10		12
3.	Fear of a conspiracy	14	13	2	29
4.	Necker dismissed	25	1		26
5.	People awaken	3	2		5
6.	Palais-Royal	15	6	1	22
7.	Cockades	24	1	2	27
8.	Demonstration	15	4		19
9.	Repression	15	5	1	21
10.	Guards go over to the people	27	2	1	30
11.	Citizen's militia	33	2		35
12.	Patrols	16	3		19
13.	Search for weapons	26			26
14.	Invalides' barracks	30	1		31
15.	To the Bastille!	22	4		26
16.	Delegations	18	2		20
17.	De Launay's treason	23	8	5	36
18.	Storming of Bastille	40	4	2	46
19.	March to city hall	10			10
20.	Popular justice	28	10	2	40
21.	Justification	4	5		9
22.	Prisoners free	2	15	4	21
23.	Victors of Bastille	13	12	2	27
24.	Razing of Bastille	13	5		18
25.	Bastille monument	10	1		11
26.	Vive le Roi!	18	4		22
27.	Retrospective appreciation	3	13		16
28.	Tour	1	5		6
29.	Conspiracy confirmed	1	1		2
30.	Bastille archive	12	2		14
31.	Terror of the dungeons	2	10	2	14

Note: Table 4 is based on table 3.

Table 4. Early Accounts of 14 July 1789: Content and Perspective

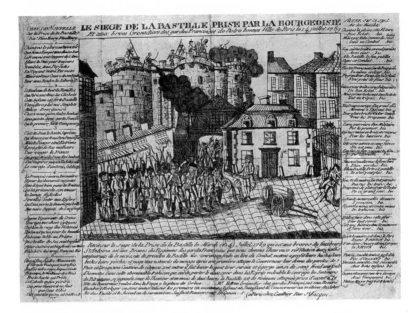

Figure 9. Siege and conquest of the Bastille by the citizens' militia. Anonymous etching, 172 by 322 mm, published by Gautier, Paris, 1789 (Bibliothèque Nationale, Estampes, Coll. Hennin 10330).

which political analysis and evaluation are formed and articulated. From the beginning, as the weakness of dissenting opinion illustrates, journalistic accounts were decidedly in favor of the revolutionary interpretation. It even seems as if supporters of the ancien régime had lost their voice in the face of the prevailing enthusiasm over the storming of the Bastille. A consistent counterrepresentation such as that of the Royalist lawyer Montjoye of 1791 (no. 48) was a major exception. The example of Beffroy de Reigny demonstrates how little effort went into critical reporting and self-correction. Beffroy already qualifies his first report by saying that there are "so many versions of the details [of 14 July] that the public until now has been only imperfectly informed of the truth" (no. 9:1). In his expanded account, he laments the "unceasing litany of anonymous pamphlets" whose authors are swept away by the "stream of momentary opinions" and give "their fantasies the significance of truth" (no. 32:3–4, 81), with a pointed dig at the *Révolutions de Paris* (no. 15). Beffroy even distanced himself from his *Précis exact* after the Terror, because, as he then told, he had composed it under duress and in parts untruthfully,[27] and he mocked all "the euphonious declarations [concerning the storming of the Bastille] that were flooding France."[28] But what had long since become a permanent part of the collective consciousness were exactly those first "belles déclamations" which celebrated the storming of the Bastille as a heroic victory over despotism. Even the invalides, who had hardly made a serious effort to defend the Bastille (no. 36), and the contemporary Breton historians trying to maintain the rule of law (no. 47) were not able to escape the climate of opinion.

In addition, table 3 shows a certain development through time. With growing distance from the event, not only do published accounts gain revolutionary pathos, they also increasingly shift their main emphasis from the central narrative sequences to the margins. This shift indicates that the storming of the Bastille as an event had moved into the background. Now, it served merely as an occasion for basic, confessional declarations of the horrors of the ancien régime, the perniciousness of its governments, and the liberating effects of the Revolution.

We shall try to follow this collective process of selection, interpretation, and formation of meaning in the order of the narrative sequences listed in tables 3 and 4 by means of the emphatic textual passages and supplementary leaflets concerning the importance of the Bastille. The introductory highlighting formula referring to the "unique and memorable day" of 14 July is established from the very start. According to the *Courrier de Versailles,* this day "has prepared the greatest and maybe happiest revolutions" (no. 1:129; see also no. 45:224). Surprise about the "unparalleled violent and manifold revolutions" of 12 to 17 July in Paris soon gives way to an impression of tremendous historical acceleration,[29] which "has brought about in eight days what in other places violence and laws have not accomplished in a hundred years" (no. 6:1). Beffroy de Reigny stresses above all the miraculousness of the storming of the Bastille: "This remarkable revolution will seem almost incredible to posterity" (no. 9:1). Later on he grows even more emphatic, calling the miracle divine (no. 32:69–70), in which assessment he is followed by Janinet's pictorial account (no. 42:17, 1). After August 1789, however, such general declarations on the significance of the events are supplemented by political evaluations, for instance, that the Bastille, that "monument of despotism, of tyranny, of ministerial revenge fantasies, and of the barbaric greed of its governors, . . . [had to] be abolished and destroyed in view of the rise of freedom" (no. 33:53; see also no. 44:30–34), or even dispatched to the realm of the devil, where it belonged (no. 46:1). Ultimately, the storming of the Bastille appears as the decisive victory of the people, who are reasserting their own power over their oppressors: "Despotism has no end, but the people's patience does; a moment of weakness or a great crime is all it takes for the tyrant to be finally delivered to the mercy of the crowd, which is tired of its long sufferings." The freedom that England had to gain bloodily in several centuries of civil war, France had won without great sacrifices in three days (no. 47: vol. 1:1, ix).

To the same degree that the storming of the Bastille no longer appeared as a mere sensation but as a revolutionary act of freedom, the hour of birth of a new, better age, the ancien régime gained prominence as an age of despotism under the sign of the Bastille. "The princes, the great, and the ministers had plotted against the people and wanted to crush them under the heavy chains of despotism" (no. 6:1). Accusatory references to the old "ministerial power politics" (no. 7:6) and "ministerial tyranny" (no. 11:1), which were initially quite general, soon became concrete denouncements of the lettres de cachet (no. 26:4), the "tyranny" of the landlords and the rule of clergy and aristocracy (no. 16:3–7), the millennial arbitrary rule of the army (no. 42:17, 2), the "absolute monarch," the upper courts, or "parlements," the "feudal system," and the privileges of clergy and aristocracy (no. 47: vol. 1, iii–iv; see also no. 46:2, no. 49:8–13).

One pamphlet illustrates this "despotism" as a twelve-headed hydra featuring the ministers of the ancien régime from Richelieu to Lamoignon, all of whom had made use of the Bastille as an instrument of repression: "Without the fortunate insurrection of 14 July, these tormentors would have perpetuated despotism. On this day, ministerial despotism fell along with the Bastille."[30] Accordingly, a number of revolutionary pictorial broadsheets celebrated the storming of the Bastille as a victory of the citizens over the many-headed dragon of despotism.[31]

A consequence of this despotism theme forms the third narrative sequence: Despotism becomes concrete prior to 14 July in the form of conspiracies. Originally, they are only vaguely inferred from the concentration of troops in and around Paris (no. 1:30; no. 2:3; no. 6: 1–2; no. 11:2; no. 16:7; no. 21:3; no. 32:14–17; no. 42:17), but by July 17 the press claims to know of plans for a new Saint Bartholomew's massacre, during which the capital is to be silenced in a sea of blood:

> Fifty thousand men, six cannons, six thousand plunderers, and six princes are supposed to turn this realm upside down on Monday [13 July]. The States General are to be massacred, the houses of Parisians burned to the ground, the public libraries left to the flames, the Palais-Royal plundered, devastated, and annihilated. Everything was ready—torches, daggers, gallows, and proscription lists. (No. 8:1–2)

Count Mirabeau confirmed it:

> The Constituent Assembly, the most holy of laws was to be altered; . . . the capital was to be besieged and conquered; preparations were made for a civil war, even for a terrible slaughter that all known or suspected friends of the people were to become victim of. . . . two hundred years of public and private, political and fiscal, feudal and judicial repression were supposed to be crowned with the most horrible conspiracy known in world history. . . . Only that led the people to rise up. (No. 19:56)

The pamphlets adopt this description and name the court clique around Marie-Antoinette and the Marshal de Broglie as the initiators of the aristocratic conspiracy, which was preempted by the storming of the Bastille: "From all sides, hordes of murderers and servants of tyrants are approaching to fall on your city, to cut down your wives and children."[32] In vain, the conservative critics answered that this "conspiracy novel" served only to help the rebels mobilize the mob (no. 43:18–19)—the first comprehensive account of the Revolution repeated the newspaper item quoted above (from no. 8) word for word, adding five pages of its own (no. 47: vol. 1:305–10). One revolutionary caricature sums it all up as a kind of political witches' sabbath under the leadership of murderous Discord: The court under the chairmanship of the king, who has degenerated into an alcoholic, and the upper clergy, whose executive clerk in the left foreground is the Marshal de Broglie, are preparing what both pictures conjure up—a new Saint Bartholomew's massacre, which is depicted as tantamount to the crucifixion of a peace-loving and merciful God.[33]

This tripartite, partly speculative ideological introduction determines the orientation of the account before the events leading up to the storming of the Bastille are even mentioned. After such presuppositions, the dismissal of Prime Minister Necker on 11 July (sequence 4) is seen as nothing less than confirmation of the feared conspiracy. It is understood as the first step in the execution of the "infamous aristocratic plot." The mobilizing effect described in the German press mainly as an "awakening of the people" and demonstrated with the coming into fashion of the national cockade (sequences 5 and 7) takes on a more political cast in French accounts of the inflammatory speeches given at the Palais-Royal (sequence 6): "In the midst of numerous listeners, someone climbed onto a table or bench, got agitated concerning the fatherland, developed an enthusiastic eloquence that was sometimes reckless but was usually based on thorough deliberation and intelligent judgment" (no. 32:18).[34] We find a similar description in the *Gravures historiques:* "citizens gathered at the Palais-Royal, where they discussed how to dispose of tyranny, regain their inalienable natural rights, and save the fatherland" (no. 42:17, 6). If these accounts give the incipient people's rebellion an almost orderly and planned profile suggestive of grassroots democracy, others dramatize it in a manner consistent with the famous letter that Camille Desmoulins wrote to his father on 16 July 1789:[35] "At the Palais-Royal, one violent appeal followed another with incredible speed; the most violent orators jumped onto the tables, inflaming the minds of their audience, which crowded around only to spread in the city like the burning lava of a volcano afterward" (no. 47: vol. 1:336; see also no. 45:190, 206). Even critics of the radical revolution such as Pitou confirmed as late as fall 1794 that "the foundations for our revolution and of France's glory [were] laid at the Palais-Royal" (no. 51:21–22).

The demonstrations of 13 July against the dismissal of Necker began at the Palais-Royal, and the bloody dispersal of the demonstrators by Lambesc and his troopers (sequences 8 and 9) is portrayed fairly consistently. While accounts hostile to the Revolution tacitly ignore these events (nos. 22, 43), the overwhelming majority of the portrayals friendly to the Revolution stress the popular, patriotic character of the demonstration:

> I saw six to seven thousand people walk through the street [Boulevard du Temple] rather quickly and without any special discipline; some of them were armed with muskets, others with sabers, pikes, and pitchforks; they carried with them in triumph the wax busts of the Duc d'Orléans and of Mr. Necker, which

they had requested from Mr. Curtius. Next to these busts, they carried black banners lined in white as a symbol of their grief over the dismissal of the honored minister. (No. 32:24; see also no. 33:57–58)

In the middle of all the hustle and bustle, this solemn occasion is celebrated with religious deference. All passersby are asked to take off their hats to show reverence for these two objects of public veneration. (No. 15:119)

The defection of part of the royal troops to the cause of the Parisian citizens and the organization of a militia (sequences 10 and 11) are also reported unanimously and without temporal displacement. The more friendly the account is to the Revolution, the greater is the enthusiasm expressed for the new "Soldats Nationaux" (no. 6:8) or "soldats de la patrie" (no. 15 [French original: 5]), to whom the political song-writer Déduit dedicates a chanson.[36] One leaflet characterizes them as follows: "Yes, by bursting the chains of despotism themselves, the French Guards gave us a courageous example of how to take by storm the diabolical dungeon in which the unfortunate victims of tyranny had languished for so many centuries."[37]

The same is true of narrative sequences 12 through 14, from the patrols of the new militia to the plundering of the weapons arsenal in the barracks of the invalides. Some accounts deserve special attention for their extension of the introductory motif of the "aristocratic plot" to the inspection of incoming and departing travelers (no. 15: 12). Of these, the most radical version in the pamphlet *Le Grenadier patriote* of July 1789 is literally repeated in the "patchwork" of texts from spring 1790:

All carriages and horsemen were inspected as well, everything was searched. This precaution exposes the traitors, some of whom are convicted of treason and hung on Grève Square; weapons and sums of money are found in some carriages. . . . a lot of aristocrats, eager defenders of despotism who wanted to go to the country with their weapons and their gold, are arrested. (No. 16:15–16; no. 42:11, 4)

One important point in the narrative strategy of our texts is then marked by sequence 15. This sequence focuses on why the Bastille caught the attention of the citizens, and how the march to the Bastille came about. The earliest accounts—according to which several hundred citizens went to the Bastille "without any malicious intent" to demand gunpowder (no. 3:1; see also no. 2:2; no. 17:13)—are probably closest to the actual facts. In places, this version stands until August 1789 (no. 32:59; no. 33:66, 69), and as late as the end of November the wine merchant Cholat lays claim to having issued the following appeal to his fellow citizens: "Let us go to the Bastille, it is ours, we will receive weapons and gunpowder there" (no. 37:4). The *Journal général de l'Europe,* for its part, reported that the general cry "A la Bastille" had issued from the Palais-Royal (no. 14:135). This assertion was expanded upon three weeks later by Vainqueur La Reynie, becoming the grandiose claim that he had already "suggested the siege of the Bastille" on 13 July at the Palais-Royal (no. 30:9). Finally, the *Gravures historiques* devotes a dramatic sentence to the orators of the Palais-Royal in the spring of 1790: "One of them suggests the siege of the Bastille, this terrible and threatening fortress which was considered impregnable; and this suggestion, which would have been dismissed as insane earlier, meets with general consent" (no. 42:17, 6; see also 42:12, 1–2). As a result of this decision of the people the cry "We want the Bastille!" appears, with which the poorly armed crowd supposedly made its way to the fortress on the morning of 14 July according to three other accounts (no. 25:7; no. 36:113; no. 48: vol. 2:12–13). The version that the rallying cry to storm the fortress was provoked by the (supposed) ambush set by the defenders of the Bastille attained special publicity and elaboration. Vainqueur Boucheron simply reports: "On hearing the rumor that the Bastille had opened fire on the people, I went there" (no. 4:1; see also no. 6:9; no. 34:6–7). Four days later, Beffroy de Reigny quotes an inflammatory speech that the laundry owner Hulin supposedly addressed to the royal soldiers on the square in front of city hall around noon on 14 July:

> My friends, are you citizens? Yes, you are. Let us march to the Bastille; the citizens and your comrades are being slaughtered; the former are your brothers as much as the latter. Do you want to let them become victims of the cruelest treason? (No. 10:1; see also no. 32:62)

At least a year later, Pitra dramatizes this to the following appeal:

> Are you citizens, valiant French Guards? Can you hear these cries? . . . Can you hear the cannons . . . which this scoundrel de

Launay is using to murder our fathers, our wives, our children, who are standing in front of the Bastille unarmed? . . . The Parisians are being slaughtered like lambs, and you are not marching to the Bastille? (No. 44:39–40)

Another Vainqueur professes to have "felt the entire importance of the Bastille" on his arrival at city hall, and to have announced this publicly: "He [the famous liberator Cavanagh] procured a wagon, let two men climb into it, . . . and gave them order to cry: 'To the Bastille, to the Bastille! Unite your force at the Bastille! Go to the Bastille with all your force!' In the meantime . . . he himself cried at the top of his lungs: 'Take the Bastille! Men, take the Bastille!' "[38] Another source informs us that the attack on the Bastille had been "decided on" (no. 3:7) at city hall on the discovery of the treasonable correspondence between de Launay and the Baron Bezenval and that it had been announced by an old man in the council hall: " 'My friends, what shall we do with these traitors? Let us march to the Bastille' . . . And the crowd followed him" (no. 44:19).

Despite these inconsistencies, as time goes by the accounts show an increasing tendency to present hatred of the Bastille itself as the real reason for the march on the prison instead of the search for weapons. We find evidence of this tendency in the repeated phrase that the citizens of Faubourg Saint-Antoine had been "informed of the necessity to take the Bastille" (no. 11:4; no. 20; see also no. 15:18). In several accounts, it obviously seems unnecessary to explain the march on the Bastille; it suffices to invoke "this despised fortress of the royal and ministerial desire for revenge" (no. 16:19) or simply to declare: "Everyone thinks of the Bastille and desires its siege" (no. 21:13; see also no. 18:1). That the old hated image found in prison stories is in the background here is illustrated by the *Relation véritable,* according to which distress calls had been heard from a tower of the state prison on 13 July (no. 41:2), as well as by the recollection of a conqueror: "At the sight of the Bastille, this horrible monument, we were suddenly overcome by patriotic fire; as true Frenchmen and conscientious citizens we wanted to start the siege, even if it might cost us our lives."[39] Here, the march to the Bastille is finally fully depicted as a revolutionary people's conscious rebellion against the bulwark of despotism which is sung of in a song using the popular melody of "Du pas-de-charge": "The fire of the uprising shines in their eyes, / The cry 'Long live the Nation' threateningly rings out to the Bastille, / In vain, this horrible

dungeon with its enormous towers / And its drawbridge tries to resist a veritable siege" (no. 51:24).

Descriptions of delegations sent by one city district and by the electors assembled at city hall to de Launay (sequence 16) are less important than the emphatic depictions of how the rebels' march to
the Bastille came about and are mentioned in detail by only some of
those involved. De Launay's "treason" (sequence 17), which functions
as the triggering moment of the actual storming of the Bastille in
our texts, is a different matter. Supposedly, the governor of the Bastille had shown understanding for the citizens requesting entry and
had "guaranteed them safe-conduct; but as soon as one hundred val-
iant men had entered [the first courtyard], he had the drawbridge
pulled up, had the men fired upon, and thus massacred a lot of up-
right citizens in cold blood who trustingly wanted to offer him their
hand" (no. 11:4–5; repeated in no. 20). Even though not only the eyewitnesses from the ranks of the defenders of the Bastille (no. 24:296;
no. 25:7–8; no. 36:114) but even Beffroy de Reigny (no. 32:73) stressed
that the rebels themselves let down the drawbridge, and even though
de Launay had them fired on only when he was pushed up against
the wall, the overwhelming majority of the accounts speak of a "detestable ambush" (no. 3:2; see also no. 15:18–19; no. 18:2; no. 19:25;
no. 26:7; no. 44:5–6, 12), of the "most terrible betrayal" (no. 33:68), of
a "barbaric" act committed by a "lackey of despotism" (no. 47: vol. 2:
12, 28). One puts the words "Enter, I will give you weapons" (no. 16:
19) into de Launay's mouth. *Gravures historiques* devotes an entire series
of plates to the "betrayal," and the accompanying etching shows de
Launay giving the order for the massacre (no. 42:12).

The subsequent siege and conquest of the Bastille (sequence 18) are re-
counted at great length in almost all accounts. Military details are not
as crucial to the image of the storming of the Bastille constructed in
these accounts as are the stylizations that idealize and exaggerate the
events. The decision to lay siege to the fortress seems all the more fool-
hardy given that the prison actually was impregnable, as several patriots warned (no. 3:7; no. 4:2). The siege, which was chaotic and not
very effective in military terms, is reinterpreted as a well-aimed bom-
bardment, one viewed as "making a great breach" in the walled circle
of the Bastille (no. 18:2; see also no. 17:16; no. 30:9). Individual victors
of the Bastille stage themselves as leaders of a charge; the wine mer-

chant Cholat claims to have shouted at the invalides: "Get out of there, you traitors against the nation, surrender, it is time" (no. 37:6). Critics and eyewitnesses might object that the so-called conquest of the Bastille was really nothing but an "appropriation" (no. 22:53), that the fortress had been handed over without any real defense, that no breach had been made, no charge led (no. 36:131, 146), that nobody had even thought of a charge (no. 32:87). The image that is generally accepted, however, is that of the irresistible power of the rebellious people and their heroic conquest: "A breach is made, the mass of fighters advances like a flood; everything that tries to block their way is cut down; tremendous bolts shatter, iron doors are forced open with axes" (no. 27: 18; see also no. 15:21–22). A contemporary pictorial leaflet describes the storming of the Bastille as a murderous fight of man against man during which scaling ladders were employed (figure 10). In 1790, the conquest is exaggerated even further in moral and symbolic terms:

> In this battle of humanity against the impotent fury of de Launay . . . our heroes push forward into the breach and enter the fortress; everything that tries to block their way is cut down; chains, bridges, and doors open under their redoubled blows; they advance everywhere, and the holy flag of freedom waves over the destroyed bulwark of despotism. (No. 42:17, 8–9)

We find the following version in the abridged memorial account of an almanac: "Fifty to sixty thousand men were divided into orderly battalions. The Bastille was taken by storm."[40]

The subsequent procession of the victors of the Bastille to city hall (sequence 19), which offered a "superb and terrible" spectacle to onlookers (no. 15:23), comes after the description of the execution of the "traitors" de Launay and Flesselles on the square in front of city hall (sequence 20) in most texts. Above all, the lynch law to which the governor of the Bastille was subjected is regarded as a salutary "lesson for tyrants" (no. 6:11). Earlier, members of the crowd had torn off the governor's cross of Saint Louis,[41] and on his way to the square he had abusively referred to the people as "sycophantic rabble" (no. 16: 27; no. 46:14). Therefore, spontaneous cries from the revolutionary crowd seemed doubly justified: "Let's cut this traitor's throat!" (no. 37: 10); "He's deserved that for twenty years!" (no. 41:7). The influential summary report in *Révolutions de Paris* says:

Figure 10. Conquest of the Bastille, 1789. Anonymous etching, 260 by 338 mm, 1789 (Bibliothèque Nationale, Estampes, Coll. Hennin, G 161636).

However, the traiterous Governour was safe in the hands of his conquerors, they tore from him his ensigns of honour, he was treated as an infamous person, and haled along amidst an innumerable concourse of people. . . . *Ah,* said he, racked with remorse, *I have betrayed my country!* and sobs stifled his voice. . . . Having arrived at La Grève, the people impatient of revenge would not suffer De Launai [*sic*] and the other officers to go up to the tribunal of the city, they tore them out of the hands of their conquerors, trod under foot one after another, and gave De Launai a thousand stabs. In the end they cut off his head, stuck it on a lance, and carried it about, the blood trickling down on every side. (No. 15:22–23)

While agitative revolutionary prints justify these as inescapable acts of popular justice (e.g., figure 11 and *Gravures historiques* speaks of the terrible punishment "of the crimes of the servants of despotism" (no. 42:17, 9), the few conservative replies to revolutionary rhetoric use this bloody scene to discredit the storming of the Bastille as a whole, even going so far as to reduce it to the speared heads of de Launay and Flesselles (no. 43:19). The royalist lawyer Montjoye goes furthest in 1791:

> From one moment to the next, the people of Paris turned into a tribe of cannibals. Those who called themselves the conquerors of the Bastille . . . marched around the various districts of the capital with the signs of their victory—on Place de la Grève on the quays of the Seine, in the Rue Saint-Honoré, at the Palais-Royal. Good Lord, what trophies of victory were these! Heads on spears, horrible to behold, opened the march. . . . Under the speared head of de Launay, a panel was fastened that read: "De Launay, governor of the Bastille, disloyal traitor to the people." (No. 48:126)

However, such negative descriptions were fairly rare. They met less public response than a number of other texts that returned to the act of popular justice, after reporting the events, in order to stress its legitimacy once more (sequence 21). De Launay's fate, in particular, received a great deal of attention:

> It would have been difficult to find a person more guilty, and more deserving of being sacrificed to common vengeance. Hard-

Figure 11. The just punishment for the traitors. Anonymous aquatint etching, 146 by 109 mm (Biblio-thèque Nationale, Estampes, Coll. Hennin, G 161796).

hearted and deceitful, conceited and groveling by nature, he seemed just right for his job and meant to become one of the foulest henchmen of despotism; he played games with the possessions, the freedom, and the blood of the wretches he was entrusted with; he delighted in their tears. (No. 14:148; see also no. 46:43)

A number of pamphlets took the same line. A fictitious will indicated that de Launay had left his job at the Bastille to the executioner of Paris, his cross of Saint Louis to a police spy, and the riches he had stolen from his prisoners to the former chief of police Le Noir, Cardinal Rohan, and Mme de Polignac.[42] "News from hell" reported that Beelzebub had appointed de Launay commander of the fortress on the banks of the river of the dead.[43] In a dialogue among the dead, the "detestable henchman" de Launay is accused by invalides of having bound the prisoners in the underground dungeons of the Bastille in chains. Even in hell, he declares himself in favor of despotism: "The sovereign must be master, the nation must prostrate itself before him; a king is born to give order, the people to obey."[44] The crowd's resort to lynch law is justified mainly with respect to de Launay, because two reasons can be established in his case. The just punishment was meant not only for the "traitor" but also for the governor of the Bastille as such. This two-part justification is illustrated in an etching that deduces de Launay's execution equally from his function and from his order to shoot (figure 12). Several of our reports confirm this: "De Launay deserved his fate just for being governor of the Bastille" (no. 36:146; see also no. 47: vol. 2:48). No less than Count Mirabeau traced the problem back to its roots by setting the violence of the crowd during the storming of the Bastille off against the governmental misuse of power characteristic of the ancien régime:

Compare the number of innocents who fell victim to the disregard for justice and the bloodthirsty principles of the courts, who fell victim to the secret vengeance of ministers in the prison tower of Vincennes and in the dungeons of the Bastille, with the crowd's sudden and impetuous acts of vengeance, and then judge which side was barbarism. (No. 19:56)

If these had been the motives for storming the Bastille, its main aim should have been the liberation of the prisoners. Since the earli-

LE MARQUIS   DE LAUNAY

Gouverneur   de la Bastile

Décapité le 14 Juillet 1789.   *En la Place de Grève à Paris.*

Pour avoir fait tirer sur le peuple   *après avoir arboré le drapeau blan.*

Monstrum horrendum, informe, ingens, cui lumen ademptum

Virg.

Figure 12. The Marquis de Launay, governor of the Bastille. Anonymous etching in dotted fashion, 225 by 170 mm, 1789 (Bibliothèque Nationale, Estampes, Coll. de Vinck 1571).

est reports concerning 14 July don't even mention the liberation of the captives (sequence 22), however, it would appear that the victors of the Bastille originally were after only weapons and revenge on de Launay. Nevertheless, the liberation of the prisoners is gradually transformed into a ritual action of freedom fighters. A short version of events reads: "they opened all the cells, and restored innocent captives to liberty, among whom were some venerable old men, who were astonished once more to see the light" (no. 15:22). This report is followed by a more emphatic description: "The Parisians force their way into the most horrible of prisons. The miserable victims of despotism emerge from their graves, which had swallowed them alive, and greet the daylight" (no. 16:25). One of the conquerors boasts of having "immediately liberated the victims of despotism" (no. 30:11); French Guards who participated in the storming of the Bastille declare that generally "everyone [had] rushed to liberate the state prisoners" (no. 34:8). Years later, a fictitious report based on the experience of one participant confirms: "Our first worry was to reach those underground dungeons in which the miserable victims . . . of tyranny were languishing" (no. 51:26–27). In a memorial paper dedicated to the sansculottes, the liberation of the prisoners finally becomes the driving force behind the entire storming of the Bastille. Not only is it the reason for the uprising of the people: "The voice of subjugated innocence resonated from the depths of the dungeons of the Bastille"; it is also the first thought of the conquerors:

> They found the miserable victims of the barbary and dastardliness of the governor. . . . They opened the doors of the dungeons and liberated the miserable victims of despotism, among them several venerable old men; they were astonished to see the sun, which they had been robbed of for so long. (No. 52:42, 46, 49)

This revaluation of the act of liberation in retrospect, and the demonization of the conditions of imprisonment at the Bastille, corresponds to the stylization of the prisoners as ideal types. It is also expressed in an occasional increase in their number—the *Relation véritable* speaks of fourteen prisoners (no. 41:7)—in their identification with well-known symbolic figures—Pitra wants to give the Marquis de Sade a prominent place among the liberated (no. 44:54)—and in poems by fictitious prisoners on the horrors of the Bastille and the miracle of their liberation.[45] Most frequently, however, it is expressed in the sentimental picture of a venerable old man, weakened and almost blind from lifelong imprisonment in the dungeon:

> A beautiful man, at least five feet and eight inches tall, who according to his own statement had been imprisoned for thirty years; he is around sixty-five to seventy years old. It is the Count d'Estrade; on the complaint of a schemer who accused him of "lèze-majesté," the despotic government had sentenced him to lifelong imprisonment. Supported, he was led through all of Paris; at the Palais-Royal, an unusual and very memorable scene met the eye: on the one side this courageous old man among his liberators, on the other side the speared heads of the governor, his deputy, and a warder, who had tyrannized this miserable old man for thirty years. (No. 18:2–3)[46]

This description is finally extended to all seven captives liberated on 14 July. De Launay's head with its placard was held up to them: "At this sight, tears ran from their eyes, and they lifted their hands toward heaven to praise the first moments of their liberty" (no. 47: vol. 2:44).

However, there were some opposing views. Beffroy de Reigny, for instance, remarks that the small number of prisoners "did not correspond to the idea of numbers held by public opinion; for it was said that this prison was bursting with captives" (no. 32:82). And the editor of a serial work on the Bastille established that "only seven prisoners were found, all of them alive and well; but neither corpses nor human skeletons nor men in chains—these are rumors circulating in the population that lack any evidence or basis" (no. 36:102–3; see also no. 48:123–24). The extent to which such demythologizing attempts were isolated and ineffective can be seen in the growing popularity of the legendary "Count de Lorges," the imaginary ideal captive of the Bastille. Initially, perhaps following the account of the "Count d'Estrade" quoted above, there was talk of a "harmless old man" who had been imprisoned at the Bastille "near thirty years" (no. 15:22). Then, a "Count Straze," liberated on 14 July, was mentioned and said to have languished there for "thirty-two years." "His beard reached his stomach" (no. 17:17). A few days later, an even more uncertain rumor had developed from this one. "We did not see this, but several people have assured us that they saw an old man emerge from this place of horror [the Bastille]; his massive gray beard was more than a foot long. If the reports can be believed, he languished in the dungeons for thirty years."[47] By the end of August, this old man had a fixed name—"Count de Lorges"—and his time in prison had lengthened to forty years (no. 33:82). In September, a pamphlet imagined the tale of woe of this "martyr of freedom."[48] By the beginning of 1790 he had become such a well-known figure that Curtius was representing him in chains at his waxworks.[49]

Narrative sequence 23 forms gradually as well. It follows reports in which some Vainqueurs boast:

> I was the first to climb up to the house of the governor. . . . I arrested a knight of Saint Louis. . . . With the keys in my hands, I had the sweet satisfaction of liberating and embracing five prisoners. . . . A procession of three thousand people headed by drums led me in triumph from the Palais-Royal to city hall. (No. 30:11)

There were some incorrigible skeptics who dissented, declaring that so many men were claiming the status of heroes that half a dozen Bastilles must have been conquered (see no. 10: supp. 1; see also no. 32:85; no. 33:83–84). A conservative opposing view even described the march—in which ecstatic and bloodstained Vainqueurs liberated prisoners looking rather demented, while speared heads were carried through the streets in triumph by a hysterically screaming mob— as a "satanic funeral march," "a gruesome celebration" (no. 48:124– 25). But the overwhelming majority of accounts portrayed the solemn escort of Bastille victors, decorated with "citizens' crowns" and what was alleged to be the cross of Saint Louis formerly belonging to de Launay, as a much-deserved public recognition of national heroes: "The heroic grenadier who . . . was the first to climb the tower of the Bastille is escorted to the Palais-Royal sitting in an elegant one-horse carriage. He is wearing a floral wreath on his head, and on his breast the blue-ribboned badge of Saint Louis" (no. 21:26; see also no. 15: 24; no. 23:9). The masses held in the individual parishes of the capital for the fallen victors of the Bastille receive a great deal of attention (see no. 11:7–11; no. 14:65; no. 34:45–51). The veneration is consciously meant for the "heroes" ("héros") from among the people who suppos- edly removed the stigma from the word "mob" ("populace") (no. 36: 151). Immortal glory was due not to princely commanders of the army but to "plebeian warriors" (no. 47: vol. 2:47). In addition to the accounts forming the basis of this analysis, the victors of the Bastille caused a lot of journalistic ink to flow; we will consider that corpus in "The New Heroes" section of chapter 3.

Since the storming of the Bastille was interpreted as a heavily symbolic act even as early as the evening of 14 July, the matter could not come to rest for the rebels with the capture of the fortress, the punishing of its defenders, and the honoring of the victors. "It was generally desired that the Bastille be razed at once. . . . It would not do to guard the fortress. . . . rather, what mattered was to level a hated prison, a ministerial prison, to the ground."[50] Accordingly, a number of our core accounts emphatically report the "uplifting spectacle" (no. 14:187) of the razing of the Bastille (sequence 24), which was spontaneously initiated on 15 July. "Massive stones tumbling into the muddy ditches and creating a din were the first signs of freedom" (no. 27:19). In these accounts, the significance of the razing goes beyond that of the events themselves:

> Finally, the fervent desire expressed by so many miserable and innocent victims of arbitrary power in groans, amid tears, and in desperation was fulfilled. . . . Magnanimous renewers of French freedom, complete your glorious work! Destroy and annihilate this fateful fortress to its very foundations, leave no stone unturned. (No. 14:188)

At the same time, this symbolic act was emblematically reduced and condensed in pictorial leaflets (figure 13). So obvious to observers is the meaning of that act that everything becomes clear even to a deaf-mute who has not understood the general excitement on 14 July as soon as he sees the razing of the Bastille.[51]

In the consciousness of contemporaries, however, the tearing down in itself was obviously not sufficient to completely erase the old symbol of despotism.[52] A new symbol was required to take the place of the old. As we will demonstrate in our discussion of anniversaries and memorials, in chapter 3 below, the revolutionaries were virtually obsessed with the magical idea of symbolically turning the location of the Bastille from a place of oppression and horror into a place of public joy and freedom. For that reason, reports of the razing merge with references to first plans for a memorial (sequence 25) in several of the texts concerning 14 July and its consequences:

Figure 13. Razing of the Bastille. Etching by Roger after Pernet, diameter of medal 60 mm, 1789 (Bibliothèque Nationale, Estampes, Coll. de Vinck 1665).

The first sacrifice that patriotism had to make to freedom was the razing of the Bastille; a thousand workers are occupied with that; already only the ruins of this colossus of despotism are left standing, and its complete downfall is certain. It has been suggested that a monument to Louis XVI, the "restorer of French freedom," be erected in its place. The plan for this monument is in everyone's heart, but it is left up to genius to give it the proper form and execute it. (No. 33:94–95)[53]

The originally German Parisian by choice Anton Peters, for instance, suggested an allegorical form (figure 14) by borrowing an idea from Linguet's picture of 1783 (figure 5) and modifying it to fit the new situation. The ruins of the Bastille have completely given way to the monument; as "Restaurateur de la Liberté Française," a title bestowed on him by the National Assembly, the marionettelike Louis XVI crushes the hydra of despotism. Meanwhile, a clergyman sacrifices his benefices to the nation and an aristocrat his feudal rights; "Francia," having awakened from a long sleep, raises the members of the National Guard tested in the storming of the Bastille (depicted in

Figure 14. Jean Antoine de Peters, The new Place de la Bastille. Colored etching, 214 by 166 mm, 1789 (Bibliothèque Nationale, Estampes, Coll. de Vinck 1712).

engraving on the ground in figure 14). But as such plans became antiquated with the king's loss of prestige, the monument on the site of the Bastille was rededicated—in concrete plans as well as in texts on the subject of 14 July. "Never have workers toiled more courageously than at the destruction of this hellish dungeon. From its stones, a sublime temple will be erected to freedom, justice, humanity, and the highest being" (no. 52:50).

On 17 July, Louis XVI visited Paris and practically sanctioned the storming of the Bastille, an occurrence that is enthusiastically reported by revolutionary accounts (sequence 26). New songs were composed and printed just for this event.[54] Subsequently, almost a third of our texts deems necessary a retrospective appreciation of the events of 14 July (sequence 27) that can be said to correspond with the introductory narrative sequences. Here, it is again confirmed that even in the consciousness of the time the original—military—cause for the storming of the Bastille takes a back seat to its symbolic significance. Beffroy de Reigny makes a distanced, almost historical-critical assessment: "The Bastille was perceived as the right arm of depotism in all of France. . . . Therefore, its conquering has strongly influenced all subsequent events; no patriot can look at it indifferently" (no. 32:75; see also no. 44:31). But more often our texts once again emphatically stress the miraculousness of the storming of the Bastille (see no. 15: 22–24; no. 33:80; no. 47: vol. 2:44–45) and see in it the fulfillment of Voltaire's prediction of a revolution, a realization of Enlightenment philosophy in general (no. 40:69–70; no. 46:16), an incredible acceleration of history (no. 9:14; no. 13:5–6), and a break in world history (no. 36:156) opening a new era of freedom and removing feudalism along with despotism (no. 16:44).[55] This interpretation became an article of faith for the sansculottes. There, the question of "what the revolt of 14 July was" found an answer: "It laid the groundwork for the vigor and courage of the French, who won their freedom by fighting death and the fury of despots."[56] From the beginning, the basis of this interpretation had less to do with the Bastille and its conquest than with the Bastille as a *symbol*. This can be seen first in the fact that hardly any of our reports can mention the Bastille without immediately conjuring up a vision of terror. It becomes even clearer in pamphlets that see a symbolic act of destruction in the events of 14 July: "The Bastille is no more. . . . The chains of an entire oppressed nation fall with this terrible colossus, and the day of its fall becomes the memorable day of the foundation of the freedom of the French." [57]

But which "Bastille" is meant here and — more or less distinctly — in other revolutionary interpretations of 14 July? Not only the old well-known dungeon of despotism but also now — since its conquest — the symbol of a victorious fight for freedom. In other words, the Bastille has become a *double symbol:* "It is simultaneously the cradle of *national freedom* and the grave of the most disgraceful *aristocracy*" (no. 3:8). Or in the words of a historical commentary of September 1789, "This maw of despotism has turned into a shelter of freedom that radiates the light of the Enlightenment; it illuminates all of France, has already had an invigorating effect, and eventually will also change the face of the nations surrounding us." [58] Thus the Bastille, which was hitherto determined negatively, has won an equally strong positive dimension and has now achieved the ambiguity that makes up its symbolic character. The new bipolar tension in the symbol of the Bastille found its pictorial expression in numerous etchings, most concisely perhaps in the dance of freedom performed by members of the petite bourgeoisie in front of the prison as it is about to be razed,[59] as well as in the popular Bastille festivals launched by the plebeian Palloy.

It is characteristic of the unsettling effect of the attack on the Bastille that a number of texts are not content with a retrospective appreciation of 14 July but need to reconfirm its meaning in further accounts. These supplements, as well as some brochures,[60] are primarily concerned with the Bastille as a destination for something like revolutionary tourism (sequence 28), beginning with numerous representatives of the National Assembly:

> As soon as the representatives appeared up on the towers, they received applause from the citizens who were crowding into the Rue Saint-Antoine, the Place de la Bastille, and the Porte Saint-Antoine and appearing at the windows of the surrounding houses. The representatives answered with new cries of applause and joy, and that did not go without tears of emotion and gratitude. (No. 34:22)

The writer Cubières-Palmézeaux describes such an ascent of the Bastille, undertaken on 16 July with the representative and later historian of the Bastille Dusaulx, and reports that his companion let chunks of stone fall, crying, "Liberté": "This example was generally imitated; each of us threw down a stone crying, 'Liberté!' Proud of our contribution to the razing of the Bastille, we saw ourselves as restorers and founders of *freedom* with complete justification."[61] This same scene is captured by an illustrated pamphlet of the same time (figure 15). But the new double meaning of the Bastille can also be detected in these impressions of a visit on an August evening:

> The workers had already left their places. . . . more than twelve hundred citizens were already scattered over these walls that despotism had erected. . . . the memory depressed my soul and reminded me of all the alleged criminals whose freedom was buried in the Bastille. . . . O Frenchmen, you free people, I told myself, now you can walk all over this despicable monument of tyranny![62]

Meanwhile, citizens were flocking to the Bastille not only to participate in the liberating act of razing but also "to visit this place of slavery and horror" (no. 34:23), "to descend into those grim underground dungeons and weigh in our hands the chains of our friends, our defenders" (no. 19:56)—as Mirabeau did in the company of a lady. So tours also included a search for confirmation of the terrible old image of the Bastille: "People came running finally to see with their own eyes the dreaded dungeons where tyranny had far too often chained innocence" (no. 9:8). It is a matter of seeing, hearing, and feeling the old despotism of the Bastille, and of comprehending it with all the senses:

> I have seen the disgusting caves where innocent human beings languished for fifty years. I have seen graffiti etched into the walls with shaking hands. . . . At the bottom of those grim holes, I almost thought I could still hear the sobbing of the victims of hated despotism. I thought I was dreaming when I saw the doors broken, those open, horrible dungeons, these chains torn from the walls bit by bit. (No. 7:19; see also no. 45:235)

The revolutionary reports of 14 July ended as they had begun. While in introductory accounts "despotism" had become concrete in the "aristocratic plot," now the repressive role of the old Bastille was confirmed by new reports of a planned conspiracy that had been preempted by the storming of the Bastille (sequence 29). In a footnote, a report published on 23 July adds the following news:

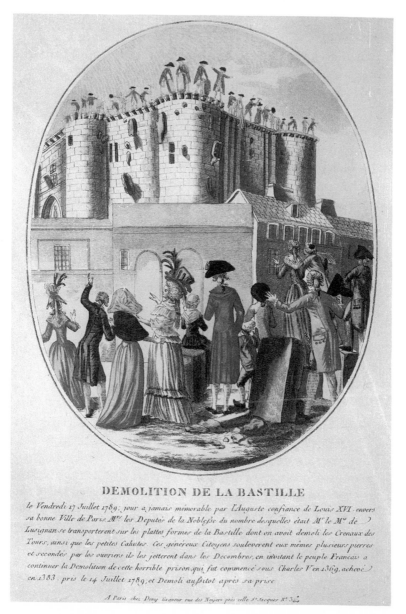

DEMOLITION DE LA BASTILLE

le Vendredi 17 Juillet 1789; jour a jamais mémorable par l'Auguste confiance de Louis XVI envers sa bonne Ville de Paris. M^{rs.} les Députés de la Noblesse du nombre desquelles était M^r le Mis de Lusignan se transporterent sur les plattes formes de la Bastille dont on avoit demoli les Creneaux des Tours, ainsi que les petites Cahutes. Ces généreux Citoyens souleverent eux mêmes plusieurs pierres et secondés par les ouvriers ils les jetterent dans les Decombres, en invitant le peuple Francais a continuer la Demolition de cette horrible prison qui fut commencé sous Charles V en 1369, achevé en 1383, pris le 14 Juillet 1789, et Demoli aussitot après sa prise.

A Paris chez Deny Graveur rue des Noyers près celle St Jacques N.° 30.

Figure 15. Destruction of the Bastille. Anonymous colored etching, 157 by 263 mm, published by J. Chéreau, Paris, 1789 (Bibliothèque Nationale, Estampes, Coll. Hennin, G 161712).

It is quite correct that Mister Bro[glie] and Prince Lambesc were supposed to fire cannons on the city in the night between 14 and 15 July and were to open it for looting for four hours. They had promised to force the Parisians down within two weeks by sword and hunger. (No. 16:19)

Four weeks later, this menace has developed into Prince Condé's "carefully prepared conspiracy" to conquer Paris, led by Marshal Broglie and Prince Lambesc, and to invade the city under the cover of fire from the cannons of the Bastille (no. 33:91–94). This report is hardly surprising, for in the meantime several leaflets had uncovered alleged plans for a new Saint Bartholomew's massacre:

> On the evening of Thursday the sixteenth, Necker was to be dismissed. That same night, troops were to move into Paris, occupy the strategic points, and set up cannons there. . . . The National Assembly was to be dissolved. . . . Forty-seven members of the National Assembly were to be arrested. The proscribed were three archbishops, four priests, seventeen noblemen, and twenty-three members of the common people. . . . When someone in the crown council dared to object that perhaps the national troops might refuse to obey orders, one of the royal councilmen angrily answered: "Well, then just promise to let them loot Paris, and they will obey."[63]

This was the "discovery" that was taken over by the German press and that fashioned German reports on the storming of the Bastille.

Some of our texts on 14 July come to an end with remarks on the history of the Bastille that are occasioned by the discovery of the prison archives and that turn into anecdotes of prison horrors (sequences 30 and 31):

> At the same time the first stone was broken off [the Bastille] amid signs of festivity, the archives, the prison cells, the dungeon stuffed with confiscated books were given over . . . to outright looting and revenge. Many registers were brought to city hall; but many documents were stolen by ignoramuses and sold to collectors and experts piece by piece. For three livres, someone purchased a register recording the names and reasons for im-

prisonment of all persons who were incarcerated at the Bastille between 1720 and 1761. (No. 14:188)

While Beffroy de Reigny skeptically predicted that business-minded journalists would exploit these documents "in order to give their fantasies the appearance of truth" (no. 32:81), a number of current pamphlets stress the significance of this "Archive du Despotisme" for a future history of the Bastille.[64] In this context, our accounts use public access to the Bastille and the discovery of the archive more and more as an opportunity to recall the man in the iron mask, the captivity of Voltaire and Linguet, Latude's escape, and the moving story of the mouse tamed by a prisoner (no. 9:8–9; no. 44:56; no. 46:17, 23–24, 30–44).[65] Reports tried to put into words what revolutionary engravers were at the same time arranging into scenes of horror: "Perhaps we can imagine the dark night of these horrible underground dungeons and demonstrate to the citizens how their fellow citizens dragged their chains behind them and were tortured by the ghost of tyranny" (no. 47, vol. 2:53). As late as 1795, a short collection of poems repeats almost literally what the newspaper *Révolutions de Paris* had reported from the conquered Bastille in 1789: "It is impossible to describe all the horrors that were found in this detestable cave; machines of death were found previously unknown to man" (no. 52:50).[66]

All in all, the collective public discourse on the storming of the Bastille, its immediate causes, and its consequences, as that discourse develops in the journalism analyzed here between 1789 and 1795, increasingly functions as a self-fulfilling prophecy. Since the despotic character of the old state, which had materialized in the Bastille, is settled from the start and is confirmed by aristocratic conspiracy plans, the storming of the Bastille appears to be the act of self-liberation of a people in extremis. Nonetheless, most of the narrative sequences fulfill the function of additionally justifying the storming of the Bastille and its bloody circumstances. A black-and-white political and historical portrayal is predominant in the majority of the reports, which contrast the forces of the ancien régime, its instruments of power, and its thugs with the glorious deeds and accomplishments of the Revolution. Both sides of the picture support each other, and the individual elements of the narrative closely engage one another. Not only is the attack on the Bastille the more inescapable and consistent, the more menacing the old despotism, its tyrannical arbitrariness, and its conspiracy plans appear; the fortress is also a more radiant sign for the present and the future, the more heroic it is and the greater its liberating effect seems. In this respect, the overwhelming majority of the analyzed reports mystifies the basically banal, almost militarily insignificant event of 14 July 1789, transforming it into a symbolic act of importance for world history by misconstruing and reinterpreting numerous facts and fashioning an ideal picture out of them. This unconscious formation of meaning, which satisfies a social desire for self-assurance and sociopolitical orientation, is guided by the symbol of the Bastille, which is latently or openly present in most of the narrative sequences examined. Thus the power of the Bastille as a symbol has not only formed the public sphere of the late Enlightenment in a manner at odds with the facts—as we have seen above—but has also, as we can say now, determined the social perception of what happened on 14 July 1789, transforming the attack on the state prison into the world-historical event we see it as today.

3. REVOLUTIONARY SYMBOLISM UNDER THE SIGN OF THE BASTILLE, 1789–1799

A Prime Example of the Self-Mystification of the French Revolution

---

Radicalization and Diversification of a Collective Symbol

LIKE A DETONATION, 14 JULY 1789 SET IN MOTION A PROCESS, lasting several years, of increased popularization, extension, and intensification of the content and diversity of the symbolism of the Bastille. The storming of the Bastille, represented as the victory of a nation fighting for freedom against despotism, had such an overwhelming importance for contemporaries that throughout the country it let even ordinary people forget the daily grind, and found expression in local arts and crafts. Showmen, for instance, made good profits exhibiting the events of 14 July in their showcases.[1] In the flat country south of Bordeaux, village youths instead of "spiritual music now [sing] patriotic songs, mainly one about the storming of the Bastille, which is performed very coarsely" at their evening meetings.[2] In Paris, the eight-year-old daughter of a bourgeois family illuminates the entire house with candles to "celebrate the conquering of the Bastille and the liberation of the poor captives";[3] children play — as broadsheets show (figure 16) — "storming of the Bastille," marching through the streets with heads of cats skewered on spears.[4] Citizens of the petite bourgeoisie donate an "equally pious and patriotic" votive picture to the church of Sainte-Geneviève that shows lightning destroying the Bastille, and a soldier on his knees giving thanks to heaven for this miraculous deliverance.[5] The National Guard of the Paris parish of Saint-André-des-Arts provide their church with "consecrated bread of considerable size in the shape of the fortress of the

Figure 16. Villeneuve, The storming of the little Bastille. Colored aquatint etching, diameter 91 mm, Paris, 1789 (Bibliothèque Nationale, Estampes, Qb1, M 98779).

Bastille."[6] The ceramics industry, centered in Nevers,[7] manufacturers of knives[8] and barometers,[9] fan makers,[10] the prospering textile factory Oberkampf,[11] and ladies' fashion in general all seize upon this profit-promising topic of current interest:

> Our speculating manufacturers of knickknacks have had stones for rings and the like cut from the gray building stones of the Bastille, and have had them set as jewels. So now rings and earrings are worn *à la Liberté nationale,* buttons, fans, and boxes *à la Bastille* . . . ; the army of makers of the frivolous and shopkeepers in the provinces . . . fabricate buttons *à la Bastille.*[12]

To dismiss such products of the new trade in political devotional objects as highly elaborate "revolutionary kitsch"[13] does not do justice to their importance as indicators of social history. The Bastille was quickly banalized and rapidly advanced into areas of everyday practice and material culture far removed from politics. These facts make it possible to gauge the extent to which ordinary people, too, experienced the obvious importance of 14 July and wanted to reassure themselves of it, as well as the extent to which the Bastille had penetrated the general social consciousness and become a recognized collective symbol.

The most important medium for the general naturalization of the symbolism of the Bastille—redefined as a symbol of freedom—was democratically distributed, up-to-date, and politicized revolutionary journalism in the broadest sense. This included publications of pictures and songs as well as the minting of coins;[14] Palloy's specialty was using the iron chains from the dungeons of the Bastille that "had fettered and locked the victims and purging them in the fire,"[15] refashioning them into medals of freedom (figure 17). The series of accounts and public statements concerning the attack on the Bastille analyzed in chapter 2 was followed by a flood of further pamphlets that greedily took up every manuscript that surfaced from the archives of the Bastille, and every discovery that was made while tearing down the fortress, to substantiate the thesis of the despotic character of the Bastille. From August 1789 to fall 1790, the publisher Desenne at the Palais-Royal issued a nine-volume documentation of all prison records in no particular order under the title *La Bastille dévoilée* (The Bastille unmasked). Abridged versions of this documentation appeared in three different German translations:

The conquering of the Bastille, this monument of tyranny, . . . offers us a superb source of curious records, . . . which can serve as examples of how far the despotism of ministers in France once went. This discovery is a subject of curiosity not only to France but to all the rest of the world as well. . . . It would be desirable for all papers belonging to this archive of injustice to be under public scrutiny; they would clearly prove how important the conquering of this prison was for us; they alone could bring us to undertake the conquering a second time, if circumstances should require it again. . . .

While people are currently busy with the demolition of the

Figure 17. Pierre-François Palloy, Memorial medal for the razing of the Bastille, presented to the representatives of the National Assembly on 31 December 1789. Iron, diameter 40 mm (Bibliothèque Nationale, Médailles, Coll. Hennin 74).

palace of vengeance, we, too, are making an effort in our own way to strike a blow against one of the most dangerous heads of the hydra of despotism. Discovering the secrets of despotism seems to us to be the strongest means of multiplying several times the hate that this despicable process has instilled in everyone.[16]

A rival enterprise, which is attributed to the revolutionary journalist Jean-Louis Carra, at the same time delivered an extensively documented and annotated chronological catalog of former prisoners of the Bastille under the motto "The Bastille was the symbol of your enslavement."[17] The revolutionary press, which developed across a broad range after 14 July and was widely circulated, also made an important contribution to the interpretation and dissemination of the symbolic power of the Bastille. This journalism also reached the "uneducated" strata of the population through readings in public forums. From radical revolutionary newspapers such as Carra's *Annales patriotiques,* Marat's *Ami du Peuple,* and Desmoulins's *Révolutions de France et de Brabant* to more moderate publications such as *Bouche de Fer,* published by the Cercle social, or the *Chronique de Paris,* which was close to later Girondists, to liberal-conservative papers such as Fréron's *Orateur du Peuple* or the semiofficial *Moniteur,* many of the leading papers published news on the Bastille for years and reviewed new releases concerning it. The most regular and committed of these newspapers were probably Antoine-Joseph Gorsas's *Courrier* and *Révolutions de Paris,* which was put out by Louis-Marie Prudhomme under the editorship of Elysée Loustalot. The latter paper had come into being with a report on the storming of the Bastille, contained the column "Papiers de la Bastille" for six months, published a number of etchings with the Bastille as their topic, and also gave a Bastille design on the title page of their first volume so much prominence that the paper can—at least in the beginning—be described as being published under the sign of the Bastille. If one counts the articles that these two newspapers devoted to the subject of the Bastille (table 5 and figure 18), there emerges a journalistic trend that peaked around the anniversaries of 14 July and remained significant over three years, before dropping off considerably after the caesura of the second revolution of 10 August—by which time the symbolic power of the Bastille had long been established. The individual thematic focuses of these articles on the Bastille usually correspond with those found in other pamphlets and other media appearing contemporaneously and mirror a growing diversity of symbolic meanings connected with current events, meanings we will trace in the following chapters.

Right now, we will mention only one example: a news item that Gorsas published on 17 May 1790: "A *vast number of carcasses* that were found when the Bastille was torn down prove in the most gruesome fashion what kind of tyranny was practiced there. In the Bastille gagging freedom and torturing the body did not suffice; men were also *strangled, beaten to death, buried alive.* But it seems that despotism lacked foresight, for it *devoured these victims,* but it forgot to *grind their bones* as well."[18] Gorsas uses these words, which were spoken by the chairman of the district adjoining the Bastille, Saint-Louis-de-la-Culture, on the occasion of the presentation of a record concerning these skeletons, as an introduction to the reprinting of an "authentic" report, which

		Celebrations		Victors of the Bastille		Prisoners		Bastille models		Archives		Horrors		Other "Bastilles"		Theater		Palloy	
		a	b	a	b	a	b	a	b	a	b	a	b	a	b	a	b	a	b
1789	July					2								1	1	1					
	August			1	1	2	1			1				4							
	October			1	1	1						2 3		3							
	December					1						4									
1790	January					2						1									
	February					3 4															
	April			1	1	3 2	1			1	1				1 1	1	1				
	June	2			3	1 1	4 4							1		1					
	August						1 1									1				1	
	October																	1			
	December				2							2 1						1		1	
1791	January			1														2		2	
	February									1						2					
	April			1 1								1									
	June			2 8					1			3									
	August	1														1		1		1	
	October											2									
	December																				
1792	January	1				3						1						1		1	
	February											2									
	April			4 4		1 1										1		1		1	
	June															1					
	November	3		3												1					

Table 5. Articles on the Bastille in Prudhomme's *Révolutions de Paris* (every first column) and Gorsas's *Courrier* (second column)

was published as a pamphlet at the same time.[19] Earlier, another journalist had also asked skeptical citizens: "Come with me to the Bastille in the twilight of the moon; do you see these two skeletons? Do you see the chains still surrounding their arms and feet? Alas, if only these miserable remains could still raise their voices; they would tell us that

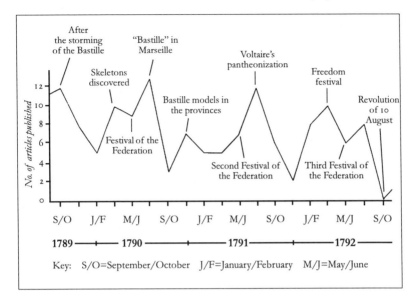

Figure 18. Summary bimonthly curve of articles on the Bastille in the newspapers *Révolutions de Paris* and *Courrier* (table 5).

the henchman of despotism had thrown them into this terrible underground dungeon."[20] These were the bones of only two men, and an investigating committee from the Academy of Sciences could not find any traces of torture or chains on them but established that they were the remains of construction workers who had had an accident a hundred years earlier.[21] Nevertheless, Palloy held a solemn procession with his workers, the National Guard, and the clerics of the district; had the skeletons buried at the cemetery in place of all the martyrs of the Bastille; and made memorial slabs for them from the stones of the Bastille as well as a plaque with the inscription "Rest in peace beneath the same stones under which you languished during your lifetime" (figure 26).[22] A popular almanac that reviewed the events of 1790 explicitly rejected the report of the scientists, and then succinctly declared: "It is certain that those who had the bad fortune to draw upon themselves the disfavor of a minister or a whore were buried alive in these places of horror [the dungeons of the Bastille]."[23] Its symbolic power intensified by the events of 14 July, the Bastille shaped the social perception of "reality" more than ever, but now in a revolutionary way.

The New Heroes: The Role-Model Function and
Self-Staging of the Victors of the Bastille

At the end of July 1789, a pamphlet called *La Journée Parisienne, ou Triomphe de la France* (The day of Paris, or the triumph of France) read:

> VICTORY, . . . victory! An army gathered in twenty-four hours has its cannons and its heroes! And the Bastille has been taken! Would you have believed that these people, who like to sing and laugh, had the courage of a Hercules and the bravery of a Pirithous? I saw those brass gates, which seemed to fear only the end of the world, fall under the blows of their axes; and my quiet foot trampled those vaults in which the thunder of kings darkly rumbled only yesterday.[24]

This pamphlet by an anonymous Parisian journalist, who appears to have personally observed the demolition of the Bastille begun after 15 July 1789, offers a typical example of the spontaneous cult of the Vainqueurs de la Bastille as new "national heroes" that sprang up immediately after the storming of the Bastille. The author of the pamphlet compares their bravery to that of ancient heroes—Hercules and Pirithous—and thus invests the "heroes of 14 July" with a legitimation based in mythology.

At the same time, he emphasizes their descent from simple people ("le peuple"), who in revolutionary imagery are embodied by Hercules.[25] The author stresses that the victors of the Bastille are descended not from the privileged aristocracy but from the ordinary people. In his view, as a "people's army"—it is explicitly pointed out that this "army" was formed spontaneously within twenty-four hours—they represent the vanguard of the entire French nation fighting for its liberty. Their enemy is despotism, ambiguously imaged as the "thunder of kings" in the pamphlet.

This glorification of the conquerors of the Bastille sets in immediately after the event itself. On the evening of 14 July, a spontaneously gathered crowd was already carrying a certain Henri Dubois through the streets in triumph and decorating him with the cross of Saint Louis. This award for military valor had supposedly been snatched from de Launay, the governor of the Bastille, after the fortress had been taken, and shortly before de Launay's death. The completely surprised Dubois passed the medal on to General La Fayette, chief of the

Parisian National Guard, since he did not think he had performed any extraordinary feat in storming the Bastille. The following day, it was presented to a grenadier named Arné, a soldier in the royal army who had run over to the rebels and had been one of the first to enter the state prison (figure 19).

Following the model of the triumphal march of the Roman emperors, Arné was led through Paris, conducted by the people's militia, on a victory chariot ("char"). According to contemporary reports, his forehead was decorated with a "people's crown" (a laurel wreath), the symbolic reward for saving their lives. On his breast, he proudly carried the cross of Saint Louis that La Fayette had presented to him. Even Bailly, the mayor of Paris, bowed before this bizarre triumphal chariot and joined in the general cheers for the wreathed victor of the Bastille.[26]

Two days later, on 17 July 1789, the Paris district Petits-Augustins decided to mint a medal honoring the Vainqueurs de la Bastille at its own expense. A week after that, on 22 July, a certain Cretaine as the first of the conquerors of the Bastille had eighteen other Vainqueurs confirm in writing that he had participated in the storming of the Bastille and, armed with a sword, had forced the governor to hand over the fortress close to the tower bridge ("Pont de tours").[27]

Finally, in the last days of July 1789, a committee made up of Bastille conquerors Dusaulx, Oudart, La Crosnière, Thuriot, La Grey, and Desmond met in the Quatre-Vingts church in Paris. The task they set themselves was to compile an official and definitive list of the participants in the attack on the Bastille, and to present these officially recognized Vainqueurs with a document attesting to their status. Within the corps of Vainqueurs that was being constituted here, an armed company called Volontaires de la Bastille was formed on 15 October 1789. Pierre-Augustin Hulin, the former royal officer in the French Guard already mentioned above, took command of this company. Those Vainqueurs who had shown special courage during the storming of the Bastille and were able to provide "authentic proofs of their bravery"[28] were—according to the group's own charter—supposed to be made members of the Volontaires de la Bastille. The company of the Volontaires de la Bastille was given its salary by the Paris city administration and housed in a barrack specifically made available for this purpose.[29]

On 6 March 1790, the Vainqueurs de la Bastille, who by then had been officially recognized, even elected official political representa-

Figure 19. Portrait of the grenadier Joseph Arné. Anonymous colored etching, 207 by 147 mm, published by A. Le Grand, Paris, 1789 (Bibliothèque Nationale, Estampes, Coll. de Vinck 1651).

tives of their interests in a kind of plenary session. This committee of eight members was given the mandate to conscientiously investigate any new applications for membership in the corps of Vainqueurs, and to represent the company's common interests to the public, to the Paris commune, and to the National Assembly. On 19 June 1790, the French National Assembly then decided to meet the demands of the Vainqueurs for official recognition of their patriotic deeds, which they had been making since March. This decision was also arrived at in view of the imminent first anniversary of the storming of the Bastille. The National Assembly bestowed a number of privileges and honors on the 863 officially recognized Vainqueurs in consideration of the "heroic intrepidity" (héroïque intrépidité) with which "they had risked their lives to liberate their fatherland and shake off the yoke of slavery." [30] Among these privileges was the right to receive a uniform individually manufactured and put at each Vainqueur's disposal free of charge along with a complete set of weapons and the right to carry them in public. The weapons were engraved with the national coat of arms, the name of the individual owner, and a coping that symbolized the Bastille. Furthermore, every victor of the Bastille was supposed to receive a document made out by the National Assembly that gave its owner the right to publicly carry the honorary title Vainqueur de la Bastille and add it to his name. According to the decree, the Vainqueurs were to occupy a place of honor in the National Guard during the festivities of 14 July and receive a monetary award—the amount of which was to be specified. [31]

The official recognition of the Vainqueurs by the representatives of the nation was the conclusion and at the same time the climax of a number of spontaneous, mostly popular salutes that had been staged since the evening of 14 July 1789. The enthusiastic crowd had carried Henri Dubois through the streets of the French capital in triumph and presented to him the cross of Saint Louis as the highest military honor. Within the same hour, the Marquis de la Salle, at this point commander of the Parisian National Guard, received a motley group of Vainqueurs at city hall, simple citizens without any military training or rank, and delivered to them the military medals of honor of the royal army. "He embraced the stormers of the Bastille, congratulated them on their action," an eyewitness wrote, "presented them with some medals of honor, which they desired much more than monetary awards, and asked them their names" (app., no. 45:44). Bessin, the commander of the National Guard in the Paris district of Saint-Méry, emotionally evoked the heroic deeds ("faits héroïques") of the Vainqueurs de la Bastille in a speech held on 18 July 1789 and then generously gave his richly filled purse to those wounded in the assault on the Bastille, and to the survivors of the ninety-eight who had died in the attack.[32] On the two following days, 19 and 20 July 1789, memorial masses honoring the fallen Vainqueurs took place in the church of Saint-Etienne-du-Mont, situated in the middle of the old market district. These masses were celebrated with an unusual mixture of religious ceremonies — among others, the traditional Te Deum Laudamus was festively sung — and military pomp (flags, a military band). In a leaflet circulating the following day, significantly entitled *Les Lauriers du Fauxbourg Saint-Antoine* (The laurels of Faubourg Saint-Antoine), an eyewitness emphasized the patriotic achievements and military deeds of the conquerors of the Bastille — most of whom were from the Paris suburb Saint-Antoine, 90 percent of them craftsmen and retailers.[33]

> It is undisputed that the fatherland owes its salvation to the citizens of the Faubourg Saint-Antoine and the National Guard. . . . So the fatherland owes the needy among them support; . . . it owes it to them because they defended the fatherland. They are our brothers, our friends, our fellow citizens, who after having shed their blood for us demand a piece of what we could not deny even our enemies for their women and their children.[34]

At the same time, the anonymous author of this pamphlet calls special attention to two individual figures who had distinguished themselves and had already become celebrated national heroes in the second half of July, the — unnamed — grenadier Jacques-Joseph Arné, who had led the assault on the former fortress and had seized the governor, and Jean-Baptiste Humbert, a clockmaker's apprentice from Langres in Burgundy, who had entered the fortress as the second person after Arné, had disarmed a Swiss soldier by surprise, and disabled a cannon that was pointed at the attackers.

Arné and Humbert, who in 1789 published an autobiographical account of his role in the events of 14 July 1789 (app., no. 28), became figures in contemporary popular literature — above all, in ballads and popular broadsheets (figure 20). In 1790, the citizens of Langres, the city where Humbert was born, even intended to erect a monument in his honor — an ambitious project that was carried out at least in part.[35]

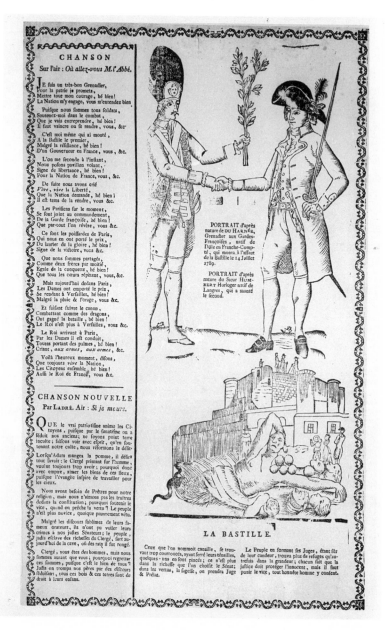

Figure 20. Victors of the Bastille Arné and Humbert. Anonymous transfer woodcut, 396 by 246 mm (Bibliothèque Nationale, Estampes, Coll. de Vinck 1647).

Even more popular than Humbert, who after the storming of the Bastille had returned to his occupation as a simple apprentice in the Paris workshop of the master clockmaker Belliard in the Rue Hurepoix, was Joseph Arné. Arné, who had been drawn through Paris in a triumphal chariot on 15 July, became the protagonist of the first French play on the storming of the Bastille, which premiered on 3 September 1789 under the title *La Fête du Grenadier* (The festival of the grenadier) and quickly became a great success with the audience. The premiere at the Paris Théâtre de l'Ambigu took place in the presence of Arné himself. He was enthusiastically celebrated by the spectators and at the end of the piece went onstage to standing ovations. In April 1790, the newspaper *Orateur du Peuple* reported that during the performance of another play, *La Liberté Conquise, ou le Despotisme renversé*—which also dramatized the attack on the Bastille—the same grenadier Arné was spontaneously crowned ("couronné") by the spectators in the theater. There being no real crown at hand, he was given a worker's cap ("bonnet d'ouvrier") instead, to loud applause.

Just as the presence of Vainqueurs at the many drama performances based on the events of 14 July, and their signatures on the tickets that were sold to the numerous visitors to the ruins of the Bastille, served to confirm the authenticity and historical truth of what was shown, pieces of clothing worn by the Vainqueurs gained the status of patriotic relics. The former gunner François-Louis Martin, for instance, who with Arné and Humbert had been one of the first to storm the courtyard of the former state prison, carefully kept the pants he had worn, which were covered with bloodstains, and, full of pride, showed them at the proper occasions as signs of his heroism.[36]

Humbert and Arné but also Maillard, Hulin—the owner of a laundry—and the former royal officer Elie, who had played prominent roles in the conquest of the Bastille, soon found a place in the new heroes almanacs of the Revolution. The *Petit Dictionnaire des Grands Hommes,* for instance, published in 1790, devoted extensive entries to Hulin and Elie. Léonard Bourdon, a representative in the National Assembly and a Vainqueurs de la Bastille himself—and in addition son of the tax official Louis-Joseph Bourdon des Planches, who had been imprisoned at the Bastille in 1785 because of his reform project for the improvement of the grain trade—published the biography of Jean-Baptiste Humbert in the first volume of his large-scale *Recueil des actions héroïques et civiques des Républicains français* (Collection of the heroic and patriotic deeds of the French republicans, 1792). This biography—like the other texts in the collection—was meant to displace antique and classical role models and was to be read at public assemblies ("assemblées populaires") as well as in schools.[37] A panegyric poem entitled *Eloge des Héros de la France* (Eulogy for the heroes of france), penned by an anonymous author, explicitly took up the ancient rhetorical tradition of the eulogy but instead of princes and noble generals now praised the actors of the Revolution of 1789: along with Bailly, the mayor of Paris, and Mirabeau, who delivered the ballroom oath of 20 June 1789, most of them Vainqueurs de la Bastille. The author of this epic poem believed that several generations after his time posterity would still "repeat with reverence" the name of Arné, an "intrepid hero" (héros intrépide), the son of a tanner from the village of Dôle in the eastern French province of Franche-Comté. By the same token, they would speak "with abhorrence" the names Conti and Polignac, names belonging to members of the court who, like many of their peers, had already emigrated in the summer of 1789.

But the cult surrounding the Vainqueurs de la Bastille, and above all the medals of honor presented to them on 19 July 1790, did not remain undisputed. Especially in the politically radical journalism of the time and in the numerous district meetings of the capital, a storm of indignation arose in the face of the privileges and honors officially awarded to them, particularly since—by chance—they had been awarded on the very day the French National Assembly had solemnly passed the abolition of the old hereditary aristocracy. In a circular letter addressed to all districts of the capital that was also published in the *Journal de la Municipalité et des Sections,* representatives of the Paris National Guard protested against the reintroduction of "usurped rights" (droits lâchement usurpés) at the very moment when all other "frivolous honors" (distinctions frivoles) were being abolished. In this circular, the National Assembly was asked to immediately rescind the decree and thus to nip in the bud any future arguments about the subject.[38] In his newspaper *Courrier des LXXXIII Départements,* Gorsas accused the Vainqueurs of having appropriated titles and medals of honor that only regular soldiers and officers were entitled to. "We are not afraid to say," Gorsas derisively remarked,

that this handful of supposed besiegers, who after the decree did not hesitate to shamelessly decorate themselves with the sub-

lime title of Vainqueurs de la Bastille, confused true fame with
a cowardly usurped right; some of them even having "the cheek
to decorate their signatures with this title." . . . No, you have to
make simple citizens of these supposed Vainqueurs, who must
be linked with and integrated into the national army, and will
there learn to serve the fatherland "without pride."[39]

Jean-Paul Marat adopted a similarly harsh attitude in his newspaper, *Ami du Peuple,* in June 1790. In his usual succinct and sharp
manner, Marat stressed the fact that all medals of honor—those of the
Vainqueurs de la Bastille too—were vain and superfluous. Marat fundamentally questioned limiting the number of victors of the Bastille
to the 863 officially recognized Citoyens-Soldats ("citizen-soldiers").
He believed that the revolution had been accomplished not by a few
hundred select individuals but by the mass of simple people ("le petit
peuple"). Hence Marat wrote:

> It is beyond doubt that the revolution originated in the rebellion
> of these simple people; and it is no less beyond doubt that the
> storming of the Bastille was mainly accomplished by ten thou-
> sand poor workers.[40]

Under pressure from parts of public opinion, the Vainqueurs de la
Bastille on 25 June 1790, again in a kind of plenary session, decided
to return the rights solemnly gained six days earlier, and to officially
renounce them. In a tumultuous internal debate, the group ready
to compromise led by Dusaulx, Parein, Bourdon, Fauchet, and La
Reynie—the "intellectual spokesmen" among the Vainqueurs—managed to convince the majority of the others of this decision. That same
day, a delegation of conquerors of the Bastille laid down the ribbons of
all Vainqueurs de la Bastille at the altar of the fatherland ("Autel de la
Patrie"). Along with this official declaration of renunciation, the Commune of Paris on 28 December 1790 explicitly prohibited any meetings of the Vainqueurs. In order to circumvent this prohibition, the
Vainqueurs in turn decided to reconstitute themselves as the Société
fraternelle des Amis des Droits de l'Homme, ennemis du Despotisme
(Brotherly society of the friends of human rights and the enemies of
despotism) and to join the Jacobin club.[41] The company of Volontaires
de la Bastille, which was not officially dissolved until 8 August 1791,
was made part of the 103d, 104th, and 105th regiments of the National

Guard and in the summer of 1792 integrated with the 35th Gendarmerie division, which saw action in the battles of the civil war in the Vendée. The Volontaires' request to keep their own coat of arms — an overturned tower as a symbol of the destruction of the Bastille [42] — on their flags was not met. The reason given was the fundamental principle of the equality of all soldiers in the French revolutionary armies.

So the corps of Vainqueurs formed immediately after the storming of the Bastille in July 1789 was finally dissolved in the summer of 1792. Nevertheless, its former members would unite once again in two later episodes. First, in September 1804, according to the reports of the Police Générale regarding the matter, a relatively small group of Vainqueurs gathered in the Paris Faubourg Saint-Antoine and demanded — loudly but unsuccessfully — admission to the newly founded French Legion of Honor of Napoléon Bonaparte, who was still consul then. Second, on 28 November 1831, following a petition brought forward by La Fayette in the Chamber of Deputies, a vote was taken awarding five hundred francs to the 401 surviving Vainqueurs de la Bastille, each of whom received the one-time monetary award on 8 May 1832. Ninety-three of them, who were classified as needy, in addition drew a small annual pension of 250 francs after January 1833.[43] King Louis-Philippe, the Citizen King from the house of Orléans who had come to power in the July Revolution of 1830, at least symbolically tried to emphasize his attachment to the Revolution with measures such as this one.

The dissolution of the Vainqueurs de la Bastille as an institution, as an officially recognized paramilitary corps, had little effect on the public-role-model function or the self-staging of the conquerors of the Bastille. Even though on 25 June 1790 they had solemnly renounced all medals of honor and titles, most of them continued to publicly call themselves Vainqueurs de la Bastille. They attached this title to their signature out of unconcealed pride, and as proof of their own patriotic conviction. In the second half of 1790, almost all of the 863 officially recognized Vainqueurs still demanded the promised decorations in *personal*, individually presented petitions. Silently circumventing the declaration of 25 June 1790, they finally received them bit by bit — as *individuals*, not as members of a corps. They received certificates and sword belts specifically manufactured for the Vainqueurs de la Bastille as well as rifle slings engraved with the names of their owners. The

Vainqueurs de la Bastille were present at official Revolution festivals after June 1790 too. At the festivities on the occasion of the transfer of Voltaire's remains to the Panthéon on 11 July 1791, for instance, a unified delegation of Vainqueurs followed the triumphal chariot on which the coffin of the great philosopher was laid out. Less than a month after the official renunciation of military certificates of honor, on 24 July 1790, the Vainqueurs de la Bastille gathered around noon for a memorial service in honor of their fallen comrades on the ruins of the former state prison. According to contemporary reports, after joint prayers and a memorial speech ("Eloge funèbre") for the Vainqueurs who fell in the assault, all present solemnly swore the citizen's oath ("serment civique").[44] Even the Committee of Public Safety, the official government of France in the years 1793–95, occasionally used the title in public documents. When General Elie was given an equipment grant of two thousand livres by the state in 1794, for example, his status as a Vainqueur de la Bastille was explicitly emphasized in the reward certificate as proof of the recipient's patriotic conviction.[45] So even after their official dissolution in June 1790, the Vainqueurs de la Bastille still appeared to be the vanguard of the Revolution and the embodiment of the patriotic military tradition—in their self-presentation as well as in the public consciousness. They seemed the incarnation of the Citoyen-Soldat, the combative and yet patriotic citizen defending the fatherland ("Patrie") with a weapon in his hand. Until 1795, active participation in the storming of the Bastille remained an almost obligatory means of establishing and justifying revolutionary identity among political activists.[46]

The self-presentation of the Vainqueurs—in the public sphere, at the revolutionary festivals, and before the National Assembly—was a decisive factor in establishing the public importance of these role models. Most of all, however, the Vainqueurs' self-staging took place in the large number of literary and journalistic texts they wrote themselves—even though only twenty-four of the 863 officially recognized stormers of the Bastille became "authors" in the real sense of the word, that is, writers of printed and published texts (figure 21). If the—often no longer preserved—handwritten manuscripts as well as the—hardly ascertainable and potentially limitless—mass of newspaper articles written by Vainqueurs were taken into account as well, the number of writing stormers of the Bastille would rise to about sixty or seventy.[47] In addition, some writings by Vainqueurs take the

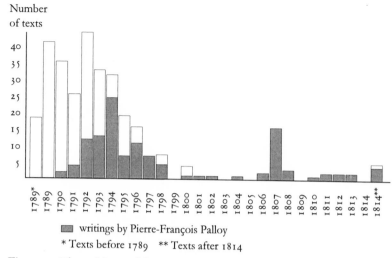

Figure 21. The writings of the Vainqueurs de la Bastille (quantification of the writings appearing annually between 1789 and 1823).

form of collective publications. A text with the title *Récit relatif à la prise de la Bastille* (Account of the storming of the Bastille, see app., no. 31), for example, whose supposed main author was Thuriot de la Rozière, carries the names of another twenty-eight Vainqueurs de la Bastille next to his. As eyewitnesses and fellow signatories, they attest to the truthfulness and authenticity of the account. The main author appears as the spokesman and mouthpiece of his comrades, who are less familiar with writing and the pen, and whose reports he has, as it says, "literally recorded on 16 August 1789" (app., no. 31:15–16).

Numerically, the pragmatic texts clearly dominate among the altogether more than 350 documents written by Vainqueurs de la Bastille during the years of the Revolution: petitions and circular letters; published speeches given before the National Assembly, in public societies, political clubs, and at revolutionary celebrations; resolutions ("arrêtés") and official declarations ("déclarations/proclamations"). These texts usually concern the entirety of the corps of Vainqueurs, who until their dissolution often appeared in public with collectively authored writings in order to give their claims to medals of honor and pensions more force.

The relatively high number of pamphletary publications and political posters ("affiches," "répliques," etc.) also shows that the writing minority of the victors of the Bastille of 14 July 1789 played an active role in the political public sphere in the following years. They saw their new task as political writers and journalists as a kind of continuation of their fight by other means: in their eyes, pen and writing were instruments of the completion of the "conquest of liberty" (Conquête de la Liberté) begun with the storming of the Bastille.

The case of Pierre-Mathieu Parein (1755–1831) can be considered typical of the way Vainqueurs "took the floor" journalistically between 1789 and 1799, in a manner deriving immediately from their historical role on 14 July 1789. Parein was the son of a saddler in the village of Mesnil-Aubry southwest of Paris and before the Revolution worked as an office scribe for a Paris lawyer. The fourteenth of July 1789 was a turning point in his life. Parein, elected to the Comité des Vainqueurs de la Bastille as someone capable of writing and experienced in legal matters, stepped forth after the storming of the Bastille from his hitherto obscure existence as a subaltern office scribe and henceforth became publicly known as one of the spokesmen for the Vainqueurs. Together with the engineer Estienne, the Academy member and author Jean Dusaulx, and the glazier's apprentice Jean Rossignol, Parein was one of a small but active and vociferous number of Vainqueurs who represented the other members of the corps to the public and appeared as their political mouthpieces again and again. Alongside the three other members of this group, Parein signed the petitions and requests presented to the National Assembly in the name of all Vainqueurs. Acting as a deputy for all, Parein on 16 June 1790 wrote an article for the *Chronique de Paris* about the impressive funeral ceremony honoring a deceased Vainqueur called Fausset, to whom last respects were paid by the twenty thousand Paris citizens, along with four hundred conquerors of the Bastille, who filed past his coffin. And it was Parein who in 1791 wrote the only drama on the assault composed by one of the participants themselves: *La Prise de la Bastille, fait historique en trois actes en prose, et mêlé d'ariettes* (The storming of the Bastille, historical prose drama in three acts, with sung interludes). At its end, the text of the drama bore the signatures of more than sixty other participants in the storming of the Bastille, who expressly confirmed the truthfulness and authenticity of the portrayed events. Not without vanity, Parein in his foreword stressed the view that a truthful account of the great event could be given only by one who had actively participated in it. In two somewhat pretentious-sounding sentences, he dispensed with all previous dramatizations of the matter, among which Harny's *La Liberté Conquise* (Conquered liberty) in particular had been an overwhelming success:

> Among all the depictions that have previously been written of the *storming of the Bastille,* there is—I am not afraid to say—not one that deserves the approval of the audience. This is not to say that I want to belittle the works of the esteemed gentlemen who have treated this subject, but they simply were not part of the siege of the Bastille. In order to describe the historical events exactly, it is necessary to have seen them with your own eyes, and one should not be surprised at the contradictions one finds in their writing.[48]

Parein's drama was a complete flop. It was rejected by the Théâtre des Italiens and then received without enthusiasm in the few performances it experienced (for example, in Rouen in 1795). In attempting to meet its own standard, by delivering "facts and circumstances of the most exact truth,"[49] Parein's drama turned out stilted and simplistic. This was perhaps because even though the author was able to read and write and was familiar with the style of political pamphlets and administrative documents, he had hardly any literary education, and absolutely no experience of the theater. Instead of popular identification figures such as Arné, Hulin, or Humbert, whom everyone knew and who were revered as "heroes of 14 July," Parein put the entire people onstage as "Peuple," "Citoyens," or "Hommes du Peuple," groups that were each represented by one actor. Parein also had no feel for the spectacular theatrical effects that had helped make Harny's *La Liberté Conquise,* which was written at approximately the same time, such an overwhelming success: parades, cannon thunder, impressive stage decoration, immense papier-mâché constructions that were supposed to represent the towers of the Bastille, gun salutes, and fighting scenes—dramatic effects, that is to say, that let the contemporary audience sensually experience the heroic deeds of the conquerors.[50]

The former office scribe Parein seemed to feel more in his element in the medium of the pamphletary broadsheet. Between 1789 and 1791, he published a series of virulent pamphlets with titles such as *Les Crimes des Parlements* (The crimes of the high(est) courts, September 1791) or *Extrait du Charnier des Innocents, ou cri d'un plébéien immolé* (Insight into the pile of corpses of innocents, or the cry of the butchered plebeian, 1789), in which he attacked the court and prison practices of the ancien régime in an extraordinarily sharp fashion. In these pamphlets, Parein connected his self-representation as a glorious conqueror of the Bastille with a radical critique of the judiciary system of the ancien régime, which remained in force until 1791 and which he—if only in his position as a subaltern office scribe—had got to know from a personal experience of over twenty years. In his writings, the prison practice of the Bastille is described not as an exception but on the contrary as a symptom of a "despotic" system of justice that claimed innumerable victims in the course of centuries. Parein depicts the judiciary system of the ancien régime and its representatives in an extremely political language reminiscent of the street slogans and political prints of the period, a language at the same time that is full of hate. He calls the judges of the high(est) courts of France, the parlements, "parliamentary vermin" (vermine parlementaire) or "detestable bloodsuckers" (vampires détestables) and their sentences "crimes"; in discussing the prisons, he speaks of "the darkness of dungeons where the sun has never shed its light."[51] A great part of the French population saw the Bastille not only as an abstract symbol of despotism but also as one embodiment of a detested judiciary that had a great impact on the conflicts of daily life and was usually completely impenetrable. Sharing these sentiments, Parein set up his participation in the events of 14 July as a long overdue personal settling of scores with its prominent representatives. "The memory of the tortures I had endured, patriotic enthusiasm," he writes about his participation in the storming of the Bastille,

> the thirst for revenge, and the certainty that I would be murdered with other patriotic authors after the assault on the Bastille—all these compelling arguments made me defy death as it spewed from the cannon barrels of the fortress; I was one of the first to penetrate it, and to sing a hymn to freedom from its menacing towers.[52]

Parein mentions his part in the storming of the Bastille more or less in passing—perhaps because his claim to have been one of the first who penetrated the fortress was an immoderate assertion not confirmed by any eyewitnesses. Other writing Vainqueurs de la Bastille made the presentation of their role in the attack into extensive autobiographical histories. As early as the second half of July 1789, several eyewitness accounts of participants were published. These responded to the public's desire for "authentic reports" from the mouths of the Vain-queurs. On the evening of 14 July, Louis-Abel Beffroy de Reigny, one of the most original and productive journalists of his time, visited the Bastille, interviewed witnesses, and took notes, which he transcribed into a report that very night. His pamphlet *La Semaine mémorable* (The memorable week, app., no. 7) was published several days later as one of the first accounts of the storming of the Bastille. On 16 July, among a multitude of curious visitors, an entire delegation of Paris authors and journalists (among them Brizard and Cubières) flocked to the towers of the former state fortress, which was already being torn down, in order to inspect the inside of the prison, the dungeons, the instruments of torture, and the basement. During this visit, they let the Vainqueurs de la Bastille who were acting as tour guides tell them the course of events firsthand (see app., no. 45:62). These early re-ports, written by journalists and literary men — outsiders to the events of 14 July — were soon followed by accounts composed by the partici-pants themselves: all in all there were seventeen texts, most of which were published in the summer of 1789. One of the first autobiographi-cal accounts was penned by the clockmaker's apprentice Jean-Baptiste Humbert, who was born in the same city as Diderot, Langres, and who was one of the first to climb the towers of the Bastille on the early afternoon of 14 July. His *Journée de J. B. Humbert* (The day of J. B. Humbert) was published in the last days of June 1789 as a pamphlet and was immediately excerpted or reprinted in its entirety by several newspapers. As early as the beginning of September 1789, translations of this document appeared in German periodicals. On 10 September, for instance, the *Bayreuther Zeitung* published the "Protokollirte Aus-sage des J. B. Humbert, welcher der erste war, so auf den Thurm der Bastille stieg" (Statement in testimony of J. B. Humbert, who was the first to climb the tower of the Bastille) in its numbers 109 and 110. Humbert's autobiographical account is sober, like a chronicle, with-out pathos. The first sentences, in which he immediately speaks of the events of 14 July, read:

> My name is J. B. HUMBERT, and I am a native of Langres, work-ing and living in Paris, at Monsieur Belliard's, watchmaker to the King, Rue Hurepoix.
> Assuming that I belonged to the district of Saint-André-des-Arts, I went to that Parish on Monday morning with the rest of

the citizens, and patrolled the streets with them all that day and night; we were armed with swords, the District having no firearms or only a few. (App., no. 28:280)

And several paragraphs further down, one reads about Humbert's decision to hurry over to the Bastille:

As I learned on the way that they were handing out powder at the Hôtel de Ville, I hurried thither and was given about a quarter of a pound, but they gave me no shot, saying that they had none.

As I left the Hôtel de Ville I heard someone say that the Bastille was being besieged. My regret at having no shot prompted an idea that I immediately carried out, namely to buy some small nails, which I got from the grocer's at the Coin du Roi, Place de la Grève.

There, I prepared and greased my gun. . . .

I immediately set off for the Bastille, loading my gun as I went. (App., no. 28:281–82)[53]

The autobiographical account shows how the clockmaker's apprentice Humbert became a hero unwittingly and more or less by chance. But at the same time his actions seemed to be following an inner instinct, an unconscious drive that the political thinkers of the time in the pompous language of the philosophy of history interpreted as the "awakening of the people" (le réveil du peuple) or the "manifestation of the will of the people" (la volonté du peuple). In Humbert as in the writings of other Vainqueurs who came from the lower classes— the wine merchant Cholat, the building contractor Palloy, the beer brewer Santerre, the grocer Pannetier, or the craftsmen Rossignol, Boucheron, and Rousselet—the storming of the Bastille is depicted as an event that unexpectedly descends on them, draws them in like a vortex, and arouses immense, dormant powers in them. "On 12 July," the craftsman and later revolutionary general Jean Rossignol writes in his autobiography, "I knew nothing yet of the Revolution, and I had no idea of all the things one could do."[54] This view of the events is embodied in the extreme by the obscure kitchen assistant Dénot, who on the evening of 14 July cut the throat of the governor of the Bastille with his kitchen knife. Called to account for his action the following day by the Châtelet court, the surprised Dénot stated during the interrogation that he thought he had performed a "patriotic deed" (un acte patriotique) and believed himself to be worthy of a medal of honor ("mériter une médaille") for executing the governor—an act that, after all, was cheered by the incensed mob with great enthusiasm. Dénot in turn surprised the examining magistrates by saying in response to their question about why he had run to the Bastille on the morning of 14 July in the first place that he had been unemployed for over six months and had been bored sitting at home that day. Armed with a kitchen knife for lack of a gun or a pistol, he had followed the crowd that was streaming past his window to the Bastille to see what was happening there.[55]

Those authors among the Vainqueurs de la Bastille who had a more extensive scholastic education and more philosophical knowledge presented the events of 14 July 1789 and their own role in them in a completely different light. They saw the storming of the Bastille as the consequence of a long-term development, and their own involvement as the result of an individual dawning of consciousness. La Reynie de la Bruyère (1759–1807), who had fled the seminary in Angoulême in 1784 because he had seduced a girl in the confessional, saw his participation in the attack as grounded in his enthusiasm for the writings of Rousseau, Raynal, Pope, and Helvétius, which he had already secretly devoured while at the seminary. "Through these writings," La Reynie states in his autobiography, *A mes concitoyens et à mes camarades* (To my fellow citizens and comrades, app., no. 30), he was able to "reinforce this love for freedom," which drove him on 14 July as well. Unlike Humbert, Cholat, or Dénot, who more or less by chance had arrived at the square in front of the Bastille following the movement of the crowd, La Reynie in his description from the very beginning sees himself as an acting hero setting events in motion. He claims to have run through the streets of the capital on the morning of 14 July and to have mobilized the incensed people with the cry "Citizens to the Bastille! To the Bastille!" An increasingly large crowd is supposed to have answered his appeal, and he himself to have pretty much organized the siege, since it was he who had sent for the cannons and had them aimed at the drawbridge of the Bastille. Finally, he claims to have forced his way into the apartment of the governor of the Bastille, de Launay, at the risk of his own life—a bullet went through his hat—in order to negotiate the handing over of the fortress to the besiegers.

La Reynie's account is conceited, showy, full of exaggerations— but at the same time a typical example of how the storming of the Bastille was perceived as a heroic act of patriotism. In contrast to writing Vainqueurs such as Rossignol and Humbert, who came from the lower classes, La Reynie gives the readers and the public a philosophical justification of the storming of the Bastille—which legally was a crime of "lèze-majesté" punishable by death—into the bargain. The radical movement of Enlightenment philosophy (Rousseau, Raynal, Diderot, Helvétius) provided the basis for the legitimation of political violence and popular justice with its conceptions of freedom and sovereignty of the people, as well as with the concept of the "right to resist despotism." Victor of the Bastille Dusaulx, who as a member of the French Academy of Fine Arts and translator of the works of Juvenal was certainly the most educated of the 863 Vainqueurs, added an aesthetic justification to this one from the philosophy of history. In his report on the storming of the Bastille, Dusaulx compared the participants to the Spartans, the conqueror of the Bastille Elie to the Roman general Marius, and the entire corps of Vainqueurs to that "famous troop of old Thebes" which was called the "Sacred Battalion" (app., no. 45:156).

The self-portrayal of the Academy member Dusaulx and the completely different, sober autobiographical account of the clockmaker's apprentice Humbert are linked by their common depiction of a role model that the public in 1789 identified surprisingly quickly with the Vainqueurs de la Bastille, that of the Citoyen-Soldat, a combative, patriotic, freedom-loving citizen. The actors of 14 July from the very start managed to present the storming of the Bastille as a *military* action, as a grand victory that had been won not by the royal army but by the "people," not by a general from a noble family such as Condé but by obscure craftsmen such as Humbert and Rossignol. The calm assurance of the Vainqueurs de la Bastille that that group represented the patriotic as well as the military vanguard of the Revolution showed in their attempt to form a kind of patriotic elite troop in October 1789 in the guise of the Volontaires de la Bastille; then in the deployment in 1792 of the Volontaires who had been integrated into the regular army in the Vendée, the center of the royalist counterrevolution; and finally also in the military careers of individual Vainqueurs. Parein and Rossignol, for example, actually made it to the rank of general. Both gave up writing in 1792 and instead fought weapon in hand for the new French republic. With their autobiographical writings, both understood themselves as Citoyens-Soldats and—like most of the victors of

the Bastille—proudly added the title of honor Vainqueurs de la Bastille to their signature—even after 1792 and during the Directoire. And
while most other former members of the corps of the Vainqueurs de la
Bastille disappeared from public view in the years 1796–99, fell silent,
and did not speak of their revolutionary past, Parein was arrested in
1803 in Caen on the order of Consul Napoléon, and Rossignol at the
same time was exiled to Devil's Island in French Guiana for activities
hostile to the state. Jean-Joseph Dusaulx was the author of what was
considered throughout France during the early stages of the Revolution to be the official "authentic" account of the storming of the Bastille, *De l'Insurrection parisienne* (On the Paris insurrection). Yet in 1796,
after the stormy years of the Revolution, he returned to literature and
continued to work on the *Voyage sentimental dans les Pyrénées* (Sentimental journey in the Pyrenees), which he had begun eight years earlier.
In 1798, a year before his death, Dusaulx's nostalgic and critical retrospective work on his encounters with Jean-Jacques Rousseau was published.[56] By 1803 at the latest, with the abolition of 14 July as a national
day of commemoration, the "heroes of 14 July" were thrown from
their pedestal, their spokesmen silenced. There was one exception,
however: Pierre-François Palloy, a former journeyman bricklayer and
later a building contractor, who between 1789 and 1791, first on his
own and then with an official commission, had destroyed and leveled
the former state prison of the Bastille. As late as 1809—as the last of
the writing Vainqueurs de la Bastille—he published a four-page ballad
at his own expense that was sung to the melody of "Au pas redoublé"
and was entitled *Aux Fils aînés de la Révolution Française; Enfants de 1789;
Hommes de 1809* (To the oldest sons of the French Revolution; children
of 1789; men of 1809).[57] This ballad, which it cost the author—who had
become more and more impoverished since the Revolution—several
hundred livres to publish, went almost unnoticed by the public. And
yet Palloy had with his stylistically unpolished song touched a chord
that resonated more deeply in the consciousness of the French living
under Napoléon's empire than the high-handed emperor was willing
to admit. This was the connection between the "heroes of 14 July" and
the soldiers of the imperial armies, who were joined by a similar patriotism and a similar self-assurance as Citoyens-Soldats, warlike citizens
in the service of the newborn nation. The image of the victors of the
Bastille that even the *Bayreuther Zeitung* was able to come up with less
than a fortnight after the event seems like a premonition of the vic-

torious republican and later Napoleonic armies that German princes and armies had nothing to equal for a long time: "One could see these young heroes attack the Bastille and in two hours take control of a fortress that had resisted the armies of Louis XIV for over six months."[58]

Martyrs of Freedom, Victims of Despotism: The Triumph of the Prisoners of the Bastille

After the stormers of the Bastille, the second group of heroes of 14 July 1789 were the liberated prisoners. A contemporary copperplate engraving shows them on their way from the Bastille to the Paris city hall, surrounded by an enthusiastic crowd, protected by the National Guard, in a triumphal procession that made its way through half of Paris, from Faubourg Saint-Antoine to the center of the capital. There are seven captives in all, an old man with a long white beard leading the way—a dignified figure who impresses the spectators. The English traveler Rigby, who had gone to the Bastille on the evening of 14 July immediately after hearing of the storming of the notorious state prison, was part of the immense crowd that accompanied the liberated prisoners of the Bastille to the city hall. In one of his letters, Rigby writes about the event:

> Every one who witnessed this scene probably felt, as I did, an emotion which partook of horror and detestation of the Government which could so obdurately as well as unjustly expose human beings to such sufferings; and of pity for the miserable individuals before us. . . . I was no longer able to bear the sight, I turned from the crowd, I burst into tears.[59]

In contrast to the conquerors of the Bastille, however, the liberated prisoners in no way matched the expectations of the public, not only because of their "incredibly small" number, as contemporary witnesses already remarked, but also because of their biographies and fortunes. Four of the seven former prisoners of the Bastille were even transported to another prison (at Bicêtre) several days after their "liberation," because they turned out to be not innocent victims of despotic persecution but unscrupulous counterfeiters. Two other prisoners, the Irish nobleman Jacques-François-Xavier de Whyte de Malleville and Count Gabriel-Charles-Joseph-Paulin-Hubert de Solages from the southern French province of Languedoc, had been

Délivrance de M. le Comte de Lorges, prisonnier à la Bastille depuis 32 ans.

Figure 22. The liberation of the Count de Lorges from the Bastille after thirty-two years of imprisonment. Anonymous colored etching, oval 137 by 181 mm, published by Bance, Paris, 1789 (Bibliothèque Nationale, Estampes, Coll. de Vinck 1642).

forcibly delivered to the Bastille by their families for engaging in perverted sexual practices. Only a certain Tavernier, who had been incarcerated since 1757 because he supposedly was an accomplice of Robert-François Damiens, who had tried to assassinate Louis XV, exhibited at least some of the features that fit the image of Bastille prisoners held by contemporaries, namely, that of a man who was simultaneously an enemy and an innocent victim of despotic rule.

Since none of the true prisoners matched the expectations of society, journalists and writers created a kind of ideal prisoner in the figure of the Count de Lorges. His "story" was written and started circulating right after the events of 14 July 1789. The Count de Lorges, who is depicted in popular copperplate engravings as a venerable old man with a white beard (figure 22), is reminiscent of the figure that ten thousand Parisians had seen with their own eyes in the late afternoon of 14 July after the storming of the Bastille. His name was similar to that of the Count de Solages, who was named in the newspapers as one of the liberated captives. His history borrowed from that of the liberated Tavernier and, more important, conformed to ideas concerning the Bastille that had been widespread in the eighteenth century since Constantin de Renneville's volume *L'Inquisition française* (The French inquisition). In the story of the Count de Lorges, historical fact and audience expectations, oral rumors and journalistic imagination met in a mixture typical of its time, one that emerged during the summer of 1789 in a wide range of genres, from popular broadsheet to political leaflet, from newspaper article to popular song.

Jean-Louis Carra, for example, in a short book taking up the tradition of the inexpensive chapbook, reports that the Count de Lorges had been committed to the Bastille in 1749 at the behest of the Marquise de Pompadour because he had denounced the scandalous lifestyle of Louis XV's mistress in a pamphlet. Interrogated by the Paris police chief Sartine, whom Carra portrays as a pompous despot, de Lorges was thrown into a dark dungeon in the Bastille and put in heavy irons. Several prison breaks failed, as did the plan to escape the Bastille through sawed-up bars with a rope ladder made from pieces of clothing. "The years flew by," Carra lets his hero say in the first person, "and brought no change at all in my fate; sad and in low spirits I let my days pass in bitterness and sorrow and cursed Despotism and its accomplices."[60]

As in a street ballad that was probably sung to a favorite French melody, "Il pleut, il pleut bergère," and that was published together with the popular broadsheet recounting the story of de Lorges, 14 July in Carra, too, is depicted as a day of liberation from inhuman solitary confinement, as the victory of the "nation" over despotism.[61] And as the anonymous ballad's last stanza sets the courage of the victors of the Bastille above the bravery of the Roman Scipio,[62] Carra at the end of his tale lets the liberated Count strike up a hymn of praise for the day the Bastille was stormed:

> I want to celebrate forever, yes I desire that the fourteenth of July be a day of festivity in eternity, and that the rest of my fortune be used every year to help five innocently incarcerated captives regain their freedom.[63]

Figure 23. The liberation of the Count de Lorges and the discovery of the iron mask by the nation on 14 July 1789. Anonymous etching, 230 by 339 mm, published by Gouthier, Paris, 1789 (Bibliothèque Nationale, Estampes, Coll. de Vinck 1631).

The figure of the Count de Lorges, whom Carra claims to have personally met after his liberation on 14 July, shortly before his disappearance,[64] and questioned about his fate,[65] became a popular image primarily through his depiction in the above-mentioned broadsheets (known as "canards") during the summer of 1789. Following traditional patterns, the canard entitled *Délivrance de Mr le Conte* [sic] *de Lorges par la Nation* (The liberation of the Count de Lorges by the nation) consists of three parts (figure 23). On the left side of the broadsheet, the above-mentioned street ballad is printed; in the lower part there is a short narrative text telling the Count's story; and in the middle, as the central component of the piece, a picture. This picture shows the conquerors of the Bastille coming through a door on the right with torches, greeted with a gesture of welcome by the old, long-bearded prisoner sitting in a chair. To the right of *Délivrance,* as a kind of mirror image, appears the story of the man in the iron mask, it, too, consisting of a picture, a popular street ballad (sung to the melody of "D'Adélaïde"), and a short narrative text.

The story of the man in the iron mask, behind which was suspected a brother of Louis XIV who had been brought to the dungeons of the Bastille at the behest of the Sun King, received a fresh impetus from the discovery of skeletal remains after the taking of the Bastille. In the summer months of 1789, thousands of visitors were led through the jail rooms and dungeons of the fortress by accredited guides for a small entrance fee. These guides were workers of Palloy's, many of them participants in the storming of the Bastille who were helping to tear down the former state prison. In the fortress, visitors were shown instruments of torture that had been found, the remains of bones, and "death machines unknown to man,"[66] as well as the extensive archives of the state prison. The press of the Revolution years published inscriptions written by captives that had been found on the walls of the Bastille and deciphered. As late as 13 August 1793, the *Chronique de Paris* claimed to have read on a stone there that "an old man bathed this stone with his tears," or "I have been chained to this stone for forty years. They covered my face with an iron mask."[67] Stories such as that of the Count de Lorges or the man in the iron mask and legends concerning dungeons in which prisoners had purposely been "forgotten" until they died a horrible death from starvation[68] were retold by the "tour guides" ten thousand times, and eagerly taken up by journalists and authors such as Carra, Manuel, Beffroy de Reigny, and Cubières. Within several weeks, they gained huge popularity. Germans traveling to Paris such as Halem, Campe, and the Baron von Trenck, who never missed a sensation, combined these tales—transmitted half orally, half in written form and situated between historical truth and exorbitant exaggeration—into a new form of the Bastille myth, one in which the prisoners played a central role as the victims of despotism. Trenck comments on the Bastille's "jaws of hell," which were revealed to the public for the first time in 1790–91. He writes of the tortures that were common practice at the Bastille, of the "corpses of some unlucky men who had rotted in their chains" and who were found after the storming of the Bastille.[69] Trenck also claims to have personally seen the liberated prisoners of the Bastille during their triumphal procession through Paris; in a few sentences he describes the mythical figure of the Count de Lorges, who for his contemporaries embodied the "ideal" prisoner of the Bastille:

I have seen them all led around the Palais-Royal in triumph. One of them was an old nobleman who for thirty-nine years had languished in this dungeon with hardly any daylight. And what was this man's crime? As a witty young man without any experience in the world, he had written a small satire against Madame de Pompadour.[70]

"The horrors of the Bastille" (les horreurs de la Bastille) were at the center of a great number of publications during the second half of 1789 in which—starting from the sensual impressions of the innumerable visitors of the Bastille—the fate of the former prisoners was portrayed in glaring colors reminiscent of contemporary Gothic novels.[71] Louis-Pierre Manuel, a former private teacher and later a bookseller, published a bestseller in this literary genre with his *Histoire des plus célèbres prisonniers de la Bastille* (History of the most famous captives of the Bastille, 1790). In this book, the story of the Count de Lorges and the mysterious legend of the man in the iron mask took a central place. As early as August 1789, one Mauclerc, an office scribe like Parein from Châlons in Burgundy, had composed a pamphlet with the almost programmatic title *Le Langage des murs, ou les Cachots de la Bastille dévoilant leurs secrets* (The language of the walls, or the dungeons of the Bastille unmask their secrets) after his visit to the Bastille. Mauclerc took the numerous inscriptions on the walls of the dungeons of the Bastille as an occasion to follow the fate of individual prisoners—such as the fate of the Count de Lorges, whose dungeon the "tour guides" at the Bastille had showed him first of all.

The figure of the Count de Lorges, which can also be found in the second large contemporary collection of horror stories concerning the Bastille, the *Remarques et Anecdotes sur le château de la Bastille* (Remarks and anecdotes concerning the castle of the Bastille, fall 1789),[72] did also encounter skepticism. An anonymous journalist with a feel for history who reappraised the history of the Bastille raised doubts about the existence of the Count de Lorges after looking in vain for his name in the prison register.[73] Nor did Manuel allow himself to be swayed by the legends that had formed around the Count de Lorges, who had already found his way into Curtius's famous waxworks. Instead, he compared the names of the prisoners, the time they spent in the Bastille, and the reasons given for their imprisonment and finally came to the conclusion that the Count de Lorges had never existed, and that no one else was hiding behind that name either. His story, which had been considered true, was nothing but a web of lies, a "novel"—the Count himself a made-up "novelistic hero" (héros de roman).[74]

The symbolic figure of the Count de Lorges was joined in the spring of 1790 by Henri Masers de Latude, born in 1725, who had endured a prison sentence inflicted at the behest of the Marquise de Pompadour from 1749 until 1784, mostly in the Bastille. Latude was liberated not on 14 July 1789 but five years earlier by a royal pardon; and he had been locked up in the Bastille not because of critical writings but because of a youthful prank that the Versailles court had mistakenly suspected to be a conspiracy against the king and his mistress. Latude, an illegitimate child and a barber in the army by profession, had in 1749 come up with the idea of revealing a conspiracy that he had supposedly discovered but that he had actually invented himself. He then disclosed the plot to the Marquise de Pompadour and warned her of a poison that he himself had sent to her in the form of a harmless vitriol.[75] The ruse of the guileless Latude, who had hoped to gain a princely reward for discovering the supposed conspiracy, was uncovered by a simple comparison of handwriting—his hand and that on the address of the package were the same—and he was taken to the Bastille with a royal lettre de cachet. Having staged several spectacular prison breaks, each of which made the conditions of his imprisonment worse, Latude was released after thirty-five years of captivity in the Bastille—as well as in the prisons of Bicêtre, Charenton, and Vincennes—at the instigation of a private plea for clemency.

Even though the reason for his imprisonment—which shows him aspiring after money and fame—did not quite fit into the picture of the patriotic "martyr of freedom," Latude managed to turn himself into a former prisoner of the Bastille who was celebrated and acclaimed on all sides within several months of the storming of the erstwhile state prison. Even before 1789, Latude had not been an unknown figure. On a winter day in 1782, an obscure knitwear trader from Paris had found a package with an unreadable address in the street and had opened it. Inside, she found a letter from one "Masers de Latude, prisoner for thirty-two years at the Bastille, at Vincennes and now at Bicêtre, on bread and water, in a cell 10 feet underground,"[76] which contained a plea for mercy obviously addressed to the king. Madame Legros—the knitwear trader—was deeply moved by the fate of Latude. From then on, she spent almost three years fighting for his release. She circulated copies of his plea for mercy, secured two attorneys at the Paris court, Lacroix and Comeyras, for the case, and finally managed to interest influential circles at court in the former prisoner of the Bastille. Certain members of the high nobility, such as the Marquis de la Villette, a friend of Voltaire's, gave their support to Latude, and in 1784 finally succeeded in obtaining his release. That same year, the French Academy presented its newly founded "Prize of Virtue" (Prix de la Vertu) to Madame Legros, who had selflessly and with great financial sacrifices fought for Latude. Writings such as the *Histoire d'une détention de trente-neuf ans dans les prisons d'Etat* (History of a thirty-nine-year imprisonment in the state prisons, 1787), published by one Marquis Beaupoil de Saint-Aulaire, which circulated illegally and connected Latude's story to a scathing critique of the despotism of the lettres de cachet and the justice system in general, made Latude a well-known celebrity even before the Revolution. Hundreds of visitors came to his Paris apartment, sent him money, and heard the account of his tale of woe from his own mouth, since he did not dare to publish it for fear of being incarcerated again.

After the Revolution, Latude saw that his longed-for opportunity had come to go public with his own writings, and to sue the heirs of the Marquise de Pompadour, who had died in 1769, for compensation. As early as the day after the conquest of the Bastille, he was seen climbing down into the dungeons in which he had spent more than twelve years of his life, accompanied by Palloy's workers, who had begun tearing down the state prison. Together with these workers, he discovered the very instruments he had used in his escape attempts in a dungeon that was used as a room for archives and documents. Most prominently, they found the 180-foot-long rope ladder he had tied with his fellow inmate Antoine d'Alègre from shirts and bedsheets. Several weeks later, in August and September 1789, Latude published the first of his writings. These were printed versions of his pleas for mercy to the Marquise de Pompadour and the Paris police chief Sartine, as well as a narrative of his sensational escape through the chimney and over the tower walls of the Bastille,[77] for which he had used the much-admired rope ladder. In one stroke, Latude, who before had been known mostly in the enlightened Paris salons that had taken up his case and in Versailles court circles, became a national celebrity. In August 1789, the painter Vestier created the famous portrait of Latude that was spread by the thousands as a print. This

Figure 24. Jean Dominique Etienne Canu after Vestier, Mr. Masers de Latude. Etching in dotted fashion, plate 138 by 100 mm. Frontispiece for *Le Despotisme dévoilé, ou Mémoires de Henri Masers de Latude, détenu pendant trente-cinq ans dans diverses prisons d'Etat . . .* (Paris: Lejay fils, 1790), vol. 1.

picture shows Latude in front of the Bastille, which is about to be demolished, looking at the spectator while pointing at the former state prison towering in the background (figure 24). The painting itself—together with the rope ladder—was displayed in the fall of 1789 in the public art exhibition of the Louvre. In 1790, an impresario presented the ladder at innumerable markets throughout France and England and told Latude's tale of woe; the former prisoner himself, as he regretted to inform Lord Grosvenor, was unable to take part in these exhibitions because of his advanced age.[78] A miniature of Latude's rope ladder and the inscription "Replica of the self-made ladder with which M. de Latude escaped the Bastille"[79] was included with all models of the Bastille that Palloy began sending out after November 1790. In July 1790, the members of the Paris Jacobin club elected Latude, "known all over Europe," as the *Chronique de Paris* noted, "for having spent thirty-five years in the Bastille," to their circle by acclamation. In addition, his benefactress, Madame Legros, was awarded the citizen's crown ("couronne civique") for her "courage" and "perseverance," and it was solemnly given to her by a delegation of twelve.[80] Latude's autobiographical self-portrait was first published in 1790 and became a bestseller of the revolutionary years with more than twenty editions. Along with Dusaulx's *De l'Insurrection parisienne et de la prise de la Bastille*—the official description of 14 July from the perspective of the Vainqueurs—and his Bastille stones, it was one of the objects that Palloy had sent to all départements in France, and had carried through the streets on biers. In this five hundred-page autobiography, which was published by his lawyer, Latude for the first time gave the numerous fragmentary descriptions of his life that had been circulating since his liberation from prison in 1784 epic scope. The illegitimate child of the laundress Jeanneton Aubespry from Montagnac and the impoverished Count de Latude who after meager schooling had become a barber by profession, Henri Masers de Latude started out by creating a refined education for himself that included the study of engineering. Next, he glossed over his attempt to ingratiate himself at court by discovering the alleged plot by presenting the conspiracy as real. At the center of his story, however, are the descriptions of the horrible prison conditions at the Bastille, Vincennes, and Charenton, the luridly depicted and increasingly cruel persecutions by the Marquise de Pompadour and the Paris police lieutenants Sartine and Le Noir, and finally the account of his three ingenious prison breaks, each of which earned him some days or weeks of freedom.

Latude's carefully crafted autobiography reads like a political pamphlet, and yet it is in large part a Gothic novel trying to rouse and shock the reader:

Yes, for thirty-five years I have vainly belaboured these infernal vaults with my sighs and my despair: my spirit bruised incessantly by fits of rage and distressed by endless pain; all my limbs seared, torn by the weight and friction of my chains; my body gnawed by the most repulsive animals, breathing only putridities in place of air, and, as the acme of horror, succoured and saved whenever death seemed willing to make end to my anguish by snatching me from my tormentors: such was my fate throughout this long sequence of years.[81]

Latude's political Gothic novel caused a considerable sensation, especially since its effect was constantly increased and reinforced by its author's numerous public appearances. The newspaper *Mercure de France* called the publication of the book a "memorable event" and the book itself a work all should choose to peruse who were capable of reading and writing.[82] Jean-François de La Harpe, literary critic and founder of the Paris Lycée, a kind of free university, in his enthusiastic fifty-five-page review of Latude's book went so far as to suggest the work as a primer for beginning lessons in primary schools:

> I want this terrible story to become a schoolbook from which all children should learn to read. One believes that blood and tears of misery flow from every line; if every line were squeezed, a crime would come out of each one: this is the lesson that must be taught to people who have only recently been liberated.[83]

Together with his lawyer Thiery, who spoke for him, Latude presented himself to the National Assembly twice. The first time, in May 1790, he wanted to secure a state pension;[84] he returned on 27 January 1792, as his request had initially been denied, mainly because of the rather ambiguous reason for his arrest.[85] On this second attempt, his petition was received with applause by the representatives of the new Constituent Assembly. Representative Lasource spoke emotionally of Latude's innocence, which humanity as a whole was obliged to compensate, and explicitly mentioned the famous passage from the memoirs in which Latude describes how he just continued to write with his own blood on cloth rags when the governor of the Bastille punished him by depriving him of paper and ink.[86] After Latude had been granted the pension he had asked for, in 1793 he also managed finally to push through his claims against the heirs of the Marquise de Pompadour before a Paris court. "Latude," the *Moniteur* reports in its 15 September 1793 edition, "whose story and whose misery everyone knows, petitioned for damages against the inheritors of Pompadour" and was awarded the considerable sum of sixty thousand livres, a sixth in cash, the rest in the form of land.[87] A year earlier, he had already taken a symbolic and posthumous revenge on King Louis XV—who had died in 1775. When on 10 August 1792 the statue of Louis XV on what was to become the Place de la Révolution was torn down by the rebellious crowd after the sacking of the Tuileries and the arrest of the royal family, Latude at his own request received the right hand of the bronze statue from the rebels—a symbolic embodiment of the hand that had signed his warrant for the Bastille forty-three years before.[88]

Gestures such as this perhaps make it easier to understand why the autodidact Latude was more popular and closer to the people in his forms of expression during the revolutionary years than other former prisoners of the Bastille who tried to seize the moment and publish their biographies. These individuals, too, were hoping for damages and pensions from the state: the Count de Paradès, for instance, or Leprévôt de Beaumont, a clergyman who had uncovered price-fixing in the corn trade in 1769, had been imprisoned for that reason in the Bastille and other places until his liberation on 5 October 1789, and had finally received a small compensation in 1792.[89] Palloy, the Vainqueur de la Bastille and the great director of the festivals of 14 July, and Latude, whose biography like no other embodied the collective tale of woe of the prisoners of the Bastille for his contemporaries, have much in common. Like Palloy, who came from humble circumstances, Latude was at the same time a plebeian and a boastful parvenu who was ashamed of his illegitimate birth his entire life. He had already changed his original name, Danry (based on his first name, "Jean Henri"), to the noble title Masers de Latude while still in prison, even though his father had never officially acknowledged him. Like Palloy, Latude knew how to publicly stage himself and had at his command the pathetic and emotional gestures that dominated in the public sphere during the years of the Revolution. Also like Palloy, who was similarly productive "of superficial knowledge," Latude was possessed by an unrestrained enthusiasm for writing. During his imprisonment and then in the years of the Revolution until his death in 1804, he wrote hundreds of letters, requests, and petitions—over sixty just to Sartine, the Paris police chief. He drew up political and "scientific" reform projects that he sent to the Versailles court without ever receiving an answer; told the story of his imprisonment and prison breaks in dozens of variations; and—along with Palloy's Bastille relics—sent his autobiographical account to a large number of celebrities and institutions. Symbolic gestures made by Latude such as presenting to Palloy a shirt worn in the Bastille are related to the popular-religious cult of relics that Palloy revitalized in secular form and used for his own ends with his semireligious, patriotic cult of the Bastille stones. And finally, the former master builder Palloy and the son of a laundress Latude represented a bourgeois ideal to which none of the prisoners of the Bastille liberated on 14 July 1789 could lay claim for themselves: that of the industrious, ambitious, and intelligent self-made man of which Latude offered evidence with his minutely prepared escape attempts and his numerous reform projects in all areas.

At the same time, he served as the model of an uncompromising man of letters who would not be silenced either by censorship or by deprivation of paper and ink but incessantly continued to write, tried to rouse the public, and finally succeeded in spite of all the obstacles.

"The Patriot" Palloy: Conqueror of the Bastille and Vulgarizer

The best known and most fascinating of the conquerors of the Bastille was undoubtedly Pierre-François Palloy, who gave himself the nickname "the Patriot" in July 1789 (figure 25). Born in 1755, the son of a small wine merchant in Paris, Palloy had already made a dazzling ascent through society at the beginning of the Revolution. After breaking off his scholastic education, he first entered the royal army at fifteen. Six years later, having married the daughter of a Parisian building contractor, he turned to the bricklayer's trade. Palloy learned from scratch, took over his father-in-law's business, and proudly called himself not only "maître maçon" (master builder), but also "architecte-entrepreneur." In the summer of 1789, he was one of the largest building contractors in Paris, employed up to four hundred workers, estimated his fortune at more than 500,000 livres, and called seven houses his own. All in all, this was a fortune comparable to that of a "fermier général" (farmer-general), or of a large Paris businessman.

The storming of the Bastille was the decisive turning point in the career of this ambitious and talented builder. Mostly by chance, Palloy let himself and a dozen of his workers be swept away with the crowd on 14 July 1789. He witnessed the first riots and looting, took the opportunity to arm himself and his men, and finally—according to his own report, which cannot be verified, and which is probably less than truthful—was one of the first to enter the inner courtyard of the conquered state prison. "As a good citizen," Palloy wrote two years later in an account of his role in the attack on the Bastille, "I climbed onto the stage of the Revolution, without any political goals, an honestly acquired cane with a golden knob in my hand; and my only ambition is to die with a white cane in my hand."[90] And in a letter written less than a year after the assault on the Bastille to the administration of the département of Calvados, to whom he proferred a stone cut from the Bastille as a patriotic present, Palloy writes, "It did not suffice for me to have participated in the destruction of this fortress's walls, I had the desire to immortalize the memory of its terror."[91]

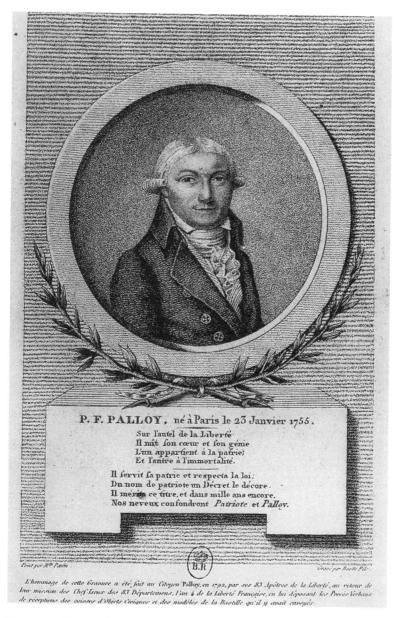

Figure 25. Ruotte the younger after Mlle Pantin, Pierre-François Palloy. Etching in dotted fashion, 201 by 124 mm, 1792 (Bibliothèque Nationale, Estampes, Inv. N²).

As early as the evening of 14 July 1789, Palloy and his workers had begun demolishing the conquered former state prison—two days before he received the official commission to do so from the Paris city government. Only after much delay—in 1791–92—was Palloy actually reimbursed for the services rendered, in which at times more than five hundred workers took part, all of them paid by Palloy. He saw the destruction of the Bastille as a symbolic act, and the reminting of its stones and iron chains into *"reliques patriotiques"* (patriotic relics) as a means of reminding the French of the birth of revolutionary France. In the summer of 1789, Palloy and his construction workers started giving paid tours through the basement, dungeons, and "torture chambers" of the notorious state prison, where they depicted the conditions of captivity in the darkest colors. Skeletons and bone parts that had been found in the cells and under walls—which probably belonged to fallen construction workers[92]—served as "visual aids" until Palloy finally had them interred in a monument (figure 26) erected specifically for that purpose in the Saint-Paul cemetery.[93] In October and November 1790, he started sending miniature Bastilles—stone blocks cut from the former state prison—to all French départements (there were eighty-three at the time) at his own expense. Delegates from Palloy, called "Apostles of Freedom," brought the Bastille stones to the provinces in carts for heavy loads and organized their solemn dedication in the individual département capitals. Next to these cut stones, which Palloy himself named "ex-votos" (votive sculptures) or "Relics of Freedom," a number of other objects with symbolic significance were carried past the amazed crowd on two additional biers in a patriotic procession: the memoirs of the prisoner of the Bastille Latude; the official history of the storming of the Bastille (*De l'Insurrection parisienne et de la prise de la Bastille*), written by one of the conquerors, Dusaulx, himself; several framed engravings showing the monument for the victims of the Bastille buried in the Saint-Paul cemetery in Paris (see figure 26); portraits of King Louis XVI, La Fayette, and Bailly, the mayor of Paris; and finally a cannonball and a breastplate, which as trophies were supposed to symbolize the disarming of the defenders of the Bastille.[94]

Palloy pursued the patriotic cult of the Bastille stones that he had initiated with immense energy. He combined it with the idea that only the authentic "Relics of Freedom," which every French citizen

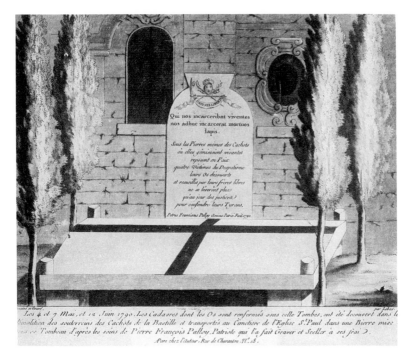

Figure 26. Lebas, Funeral monument for the mortal remains of the victims of the Bastille whose bones were discovered during the razing. Aquatint etching, 189 by 256 mm, 1790 (Bibliothèque Nationale, Estampes, Coll. de Vinck 1684).

should see and touch, could in the long term ensure the unity of the newly born French nation regenerated from centuries of slavery and despotism. Palloy's speeches on the symbolic meaning of the Bastille, which he had his "Apostles of Freedom" read publicly in the départe-ment capitals, show a peculiar combination, typical for its time, of traditional popular-religious ideas with the new political language, which had its roots in the works of Rousseau, Voltaire, Montesquieu, and Raynal. In a speech delivered in 1792 and printed afterward, Pal-loy said:

> I have sworn to devote all my energy to propagating the fruits of our newborn constitution. France is a new world, and in order to hold on to this achievement, it is necessary to sow the rubble of

our old servitude everywhere, as Leviticus in the book of Moses scattered the limbs of his wife into the four winds to take revenge.[95]

Palloy called the Bastille a "detestable monument," a "temple of despair," a "damned bit of earth," and an "infernal colossus" that the people of Paris had brought down. He saw the Bastille stones themselves not only as "relics" of a new patriotic cult but as "emblems" and "gages de la liberté" (guarantors of freedom).[96] They were supposed to indissolubly join the regenerated body of the nation, and at the same time give new strength to those parts which were still infested with superstition and lethargy. "These impressive artifacts will remind all spectators of the memorable days when the French, after eighteen centuries of disgraceful servitude, were led to freedom and equality," Palloy wrote to the Société populaire in Nantes concerning this matter in November 1793. He had presented them with a Bastille stone and some other patriotic accessories, and advised the chairman of the political club to give the public dedication as solemn a setting as possible: "These striking artifacts will remind posterity of the memorable times that led the French to liberty and equality after eighteen centuries of disgraceful slavery. Let the dedication of these valuable items be part of a great celebration, for only public ceremonies will make those men who are still numbed by the burden of their toils emerge from their stupor, and only when they have seen the light will reason replace their prejudices."[97]

Palloy became obsessed with his self-chosen mission, sparing neither trouble nor expense. In 1793, he sent out stone slabs fashioned from what remained of the walls of the Bastille to all 544 French districts, to a large number of political clubs (Sociétés populaires, Jacobin clubs), and to individuals who in his opinion had rendered outstanding services to the nation through their patriotism. At Palloy's behest, Bastille stones with the respective accessories and prints made their way to the new French départements of Mont-Blanc (Chamonix) and Alpes-Maritimes (Nice), to the département of Mont-Tonnerre west the Rhine, and to the overseas colonies of Saint-Domingue (the present-day Haiti) and Guadeloupe. Three days after the assassination of Jean-Paul Marat by Charlotte Corday on 13 July 1793, Palloy presented the Théâtre-Français section in Paris (an administrative subdivision, also called the "Marseille section") with twelve stone blocks

cut from Bastille stones inscribed "Rue Jean-Jacques Rousseau," "Rue
Marat," and "Place de l'Ami du Peuple" (Square of the friend of the
people), which were supposed to be used as street signs.[98] At its request, the city administration of Orléans in September 1793 received
three Bastille stones from Palloy, which were to serve as pedestals for
busts of the "martyrs of the Revolution" Marat and Lepelletier, and
for one of Caesar's assassin, Brutus, who in the years 1791–94 was revered throughout France as a patriotic role model.[99] In October 1791,
Palloy donated a Bastille stone bearing a portrait of Mirabeau, who
had died in April, to the Constituent Assembly. In January 1794, he
gave the deputies another stone bearing the Declaration of the Rights
of Man and Citizen—gestures that were widely commented on in the
press and that transformed Palloy, the official Démolisseur de la Bastille (demolisher of the Bastille), into a popular and publicly celebrated
patriot. Earlier, in March 1792, Palloy had had small medals made
from the iron of bars, balls, and chains from the Bastille for the over
nine hundred representatives of the French parliament. They bore an
image of the freedom column that Palloy had designed for the Place
de la Bastille (figure 27).

> These medals, symbols of freedom, will be indissoluble bonds
> of brotherhood; I have had them cleaned and purified with fire.
> Placed on the hearts of the deputies, they will remind them of
> their former servitude, and of the courage they need to resist the
> harassments of despots.[100]

But the Revolutionary celebrations, conceived and organized in
part by Palloy himself, provided the real forums for the public staging
of the Bastille stones as "patriotic relics." Not only did Palloy give the
impulse for patriotic processions in the provinces by sending out Bastille stones to all département capitals; he was also one of the most
prominent directors of the Fêtes révolutionnaires, especially the festivals celebrating 14 July 1789 in Paris from 1790 to 1796.

When Palloy held his own festival commemorating the first anniversary of the storming of the Bastille from 18 to 20 July 1790 on the
site of the former state prison, which had already been completely
dismantled, his contemporaries saw it as a popular counterpart to the
official Festival of the Federation, which was celebrated on 14 July on
the Champ de Mars. In contrast to the grandiose but also meticulously
planned and geometrically formal Festival of the Federation, Palloy's

Figure 27. Pierre-François Palloy, Medal of a freedom column on the ruins of the Bastille. Iron, diameter 69 mm, 1792 (after Weil, W 17).

event was designed as a spontaneous popular festival. The large signs that Palloy had put up at the entrance of the celebration read "Ici l'on danse, ah ça ira, ça ira" (Here, people dance, and all will be well) (figure 28). On the dance floor, which rested upon Bastille stones, an orchestra hired by Palloy played old popular melodies (such as "Vive Henry" or "Il pleut, il pleut bergère") as well as new, patriotic airs so that people could dance. Festoons of garlands and Chinese lanterns surrounded the spacious dancing floor, as did wooden benches and tables that had been set up. Sellers of lemonade, wine, and sausages gave the festival, which the Paris city administration had initially resisted, the atmosphere of a public celebration at which wine flowed like water. Palloy's construction workers made some money on the side with "guided tours" through an underground dungeon they had built and fixed up as a horror and torture chamber.

The festivals Palloy arranged in later years featured more political symbolism than had the "alternative national festival" the Démolisseur de la Bastille organized in July 1790, and once again the following year, on the ruins of the Bastille. As Palloy proudly and publicly announced, both celebrations relied on his own generous funding.[101] On 14 July 1790, he had already directed a dramatic reenactment of the storming of the Bastille in Sceaux (a small town south of Paris where he owned a house) that was to become the model for numerous other open-air dramas of the same kind. Palloy had a miniature Bastille built out of papier-mâché, which was symbolically conquered. Afterward, an old man with a white beard, laden with chains, was "liberated" to the cheers of the crowd and then led through the streets of the village in triumph.[102] At the celebrations on the occasion of the transfer of Voltaire's remains to the Panthéon on 11 July 1791, Palloy headed a large delegation of conquerors of the Bastille exhibiting a Bastille stone on three biers in their midst; a plaque borne in front figuratively recalled the storming of the Bastille and celebrated it as "la dernière raison du peuple" (the people's self-defense). In another part of the procession the works of Voltaire were displayed on stones from the Bastille, where the author had been imprisoned twice,[103] in a manner reminiscent of both military triumphal marches and the exhibition of religious relics. In the years 1792 to 1794, Palloy finally became one of the great organizers and directors of the *official* Revolution festivals in

Figure 28. View of the Bastille on the day of the festival of 14 July 1790. Anonymous colored etching, diameter 96 mm, 1790 (Bibliothèque Nationale, Estampes, Qb1, M 100179).

Paris as well as in Sceaux, where he was elected president of the local Société populaire—a Jacobin club—in 1793. He was involved in producing the Festival of Reason and the Festival of the Supreme Being, in the ceremonies on the occasion of the funeral of Mirabeau (4 April 1791), and in the annual organization of the national holiday commemorating 14 July 1789. He gave the latter events a popular feel not only by displaying Bastille relics but also through his hospitality. For instance, he and his family invited a number of patriots from the provinces to Faubourg Saint-Antoine to a "repas fraternel," a brotherly feast, for which they bought wine and ham.[104] During the Revolution and into Napoleonic times, Palloy would celebrate the anniversary of the execution of Louis XVI on 21 January with a patriotic banquet for which friends and members of the Société populaire de Sceaux were invited to his house. In the sansculottic tradition, a cooked veal's head in sauce was on the menu, which the patriots feasted on while telling obscene jokes about the executed king and his consort Marie-Antoinette. Even when he was held in prison for two months during the Terror in March and April 1794—Palloy was accused of embezzling public funds and of being an accomplice of the "Hébertistes" by the Commune of Paris—his self-portrayal showed a sense of popular theatricality. In his printed defense, his last wish, after being guillotined, was to be buried under a Bastille stone with the following inscription: "Here lies Palloy, who in his youth laid siege to the Bastille, destroyed it, and scattered the limbs of this infernal monster over the face of the earth."[105] And in a letter in which he justified himself to the National Assembly, Palloy described how even in prison he surrounded himself with symbols of the Bastille—providing a significant example of theatrical self-staging by a "patriot of 1789":

> The Bastille stone on which I was sitting made me guess the motive behind my imprisonment. My dog stayed faithful and close to me, and my records of the costs of destroying the Bastille, which I had delivered and checked anew, became a sentence against my enemies and served for my own justification.
>
> I had decorated my cell with a picture of the fortress whose remains I have scattered to the four winds. The republican commandments I wrote served as proof of the epoch of freedom, the Declaration of Rights and the text of the constitution as morning and evening prayer; the patriotic oath was the short version of this, and a medal from the rubble of the colossus of tyranny

was my relic. Even in these three months, I have devoted all my energy to the public good, and here I swear that I will always remain true to myself.[106]

Palloy's gestures of self-portrayal, which sometimes seem bizarre and occasionally strange or naive, were grounded in the cultural syncretism that also characterized the staging of the Bastille stones. The latter mixed popular-religious ideas with the new political language of the Revolution, the cult of political relics with a form of traditional popular culture that was rooted in excessive feasts (the "ripaille"), in carnivalesque mirth, and sometimes in obscene buffoonery. The patriotic art of the builder and wine merchant Palloy was based on the intuitive conviction that abstract ideas such as "tyranny," "freedom," and "equality" could achieve broad social effectiveness and political effects only through sensual and physical experience. This explains the occasionally disconcerting juxtaposition of theatricality and bits and pieces of abstract political language, the mixture of popular festivity and political ceremony, and the desire to translate historical events such as the storming of the Bastille and political concepts such as "despotism" into tangible pictures, objects, and gestures. It was not the spoken, written, or printed word that Palloy thought could achieve a political effect, "electrify" people and motivate them to act, but only its anchoring in physically experienced sensual impressions. For Palloy, these included the exhibition of Bastille stones and the authentic-as-possible dramatic reenactment of the storming of the Bastille, the patriotic orgies of eating and drinking accompanied by renditions of the *Marseillaise* sung at the top of one's voice, the touching of the "Relics of Freedom" and their use as patriotic lucky charms, charms that—before they could, for instance, be given to the representatives of the National Assembly—first had to be cleansed of the "dirt" of their past in a fire.

Palloy's almost fetishistic relationship to writing, and above all to the printed word, only appears to contradict his intuitive emphasis on the sensual and physical dimension of patriotic popular art, the most prominent part of which for Palloy was the energetically pursued cult of the Bastille stones. Before 1789, Palloy had almost exclusively used his knowledge of writing for professional purposes—building sketches, business correspondence, accounting, and bills. Between 1789 and 1799, he published more than one hundred monographs at his own expense: from political speeches to large-scale posters, from autobiographical texts to patriotic songs and extensive designs for national monuments that he repeatedly dreamed of erecting on the site of the Bastille. He saw himself mostly as an educator of the people who had to fall back on popular, publicly effective media to strengthen the patriotic spirit of the bulk of the population. In a speech he gave before the Société populaire de Sceaux in October 1793, which he afterward had printed and gave away for free at the Festival of Reason, he explained:

> Let the patriotic writer especially train his abilities. By joining the fire of the republican spirit with his own proud self-esteem, let him resist the vengeance of the mighty, the hatred of the envious, and the ingratitude of nations; if necessary, let him cast the lightning bolt of eloquent truth. In this fashion, let all patriotic writers contribute to the progress of our rebirth, and express their deep respect and their disdain before the feared tribunal of public opinion.[107]

Palloy, who came from a humble background himself and knew the limits of written literature—at the end of the eighteenth century, almost two-thirds of the entire French population was illiterate, in Paris about half of the citizens—mainly wrote short, catchy publications that were also suited to being read or sung. In 1792 and 1793, he had several thousand copies of the text of the *Marseillaise,* the new revolutionary hymn that had been composed in Strasbourg in May 1792, printed and given out to the citizens of Paris free of charge.[108] In 1801 he had the *Hymne dédié aux Citoyens Français . . . à la gloire des braves guerriers,* which he had composed himself, sent to the soldiers of the revolutionary army.[109] Continually, especially in the years 1790–94, he wrote not only speeches to be read at dedications of the Bastille stones but also large-scale placards that he had posted on the walls of Paris by the thousands and had sent to the provinces. On placards such as *Les XVI Commandements patriotiques, par un vrai Républicain* (The XVI patriotic commandments, by a true republican, 1794), *Le Serment Républicain* (The republican oath, 1794), or *Les XXX Conseils de la Raison* (The thirty recommendations of reason, 1793–94), Palloy proclaims principles of a patriotic morality that in its form is clearly adapted from religious models—the ten commandments and the catechisms. For example, the first of the *XVI Commandements patriotiques,* which he proudly signed "Palloy, the Patriot," reads, "Love God above all things, and your fatherland like yourself: Your life is only a transition, it belongs to them. Remember that you came into this world naked, and that you will leave it in the same manner." The tenth commandment in turn exhorted readers to remember the two most decisive events of the French Revolution, the storming of the Bastille and the abolition of monarchy: "Always preserve the memory of the days of 14 July 1789 and 10 August 1792 and pass it on to your progeny."[110] The sixteenth and last commandment, too, is related to the assault on the Bastille through its metaphors, and it connects the collective memory of 14 July 1789 with a moral and political obligation: "Remember that you broke your chains; and that despots show no traces of humanity. Choose your legislators prudently, and carefully observe the ministers, who have always done evil and could continue to do it."[111]

In his autobiographical account of 1794, in which he defends himself against attacks from his enemies, Palloy stresses that his correspondence has become huge[112] and that he has been financially ruined not only by the demolition of the Bastille and the production and distribution of the Bastille relics but also and above all by the publication of a large number of his own writings. In 1792, Palloy commissioned 1,060 copies of his speech *Discours prononcé en présence des Bataillons de Volontaires et Citoyens d'Epernay* and passed them out free of charge. In 1794, he had the mayor of Sceaux give out several hundred copies of his *XVI Commandements patriotiques,* and of the Declaration of Rights of 1789. That same year, he sent out a thousand copies of the *XVI Commandements* to the Société populaire de Menton, to which he had already sent a Bastille stone—after the annexation of the earldom of Nice to France in the spring of 1793—and which then requested his patriotic poster. Fifty copies of the speech he delivered at the Festival of Freedom in Sceaux were sent to the departmental administration in Brussels.[113] In his feverish obsession, Palloy had all his speeches, his architectural sketches for patriotic monuments, and the descriptions of the patriotic festivals he produced printed, distributed locally, or— often together with a "patriotic relic" made from Bastille stones—sent to numerous institutions and political celebrities. "I am in the habit of having all the speeches printed that I give in public assemblies," he wrote to Collot d'Herbois, author of the *Almanach du Père Gérard,* which he saw as a model of a new patriotic popular literature.[114] Time constraints, and dwindling resources, forced him in 1794 to give up his intention of sending a copy of his *XVI Commandements* to all 44,000

municipalities in France, so that they could be read by—or read to—
every French citizen. How dearly this commitment cost him shows
in the accounts of printers' bills from the years 1791 to 1794, some of
which are still preserved. For the printing of one thousand copies of
a speech given before voluntary battalions and the citizens of Epernay alone, for instance, Palloy paid 744 livres in August 1792—a sum
that equals approximately two years' salary for a construction worker
at the time.[115]

Palloy's obsession with the written and printed word—integrated
though it was into nonwritten, publicly effective media aimed at immediate sensual impressions—is typical of its time. Like thousands
of other social climbers who came from the lower strata of society,
Palloy understood the transformation of the public sphere and the
explosive development of new literary and journalistic forms of expression (pamphlet literature, the political press, political songs, and
broadsheets) as a solicitation to take up the pen and participate in the
public discussion over the shaping of the new, revolutionary France.
But in contrast to most of the other "self-styled" authors of the Revolution, he did not give up writing during the Napoleonic empire and
the Restoration. Until the 1820s, he made public appearances, mostly
with political chansons in which he celebrated Napoleon's victorious
armies as the heirs of the glorious conquerors of the Bastille[116] and depicted Napoléon Bonaparte as the finisher of the Revolution. The fate
of Palloy, who in a way outlived himself and even after the rigorous
limitations of political and literary expression during the Napoleonic
era understood himself as a patriotic author in the tradition of 1789,
is almost tragic. He never again was able to tend to his construction
business, which had flourished before the Revolution, with any energy
or ambition. He lived as an "early retiree" on what was left of his fortune, which had declined during the years of the Revolution, and in
vain tried again and again to acquire a state pension as a Vainqueur de
la Bastille. Only three years before his death were he and thirty of his
former comrades granted this pension by King Louis-Philippe. Palloy
died in 1835, almost completely impoverished, at his house in Sceaux,
cruelly and unjustly mocked by the historians of the Revolution of the
time, among them Alexandre Dumas and Jules Michelet, as a puppet
of the Revolution.[117]

But Palloy's "seizure of the word" remains an excellent example of
the cultural creativity of the revolutionary era, which is often wrongly

ignored in literary and cultural history, or—because of the lack of "great" authors and "classic" works—consciously repressed.[118] In Palloy's biography, 14 July 1789 functioned as an electrifying, catalytic event. The fascination that emanated from the symbolically significant storming of the Bastille caused Palloy to undergo a kind of "conversion" to revolutionary politics, and prompted a feverish journalistic and literary activity whose forms of expression seemed strange and bizarre even to some of the patriot's contemporaries. In this very fact, however, lies the condition for its broad effect: as a semiliterate autodidact with close connections to the nonwritten culture of ordinary people, Palloy was better acquainted with the people's ideas than were the representatives in the National Assembly. Palloy immediately recognized how much the Bastille as a symbol corresponded with the people's need for a magical formation of political meaning that could be concretely experienced. He wanted to break down the barriers between popular and elite culture that he had experienced so rudely and immediately when he broke off his scholastic education, between the written and the oral traditions, between the rationalism of the enlightened elites and the religiousness of the ordinary people, which sometimes turned into the carnivalesque. In his self-understanding as a patriotic author and educator of the people, in the theatrical aesthetics of his Revolution festivals, in the rhetoric of his patriotic teachings, but most of all in the cult of Bastille stones that he initiated, Palloy's effort to abolish these boundaries shows.

The Patriotic Cult of Relics: The Staging of the Bastille Stones in Paris and in the French Provinces

In March 1791, Palloy gave a delegation of pupils from the Collège Henri IV, a military school, a set of dominoes made from the marble of the governor of the Bastille's window sills. The pupils in turn gave the dominoes, on which the portrait of King Louis XVI was engraved, to the crown prince, who was also a student at the school. When he proudly showed the set of dominoes featuring the royal likeness to his father, Louis XVI—according to a rumor circulating in the press at the time—is supposed to have said to his son and to his council of ministers:

> I am *infinitely* flattered by this portrait of myself engraved on one of the Bastille's stones: while reminding me of the *strength* of the

French people, it will also remind me that gratitude demands that I do anything in my power for their prosperity. . . . it will be a great lesson to all of us and teach us what we owe to the people.[119]

Similar to Palloy's Bastille relics were the plaster Bastilles that the Paris businessman Pommay sold for forty-eight livres each in July 1790 (figure 29)—a luxury at this price that no craftsman of the Faubourg Saint-Antoine but only a well-off Paris lawyer or gentleman could afford.[120] Pommay's plaster Bastilles—an idea that Palloy was to develop on a grand scale and with real Bastille stones in the fall of 1790—and the anecdote concerning the set of dominoes given to the king reveal an important symbolic dimension of the patriotic Bastille relics: They were seen as "Gages de l'union,"[121] as symbolic securities of the nation's unity achieved on 14 July 1789, of which even Louis XVI— at least until his failed attempt to leave the country on 20 June 1791— was a part. At the same time, these symbols in their concrete, tangible materiality were accorded almost mythical characteristics similar to those attributed to religious relics. Seeing and touching them was supposed to awaken the memory of the hour of the new freedom's birth ("L'Heure de la Liberté") and to give strength and confidence. No contemporary understood this semireligious dimension of the new patriotic cult of relics, which was rooted in the practices of popular religion and stood in the center of numerous unofficial, spontaneous memorial celebrations of 14 July 1789, better than Pierre-François Palloy, who since 15 July 1789 had driven the destruction of the former state prison, the demolition and reuse of its stones and iron materials, with unwavering obsession.

"Untiring like yourselves," Palloy told the representatives of the Constituent Assembly at the beginning of October 1791,

I have [since the start of the Revolution] felt that I am a human being and that I should enjoy only those rights which nature gives us. I have immortalized every epoch of the Revolution with trophies that I have dedicated to freedom. . . . I have scattered the remains of despotism, which died in the ruins of the Bastille, over the face of the earth, and especially throughout this empire; in addition I have given out Bastille stones engraved with the Declaration of Rights and the dawn of freedom.[122]

Figure 29. Pommay, Replica of the Bastille made of plaster,
370 by 150 mm, 1790 (Musée de Digne, inv. no. 653).

Palloy's dramatic words to the Constituent Assembly refer to his
large-scale attempt—which relied on his own initiative, and mostly
on his own money—to give the patriotic cult surrounding the Bastille
stones a *national* dimension. At the same time he was selling and giving
away a large number of stones and other objects from the Bastille
to public celebrities and political organizations, Palloy in 1790 began
systematically and symbolically to "cover" the entire national territory
with patriotically consecrated objects from the former state prison. In
October and November 1790, Palloy cast his first—large-meshed—
net by sending a hewn Bastille stone with a number of other patriotic
objects (such as the works of Dusaulx and Latude) to all eighty-three
départements. In 1793, he covered the French territory with a net of
closer weave by sending a stone slab made from the Bastille walls and
engraved with the Declaration of Rights to all 544 districts. Although
wider-meshed, the first net proved more effective. Palloy's initial success was due not only to a more impressive object—a Bastille stone
the size of an ashlar, cut as a miniature replica of the state prison—

but also to the carefully prepared public staging that the patriot conceived for the 1790 campaign.

In September and October of 1790, Palloy first sent a printed circular signed by himself to all eighty-three départements announcing the imminent arrival of the Bastille stones and asking each departmental council merely to reimburse Palloy's delegates for transport and postage. In addition, Palloy asked every département for an account of the celebrations that were held on the occasion of receiving the patriotic relics. In his circular, he stresses his own prominent role in the storming [123] and destruction of the Bastille as well as the symbolic significance of the patriotic cult initiated by himself:

> From one Bastille, I have fashioned eighty-three, which I have presented to each individual département so that its ruins, so to speak, are spread all over France to remind virtuous citizens of the cruelty of despots forever. From the stones of the dungeon itself, I have formed a new image of this grave of the living; and the ground slabs, on which so many innocent victims died, I will embellish with portraits of the King, the sacred pillar of our constitution. [124]

Palloy's enterprise, which he carried out with incredible tenacity and with great financial sacrifices, was only partly successful. But alongside départements that received his letters and patriotic gifts as a matter of course, almost indifferently—or even, in a few cases, turned them down—there were triumphal celebrations, meticulously produced public dedication ceremonies for which local political organizations (usually Jacobin clubs) or the chairmen of departmental councils were responsible. The way in which Palloy's Bastille relics were received and staged in the provinces—the analysis of their reception—yields a differentiated picture of the political landscape of France in the fall of 1790. Letters thanking Palloy, many of which are still preserved in archives, some of them in printed form, and above all the travel diaries of two of Palloy's delegates—who were called "Apostles of Freedom" and who delivered the objects, which were transported by post, in every departmental capital—can add a bit of detail to our "political seismology" of France (figure 30).

The two preserved diaries ("journaux de route") of the Apostles of Freedom Le Gros and Titon-Bergeras, who traveled to the provinces on Palloy's orders at the beginning of 1790, reflect the improvised and

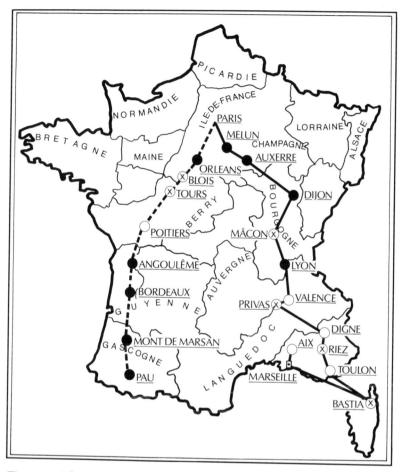

Figure 30. The journey of Palloy's "patriotic relics" through the provinces: the routes of Le Gros and Titon-Bergeras (1790–91).

Legend:

—   Le Gros's route

---   Titon-Bergeras's route

●   Enthusiastic welcome of the Bastille stones

⊕   Routine welcome of the Bastille stones

○   Refusal to receive the Bastille stones

□   No information

individual character of the entire enterprise. Both belonged to the association Apôtres de la Liberté—with sixty members altogether, all of them officially recognized conquerors of the Bastille and some of them construction workers in Palloy's employ—which Palloy founded in February 1790 and whose patriotic commission he defined in its statutes as follows:

> *Observation.* Since 14 July 1789, since the storming of the Bastille, the mission of the Apostles has been to support their teacher ["Instituteur"] P.-F. Palloy in all his patriotic actions, which he has continuously performed in order to propagate confidence in the Constitution and the maintenance of freedom.[125]

In their travel notes, Titon-Bergeras and Le Gros evoke the precariousness of their mission, and describe the almost picaresque adventures they experienced in carrying it out. In Digne, where the circular sent out by Palloy had not arrived, Le Gros was taken for an "adventurer" until he was able to convince suspicious departmental administrators of the contrary with the papers he carried. In a forest near Nîmes, he was assaulted and robbed by brigands, and his horse was shot to death by a bullet meant for him. His hands and one leg injured, Le Gros dragged himself to the nearby village of Pellissance, where he spent twelve days almost motionless in bed; and ever after—as he remarks in his diary again and again—he suffered from intense pain in his leg.[126] In Riez, the largest city of the département of Basses-Alpes, Le Gros in turn was mistaken for a representative of the National Assembly and received with the appropriate honors. Since he had now formed a firsthand impression of the local situation, the mayor asked him to write to Mirabeau or Barnave, who "kept the great machine [of state] in motion," in order to have not the neighboring village of Digne but the more populous and economically much more significant Riez declared capital of the new département.[127] Le Gros, a former actor, flattered by the significance he was suddenly accorded and delighted by the generous hospitality, did what was asked of him, let the citizens of Riez go on believing what they believed, and even let himself be escorted to the departmental capital with military honors by the soldiers of the citizens' militia.

Toward the end of his journey, Le Gros ran out of money, which Palloy had not given out very generously. In Aix-en-Provence, where the conservative local departmental council was not inclined to receive the Bastille relics sent by Palloy at all, much less pay for their transport,[128] Le Gros's financial resources were finally completely exhausted; he was unable to pay his accommodation. Without further ado, he signed on for a time with a local theater company—whose director had seen him play tragic roles onstage in Paris—and played in a production of Voltaire's tragedy *Zaïre*. Curiously, he acted the role of the unhappy Orosmane, whose "I hate the entire world, I despise myself" the desperate Le Gros related to his own situation in his diary.[129]

Le Gros's colleague Titon-Bergeras did not fare much differently. Palloy had assigned him the duty of transferring Bastille stones to the départements of western and southwestern France, from Orléans on the Loire to Pau in the Pyrenees by way of eighteen further stops, which included, among others, Blois, Tours, Poitiers, Bordeaux, and the Breton departmental capitals Quimper, Saint-Brieuc, and Rennes. In Poitiers, for example, Titon-Bergeras reports to Palloy, the administration first let him wait three days and then adamantly refused to officially dedicate the Bastille relics in a public celebration. Giving up, Titon-Bergeras writes that "the officials have decided that it is better not to cause any sensation with a ceremony, since they fear that the numerous priests of the city would use the opportunity to incite the ordinary people to a rebellion against the departmental council." [130] Like Le Gros, Titon-Bergeras was impoverished by the end of his journey and, moreover, became seriously ill. He found food and lodging with his brother, who lived in Pau, but during this time neglected his "patriotic mission" and his correspondence with Palloy, who in increasingly harsh words accused him of negligence, corruption, and a lack of patriotic enthusiasm—and finally excluded this Apostle of Freedom, fallen out of favor, from the association of the *Apôtres de la Liberté*.[131]

Titon-Bergeras and Le Gros—no diaries or letters of the other Apostles of Freedom who traveled through the provinces with Bastille stones at Palloy's command have been preserved[132]—thus met quite diverse responses to their patriotic mission (see figure 30). The majority of departmental councils welcomed the Apostles with rather restrained enthusiasm but did give the dedication ceremonies a certain official atmosphere, sent Palloy the requested account ("procès-verbal")[133] afterward, and conscientiously paid the costs of transportation. In other places, however, the Apostles met suspicion and open rejection—most of all in Aix-en-Provence and Poitiers, a city of

MODÈLE DE LA BASTILLE.

Quatre hommes portoient ainsi ce Modèle dans les marches ou processions civiques,

Figure 31. Brothers Le Sueur, Model of the Bastille, Gouache on cutout cardboard, glued onto paper painted in blue watercolors, 360 by 535 mm, ca. 1790 (Musée Carnavalet, Paris, RF 36574).

which Titon-Bergeras wrote in a letter to Palloy that "one should not speak at all, since most of those who live there are aristocrats, shysters ["robinocrates"], and parsons' pets ["calotins"], and [where], after all, there is not a single member of the National Guard."[134] The officials of the département of Vienne—probably under pressure from the local municipality, who because of imminent elections to the city council wanted to avoid any unrest—preferred to receive Palloy's Apostle of Freedom behind closed doors, to fulfill their patriotic duty by accepting the Bastille relics but—as it says in the record—"determined that these stones will provisionally remain in the conference hall."[135]

In Bordeaux and Lyon, in Auxerre and Digne, by contrast, and most of all in Orléans and Dijon, political leaders consciously celebrated the dedication of the Bastille relics and the reception of Palloy's delegates with grand, often even pompous ceremonies (figure 31). Here, the dedication of the objects from the Bastille took place in public, and political figures used the opportunity to rhetorically stage themselves. Afterward, accounts of these celebrations were printed alongside texts of the speeches given on the occasion, which were often handed out to citizens by the thousands free of charge and sometimes excerpted in the national press (in Gorsas's *Courrier* and Prud-homme's *Révolutions de Paris,* among others). In Lyon, for instance, departmental council decided to hold the dedication celebration not right after Le Gros's arrival but the following Sunday, "since it was important for the people to witness this ceremony."[136] After the solemn dedication of the Bastille relics in Bordeaux, the departmental authorities decided that the Bastille stone should be "carried in triumph through the streets" every 14 July and then set up with the flag also sent by Palloy on the altar of the fatherland, and that members of the National Guard should renew their oath in the process.[137]

In Orléans, it was most of all the local Société des Amis de la Constitution (Society of the friends of the constitution), from which the local Jacobin club was to emerge, that organized the public exhibition of the Bastille relics with patriotic fervor. The president of the political club was also the chairman of the département's council; Palloy's patriotic gift and the presence of the Apostle of Freedom Titon-Bergeras gave him a welcome opportunity to demonstrate the power of the two new political institutions that had come into being in 1789, and to anchor them in the new collective symbols of the Revolution. After he had participated in the ceremonies at the dedication of the Bastille relics in the morning, Titon-Bergeras spoke to more than six hundred members of the Société des Amis de la Constitution in the evening. Then the final speaker, the bookseller Jacob, took the stage. This friend of Titon-Bergeras's, a member of the political club, gave a "speech full of fire and energy" and praised Palloy's patriotic conviction. Through the Parisian patriot's delegate, Titon-Bergeras, Jacob conveyed the request of the Société des Amis de la Constitution that

Palloy send another Bastille stone for their conference hall—a request that met with the "unanimous approval" of the audience and that was supported by loud "cheers."[138]

In Dijon, the model of the Bastille gained so much political importance that we wish to investigate this example in more detail. Palloy's Apostle of Freedom, Le Gros, found a situation here in the fall of 1790 that was almost perfectly suited to his patriotic mission. Two opposing political factions had formed in the city since the beginning of the year: on the one hand the Société des Amis de la Constitution, a group with ties to the Paris Jacobin club that dominated the departmental council of the Côte d'Or, established in January 1790, and on the other hand the conservative Club des Amis de la Paix, which had emerged as the winner in municipal elections held in February 1790.[139] This club, also called the Club Tussat after its meeting place in the house of a carpenter, formed the largest group in the Burgundian metropolis, measured by the number of members, in the summer and fall of 1790. It recruited mainly among craftsmen and members of the middle classes (doctors, lawyers, businessmen), who were suffering the most economically from the beginning emigration of the aristocracy to foreign countries. With the abolition of the Burgundian court of justice (Parlement de Bourgogne) and the increasing emigration of the aristocracy, the city, which had a population of twenty-four thousand in 1789, had lost an important pillar of its economic activity. The service sector as well as the producers of luxury articles, but also tailors, carpenters, upholsterers and other skilled tradespeople, suffered from these losses.[140] The Club des Amis de la Paix, in which these economic "victims of the Revolution" had met, demanded that most of the changes of 1789 be revoked in 1790, that the power of the monarchy be strengthened, and that everything be done to bring about the return of the aristocratic emigrants. In February 1790, the lawyer Pierre Landes became the spokesman for these political demands and published a pamphlet entitled *Discours aux Welches* (Speech to the barbarians).[141] In this pamphlet, Landes, who had been a member of the Parlement de Bourgogne until its abolition, writes:

> Break the chains that have been put on our unfortunate ruler, and pour the balsam of your tears on all the wounds that you have inflicted on him. Demand of him the dissolution of a con-

vention [the Assemblée Nationale] that has hurled this kingdom into an abyss of need and misfortune. May he declare all decrees that this convention has passed invalid, and may this act of determination finally bring about the dawn of that happy day which you have been longing for so long.[142]

Even though he believed that such reforms as the abolition of exceptional royal justice (the lettres de cachet), the granting of extensive freedom of the press, the abolition of individual, humiliating feudal rights, and a thorough restructuring of the judicial system were necessary, Landes firmly stressed the disastrous economic consequences, from his point of view, of the constitutional Revolution of 1789. According to Landes, the abolition of feudal rights and the nationalization of church property had led to a general decline in prosperity that only the new rulers in Paris profited from and had simultaneously ruined the luxury trade and the class of craftsmen. By abolishing venal offices, the *Discours* claimed, the National Assembly had destroyed "half of the riches of the kingdom."[143]

This pamphlet caused quite a sensation in Dijon. Its author was arrested on 30 April 1790 but managed to escape from prison and fled to Switzerland, where he stayed until 1802. The arguments between the two quarreling political clubs became more and more heated. On 9 November, four days before the dedication of Palloy's Bastille relics, a bloody brawl between supporters of the two factions occurred in the Cabaret Androt after members of the Club Tussat had sung provocative songs.[144] Seven weeks later, on 29 December 1790, the political club, which as a self-help organization of businessmen in need was also known as the Club du Tire-Lire (piggy bank club), was banned at the instigation of the departmental council and meetings at the house of the carpenter Tussat forbidden. At the end of December 1790, the Jacobin club therefore dominated the political scene in Dijon. Three months later, it emerged as the clear victor from the new elections to the city parliament, after the spokesmen of the opposition had been intimidated or had left the country.

Two events in this local political "seizure of power" were decisive, had a "catalytic role": on the one hand the performance of Voltaire's drama *Brutus* on 6 December 1790 in the Dijon city theater—which members of the Club Tussat in vain tried to prevent and then to disturb with heckling and violence[145]—and on the other hand the public celebrations around the Bastille relics, which gave members of the "patriotic party" in Dijon an unexpected opportunity to show themselves.

On the morning of 13 November the three blue crates were opened with great pomp and their contents carried through the streets on biers, escorted by the National Guard. They were led by the top officials of the département of the Côte d'Or, Louis Bernard Guyton de Morveau and Claude-Bernard Navier, who were also the leaders of the local Jacobin club. After Le Gros had read an almost standardized text by Palloy, both officials took the opportunity to give long speeches. In a discourse that at first glance seemed ridden with clichés and that invoked the symbolic meaning of the destroyed Bastille as a monument of freedom, Dijon's citizens—who had come in great numbers—were unmistakably able to detect direct attacks on the local political enemy and competitor, the influential and large Club des Amis de la Paix. Who else could be meant by the "perverse" and "stick-in-the-mud" followers of the ancien régime, whom Navier, the president of the departmental council, harshly attacked in the central part of his speech? "May they finally give up their pernicious hopes, these perverse people," he cried out to the crowd,

> who spread the fire of civil strife among us! May their agents return to the filth and finally stop confusing our fellow citizens! We know that their conspiracy aims at restoring the ancien régime. But here, we have before us [and with these words, Navier pointed at the Bastille stone laid out before him] the picure of all evils of the ancien régime; and this will be enough to help those men and women triumph who have already tasted the fruits of freedom.[146]

The actual seizure of power by the patriotic party in Dijon was thus prepared by its symbolic seizure of power. No symbol was more suitable than the Bastille to illustrate and justify the necessity of a radical break with the past—and to criminalize the opponents of the Revolution, as Navier did extensively by using words such as "perverse," "despotic," "tyrannical," and "conspiracy" to characterize the members of the opposition and their "subversive" activities. To give the patriotic ceremony even more resonance, Navier and Guyton de Morveau had twelve hundred accounts of the reception of the Bastille relics printed and sent to all districts of the former province of Burgundy, and to numerous politically influential persons, free of charge.

A comprehensive article on the celebration showing the speeches of Navier and Guyton de Morveau in their best light was published ten days later in the *Journal Patriotique du Département de la Côte d'Or.*[147] On 23 November 1790 a delegation from the Société des Amis de la Constitution petitioned the departmental council to have all symbols of the ancien régime ("monuments de l'ancien régime") replaced by "patriotic monuments." The municipal authorities, some of whom were members of the Jacobin club themselves, agreed.[148] The Bastille relics took their official place, in the conference hall of the departmental council and at public ceremonies, but most of all in the national festival of 14 July, during which in Dijon the Bastille-stone display formed the symbolic center of the action.[149]

Palloy himself considered the ceremony in Dijon to be the greatest success of his patriotic campaign.[150] Enthusiastically, he thanked the administration of the département of the Côte d'Or and sent out copies of their report himself. He also informed Gorsas's *Courrier* and Prudhomme's *Révolutions de Paris,* which were among the papers with the highest circulation, of the eagerness of the Burgundian patriots — which suddenly gave the local arguments in faraway Dijon national importance.

Three years later, in the summer of 1793, once again without an official commission, Palloy at his own initiative and at his own expense decided to begin a second, large-scale campaign. He sent slabs inscribed with the Declaration of the Rights of Man made from Bastille stones to all 544 districts of the French republic. According to Palloy's wishes, they were to replace the busts of the deposed King Louis XVI—which all district administrations displayed up until 1792 —Louis XVI the "traitor," as Palloy called him in the letter accompanying the slabs.[151] After the proclamation of the republic and the declaration of war, which had been made in April 1792, Palloy also let his sixty Apostles of Freedom, who were entrusted with the distribution of the patriotic gifts, swear a new oath, which was called the "serment républicain" (republican oath):

As Republicans, we promise that we will exterminate all tyrants, all despots allied against us. . . . We will always be the arm of the weak and the opponent of the strong. . . . We will defend the huts of the needy and overthrow everything that might disturb freedom as long as this is in our power: no Bastille will remain on the earth, no tyrant on his throne, no people in their chains, so that the nations find their brother in us, and all our fellow citizens become imperturbable helpers of the One and indivisible French republic. We swear this on the ruins of the Bastille; we swear it on the immortal rights of human beings and citizens.[152]

More emphatically than Palloy's, Titon-Bergeras's, and Le Gros's speeches from this time, and more strongly than its 1790 counterpart, the 1793 oath of the Apostles of Freedom underlines the stronger militaristic and expansionist character of the patriotic mission of Palloy and his Apostles. The new borders of the Republic—which had been considerably enlarged in 1792 by the annexation of Savoy, the earldom of Nice, the territories to the west of the Rhine, and pieces of land in Alsace and in Walloon territory—got their patriotic legitimation in the symbolism of 14 July. The Bastille relics served to legitimize and symbolically aggrandize the act of military conquest as an act of liberation from despotism. In the spring of 1793, Palloy sent the Apostle of Freedom Woillez on his way with the very same objects that the then eighty-three départements had received in 1790: to Chambéry in the new département of Mont-Blanc, to Mons in present-day Belgium (département of Jemappes), to Nice, the capital of the département of Alpes-Maritimes, to Mainz in the département of Mont-Tonnerre (Donnersberg), and finally in 1795 also to Brussels in the newly added département of Dyle.[153] When Citizen Woillez came to Nice, for instance, in May 1793, he was met by officials of the département with an open mind for his patriotic mission, as he had been earlier in Chambéry. In a public ceremony on 28 May, Woillez and the members of the departmental council joined in opening the three huge crates containing the objects from the Bastille, and Woillez explained their symbolic significance. He exclaimed to the citizens of Nice,

> Here you see a part of the hellhole where terror, misfortune, and death ruled, of the walls that for so long knew the sobs of the aristocracy's miserable victims, were covered with their tears, and perhaps even soaked with their blood. . . . But now freedom is standing upright, and shortly her victory will be complete. . . . You, too, were slaves of tyranny, and now you have become friends of freedom. . . . The people have suffered too long under the shameless oppressors who bound them in chains again and

again, and now they have recognized their rights, broken the iron chains that scarred them all over, to welcome those who are taking revenge for so many centuries of slavery and suffering.[154]

Woillez also speaks of the "liberators," meaning the troops of the French republic that had invaded the earldom of Nice in October 1792 and thereby created the conditions under which the new département of Alpes-Maritimes was established in February 1793. On 29 May 1793, the Bastille objects presented by Woillez were carried through the streets of that city with great pomp. The festivities concluded with the storming of a Bastille made of papier-mâché, in which the mayor of Nice and the members of the city council took on the roles of the conquerors. Crying out, "Vive la Nation, vive la République," the political figures of Nice, who had been installed by France, stormed the fortress defended by men disguised as aristocrats. To the cheers of the audience, they overpowered the garrison and then carried the Bastille stone received from Palloy out in the open. This stone was inscribed as follows:

Bastille. On these stones, the French strengthened their courage and swore to maintain the law and the Republic. Live free or die; presented to the city of Nice by Palloy the patriot, 1 March 1793, in the Second Year of the French republic.[155]

The patriotic festivities of 28 and 29 May in Nice were part of the symbolic integration of the newly annexed territories into the French nation. Henri Baptiste Grégoire and Grégoire Marie Jagot, since March the new commissaries of the Republic in the département of Alpes-Maritimes, had emphatically urged everyone to attend these festivities in order to strengthen the "communal spirit and public opinion"[156] of the new citizens of the Republic. The institutional backbone of this public-relations work—in which political officials in the département and city administration also took part—was the local people's society (Société populaire de la Ville de Nice), to which Woillez had already presented a modest gift from Palloy. This was a slab cut from Bastille stones inscribed with Palloy's XVI Patriotic Commandments. After all members of the society had sung the *Marseillaise* "with passion and enthusiasm," as it says in the account,[157] the president of the society accepted the gift with the following words of thanks:

The society receives the present of your friend Palloy with great satisfaction. This present will constantly remind us of the terrors that were the order of the day in the century of tyranny, and it will sharpen our daggers in order to destroy it.[158]

With the increasing emphasis on military messianism, Palloy's patriotic cult of relics underwent a development that can also be recognized in the official speeches on 14 July. The metaphoric "conquest of freedom" that Palloy and his Apostles had invoked in their patriotic missionary journeys in the fall and winter of 1790 and 1791 became increasingly literal. In November 1790, the members of the Dijon Jacobin club and their confederates in the departmental council already understood the metaphor as an appeal to storm and destroy the counterrevolutionary "citadel" of the "aristocratic" Club Tussat. Two and a half years later, the new political officials in Nice did more than take on the role of the conquerors of the Bastille of 1789, whose courage and determination they admired with rhetorical pathos. As "liberators" of the citizens of the earldom of Nice, they also saw themselves—and the soldiers of the French army—as immediate successors of those combative, self-confident, and missionary Citoyens-Soldats of 1789, the "citizens become soldiers"[159] that the storming of the Bastille had produced.

Palloy's private patriotic and missionary enterprise made a major contribution to popularizing the Bastille as a symbol, and with it the role model of the Citoyen-Soldat, nationwide, and after 1792 beyond the borders of France as well.[160] It connected the theatrical with the religious, abstract political terms (such as "freedom" and "despotism") with the sensually comprehensible, by means of authentic objects that were impressive just to look at: the Bastille stones, which had been soaked—as Palloy's Apostles of Freedom affirmed again and again—with blood and tears, as well as iron chains and handcuffs that had inflicted "terrible wounds" on the bodies of the prisoners. Palloy's patriotic missionary campaign may sometimes seem like political grand-guignol theater, but in its semireligious and vociferous pathos it was undoubtedly closer to the people than the formal, official national festivals on 14 July that the representatives of the National Convention organized. In the end, Palloy's festivals were equally governed by his patriotic cult of relics and by the century-old popular dream of an "upside-down world," a world in which water could be changed into wine, the poor into the rich,[161] and the instruments of oppression into symbols of freedom.

For this reason, it was not just by chance that Palloy held his Fête champêtre et nationale (Rural and national festival) in memory of the storming of the Bastille on 14 July 1790 on the ruins of the Bastille. According to Palloy's ideas, there was to be vivacious dancing on the rubble of the formerly notorious state prison. The stones from the former dungeons were to be transformed into a dance floor framed by garlands and Chinese lamps. Instead of oppressive silence, vigorous and loud merriment was to rule; the place of suffering was to become a site of patriotic brotherliness. This concrete vision of the upside-down world helped the plebeian Palloy become incredibly popular and politically effective in the years 1790 to 1793.

The Symbolic Foundation of National Identity: Festivals, Speeches, and Monuments Commemorating 14 July 1789

As we have seen, 14 July 1789—which many contemporaries spon- taneously perceived as an "incredible" and "memorable" event—was soon connected with the idea of its celebration. Even at the begin- ning of the Revolution, no event in modern history seemed as suited, in the minds of both politicians and ordinary people, to provide the date for a new national holiday as the anniversary of the storming of the Bastille. Traces of this collective idea can be found in a large num- ber of contemporary writings: in the speeches and festival programs written by Palloy as well as in pamphlet literature, in numerous de- signs for monuments and festivals, in hymns and songs, and finally in official statements by *state* institutions.

One of the most popular pamphlets concerning the storming of the Bastille, the biography of the fictional Bastille prisoner Count de Lorges, ends—in a manner typical of its genre—with an emotional appeal by the author asking French citizens to make 14 July a day of commemoration forever. That appeal is voiced by the Count de Lorges:

Always remember this noteworthy day, which is unforgettable in the annals of France; the clock struck twelve, and suddenly a hollow sound could be heard that echoed into the depths of my dungeon. . . . The noise stopped, and soon shouts of triumph and joy reached my ears. The soldiers of freedom came in large numbers, the doors of my dungeon gave way and burst under the mighty blows of the besiegers. . . . I want to celebrate forever, yes, I desire that the fourteenth of July be a day of festivity in eternity, and that the rest of my fortune be used every year to help five innocently incarcerated captives regain their freedom.[162]

Once again, the figure of the Count de Lorges, who became the Bastille's prototypical prisoner, provided an expression and reflection of collective wishes and expectations. At the same time this pamphlet was published, Paris saw the first celebration commemorating the storming of the Bastille—exactly two months after the event itself. Witnesses such as the bookseller Hardy report that on 14 September around noon, a large crowd, including six or seven hundred women clad all in white, escorted by a brigade of the National Guard, went from Faubourg Saint-Antoine to the church of Sainte-Geneviève, the later national Panthéon. After a delegation of six workers had given the priest of the church consecrated bread and a crown honoring Saint Genevieve in the following solemn ceremony, the procession—all in all more than three thousand people—started moving again. To the sound of drumrolls and military music, they went to city hall and from there began to make their way back home to Faubourg Saint-Antoine via the Place de la Bastille. The curious march—unanimously called a "procession" by contemporaries because of its semireligious character[163]—recalled the storming of the Bastille not just by its route but also by numerous symbolic objects. A delegation of the citizens' militia carried a flag bearing a picture of the Bastille in their midst; other groups bore "enemy" flags captured during the assault on the Bastille, some of which had been torn and were riddled with bullets. But the most striking exhibition for all witnesses was a miniature replica of the former state prison made from cardboard and carried by citizens of Faubourg Saint-Antoine who had distinguished themselves in the siege of the Bastille.[164] The miniature replica of the former state prison also recalled the drama of the attack on the Bastille itself: miniature soldiers could be seen, as well as flames, cannons, the dead and dying, all made from papier-mâché—"nothing was forgotten," the newspaper *Courrier de Versailles* wrote concerning the matter in its extensive report, "not even the traitor de Launay's little white flag."[165]

The patriotic procession of the citizens of Faubourg Saint-Antoine, which ended in a wild party,[166] was part of a series of spontaneous, nonofficial commemorations of the storming of the Bastille that took place at the initiative of individual citizens in the summer and fall of 1789 and throughout 1790. As early as 5 August 1789, Abbé Fauchet, who had participated in the assault on the Bastille himself and who was one of the official spokesmen of the conquerors of the Bastille, had held a memorial mass for the fallen Vainqueurs de la Bastille in the Paris church of Saint-Jacques. In a passionate speech combining the fervor of a religious sermon with the pathos of political rhetoric, Fauchet also recalled the epoch-making importance of 14 July 1789. "Brutus himself would not have spoken with more energy from the pulpit," the *Courrier de Versailles* reported, comparing Fauchet's eloquence to the legendary rhetoric of Caesar's assassin Brutus, and then extensively quoted from Fauchet's speech. "Our fatherland breathes a sigh of relief," Fauchet told his audience,

> from the Pyrenees to the Schelde, from the Alps to the Ocean, France is free. . . . We thought we would need more time for this great conquest [of the Bastille]. Time! If that had been necessary, we would have perished mercilessly; as the enemies of the state were determined to slaughter our fatherland. O Providence, Providence! We adore you in our joy! You [the conquerors of the Bastille] fought for us: in a single minute, you avenged the crimes of twenty reigns; and you have prevented an immense crime which was being prepared at that very moment and which would have exceeded all earlier crimes by far.[167]

Claude Fauchet, an accredited "court preacher" (Prédicateur du Roi) by profession, had been temporarily forbidden to preach as early as 1776 by the archbishop of Paris because of his "scandalous appearance."[168] According to the commentary of the *Courrier de Versailles,* he "goes slightly beyond the normal limits of eloquence" in his speech; but, as the journalist apologetically explained, "does the subject not seem to allow this?"[169] Fauchet's speech, announced as a "funeral oration," did take place in a church and at first glance seemed to comply with the external form of a requiem mass, but it was given at the priest's own private initiative and in its structure and political spirit went beyond the usual scope. Fauchet was devoting the rhetorical genre of the funeral oration, which was traditionally reserved for high-ranking persons such as members of the royal family, great generals, and high church dignitaries, to the fallen Vainqueurs de la Bastille, almost all of whom came from the craftsmen's level of society. He praised their "heroic deeds," even though they were seen in court circles and by conservative petit bourgeois citizens such as the bookseller Hardy as "despicable" and as "resistance to state authority" that should be punished by the maximum penalty. Fauchet thus combined a funeral speech with an appreciation of the new "heroes of the fatherland" that celebrated the event he interpreted as the fulfillment of Biblical promise. And finally, in the conspiracy theory he evoked one of the most radical explanations of the attack on the Bastille itself, an explanation that was also supposed to justify such violent acts as the massacre of governor de Launay and six of his officers and soldiers. According to Fauchet, the heroes of 14 July had not only extirpated a symbol of despotism by attacking the Bastille and liberating the incarcerated prisoners but also prevented an "immense crime." Fauchet did not go into any further detail, but he consciously reminded his audience of the rumors that had caused many citizens of Paris to panic in the days before 14 July, because they were afraid of being secretly murdered during the night by the troops of the Count d'Artois.

The first two major celebrations commemorating the events of 14 July 1789, which took place in Paris on 3 August and on 14 September 1789, took forms that reappear in a large number of later observances. Since they were not prescribed "from above," from state institutions, they seemed to be based on a collective desire to publicly celebrate the event of the taking of the Bastille. Even though a militant group such as the Vainqueurs de la Bastille played a major role at least in the first celebrations in Paris, the massive participation of the lower classes, and finally the large number of spontaneous festivities in the provinces,[170] proves their anchoring in a kind of collective mentality. A mixture of religious ceremony and political rhetoric typical of its time characterized these first, "spontaneous" celebrations of the storming of the Bastille.

In the spirit of Voltaire, contemporary journalists, usually members of the enlightened elites, often dismissed popular religious practices as "superstition" with a single stroke of the pen. They observed with some disconcertment, for instance, that Fauchet offered his radical condemnation of the despotism of the ancien régime during a solemn mass accompanied by a communal singing of the Te Deum or that the triumphal march of the citizens of Faubourg Saint-Antoine on 14 September 1789 on closer examination seemed rather similar to a religious procession in which the miniature replica of the Bastille displayed on a bier and the trophies from the assault on the Bastille (flags and so forth) took the place of relics. The dedication of votive images depicting the successful taking of the Bastille also arose immediately from deeply rooted popular religious practices. The newspaper *Chronique de Paris,* for example, in April 1790 spoke of a votive picture in the church of Saint-Geneviève whose "subject is as pious as it is patriotic."[171] The (unfortunately no longer existing) picture showed the Bastille hit by a bolt of lightning from heaven ("foudre du ciel"), and next to it an injured man lying on the ground being given first aid by a woman. On the front side of the picture, the injured man who had donated the votive picture (which in its external form was quite classic) could be seen again, now recovered: he is portrayed as a former soldier kneeling on the ground, fervently thanking the heavens for having rewarded his courage, having brought the Bastille down, and having saved his life.

"On 4 August [1789] the National Assembly proposed the abolition of the feudal system, so it is in favor of a memorial day," the newspaper *Bouche de Fer* wrote on 1 July 1791.

> But the real [basis for a] national festival, that of the people, the festival of all peoples, is the overthrow of the Bastille, on 14 July, which shook up the nations, an event that caused all thrones to totter.[172]

The awareness expressed here that as the anniversary of the storming of the Bastille, it was *14 July* that had to become the *national* day of celebration, the French nation's festival of unity and freedom, can be observed not only in the months immediately following the storming of the Bastille. As early as the end of 1789, preliminary—and sometimes very detailed—designs for the actual establishment of a national festival began to surface. Like Palloy's patriotic cult of relics and the first, spontaneous celebrations of the attack on the Bastille, they intended to strengthen national unity through a communal festival commemorating the fundamental events of 14 July 1789 and thus to weld together, to "electrify" the disparate parts of the body of the nation in an almost magical fashion.[173] On 9 December 1789, Clément Gonchon, a textile worker from Faubourg Saint-Antoine, presented to the Paris city administration and to the public his *Projet d'une fête nationale pour être exécuté le 14 juillet 1790, Anniversaire de la Prise de la Bastille* (Design for a national festival on 14 July 1790, the anniversary of the storming of the Bastille), which he expressly dedicated to "the patriotic citizens of France."[174] Gonchon, with Palloy one of the prominent activists and spokesmen of the Paris sansculotte movement,[175] suggested that a huge balloon (a so-called Montgolfière) decorated with allegorical symbols (among others, an allegory of freedom and a depiction of the altar of the fatherland) should form the center of the future national festival. According to Gonchon's ideas, this balloon was to be tied to a platform, all four sides of which were adorned with monumental paintings recounting the story of the Bastille's fall in its four major stages: the capturing of arms at the Hôtel des Invalides; the siege and storming of the Bastille "by the citizens and the National Guard";[176] then an allegorical picture of France asking the king to call back Necker, finding Minerva's assistance in taking the king into custody, driving back Discord, and putting her and the troops to flight; and finally, as the fourth picture, the triumphal entry of the king into the capital on 17 July, where he is welcomed by armed citizens and shows his love and joy to the people. The release of the Montgolfière, military parades, the singing of patriotic songs, as well as a dramatic representation of the storming and destruction of the Bastille—on the Seine shore of the Champ de Mars, the site of the entire ceremony—were to be the heart of the festivities themselves.

Only some months after Gonchon, a collective of authors who remain anonymous and called themselves the Société des Patriotes suggested a completely different project in a six-page pamphlet entitled *Enterrement du despotisme, ou funérailles de l'aristocratie* (The interment of despotism, or the funeral procession of the aristocracy). The title alone reveals that these patriots' ideas of a "national festival" were much more political and radical than those of Gonchon, whose allegorical design celebrated the Revolution not only as the result of the Enlightenment and its progress in knowledge and learning—with the symbol of the Montgolfière—but also as a fulfillment of the new unity between monarchy and nation. In contrast, the *Enterrement du despotisme* suggested celebrating 14 July as a triumph of the people over its oppressors—the privileged classes—which, however, still had to be completed. The authors of the pamphlet proposed erecting a twenty-meter-high gravestone on the ruins of the Bastille supported by "four crushed lions," embodying "despotism thrown to the ground," embraced by "snakes, adders, toads, vipers, and rats," symbolic depictions of "la vermine ministérielle" (vermin ministers). Four pots of incense almost burned out at the four corners of the monument were supposed to symbolize the clergy, whose "arrogance and deceptions" had now "gone up in flames." On the sides of the monument, the Paris patriots wanted to set up four "colossal statues" representing the clergy, the aristocracy, justice, and finance crying over the death of despotism. In the course of the festivities, the entire funeral monument with its allegorical decorations was to be set on fire by an armed citizens' militia and turned into a huge pyre into which the surrounding crowd was to throw all symbols of despotism—papers, court files ("liasses de procureur"), and other objects. A funeral march of "aristocrats" around the pyre on the one hand—consisting of "old, overly made-up countesses and marquises"—and a celebration of patriots on the other hand, in which myrtle, oranges, and cherries were to be carried as "signs of luxury" and olive branches as signs of universal peace, would form the conclusion of the festival. The authors explicitly stressed that "shepherds, shepherdesses, sailors, pilgrims, freed slaves, and Indians" were supposed to present songs "appropriate to the conclusion" during the final ceremony[177]—introducing a utopian-Rousseauesque, conciliatory note into the final act of this political festival design. Otherwise, it seemed to come straight from the world of images found in satiric pamphlets and printings of the time, and significantly did not give the king any role at all.

The actual celebrations on the first anniversary of the storming of the Bastille were just as different from national Bastille celebrations as these preliminary designs. The Paris city administration hosted wrestling matches on the Seine and between the Pont-Neuf and the Pont-Royal (on the later Place de la Concorde) won by athletes wearing red, white, and blue who were celebrated with military marches as well as fireworks.[178] Palloy organized his own festival on the ruins of the Bastille from 16 to 18 July 1790. It was built around common singing, wild dancing, and drinking, in order—as Palloy wrote—to "cleanse by our dances" this dark site of "despotic and arbitrary rule."[179] The official festival, sponsored by the National Assembly—called the "Fête de

Figure 32. Allegory of the oath of brotherhood sworn on 14 July 1790 on the altar of the fatherland on the Paris Champ de Mars. Colored etching, 230 by 300 mm, published by Driancourt, Paris, 1790 (Bibliothèque Nationale, Estampes, Coll. Hennin, G 162112).

la Fédération" (Festival of the Federation) because delegations of the individual National Guards from all over France participated in it—took place on the Champs-Elysées and on the Champ de Mars and was closest to the ideas expressed by Gonchon in December 1789. Military parades from the Champs-Elysées to the Champ de Mars, where a triumphal arch had been erected; the—failed—ascent of a balloon; speeches by representatives of the new political leadership, led by La Fayette, the leader of the National Guard; fireworks; and finally the singing of political songs—above all *Ça ira,* which was composed in the spring of 1790 and became the first national hymn of the Revolution—all of these combined in the Festival of the Federation to form a kind of *Gesamtkunstwerk,* though one in which geometrical and military patterns clearly dominated (figure 32).

Looking at the Quatorze Juillet celebrations in *all* of France in 1790, the juxtaposition of traditional, often religious forms and new, revolutionary contents is striking. On 13 July the members of the Paris electoral college ("electeurs") held a mass in memory of the anniversary of the storming of the Bastille at Notre-Dame Cathedral during which the Te Deum, traditionally part of royal victory celebrations, was sung. In the same ceremony, a short drama by Marc-Antoine Désaugiers consisting completely of quotations from the Bible was performed; it represented the storming of the Bastille and compared the walls of the fallen state prison to those of Old Testament Jericho.[180] Similar festivities were to be seen in 1790 and even in 1791 in the provinces. In Douai, for instance, citizens celebrated the anniversary of the taking of the Bastille with a procession in which the city's coat of arms was carried through the streets next to a banner bearing lilies and the Latin inscription "Aeterno foedere juncti et vis unita fortior" (Joined in everlasting union and stronger as a united power), which referred to the federal idea.[181] In Quimperlé in Brittany, the local city administration erected an altar to the fatherland on the marketplace, had the members of all social classes swear an oath based on the principles of 1789, and let a delegation of the National Guard march past—but also asked the monk Dom Daveau to hold a service of thanksgiving and to conclude the ceremony with a Te Deum.[182] Similar scenes finally also took place in Montauban in southwestern France, where the service of celebration was dedicated not only to the memory of the fallen conquerors of the Bastille but to the spiritual welfare of the patriots who had fallen in the rebellions and riots of the summer of 1789 "fighting for the defense of the fatherland."[183]

Four years later, an aesthetics had asserted itself in the national celebrations of 14 July throughout France that had to a large extent eliminated the traditional religious elements, replacing them with a new patriotic and political dramaturgy. On 14 July 1794 in Grenoble, for example, a "Char de la Révolution"—a kind of patriotic chariot in which a number of armed patriots were sitting—was drawn through the streets by eight white horses. The final stop of this procession was the Temple of the Supreme Being, from which a voice invited the patriots to storm the replica of the Bastille that had been built from wood and canvas next to the temple. When the storm bells rang and a drumroll opened the imminent all-out assault, the patriots jumped from their revolutionary chariot and, according to a contemporary account, "stormed toward the bastion, cheered on by their wives and followed by their children and parents, took it at once, hoisted the tricolor on the towers of the fortress, and seized its commander."

The crowd then destroyed the rest of the artificial Bastille and erected a pyramid in its place. Inscriptions on this pyramid enthusiastically celebrated the victories of Fleurus and Ostende, milestones of the military expansion of the French republic to the north and east, which were thus represented as continuous with the first great "victory of the people," 14 July 1789. The celebration ended with fireworks as well as a drinking orgy and a "Bal populaire" that lasted until midnight. According to the Grenoble newspaper *Courrier Patriotique,* all patriots drank from the same cup on this occasion and "filled it with wine, which poured out of the pyramid, again and again, and while doing so swore an oath on the constitution."[184]

Six years later, at the beginning of Napoléon Bonaparte's Consulate, the syncretistic mixture of popular festival and political drama, of political activism at home and pressure for expansion abroad that characterized Quatorze Juillet celebrations from 1792 to 1798, had once again given way to the martial aesthetic that had been demonstrated for the first time in the Festival of the Federation on 14 July 1790. The celebration of the national holiday in the village of Forcalquier in southern France on 14 July 1800, for instance, turned into a demonstration above all of the Grande Nation's strength in foreign policy and a glorification of its First Consul, the general Napoléon Bonaparte. After military parades that were accompanied by drumrolls, the firing of cannons, patriotic hymns, and military music, the citizens of Forcalquier according to contemporary accounts congregated in the local conference hall in order to listen "in reverent silence" to the celebratory speeches of the prefect and the commanders of the court and the local regiment. The three speeches explicitly situated Napoléon's victories in the succession of the first great victory of the Revolution, the storming of the Bastille. In Napoléon's soldiers they emotionally celebrated the same Citoyens-Soldats of 1789 who without any military experience had stormed a fortress considered impregnable. Most of all, however, they stressed the courage and the military successes of the First Consul, whose return from the "Arab desert" (meaning Napoléon's Egyptian campaign of 1799) was tantamount to a "miracle": "The wonderful opportunity," one commentator writes, "to heap praise on this extraordinary military leader was taken enthusiastically."[185]

The course of the celebrations on 14 July 1800 in Forcalquier is symptomatic in several respects. The national holiday commemorating the fall of the Bastille had directed its symbolism mainly against the *domestic* enemy during the first years of the Revolution and even during parts of the Directoire at the same time strengthening the freedom and unity of the patriotic part of the nation. Now, during the era of consuls, holiday symbolism was directed exclusively against the *foreign* enemy—an expression of the determined will "to stop the Revolution" (arrêter la Révolution), as Napoléon Bonaparte and his brother Lucien programmatically stated in 1799. The majority of republicans in 1800 no longer understood commemorations of the storming of the Bastille as an impetus to military activism, seeing them rather as an opportunity to celebrate the Grande Nation and its military victories. At the end of the ceremonies in Forcalquier, toasts were proposed to the "strengthening of the Republic, concord, unity, and the forgetting of the past, the incomparable Bonaparte, and the respectable prefect of the département" [186] —symbolic actions that were almost diametrically opposed to the virulently activist aesthetics of class struggle delineated in the pamphlet entitled *Enterrement du despotisme* quoted above as well as to the plebeian and militaristic 14 July 1794 of the Grenoble patriots.

This evolution from a militant Quatorze Juillet directed against domestic opponents to a militaristic national holiday focusing on the external enemy and demonstrating the nation's strength in war during the late Directoire and the Napoleonic Consulate becomes more clearly and precisely discernible in the speeches commemorating 14 July already mentioned in passing. A detailed analysis of 28 representative speeches from the years 1798–1802 shows the most important developmental tendencies (table 6). [187] The most striking—and at first glance most banal—conclusion that can be drawn is that even as early as 1790, and increasingly in the following years, 14 July is not *narrated* but *evoked* as an event of global interest in the speeches. The account of a series of impressive, partly shattering, and shocking individual episodes—from the alleged "aristocratic conspiracy" to dramatic battle scenes to the cruel massacre of de Launay—gives way to a global impression of the storming of the Bastille, to which hardly more than one or two sentences are devoted in the speeches of 1795–1802. The event, it is argued, is already too well known—the French are familiar with all the details—to merit retelling again and again. "It is useless," Jean-Antoine Marbot, president of the Council of Ancients ("Conseil des Anciens"), for example, announced to the nation's representatives on

Table 6. Content Analysis of Selected Memorial Speeches on 14 July, 1789–1802

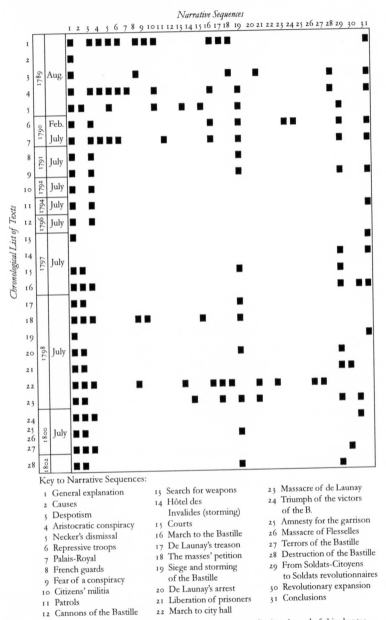

Key to Narrative Sequences:

1 General explanation	13 Search for weapons	23 Massacre of de Launay
2 Causes	14 Hôtel des	24 Triumph of the victors
3 Despotism	Invalides (storming)	of the B.
4 Aristocratic conspiracy	15 Courts	25 Amnesty for the garrison
5 Necker's dismissal	16 March to the Bastille	26 Massacre of Flesselles
6 Repressive troops	17 De Launay's treason	27 Terrors of the Bastille
7 Palais-Royal	18 The masses' petition	28 Destruction of the Bastille
8 French guards	19 Siege and storming	29 From Soldats-Citoyens
9 Fear of a conspiracy	of the Bastille	to Soldats revolutionnaires
10 Citizens' militia	20 De Launay's arrest	30 Revolutionary expansion
11 Patrols	21 Liberation of prisoners	31 Conclusions
12 Cannons of the Bastille	22 March to city hall	

Note: Sources of the speeches are listed by number in appendix A at the end of this chapter.

the occasion of the celebration of 14 July in 1798, "to recall the events of this memorable day! They are present in the hearts of all; they are inscribed on the remains of the throne and on the ruins of the Bastille, on which the sun of 14 July is now shining for the tenth time" (A22).

On closer examination, the "global view" of the storming of the Bastille that is already asserting itself in 1793 and 1794 seems to result less from an almost natural process of "sparing" details and more from a process of repressing a memory embedded in the history of a society and its mentality. While the military side of 14 July—the cannons' thunder, the siege, the assault, the spontaneously forming citizens' army—takes up more and more room in speeches on 14 July, other elements are consciously or unconsciously pushed into the background and repressed: the fear of a conspiracy, the scene of massacre, the descriptions of violence, but also the triumph of the conquerors of the Bastille and the portrayal of individual Vainqueurs such as Hulin and Arné as celebrated heroes (see the respective sequences in table 6).

But most of all, it is the domestic opponent that is repressed by the open, brutal violence legitimized by the Revolution. In his first great memorial speech on the storming of the Bastille on 5 August 1789 (figure 33), Abbé Fauchet polemically called this enemy "l'Aristocratie," meaning the court camarilla, the Paris police and its accomplices, and a large number of the king's ministers (A1). The word "Aristocratie" does not appear in any of the speeches we analyze that were presented after 1798, nor do the terms "tyrannie" or "despotisme," which had become slogans too closely associated with domestic arguments. "The citizens, who were almost devoured by it, raised their heads beneath the shadow of death and destroyed the aristocracy in one fell swoop," Fauchet had announced to his audience two weeks after the fall of the Bastille—and a day after the epoch-making session of the National Assembly at which all feudal rights were abolished—thus identifying "l'Aristocratie" as the major target of the storming of the Bastille (A1:2).

Another author, who remained anonymous, stressed the domestic and social dimension of 14 July just as radically as Fauchet in a second speech given in 1789. This speech, entitled *La Semaine mémorable*, was delivered on the occasion of a memorial ceremony—also dominated by religious forms—of the Société d'Apollon, an organization of artists, sculptors, and writers. With this ceremony, the members of the society wanted to publicly declare their support for the values of the

Figure 33. Memorial service and funeral oration of Abbé Claude Fauchet for the victims of the storming of the Bastille on 5 August 1789. Anonymous etching, diameter 90 mm, 1789 (Bibliothèque Nationale, Estampes, Qb1, M 99074).

Revolution. "Finally, that place [the Bastille]," the orator told those in attendance, "which until the day before yesterday was the bloody theater of revenge, now has suddenly become a temple of concord shining with a thousand rays of light in the middle of the night. And everything that I have related to you, like the creation of the world, was the labor of six days" (A5:13).

This speech concluded with a utopian vision that seems characteristic of the symbolic importance of 14 July in the early years of the Revolution. The vision of an egalitarian and free society is combined here with the dream of riches and luxury for all, and the idea of a new union of king and nation — a utopia typical of its time and at the same time a vision that found its pictorial expression in many contemporary engravings.[188] "Nations," this memorial speech claimed,

> none among you will ever experience humiliation or slavery again; man will respect man; the fruits of your labor will belong to you alone; you will go back to the natural law of defending your estates against rapacious birds and four-footed animals. . . . Even though you might have awakened the frightening hydra of anarchy when you abruptly threw off the yoke of despotism, good laws will suffocate her, restore order, and chase away the absence of restraint that is the sworn enemy of true freedom.
>
> If famine has oppressed you for a long time with her emaciated and dry hand, perhaps as early as tomorrow luxury shall return, crowned by ears of grain, and with her sickle in hand will bring you an abundant harvest and fill your storehouses. (A5:14–16)

One of the last speeches of the revolutionary period, a speech that resolutely stressed the social and domestic significance of the storming of the Bastille, was Marbot's *Discours,* mentioned above, before the members of the Council of Ancients on 14 July 1798. Even though Marbot's address was fairly vague in its general tone and did not narrate the event "14 July" but only evoked it as a metaphor, it did emphasize the belligerent, militant, and republican significance of the fall of the Bastille:

> The people raised their strong heads, struck out with their clubs, and all the deceptions of monarchy disappeared before them, fourteen centuries full of mistakes and fanaticism, full of prejudices and tyranny crumbled. That was 14 July, impetuous and

large like a wave in the ocean that breaks dams and carries terror to the courts of kings. (A22:4)

Marbot makes the event of the storming of the Bastille part of a series of "Journées révolutionnaires," great days of the Revolution, that every listener should vividly remember. In so doing, he implicitly underlines the system-exploding dimension of 14 July, which was anti-monarchistic from the start, a dimension that was further manifested in the storming of the Tuileries on 10 August 1792, the fall of the monarchy, and the execution of King Louis XVI on 21 January 1793.

Two years after Marbot's *Discours,* in the first year of Napoléon's Consulate, official speeches delivered on the national holiday of 14 July construct a completely different historical genealogy, situating the event in a quite distinct fashion.[189] Instead of seeing the storming of the Bastille as the trigger for a series of increasingly radical revolutionary events, they draw a straight line from it to 18 Brumaire 1799, the day Napoléon Bonaparte seized power and founded the Consulate. The years 1790 to 1799 suddenly seem like an immense detour full of unnecessary violence, anarchy, and brutality that should be repressed and forgotten. In his official address on the anniversary of the storming of the Bastille in 1800, the minister of the interior, Napoléon's brother Lucien, said:

> The eighteenth of Brumaire completed the work of 14 July 1789; everything the latter destroyed must never appear again; everything the former created must never again be destroyed. . . . Today, the nation has recovered the patriotic and generous feelings of the first day of its awakening; a pact sanctioned by its unanimous wish was strengthened on the solid foundations—freedom and equality—that were built on 14 July 1789. (A24:14, 12)

This speech is typical of the postrevolutionary domestication of Quatorze Juillet that has basically dominated the *official* discourse in France concerning 14 July 1789 up to the present day. Instead of putting his finger on the wounds that 14 July had cut in the consciousness of his contemporaries, wounds conceived by the collective imagination between 1789 and 1793 as having had a therapeutic effect on the entire nation, Lucien Bonaparte consciously and specifically repressed the domestic explosive force of the symbol "storming of the

Bastille." His description is extremely abstract and clearly pervaded by quasi-religious metaphors. "Suddenly," his narrative account of the storming of the Bastille reads,

> the holy fire shoots up and penetrates the veins of the *political body* [of the nation]; millions of arms are raised; the word *freedom* echoes from all sides. . . . The Bastille has been conquered. (A24:6)

Seeming at first glance to stay entirely in the tradition of 1789, Lucien Bonaparte then recalled the fallen heroes of the nation, meaning, however, neither the conquerors of the Bastille nor the actors in the following "Journées révolutionnaires," such as the five hundred citizens killed in the assault on the Tuileries, but the French soldiers who had fallen on the battlefields of Europe. Significantly, instead of the song dominating the first years of the Revolution, *Ça ira* with its provocative chorus "Les Aristocrates à la lanterne" (Hang the aristocrats from lanterns), the *Chant du départ* was sung on 14 July 1800, a soldierly march that in its style fit much better with the military ethos pervading Lucien Bonaparte's entire speech. For Lucien as well as for his famous brother Napoléon Bonaparte, the Bastilles to be conquered were no longer situated inside the country but found themselves, rather, beyond the traditional borders of France. This semantic use of the Bastille symbol was characteristic of the whole ruling elite of the Consulate, and before that of most of the epoch of the Directoire. "The siege of the Bastille," Citizen Desbarreaux, for example, president of the city council of Toulouse, said in a speech he gave on 14 July 1797, "was the precursor of our other triumphs and the characteristic sign that the people had not demanded the first of their rights in vain" (A16:5). Citizen Gustave Langlois, chairman of the Eure departmental administration in Normandy, expressed this hope even more clearly in a speech delivered in Evreux on 14 July 1798 in which he celebrated the recent conquest of Malta—"the Bastille of the Mediterranean, the cherished refuge of the aristocracy"—and foresaw French forces consoling "the Indians for the evils they have suffered at the hands of Europe's tyrants"[190]—here meaning the British—following their conquest of Egypt. In that same year, 1798—this, too, being a typical example of its time—on the occasion of the festivities of 14 July, the president of the cantonal administration of the village of Seurre in the Jura in eastern France cheered the Vain-

queurs de la Bastille on, only to celebrate the triumphs of the "Vainqueurs" of Jemappes, Fleurus, and Wissembourg in the same breath—
battles with which France managed to push its borders eastward to the
Rhine and the Schelde for almost two centuries. On 14 July, the orator
went on, "an army of semiarmed patriots advanced against this formidable place; the French Guards, those immortal heroes, formed its
avant-garde. . . . Frenchmen began the war of liberation in a charge,
and conquered the Bastille. Honor to the conquerors of the Bastille!
Honor to the conquerors of Fleurus, Jemappes, Wissembourg!"[191]

Finishing a process that began with the coup d'état of 9 Thermidor,
the France of the Consulate officially declared the Revolution completed ("la Révolution est terminée," A14:743)[192] and thus defused the
political controversy that surrounded the symbol "storming of the
Bastille" by consciously redirecting its meaning toward external expansion and an external mission of freedom. In this, the France of the
Directoire and the Consulate mostly followed the self-representation
of the Vainqueurs de la Bastille as patriotic soldiers, which ever since
the summer of 1789 had given the collective memory of 14 July a
military character. But instead of being a symbolic impetus for intra-
societal discussion and political argument as in the years 1789–93, the
storming of the Bastille collectively recalled on the national holiday
of 14 July now became a symbol geared to constructing a unity for
the warlike Grande Nation. Originally, it was the festival of revolutionary, armed, and patriotic citizens embodied by the craftsmen of
Faubourg Saint-Antoine, who as actors and witnesses attended Claude
Fauchet's speech of 5 August 1789 and five weeks later, on 14 September organized a patriotic procession in memory of the storming of the
Bastille at their own initiative. In 1800, it officially became a "Festival
of National Unity" (Fête de la Concorde) which consciously and specifically identified its enemies only *outside* state borders. The haste with
which Napoléon Bonaparte abolished this national holiday after his
coronation as emperor—and significantly by decree replaced it with
the anniversary of his own coronation—proves how much Napoléon,
and after the Restoration the house of Bourbon, feared the return of
the repressed in spite of the "domestication" of the storming of the
Bastille.

As the *event* of 14 July recalled in political speeches and festivals had
a prominent place in the collective memory of the French nation that

had emerged from the Revolution, the *site* where the Bastille had stood very quickly became a place of symbolic importance. The collective idea of a necessary and radical break with the past, with its mechanisms of oppression and its monuments—which had to be destroyed and exterminated in order to inaugurate a new era of equality, freedom, and universal happiness—materialized in the demolition of the Bastille, which Palloy as building contractor and participant in the assault on the Bastille had begun on 15 July 1789 and completed in the summer of 1791. The question of the new layout of the former site of the Bastille was already being discussed intensively and publicly in 1789, and it quickly became a cause of the entire nation.

The numerous responses to the competition of ideas for redesigning the site, which was announced on posters at the Palais-Royal in August 1789, all have in common the notion of destroying the former state prison as a "symbol of despotism" and spreading its remains— like the body of an executed criminal in the (still valid) legislation of the ancien régime—to the four winds. But even concerning the degree of destruction of the Bastille, opinions differed. While the majority of contemporaries favored razing the structure and, if anything at all, incorporating the notorious dungeons into the foundation of the prospective future national monument, the anonymous author of a text entitled *Idées d'un Citoyen au sujet de la Bastille, à l'occasion d'un concours affiché au Palais-Royal* (Ideas of a citizen concerning the Bastille, on the occasion of a competition announced at the Palais-Royal) suggested preserving the ruins of the Bastille as a memorial. "A triumphal arch, a pyramid, some other huge monument," the author writes,

> would appeal to the imagination less than a broken pillar of the Bastille, which dug its own grave, that is to say, the grave of despotism and of the capricious ministers. I want these remains, which are so important to the history of these times, to be maintained by the French people with as much care as they devote to their most beautiful buildings.[193]

But the idea of preserving the ruins of the Bastille as a memorial was less common than that of building a new monument. Suggestions for the latter ranged from an obelisk to an enormous pyramid, from a victory column bearing a statue of the king to a new national parliament. Several texts outlined the latter plan, seeing such a building—in place of the destroyed Bastille, the symbol of despotism—as the embodiment of the "Souveraineté du Peuple" (sovereignty of the people) won in 1789.[194]

The most bizarre suggestion was presented in July 1790 by the anonymous authors of the above-mentioned *Enterrement du despotisme, ou funérailles de l'aristocratie*. They proposed erecting a huge funeral monument bearing symbols of despotism—snakes, lizards, rats, and so forth—on top of the ruins of the Bastille and making it the center of the annual celebrations on 14 July. Other authors came up with the idea of an extensive public garden symbolizing a return to nature that was to become a place of rest and enjoyment for the citizens of the French capital. It was even suggested that a continual popular festival lasting the entire year be set up on the site of the Bastille, with carousels, dances, orchestral music, and a bar. Instead of being celebrated only one day of the year, the festival of 14 July was to become a permanent institution, a kind of living monument that would much more substantially enhance the citizens' patriotic sense of freedom.[195]

On 16 June 1792, after long hesitation, the French parliament finally decided to erect a Freedom column ("Colonne de la Liberté") on the site of the Bastille, which was renamed "Freedom Square" (Place de la Liberté).[196] On 17 July 1792, the foundation stone of this monument was laid, which in its design corresponded to a large extent with a comprehensive plan of Palloy's. Palloy had offered a very detailed proposal to completely reconstruct the entire Bastille site in a text of over fifty quarto pages, which he had printed and distributed at his own expense. In the center of the site was to be an octagonal victory column standing on a fundament in the form of a replica of the former state prison made from Bastille stones. At the top of this column, which was supposed to be taller than Trajan's Roman victory column, Palloy envisioned a statue of freedom, embodied by a female figure carrying a lance decorated with a Phrygian cap in her right hand (figure 34).[197] While the replica of the Bastille was to be framed by a twenty-three-foot rock—as a symbol of nature triumphing over despotism—plates with the Declaration of Rights and the text of the Constitution of 1791 were to be affixed to the lower part of the column.

By means of art and architecture, Palloy's design for a *Gesamtkunstwerk* offered a typical representation of the Revolution and in the process used the central terms and symbols of revolutionary self-understanding ("freedom," "despotism," "nature," "armed patriotism," "law," and "human rights"). But, though the foundation stone

Figure 34. Pierre-François Palloy, Design for a freedom column on the Place de la Bastille. Pen-and-ink drawing, painted in watercolors, 260 by 130 mm, 1792 (Bibliothèque Nationale, Estampes, Qb 1, M 98766).

had been laid, his project never went beyond the planning stage and
came no closer to being realized during the decade of the Revolution
than did any of the numerous other projects for reconstructing the site
of the Bastille. The main reason for this was certainly financial difficulty, which was followed only a few weeks after the foundation laying
by the declarations of war of Austria and Prussia against France. But
the rapid political and ideological changes that occurred during the
years following the Revolution also made a consensus over a prospective monument on the site of the Bastille difficult to reach. The lavish
monumental column that Palloy had suggested and that the National
Assembly had originally accepted was replaced by temporary memorials. On 15 April 1792, a small, provisional statue of freedom was
dedicated on the Place de la Bastille, in fact, as the newspaper *Révolutions de Paris* reported to its readers, "on the very spot where the tower
had stood in which Latude was tormented for almost forty years of
his life."[198] A year later, in July 1793, an impressive, fifteen-meter-high
plaster statue of Isis was set up, from whose breasts streamed water
that the patriots assembled on 14 July were supposed to drink—a representation of the "fountain of regeneration" that many contemporaries had dreamt of as the new symbolic center of the national body
since 1789.[199] Finally, Napoléon Bonaparte had the column designed
by Davy de Chavigné and Palloy erected, in 1806, not on the Place de
la Bastille but on the Place Vendôme—and not as a column of freedom but, in a much different form, as a victory column. On the Place
de la Bastille, he intended to construct a colossal bronze elephant that
would serve as water reservoir and fountain at the same time. However, only a plaster model of the proposed casting was set up in 1810—
this, too, a "defusing" of the symbolism of the Bastille, which had
been more radical and militant in the first years of the Revolution.
In 1844, the twenty-four-meter-high plaster elephant looked pitiful,
crumbled and damaged with its inside full of rats—"one of the most
garish monuments I have ever seen," the German traveler Frege wrote
in his *Genrebilder aus Paris* (Generic scenes from Paris).[200]

The bronze version of this "ungainly elephant made of plaster" was
never realized, which, "aesthetically, must actually be called a stroke of
luck," as Frege cynically remarked. Instead, Napoléon's delapidated,
exotic, and aesthetically completely unsuccessful elephant made way
for the July Column (Colonne de Juillet), a toned-down, ideologically
defused version of the revolutionary freedom column Palloy had de-

signed fifty years earlier and presented to the National Assembly as a proposal. The monument, similar to Napoléon's victory column on Place Vendôme, had almost nothing in common with the grand plans made during the first year of the Revolution, which had aimed at creating a pilgrimage destination for the French nation on the site of the Bastille. A world of ideas geared toward representing France's radical break with the past architectonically that at the same time was informed by popular cultural elements such as a belief in the magical powers of consecrated places and the regenerative power of consecrated water made way, here too, for a new political desire for consensus. Instead of repressing the memory of the storming of the Bastille, as Napoléon did, or "charging" it with radical political symbolism, as was often done in the first years of the Revolution, leaders began to "cool down," defuse, and monumentalize that memory during the July Monarchy—which once again called itself the Bastille's political heir. The July Column with its low-key, sparse symbolism, which recalled the victims of 1830 rather than the Vainqueurs de la Bastille of 1789, was a typical symptom of this process.

Revolutionary Activism under the Sign of the Bastille

The symbolism of the Bastille gained a positive dimension on 14 July, one reinforced by subsequent journalistic revelations, and one popularized nationwide through Palloy's political cult of relics and through the declaration of 14 July as a national holiday. But Bastille symbolism did not "only" form collective ideas and social consciousness. Rather, it showed its force by becoming a motivation for revolutionary activists.

Beyond the victors of the Bastille, who felt permanently indebted to the storming of the Bastille as the key event of their "political birth," 14 July served as an incentive and a reminder to act in a revolutionary manner, to storm such "terrible political and religious Bastilles"[201] as the monasteries,[202] the shops of price-fixing millers and bakers,[203] or the Tuileries, which were attacked on 10 August 1792.[204] When there was concern, for example, in the winter of 1791–92 with breaking Louis XVI's veto of laws passed by the National Assembly and with putting down counterrevolutionary tendencies, Hébert's radical newspaper summoned the sansculottes: "Well, damn it, behave the way you did on 14 July again. Imagine that you have to de-

Figure 35. Vieilh de Varenne, Flag of the National Guard of the Paris district Saint-Marcel. Colored etching, 210 by 160 mm, 1790 (Bibliothèque Nationale, Estampes, Qb 1, M 99279).

stroy new Bastilles; forge thousands of pikes and arm your wives and children with them." [205] Palloy joined in before the National Convention: "The thunderous fall of the Bastille has shaken all the Bastilles of the world to their foundations, all the kings on their thrones have grown pale. . . . May all of Europe's Bastilles one day fall beneath my blows!" [206] And the republican oath of the sansculottes, which also entered speeches and posters, read: "We will spare no effort to ensure that there are no more Bastilles on earth, that no tyrant stays on his throne, that no peoples are in chains. . . . We swear this on the ruins of the Bastille." [207] It is characteristic of the motivating force of Bastille symbolism that the National Guard of Paris's suburb of craftsmen Saint-Marcel got itself a flag, which it had consecrated in a ceremonial mass, showing a farmer setting out from his hut to storm a "Bastille" crying, "Death or Liberty" (figure 35).

But matters were not limited to such pictorial and speech acts; the enhanced symbolic force of the Bastille gained on 14 July also manifested itself in actual collective symbolic action in the streets. "The Bastille was conquered, but there remains another terrifying fortress of horror, which is the hope of our enemies." [208] This statement refers to the prison tower of Vincennes, where such symbolic figures as Mirabeau and Latude had been detained. The prison had been closed in 1784 owing to its dilapidation but was to be renovated in the spring of 1791. The petite bourgeoisie of Faubourg Saint-Antoine immediately suspected the preparation of a "new Bastille," went out to the castle of Vincennes in large numbers on 28 February 1791, and began razing the tower of the former state prison. The National Guard had to intervene, chasing more than three thousand people from the premises, arresting sixty-four activists and taking them into custody at the Conciergerie. The Paris city council justified this unpopular show of force:

> For several days, the people, and especially the citizens of Faubourg Saint-Antoine, have been deceived. They are told not that the repairs on the tower of Vincennes would serve to move criminals from the overcrowded prisons of Paris but that a new Bastille was being erected, a fortress in which the enemies of freedom could unite. An underground tunnel was to lead to the arsenal and into the city; cannons were to be set up on the platform of the tower in order to destroy the suburb and the capital.[209]

But almost the entire revolutionary press sided with the activists and transferred the same hate of tyrants and fear of conspiracies that it had developed concerning the assault on the Bastille in 1789 to Vincennes, calling it a "nest of tyrants" that deserved to be razed: "What the Bastille used to be, Vincennes is today."[210]

Not only in Paris but also in the provinces, the example of 14 July resulted in imitative symbolic actions. The press was constantly denouncing new "Bastilles": "The Bastille [in Paris] could be considered the main seat of despotism, but it maintained a host of supplementary seats throughout the country that still dishonor the soil of France."[211] In August 1789, the radical *Révolutions de Paris* reported: "After the example of the capital, almost all cities have taken control of their fortresses. There is no city that does not take up arms, that does not want to lay a siege; . . . every city, every small market town seems to regret not having cut off any heads, not having conquered a Bastille."[212] In this vague formulation, we find a symbolic stylization of the actual events of the summer of 1789 in the provinces, where the so-called municipal revolution mostly involved raising a citizens' guard and chasing off the old oligarchic city government,[213] and where the farmers fearing an "aristocratic conspiracy" destroyed the documents of their feudal lords but did not arrange a "storming" of their castles.[214] In the port of Brest, a crowd gathered on 17 July, entered the harbor fortress with more than two thousand workers, plundered the weapons stocks, declared themselves the "parti du Tiers Etat," adopted the new three-colored national cockade as their sign, and occupied Fort Gonête, which lay a mile outside the city, without a fight.[215] But, as this example suggests, the news of the storming of the Bastille, which spread like wildfire, was also the cause of the municipal revolution and at least to some extent led to real imitations. In Nantes in Brittany, for instance, the excited crowd was stopped from storming the city fortress with ladders only at the last minute by the prison's capitulation.[216] In Bordeaux, the garrison of the royal fortress Trompette, built after the Fronde, was preparing for a siege like that of 14 July until its commander, Funel, turned over the fortress's keys to the rebellious citizens on 29 July and put his stock of weapons at the disposal of the citizens' guard.[217]

The symbolic effect of the example of the Bastille was more lasting in Lyon, where contemporaries often compared the state prison Pierre-Scize to that of Paris.[218] Mobilized by the news from Paris, the silk workers of Lyon wanted to seize the prison on 17 July but found themselves unable to enter the impregnable fortress built on a steep cliff above the Rhône.[219] When the commander voluntarily handed over the fortress to the citizens' guard, a liberation of prisoners was staged and represented in a broadsheet (figure 36) that closely corresponds to those which formed myths around the Bastille. The caption calls Pierre-Scize a "horror for citizens" against which the "national phalanx . . . fearlessly advanced" and depicts the prisoners whom the commander liberated as crying, "Vive la liberté, mes amis, mes frères." The caption goes on to say, "The Marquis de Brunoy, who had been declared deceased several years ago, climbed from the prison as if from his grave; he covered the courageous French who returned him to the nation with signs of his gratitude." As in the example of the "Count de Lorges" in Paris, there was an entire pamphlet in Lyon concerned with the resurrection of this imaginary captive.[220] The symbolic act of razing this "hated state dungeon" did not take place immediately but rather was performed only after Pierre-Scize had served as a political prison in the first years of the Revolution and had become the site of massacres in August and September 1792.[221] When a revolutionary army took the city, which opposed Paris centralism, after a long siege in the fall of 1793, one of the first official acts of the commanding commissaries was to liberate the Jacobins held in Pierre-

Scize. On 11 October a decree announced that "the castles and houses that recall the rule of feudalism and royal despotism must disappear from the soil of freedom, . . . that the castle or state prison Pierre-Scize must be destroyed."[222] In October, the commissaries, along with a revolutionized city council as well as hundreds of workers and spectators, went there to publicly launch the razing of Pierre-Scize, "this place of pain," with solemn blows from their hammers:

> When the representatives of the people had climbed the platform of this monstrous tower which for so long has terrified humanity, they asked heaven to bear witness to their dealing the death blow to this monster in the name of the people and humanity. At this sign, thousands of armes were raised to destroy the horrible edifice.[223]

That this act followed the example of Paris is confirmed by a medal commemorating the razing of the "Lyon Bastille" that features broken

Figure 36. The surrender of Pierre-Scize to the citizens in August 1789. Anonymous aquatint etching, 250 by 387 mm, 1789 (Bibliothèque Nationale, Estampes, Qb1, 67 B 41285).

PIERRE ANCISE RENDŪÆUX CITOYENS EN AOUST 1789.

Cette Fortoresse Elevée Sur un Roc escarpé dominant la Ville de Lion, étoit l'effroy du citoyen et de tout étranger suspect, où non; mais nôtre phalange nationale s'avance et envisage avec horreur et sans effroy, ce Roc menaçant, le Gouverneur vrai patriote lui rend les Clefs de la citadelle, en delivre les prisonniers; en disant vive la liberté mes amis, mes frères, voilà le plus beau moment de non existence: M.ʳ le Marquis de Brimey que l'on avait fait mort il y a quelques année. en est sorti comme du tombeau, en comblant des marques de sa Réconnaissance les Braves françois qui le rendaient à la Nation.

chains and instruments of demolition under the sign of the Jacobin hat (figure 37).

But the storming of the Paris Bastille, including its prelude and epilogue, found no more striking imitation than in Marseille.[224] Nothing happened there immediately; events, rather, began to occur only after a delay of nine months, during which the "revolutionary news" from Paris was able to settle into the political consciousness of the Marseille patriots. As early as 17 July 1789, those patriots had addressed a declaration of solidarity to the Paris city government and had invited the governor of Provence to withdraw the cannons from the battlements of the Marseille city fortress. On 29 August they organized such violent riots against the citizens' guard, which served only the interests of the upper class, that the governor, the Count de Caraman, fled to one of these fortresses, Fort Saint-Nicolas.[225] Sparked by mass arrests and the prosecution of feudal-rights-violation cases, by the state of affairs in the local justice system, by the flight of compromised royal civil servants, by troop deployments in the city, and by a statute that prohibited the newly formed National Guard from protecting the city gates, the smouldering conflict between the old city oligarchy and the politicized petite bourgeoisie burst into flame in the spring of 1790. On 4 May of that year, the leading local newspaper finally reported the good news: "Those who saw the last hiding places of the aristoc-

Figure 37. The Lyon Bastille. Iron medal, diameter 48 mm, Lyon, 26 October 1792 (Lyon, Musée des Beaux-Arts, inv. no. 225).

racy in the fortresses of this city and called them "Marseille Bastilles" need no longer fear these dungeons. As of yesterday, they are in the hands of the nation" (B1:4). And a leading revolutionary newspaper in Paris was quick to add: "Citizens of Marseille, your affairs cannot be separated from those of the people of Paris. . . . You have followed in their footsteps; not only the circumstances, but also your motivation and your behavior were the same."[226] Indeed, the supporters of the Revolution won the upper hand at the time by holding their own "storming of the Bastille," which justified their high-handedness and proved them to be true revolutionaries. The collective discourse on this matter, as reconstructed from a corpus of two dozen relevant pamphlets and newspaper articles, shows that this was a five-act restaging under the sign of the Bastille.

In the first act, the thesis of an "aristocratic conspiracy" is transferred to Marseille. The harbor fortresses of Saint-Jean and Notre-Dame de la Garde as well as the citadel of Saint-Nicolas, located on a hill above the city—which Louis XIV had had built in 1660 under the protection of a military occupation in order to make the traditionally rebellious city submissive for good[227]—were considered the bases of the feared plot. The "despotic" origin and purpose of the fortress were considered to be common knowledge; it was called a "shame of the ancestors" (B18:722) and believed to embody a "disregard of the sacred rights of man" (B14:7). Similarly, the speaker of Marseille's city council declared before the National Assembly:

> This citadel was built not to protect citizens but on the contrary to subjugate them; for all of its batteries threaten the city. . . . The despot had the decree of our enslavement carved into the cornerstone of this overwhelming edifice . . . : "Louis the Great" had this citadel built so that the faithful city of Marseille may not give in to pretensions of freedom. (B17:68)

This notion was reinforced by the dark, forbidding appearance of the fortress: "If we did not know from reliable tradition with what purpose Louis XIV had the citadel of Saint-Nicolas erected, its mere sight would suffice to make any doubt in this respect impossible" (B4:1). So the Marseille fortresses (unlike the Paris Bastille) are considered despotic not as state prisons—which they after all were not—but as military bases of royal absolutism.

This function was apparently being actualized with the reinforcement of the garrison by royal troops, which Minister of the Interior Saint-Priest refused to withdraw. As in Paris, the patriots in Marseille, too, feared that cannon fire from the battlements of the fortress would "reduce the city to rubble" (B3:3). Popular pamphlets expressed the same sentiment in more symbolic terms:

> Repeated threats from the representative of ministerial authority, unjust machinations, the accumulation of ammunition in the fortresses—all this led to the fear that the new laws of the French empire would be destroyed, that slavery and despotism would come crawling from these aristocratic chasms to devastate our homes and those of our brothers. (B10:7; see also B19:1; B2:3–4; B23:7–9, 13)

Even though most regular troops had left the fortress between 17 and 21 April and the remaining garrison had provisions for only a few days, public opinion, based on rumor, held that the Marseille fortresses had prepared for a siege and had pointed their cannons at the city.

> Fortresses, Rousseau says, are *nests of tyrants*. Here, this word has found its confirmation. Here, fortresses threatened not only our fortunes but also our lives and our freedom. It could not remain concealed from the citizens how many provisions, how much ammunition they were amassing. (B17:65; see also B14:3)

Such certainty concerning the "planned conspiracy" (B2:4) in Marseille, too, justified, even demanded, the second act, the self-protective reaction of the threatened citizens. "Since they can no longer carry a yoke that is intolerable for a people worthy of a faithful and free life under the law, they have come to the firm resolution to seize the fortresses" (B14:3). They could not obtain weapons from the barracks, but they could get them from ships anchored in the harbor, and, with the support of the municipality, from municipal stocks (B2:4; B3:12). The fact that the rebels' cannons and rifles were not even used, because all three fortresses were taken on 30 April without a fight, did not stop the revolutionaries in Marseille from portraying their actions as a new storming of the Bastille. After they had taken the garrison of Notre-Dame de la Garde by surprise with an ambush, they set up

> several batteries of cannons that could have fired on the fortress from different sides if they had proven to be hostile. The districts

had come marching in with drums and flying flags. . . . About fifteen thousand National Troops were parading in the fortress in front of the municipality and the commander; they climbed the tower of the fortress and hoisted the flag of the nation. (B3:8)

Even though the commander of Fort Saint-Jean, Chevalier de Calvet—weakened by the refusal of one of the regiments under his orders to obey him—finally handed over the fortress without any resistance, one pamphlet imagined a heroic conquest: Provoked by a malicious volley of case shot, it claimed, the citizens had stormed the fortress with ladders, weapons drawn (B2:5–7).[228] The conquest of the fortress by the patriots also seemed necessary, however, in a more general sense: "We had to douse these embers of counterrevolution, which were smouldering among us and threatened our life. We have fulfilled our sacred duty by seizing the fortresses; for they threatened the National Assembly and even all of France" (B10:6–7).

As in Paris, the "treason" of the fortress's commander demanded a spontaneous act of popular justice: "The heads of our tyrants have fallen with our Bastilles" (B10:6). On the one hand, this statement refers to de Calvet:

Convinced that he would have to either give in or play the role of de Launay, he preferred the latter, which corresponded more closely to his well-known malice. . . . The crowd demanded de Calvet's punishment . . . , he was hung over the breach of the first ringwall; his head was stuck on a pike and carried all around the city the entire day. This memorable example is very similar to the tragic end of the governor of the Bastille; it seems to scare aristocrats and cross their cabals. (B2:5–8)

On the other hand, the reference to falling tyrants' heads evokes the lynch law practiced on Louis Sauvaire Hippolyte de Bausset, major of Fort Saint-Jean. When de Bausset attempted an escape, the crowd surrounding the fort misunderstood his actions as "treason," and in its rage knew no bounds. "It struck him down and dragged him back and forth in the dirt; his head was cut off, stuck on a pike, and carried through the city in triumph. Such are the disastrous consequences of our courts having passed down cowardly sentences as favors [to the powerful]" (B7:4). This third act of the restaging of the storming of the Bastille, too, is invested with more than local importance: "The head of the miserable aristocrat was paraded through the streets; the twenty-five thousand foreigners who were in Marseille can report in their kingdoms that they saw how traitors and enemies of the nation are treated in France" (B11:563).

An ensuing liberation of martyrs of freedom could hardly be celebrated, since the three Marseille forts had all served military ends—even though the scenes of fraternization between the "conquerors" and the garrisoned troops could to some extent be interpreted as a "liberation of prisoners" (B1:5; B3:15–16). But, absent liberated prisoners, the Marseille patriots devoted all the more effort to presenting themselves as the new "victors of the Bastille." Like their models, they published a list of members several times, that is, the names of those fifty men who had taken the Notre-Dame fort by surprise (B1:7; B14: 4–7). One of them, the locksmith Doinet, reports in an open letter how he planned the overthrow of the fortress and helped execute the plan (B1:4–6). Not only local pamphlets and speeches praise "the courageous citizens [for] having matched the conquerors of the Bastille" (B2:7; see also B23:15). Even Paris revolutionary clubs spontaneously recognized the conquerors of the forts as their brothers in arms (B20: 4–5; see also B21:47–48), and the flattered city council of Marseille responded with words of thanks and praise:

> You, brave citizens of Paris, have struck the first blow against the colossus of despotism [the Bastille]. . . . We have done no more than follow your example. With your shackles, ours have fallen as well. Without the enormous shock that emitted from the fall of the Bastille, we could never have destroyed these threatening bastions, these hiding places of tyranny. (B21:48; see also B20:5–7)

The fifth and final act of restaging consisted of the razing of the "Marseille Bastilles," especially of Fort Saint-Nicolas, which in the night of 17 to 18 May 1790 was entered by two hundred patriots equipped with picks and other necessary tools who immediately began to demolish the harbor fortress.[229] All the powers in favor of the Revolution showed their solidarity for this razing, which was also represented in broadsheets (figure 38). While women and children supported the two hundred constantly working "démolisseurs,"[230] the local Jacobin club collected more than sixteen thousand livres in a fund-raising campaign,[231] and the proceeds of a drama entitled *La Démolition des forts de Marseille* were devoted to the same purpose.[232] The magistrate and general council of the city made hardly any effort to enforce the gov-

Figure 38. The razing of Fort Saint-Jean outside Marseille. Anonymous etching, 140 by 95 mm. Frontispiece for the pamphlet *Marseille sauvée* (B2).

ernmental prohibition on the razing.[233] Although the demolition of the "Marseille Bastilles" did not unearth such horrors as were found in Paris, or inspire a second Palloy, it was still symbolically significant, as a mock funeral speech for Fort Saint-Nicolas exclaims: "I do not know if a hidden spirit is at work in the sequence of events that take place in this world . . . ; but when I see how the ruins of the nobility, the clergy, the upper courts, the Bastille, and Fort Saint-Nicolas cover the ground, I have to cry out, 'Providence, you do exist, and you are just'" (B4:2–3).

The Bastille symbolism used to enshroud the takeover of the Marseille fortresses was to contribute considerably to the fact that the minister of the interior was unable to get a punitive expedition accepted by the National Assembly,[234] that the razing was completed only after the demolition of those parts of the fortresses that were directed at the city, and that the National Assembly avoided condemning the Marseille revolutionaries and their lynch law. In this, they followed the reservations of a representative from Provence: "By razing only those fortifications which threatened the city, . . . they have followed the example of the citizens of the capital, who destroyed the fortress of the Bastille last July" (B18:721–22). Or, as Marat expressed it even more radically:

> With the destruction of a monument of tyranny that was built in their midst to extirpate them, the citizens of Marseille do today what the Parisians did when they razed the Bastille under the very eyes of the National Assembly. . . . If, however, the rebellion of 14 July is the first great deed of the Revolution, which has destroyed despotism and given the nation its rights back, and if the greatest act of heroism of the Parisians consists in this, then how can the citizens of Marseille be wrong when they imitate this model of civic virtue?[235]

But the adoption of Bastille symbolism in Marseille, and the public acceptance of its validity, was more than a retrospective attempt to justify local revolutionary acts by identifying them with a national model. To a large extent, Bastille symbolism had shaped the Marseille unrest of spring 1790 from the very beginning. Moreover, it had served as a catalyst propelling Marseille into the process of the French Revolution, at the same time forming the exemplary figure of the

Marseille revolutionary, which continued to exert its power into 1792 and beyond, on the model of the victors of the Bastille.[236]

The Marseille example is unusually well documented, but not untypical. It clearly shows the great importance of Bastille symbolism in developing the national political culture of the French Revolution — a culture not only of key words, slogans, and pictures but also of concrete collective action. On top of that, the symbol "Bastille" once again shows its potency by supporting, even bearing the main weight of, the seizure of power in local politics by followers of the Revolution.

Echo and Export of Bastille Symbolism Abroad:
Germany as a Significant Example

The fourteenth of July 1789, a catalytic "total event"[237] with far-reaching political, social, and mental consequences in France, had profound, hard-to-assess effects abroad as well. The daily and weekly newspapers of all European countries, but also the gazettes of the young United States of America, the periodicals of Spanish-speaking Central and South America, and the press of the French colonies in the Caribbean — here, most of all the *Gazette de Saint-Domingue* — reported extensively on the event and gave it prominence by reporting comprehensively and often enthusiastically on it.

As early as August 1789, for example, a pantomime on the storming of the Bastille was performed with great success in the London Drury Lane Theater.[238] A contemporary engraving shows that the military and warlike aspects of 14 July were stressed at great expense in this production. In front of the dark towers of the Bastille, made from papier-mâché, rising high in the background, the spectators saw cannons onstage as well as uniformed National Guards who opened fire on the defenders of the state prison with fake ammunition and afterward forced them down with their assault.[239] In October 1789, Covent Garden produced a second drama on 14 July 1789, though it was soon banned by the government for political reasons.[240] Further dramas followed in 1790 and 1791 in London, in the English provinces, and even in Irish Dublin, where a play entitled *Gallic Freedom; or, The Destruction of the Bastille* was performed. Here too, the spectacular character of the event was stressed by decoration and accessories —

cannons, dark dungeons, changing scenes[241]—but its significance as a symbol of freedom was emphasized as well. The announcement of the drama, which was published in the Dublin *Hibernian Journal* in November 1789, explicitly called the storming of the Bastille "that glorious Struggle which gave birth to National Freedom."[242] In July 1790, patriotic souvenirs were sold in London—small miniature Bastilles, which according to contemporary accounts were very popular.[243] In several English cities, but also in Ireland, the Netherlands, the former diocese of Liège, and in Switzerland, the first anniversary of the fall of the Bastille was an occasion for celebration. In London, Lord Stanhope launched a subscription drive to raise money for a large-scale 14 July celebration. By mid-June 1790, fifteen hundred subscribers had already come forth to "bring the French Revolution closer to the people," as one newspaper wrote.[244] A year later in Dublin, on 14 July 1791, citizens from "all social strata" marched through the streets of the Irish capital. They carried banners showing pictures of the destroyed Bastille and reading "The Glorious Revolution of 1789" and "Human Rights."[245] In Birmingham, a memorial celebration organized by a Doctor Priestley on 14 July 1791 ended in bloody riots between followers and opponents of the Revolution. The "friends of freedom," as they were called in the press, were pelted with stones, and Priestley's house was looted.[246] The crowd, supposedly incited by members of the church and the aristocracy, continued its destruction, indiscriminately looted stores, and, armed, stormed the prison—inciting a riot that was put down only with great difficulty by the royal regiment that had hurried to the scene. In other English cities—fifty in all according to witnesses[247]—celebrations of the second anniversary of the storming of the Bastille were much quieter. In London, the indefatigable Lord Stanhope, thanks to his impressive list of more than five thousand subscribers, was able to organize not only a procession but also a "patriotic dinner" with more than seven hundred special guests on 14 July 1791.[248]

Dutch patriots, for their part, had already organized illegal celebrations of 14 July in 1790—official ones had been banned—and chose "To the destruction of all Bastilles and the extirpation of all tyrants" as their toast.[249] At celebrations in Switzerland—for instance, in 1791 in Lausanne—it was not Bastille symbolism, considered subversive and martial, that was at the center of the festivities but rather a commemoration of the French Declaration of Rights.[250] In this context, the Swiss also persistently invoked their own Helvetian love of free-dom.[251] The citizens of Liège understood the message of 14 July as an appeal to destroy their own "Bastille"—the former citadel of the prince-bishops, who had been overthrown in 1787—after the Parisian example. On the site of the "Bastille liégeoise," gardens were planted after November 1790 that, according to a contemporary report, "beautify the city and will remind the citizens of their rewon freedom forever." [252]

The storming of the Bastille had its most profound and far-reaching effect, however, in the territories of the neighboring German realms. The then exclusively German-speaking Strasbourg in particular, with its newspapers, publishers, and printers, was an extremely lively center for the dissemination and translation of news and writings about the French Revolution to the entire German-speaking area.[253] German "Revolution tourists," mostly journalists and authors, had been streaming into Paris since the beginning of the Revolution and informing the German public—from "firsthand" knowledge and as eye-witnesses—of the events occurring on the other side of the Rhine. They reported on the fall of the Bastille and its destruction, begun in the second half of July, in printed texts and correspondents' reports. In his *Briefe aus Paris* (Letters from Paris), the school inspector Joachim Heinrich Campe from Brunswick, who had traveled to the French capital in the first days of July, was most affected by the overwhelming impression that a visit to the conquered notorious state prison made on him. Like countless other visitors, Campe—for a small "entrance fee"—was led through the dungeons and underground prison cells by Palloy's workers. Afterward, he wrote of seeing "cursed" places of "horror" that were at the same time silent witnesses to the

> *lawless despotism* . . . by which without any prior legal proceedings the guilty and the innocent were thrown into this place of misery, in order to bury them alive, often for their entire life, or some-times even, as is more probable, to *let* some of them *disappear, by poison and strangulation, from the living.*[254]

Campe's impressions read like an extract from the extensive pam-phlet literature—some of which, from Renneville's *L'Inquisition fran-çaise* to Latude's autobiography, *Le Despotisme dévoilé,* was translated into German—and contributed crucially to the Bastille's political my-

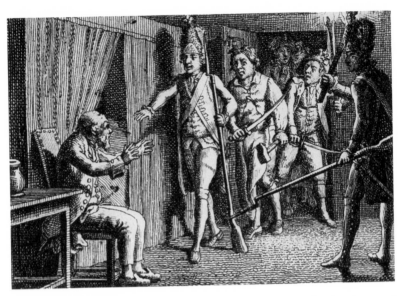

Figure 39. E. Henrie, The liberation of the Count de Lorges by the victors of the Bastille. Etching, 51 by 63 mm. Title picture in Friedrich Schulz, *Geschichte der grossen Revolution in Frankreich* (Berlin: Vieweg, 1790).

thologization on German soil (figure 39). Instead of giving his concrete, *immediate* impressions, Campe in his *Briefe aus Paris* outlined the features of a *symbol,* one with which he was familiar from the press and pamphlets, from written and pictorial sources. First describing his route through Paris in great detail, Campe changes gears when he lays eyes on the Bastille, adopting a tone replete with the pathos of contemporary pamphlet literature, one that had also dominated the rhetoric of the Bastille literature of the eighteenth century.

At the end of Rue Saint-Antoine, we find the former bastion of French despotism, the *Bastille;* this horrible chasm which swallowed many an innocent victim of tyranny; this place of terror and misery, covered by many a hot tear, and of deep and dark graves, filled with living corpses, from which many a sigh of fear and desperation climbed up through the immense walls of rock and the iron doors to the Father of Men, to the Judge of Kings, and cried out for revenge. Now they have been heard, these pitiful sighs; the dreadful castle lies there, at least in part, already in ruins, and soon it will be completely destroyed.[255]

But much more than the accounts of German "Revolution tourists" such as Campe, von Halem, or Konrad Engelberg Oelsner,[256] the contemporary German daily press helped the events of 14 July 1789 achieve a broad social echo and a symbolic effect in politics. With a delay of seven to twelve days after the event itself, almost all periodicals in the German-language area reported on the storming of the Bastille, most of them very extensively. The detailed analysis of a representative selection of twenty newspapers and magazines[257] and seven non-periodical texts—the contents of which are in some cases verbatim repetitions of the reports in periodicals but ones that through their form of publication and repeated printings were able to achieve a more lasting effect—shows that the events of 14 July were represented in a surprisingly positive fashion in contemporary Germany (table 7). While there was consensus concerning the justification of the assault on the Bastille, and concerning its importance for world history, the accounts of the individual periodicals differed in the terminological *descriptions* of the events and in the *assessment* of specific episodes. The *Politische Gespräche der Todten* from Neuwied, for instance, at first disapprovingly used the term "rebellion" (C16: 29 [23 July 1789]: 235) to describe the attack on the Bastille—the same term King Louis XVI is said to have applied in his first spontaneous reaction to news of the event. Other newspapers such as the *Frankfurter Staats-Ristretto* (C9: 115 [24 July 1789]: 494) or the *Hanauer Neue Europäische Zeitung* (C10: 115 [24 July 1789]: n.p.) initially called the events of 14 July a "civil war" but then preferred the neutral term "Staatsveränderung" (change of state) or, even more often, "revolution." In the following issues, the above-mentioned paper from Neuwied switched over to the same terms. The *Hamburgische unpartheyische Correspondent*[258] explicitly called the events a "happy revolution." The *Kurzgefasste Geschichte der Bastille* even spoke emphatically of the "famous revolution that put an end to both oppression and the matter of Bastilles simultaneously."[259]

One important element of the revolutionary dimension of the storming of the Bastille—the completely new role of the king, who was demoted in one stroke from "absolute monarch to first civil servant," as Ludwig Buri wrote[260]—was taken into account only outside the daily press. Some contemporary German press reports described the massacre of the governor of the Bastille de Launay and the glorification of the victors of the Bastille with unconcealed sympathy and open enthusiasm. None of the representative German periodicals of the time examined here demanded the punishment of the Vainqueurs

Narrative Sequences	Mainzer Zeitung	Pol. Gespräche	Augsputg Postz.	Frankf. Postz.	Frankf. Staats.	Hanauer . . . Zig.	Schwäb. Merkur	Z. des Hamb. Corr.	Berlin Nachr.	Bayreuber Z.	Leipziger Zeit.	Neueste Wdth.	Erlanger Realz.	Friedens-Courier	Allg. pol. Staten;	Berlinische Zeit.	Wiener Zeitung	Polit. Journal	Mancherlei	Buri, Sammlung	Beiträge	Beschreibung	Geschichte der . . Batt.	Erzählung der . . . Revol.	Schulz, Geschichte (see fig. 39)	Campe, Briefe	Frequency
	July														*Aug.*							*Sept.*	*Oct.*	*Nov.*			
	22	23	24			25		27							28												
1. Introduction	X	X	X	X		X		X		X	X	X			X	X	X	X	X	X	X				X		18
2. Fear of a conspiracy			X	X						X					X					X	X	X					7
3. Necker dismissed	X		X	X		X	X		X	X	X	X		X	X		X	X	X			X					16
4. People awaken	X	X	X		X		X	X	X	X				X	X	X	X	X		X	X	X	X				17
5. Demonstration	X		X	X				X	X								X			X							7
6. Repression	X	X	X	X				X	X						X		X		X	X	X						11
7. Guards go over to people	X	X	X	X	X		X	X	X	X		X			X	X	X	X	X	X		X	X	X	X		20
8. Citizens' militia	X	X	X	X	X	X	X	X	X	X					X	X	X	X	X			X	X				17
9. Cockades	X	X		X	X	X	X	X		X	X		X		X	X	X	X	X	X	X		X	X			20
10. Patrols	X		X		X	X		X		X		X	X	X			X	X									11
11. Search for weapons	X		X	X	X	X	X	X	X	X		X		X	X	X	X	X	X		X	X	X	X	X		21
12. To the Bastille!	X	X	X		X	X	X	X	X		X		X		X	X	X	X	X	X	X	X	X	X	X		21
13. De Launay's treason	X	X	X	X	X	X	X	X	X	X	X	X	X	X	X	X	X	X	X	X	X	X	X	X	X	X	26
14. Storming of the Bastille	X	X		X	X	X	X	X	X		X	X	X	X	X	X	X	X	X		X	X	X	X			24
15. Popular justice	X	X	X	X	X	X	X	X	X	X	X	X	X	X	X	X	X	X	X	X	X	X	X	X	X	X	26
16. Justification	X		X	X	X	X	X	X		X	X	X	X	X	X		X	X	X				X		X		20
17. Prisoners free	X	X	X	X	X	X	X	X		X	X	X	X	X	X	X	X	X	X		X	X	X	X			25
18. Victors of Bastille	X		X		X	X	X	X		X	X		X	X	X	X		X	X	X	X	X	X	X	X		22
19. Bastille burning	X		X		X	X				X		X		X		X		X							X		10
20. Razing of Bastille	X	X	X	X	X	X	X	X	X		X	X	X	X		X	X	X	X		X	X	X	X	X		24
21. Bastille monument	X	X		X		X	X		X		X			X		X						X	X				11
22. Vive le Roi!	X	X	X	X	X	X	X		X	X	X	X		X	X	X	X	X	X				X	X			20
23. Retrospective appreciation	X	X	X	X	X	X	X			X	X		X	X	X	X		X		X	X	X			X	X	19
24. Conspiracy confirmed	X		X			X	X		X	X			X		X		X				X		X		X	X	13
25. Bastille archive	X		X		X	X	X	X	X		X	X		X	X	X			X		X		X		X	X	17
26. Terror of dungeons	X	X	X	X	X							X				X			X		X						9
27. Book announcements		X		X	X			X	X																		5

Note: German newspapers and magazines are listed chronologically according to the date of the first major report of the storming of the Bastille (later reports are subsumed under this date). Full bibliographic documentation of periodical sources appears in appendix C at the end of this chapter; documentation of nonperiodical sources is given in the text or Works Cited.

Table 7. The Storming of the Bastille and Its Individual Events in Journalism from July to November 1789

de la Bastille, a punishment required by French law for the crimes of resistance to state authority, murder, and incitement to riot. Prosecution was publicly called for by the majority of the aristocratic emigrants, above all King Louis XVI's brother, the Count d'Artois, who had already fled to Germany on 15 July 1789. Instead, German newspaper reports (sequence 18) communicated the cult of the "new heroes of the nation," which had come into being the very evening of the storming of the Bastille, without any attempt at revision. They reported on the decorations and public honors that were accorded to the rebels, on the masses and first memorial celebrations that were dedicated to them in Paris during the summer of 1789. The *Erlanger Real-Zeitung auf das Jahr 1789,* for instance, wrote the following on the first mass celebrated on 25 July in memory of those who fell in the attack — openly or subliminally adopting the admiring tone of voice of the majority of French reports:

> On the twenty-fifth, a mass was read in Paris in the monastery of the Augustine barefoot monks, or Petits-Pères, for those who sacrificed their lives on the thirteenth and fourteenth of July for the restoration of freedom. The Marquis de La Fayette and Mr. Bailly [the mayor of Paris] attended the same. A eulogy was given for the heroes who died for the fatherland and thwarted the black plans of despotism, and a collection was taken for their widows and children. It was a beautiful sight to see the noble Mayor of Paris (Mr. Bailly) and the famous pupil of Washington (Mr. d. Fayette) teach the equality of citizens. (C7: 60 [4 August 1789]: 547)

This report from the Erlangen newspaper, which describes the half-religious, half-political and secular ceremony on 25 July 1789 in such detail, contains all the important elements of the German fascination with the storming of the Bastille: the continuity of the Enlightenment and the Revolution, of the U.S.-American and the French Revolutions, both embodied in the person of General La Fayette, head of the new National Guard; the message of freedom and equality connected with the event 14 July 1789; and finally the glorification of the "new heroes of the nation," the conquerors of the Bastille. Significantly, the *Erlanger Real-Zeitung* described them as "heroes who died for the fatherland," thus moving a new identification figure into the view of the German public too. It was the figure of the patriotic soldier from the ordinary people fighting for fatherland, freedom, and equality, who was first embodied by the Citoyens-Soldats of 1789, then by the French soldiers of the revolutionary wars, and finally—on the German side—by the patriotic defenders of the fatherland in the wars of liberation.

Even the massacre of Governor de Launay and six of his officers and soldiers, which even in parts of the French press was denounced as "barbaric" and as the "cruelty of the mob," was justified by the majority of German periodicals. The dominating view was that like could be repaid only with like, and that de Launay's despotic cruelty had almost called out for the people's cruel revenge. In its report on the lynching of 14 July 1789, the *Frankfurter Staats-Ristretto,* for instance, wrote:

> De Launay had deserved such revenge for a long time; for he was barbaric, harsh, and arrogant, and took delight in the tears of his miserable victims. (C9: 116 [25 July 1789]: 498)

Louis XVI's factual approval of the events on 17 July 1789 was certainly a crucial reason for the surprisingly positive representation and assessment of the storming of the Bastille in the contemporary German press. Almost all newspapers reported extensively on the king's response, and it seems that they at first left unpublished news of the storming of the Bastille that they had received *before* 22 July while awaiting an official reaction. But only a few German journalists recognized the fundamentally antimonarchistic, system-exploding dimension of 14 July as an "act of national liberation" to which Louis XVI had given his approval only after the fact under the compulsion of circumstances, under the immense pressure of public opinion, and because of his own lack of leadership. Of all commentators, the Neuwied Enlightenment figure Ludwig Ysenburg Buri, who in 1791 also published a drama on the storming of the Bastille that was banned because it supposedly glorified violence,[261] undoubtedly understood this most clearly in his *Sammlung der zuverlässigsten Nachrichten, die neueste Revolution in Frankreich betreffend* (Collection of the most reliable news concerning the latest revolution in France), which was published as early as September 1789:

> France alone remained to make the eighteenth century officially the century of revolution. . . . Since 11 July of this year of 1789, her capital has been the scene of the most terrible performances, and her king has been demoted from absolute monarch to first

civil servant. This revolution is certainly one of the most extraordinary events in the world in our time.[262]

A large part of German-language newspaper reports and other writings concerning the assault on the Bastille, which at first could be grasped only in its broad outlines, was directly translated from French original texts and periodicals—namely, *Révolutions de Paris, Révolutions de France et de Brabant, Mercure de France,* Gorsas's *Courrier,* and widely read pamphlets such as *La Bastille dévoilée.* The prefaces appended to these publications, and the comments of editors and translators, often underline and further amplify the almost completely positive assessment of the storming of the Bastille in the French originals. The massacre of Jacques de Flesselles—who was responsible for supplying Paris with food and was accused of being an accomplice of de Launay's—by the besiegers of the Bastille in the late afternoon of 14 July is explicitly legitimized in a footnote by the Bayreuth schoolteacher Johann Friedrich Leonhard Menzel, the German translator of *La Bastille dévoilée.* Menzel adds an additional comment to the rather neutral description of the event in the French original in which he firmly takes a stand. The pedagogue and translator of Voltaire [263] writes:

The above-mentioned Mr. Flesselles was a traitor to the people, since he informed the other party of all measures decided at city hall (which he presided over). He was convicted of this offense by a number of letters found in the boots of his courier. He turned pale over this evidence, and immediately a young man put a bullet through his head; he was carried to the Grève (place of execution), to which the corpse of Mr. de Launay had already been dragged. The enraged people cut the limbs from their bodies and carried them through different streets, screaming "the remains of the traitors!" [264]

The above-mentioned author and journalist Buri in turn prefaced his *Sammlung*—a work consisting entirely of translations of accounts from contemporary French newspapers and periodicals—with a firm profession of his belief that the events of 1789 were significant for Germany too:

The French Revolution cannot be without interest for the Germans, however. It is a magical mirror in which the princes of the earth can read what a provoked people are capable of, even if they have carried the shackles of servitude with hanging ears for centuries.[265]

A "mirror in which the princes . . . can read what a provoked people are capable of": this statement made by Buri in the preface to his history of the Revolution also encapsulates the essence of the political and social "message of 14 July" in Germany. In surprisingly positive, extensive descriptions in the daily press and periodicals, the storming of the Bastille was presented as the heroic deed of an awakened "people" against a criminal, despotic regime—and at the same time as a revolution approved of and sanctioned by the king himself. This "message" remained more restricted to the elites than it did in France, however. It hardly, and only with great delay, made its way into the communications media of popular culture—almanacs, catechisms, popular pictures, popular theater—and overall reached only a relatively small part of the population: mainly the "reasoning" public of enlightened society. Germany of 1789–99 produced neither a Palloy nor a Latude, and no Harny, who with his drama about the attack on the Bastille (*La Liberté Conquise,* published in 1791) created one of the great successes of the new political popular theater of the Revolution.[266] The German republic of letters, which—in contrast to the French—did not change its basic structure during the Revolution, aimed at the intellectual enlightenment of its members and audience —among which were counted the princes, who were supposed to be influenced, enlightened, and educated to become the "first servants of the state." And German Enlightenment society never produced the radical political pamphlet literature of the likes of Marat, Raynal, Desmoulins, Carra, or Théveneau de Morande, which connected the late French Enlightenment with the political tracts of the Revolution to form an indissoluble whole linking written words and deeds, rhetorical violence and incitement to violent action.[267]

Nevertheless, even in Germany—though to a much lesser extent than in the French provinces or in Paris—certain events can be discerned in which the storming of the Bastille became a model for action. The Saxonian peasants' revolt of the summer of 1790, for instance, if one believes contemporary eyewitnesses, owed crucial aspects to the model of 1789. A lack of food for livestock and the cruelty of landlords were definitely the basic causes of the rebellion, but only

the news of the events in France—transported by the German press—
actually ignited it. The peasants, Gotha journalist Heinrich Ottokar
Reichard wrote, were trying to copy the Bastille victors without taking
account—as the conservative author qualified—of the fact that the
French conditions were very different from those in Germany.

> They had heard the perjury and disloyalty of the Gardes Fran-
> çaises called civic virtues and praiseworthy deeds in the German
> press, and judged the loyalty of the German warrior accord-
> ing to French standards. But, o ye Vainqueurs de la Bastille! O
> ye Hommes du 14 Juillet, how many victories would you have
> achieved, or pikes hoisted, if your *premier fonctionnaire public* had
> had loyal Saxons or nothing but Swiss guards in the Bastille and
> in the good city of Paris![268]

Even more impressive than the Saxonian example is the rebellion of the peasants of Gesmold in the bishopric Osnabrück, which
finally erupted into violence after a long-smouldering conflict between farmers and their landlord in the summer of 1794. While the
landlord saw the rebellion as the excesses of a "Jacobin conspiracy,"
the farmers demanded "freedom and equality as in France" and on the
morning of 1 September 1794 stormed the prison tower of the feudal lord, which they called the "famous Gesmold Bastille." After they
had almost completely destroyed it with rods and crowbars, they celebrated their victory—imitating the Paris conquerors of the Bastille—
in the courtyard of the Gesmold castle, some of them decorated with
a "green leaf on their hat" in the manner of a cockade.[269]

But events such as the storming of the "Gesmold Bastille" remained
exceptions, even though a direct reference to the French Revolution,
and especially to 14 July 1789, can be demonstrated in a dozen similar
revolts.[270] They also remained the exception in literary sketches and
in the journalistic "dreams" of German intellectuals—even if visions
of the storming of German Bastilles could occasionally be gleaned,
most provocatively no doubt in the Hamburg *Obscuranten-Almanach* of
1798. In this publication, a double picture shocking to contemporaries could be seen on the cover pages, accompanied by an equally
provocative four-line poem (figure 40). The left side shows the Paris
storming of the Bastille, the right a picture of the state prison in Kassel. The poem, by the Viennese author Leopold Haschka, inserted in
the former picture reads:

Figure 40. The Paris storming of the Bastille as a model for the "Bastille" of Kassel. Two copperplate engravings on green-white striped ground, each 100 by 60 mm, 1798. Inside covers of Rebmann, *Obscuranten-Almanach*.

Pipe smoke, the roll of timpani and drums,
the noise of chains and whips
and the roaring of those being whipped
alone are music to this sovereign lord's ears.[271]

A comment by Georg Friedrich Rebmann on the following first page of the *Almanach* underlines the political symbolism of the images as well as the revolutionary content of the parallel depictions:

A pair of fortified monuments or slaughterhouses [are] sure signs of an impending revolution; "Prison for Dissidents," the minister of state could undersign his name at any time. . . . Here now you can see juxtaposed to its old counterpart the famous newly built Bastille located next to the bridge over the Fulda in Kassel; it looks sharp and firm all around.

German intellectuals may not have seen the storming of the Bastille as an immediate revolutionary example to be imitated, but they *celebrated* it, at least in 1790 and 1791, with an enthusiasm that was equaled only in England, if at all, outside France.

According to contemporary accounts, *memorial celebrations* on the first anniversary of the assault on the Bastille took place in Germany in Frankfurt, Göttingen, Marburg, and Leipzig. The most impressive celebration, however, was in Hamburg, where the merchant Sieveking, the poet Klopstock, and the moral philosopher and publisher Knigge turned the "Freedom Festival Honoring the French Revolution" into a festival of the enlightened Hamburg bourgeoisie. The following day, Knigge wrote in a letter to his daughter Philippine:

All just people fond of freedom living in Hamburg were invited to the event. All females were dressed in white and carried white straw hats with the national ribbon . . . , also sashes and medals of the same kind. The ladies also gave the gentlemen parts of their ribbons. When I received my little part, I took off my medal and put on this ribbon instead, which was generally applauded. We also had music; a choir of maidens who were very musically gifted sang a song composed for the occasion, and all of us repeated its chorus. We stayed together the entire day, starting at ten o'clock. The three prettiest young girls collected for the poor. *Klopstock* read two new odes. On the firing of the cannons, music and loud cheers were heard, toasts were proposed, among others, to the quick succession in Germany and the abolition of despotism. Before and after dinner, there was dancing. —It was a wonderful day, and many a tear of emotion was shed. All Americans, English, French, and Swiss who are here were invited. A certain merchant *Sieveking* had written the song that was sung.[272]

In Knigge's account, the festival in Hamburg on the first anniversary of the fall of the Bastille appears to be the realization of an imagined, thoroughly intellectual utopia of freedom, equality, and fraternity. Nothing is missing—be it charitable donations for the poor, singing and dancing, the words of a great poet (Klopstock), a staging of fair femininity (the maidens in white), or tears of emotion—from this cosmopolitan event, to which Swiss, Americans, English, and French were explicitly invited as well. The symbolic significance of 14 July was evident on an abstract and sublime level in toasts to "the quick succession in Germany" and to "the abolition of despotism" as well as in Klopstock's odes. Only the cannon fire, if anything at all, evoked the violent, brutal, popular-revolutionary side of 14 July. Actually, the siege, the almost one hundred injured and dead among the "victors of the Bastille," the attempts of the crowd to take the doors and drawbridge with rams, the evening's bloody scenes of massacre, and the triumph of the victors of the Bastille celebrated with military honors were all successfully excluded.

A completely different picture from this first anniversary in Hamburg presented itself eight years later to the spectators of the celebrations commemorating the taking of the Bastille in the Rhine metropolis of Mainz, now occupied by French soldiers. On 14 July 1798, a procession consisting of young male and female citizens, students, professors from the university, and a delegation of soldiers from the local French garrison walked through the city. The individual groups carried signs with inscriptions explaining the political and symbolic significance of 14 July to the crowd.[273] In front of the children from the primary schools, a sign was carried that read, "Children, remember that you alone enjoy the fruits of 14 July." The professors' sign, referring to 14 July 1789, said, "The synthesis of the sciences created it."

These placards were followed, before the marching regiment of the French garrison, by signs with the following inscriptions:

To the victors of the Bastille—may the fourteenth of July always remain the instructive example of the people, and the terror of tyrants.

To the spirits of those innocent people who grew pale in the Bastille.

May the people's vengeance strike down every new de Launay who would defend a new Bastille.

In the middle of the procession, there was a "colossal fasces"— a kind of bundle of rods carried by a six-horse coach—surrounded by forty young girls "who preceded with baskets of flowers and broken shackles," as the *Mainzer Zeitung* wrote, the "symbol of the united départements." The procession finally made its way to the church of Saint Peter, "which was imagined to be the Bastille." The conclusion of the festivities was formed by a dramatically staged storming of the Bastille, which the journalist of the *Mainzer Zeitung* described as follows.

> It [the church of Saint Peter] was occupied with troops; in front of the entrance there were Spanish horsemen. The besiegers advanced, there were some skirmishes; the garrison made a sortie; the besiegers fell back. The development was masterly. Marching forward and back, attacking in platoons and in columns, the cavalry intervened. Finally, the terrible *pas de charge* [rifle volley] thundered. The besieged were attacked severely from all sides. The charge of the troops was terribly beautiful. The beaten enemy retreated into the Bastille; an assault was laid on the fortress; the gates were blasted open. Gen[eral] Bastoul stormed into the Bastille, saber in hand; the garrison surrendered and the victorious tricolor flag flew from the battlements. —Now wreaths were distributed to the most commendable of the various corps that lay here. B. Cosson, Mallingre, and Lembert gave speeches; the garrison marched past one more time to wonderful music. —Nothing more beautiful can be imagined than this sight of shaking the world to its foundations.

The entire celebration—including the procession and the dramatic staging of the storming of the Bastille in front of Saint Peter's in Mainz—had lasted four hours. At noon, it was concluded with a rifle salute and the ringing of church bells, which, as the *Mainzer Zeitung* explained, "announced the point in time when the thunder of freedom sent the Bastille crashing down."[274]

The celebrations in Mainz on 14 July 1798 in many respects recall the festivities that the officials of the new département of Alpes-Maritimes had organized in memory of the attack on the Bastille in Nice five years earlier, in May 1793. Here too, we can discern a close, dramatically staged, and emotionally evoked connection between the message of freedom and military "liberation." In both ceremonies, 14 July 1789 was represented as simultaneously a product of the Enlightenment and a decisive break with despotic rule and tyranny. And in Mainz, capital of the new département of Mont-Tonnerre (Donnersberg), as in Nice, which had become French in 1792 as well, the military expansion of revolutionary France appeared to be a logical progression from the liberating deeds of 1789, just as the conquest of the west bank of the Rhine and the earldom of Nice seemed to be necessary continuations of the conquest of the Bastille on 14 July 1789. It was no coincidence that the representatives of the new political powers symbolically took on the roles of Vainqueurs de la Bastille in the dramatic reenactments of the taking of the Bastille staged in Nice and Mainz. In Nice it was the officials of the new département of Alpes-Maritimes and the "District de Nice" that played the Vainqueurs; in Mainz it was the soldiers of the French garrison, led by their commander, General Bastoul. The fourteenth of July 1798 in Mainz was a day commemorating the fall of "despotism" in France as well as the "liberation" of the west bank of the Rhine by revolutionary troops. Thus it also served to legitimate the military expansion of revolutionary France beyond its traditional borders—in a magnificent demonstration of the strength and self-confidence of the Grande Nation. Abraham Lembert, the administrative president of the new département of Mont-Tonnerre (Donnersberg), told the citizens of Mainz in his speech on 14 July 1798:

After centuries of suffering, the day of the salvation of humanity finally appeared. . . . In vain, they [the despots] had hoped the Bastille would resist; what is able to resist a people angry for their freedom? A few hours were enough to overthrow those protective walls of despotism, and the sign was given for today's rebellion against tyranny; the electric shock was delivered that communicated itself to the world's peoples from sunset to daybreak, from South to North. The nations rejoiced, and the kings were seized by terror!

Since that day, citizens, what events! what victories of freedom! what defeats of tyranny! what wonders has 14 July created!

Sublime and great are the days of the Republic's victories! Each of you inspires holy shudders, days of fame and of victorious battle![275]

Lembert concluded his speech, during which he had extended the liberty symbolism of 14 July with increasing clarity to the liberation of other nations by France, with a sharp rebuke of those who had questioned the annexation of the west bank of the Rhine by the French Republic:

So let us ignore those few voices which still wish to see a mystery in our unification with the great Republic and busy ourselves with the education of the bulk of our fellow citizens who love freedom.[276]

Hamburg 1790, Mainz 1798: the great, fundamental differences between these two celebrations of 14 July cannot be explained only by geographical distance and historical disparity. They also point to different social experiences with the France of the Revolution: here the fascination of German intellectuals with the French Revolution, there the immediate daily confrontation of the entire population with France as Grande Nation and occupational power, with its will to expand, its soldiers and bureaucrats. The disappointment of many German intellectuals with the course of the Revolution contributed to transforming the once powerful symbol of the storming of the Bastille—which had already been diluted to an abstract Enlightenment utopia in the Hamburg ceremony—into nothing more than a detached metaphor. It became a poetic metaphor for revolt, for the desire for freedom, and for the breaking of chains. Goethe used Bastille symbolism exactly in this detached and intellectual fashion in his *Farbenlehre* (Theory of colors), when he compared the Newtonian theory of color, which he believed was obsolete, to "an old castle" and announced his intention of "razing this Bastille."[277] In his novel *Der Komet* (The comet) of 1820, Jean Paul also gave Bastille symbolism a purely intellectual significance, calling for the overthrow of "Bastilles of the spirit" and seeking to begin "storming the Bastille from the inside"[278]—metaphors that announced and outlined the center of the poetic and cultural "revolution" of romanticism.

The warlike and combative 14 July that Mainz celebrated under French direction in 1798 stressed the trend toward a "militarization" of the event that could also be observed in contemporary French speeches and stagings. The celebration of the storming of the Bastille in the Rhineland, in Alsace, in the former earldom of Nice, and in the likewise annexed Savoy connected the legitimation of foreign expansion to the prerevolutionary "Grande Nation." The expansion "exported" the political and democratic freedom of 1789, but it also proclaimed the political, cultural, and sometimes linguistic forcing-into-line implied by the French idea of the nation. This other face of the "message of 14 July" became most visible in Alsace, the border country between French and German language and culture, where the French Revolution instituted a program of forced cultural and linguistic assimilation and politically justified it with the ideals, and in the terms, of 1789.[279]

"What does the fourteenth of July mean to us?" the Alsatian newspaper *Rot un Wiss,* the organ of the militant circle around René Schickele that engaged in language politics, asked in July 1976. They referred to the profound ambivalence the French national holiday had taken on since its introduction almost two hundred years earlier in the border country between France and Germany—an ambivalence in which the contradictions of Bastille symbolism emerge clearly and radically:

In Alsace, the initial exhilaration over the Revolution had soon worn off. Along with the abolition of oppressing privileges and the granting of equal rights to non-Catholic as well as Catholic citizens, the Alsatians soon experienced the other side of the Revolution. In 1793, the intolerant Jacobins won the upper hand over federally minded Girondists. This change was to restrict the rights of the Alsatians no more than the revolutionary privileges. A commissary of the National Convention even went so far as to propose that a quarter of the citizens of Alsace should be guillotined, that most should be chased off, leaving only those who had actively taken part in the Revolution. . . . If today at Quatorze Juillet celebrations we make our way to the monument for the fallen through rows of flags to the strains of the *Marseillaise* and draped with medals, it would be appropriate also to think about those things, and about the vassal's relationship we are still kept in today by the "Une et indivisible" [meaning the one and indivisible French nation] that omits the Alsatian character.[280]

APPENDIX A: SOURCES OF MEMORIAL
SPEECHES, 1789–1802

A1 Claude Fauchet. *Discours sur la Liberté Françoise, prononcé le Mercredi 5 août 1789, dans l'Eglise Paroissiale de St. Jacques et des SS. Innocens, durant une Solemnité consacrée à la mémoire des Citoyens qui sont morts à la prise de la Bastille, pour la défense de la Patrie.* Paris: Bailly, [1789].

A2 Charles Osselin. *Discours funèbre, prononcé par Me. Osselin, Président du District des Petits-Augustins, après la Messe Patriotique que l'Assemblée a fait célébrer en l'Église de Saint-Sulpice, par les R.P. Augustins, le Lundi 10 août 1789, pour le repos de l'âme des Citoyens morts en combattans pour la Patrie.* Imprimé à la réquisition et en conséquence de l'Arrêté de l'Assemblée du 12 août, et au profit des Pauvres du District. Paris: Quillau, 1789.

A3 *L'Héroïsme national, Oraison funèbre, prononcée le Mercredi 12 août 1789, dans l'Eglise des PP. de Nazareth, après le Service solemnel consacré à la mémoire des Citoyens morts glorieusement à la prise de la Bastille.* Paris: Chardon, 1789.

A4 Antoine-René-Constance Bertolio. *Discours prononcé le 20 août 1789, dans l'église de Saint-Nicolas-des-Champs, pendant la pompe funèbre que ce District a célébrée en l'honneur des victimes et des martyrs de la liberté publique.* . . . Paris: Vaiade, 1789.

A5 *La Semaine Mémorable. Discours prononcé après un Te Deum en musique, dans une Assemblée d'Artistes de tous les genres, sous le nom de SOCIÉTÉ D APOLLON.* Paris: Imprimerie de Prault, 1789.

A6 Jean-Joseph Dusaulx. *Discours prononcé dans l'Assemblée Nationale, par M. Dusaulx, l'un des commissaires du comité de la Bastille, et présenté par MM. les Volontaires de la Bastille.* N.p., n.d. (Included in a much longer version in Dusaulx, *De l'insurrection parisienne* [app., no. 45], 73–162.)

A7 Antoine-René-Constance Bertolio. *Discours prononcé dans l'église métropolitaine de Paris, le 13 juillet 1790, pendant la cérémonie du Te Deum, en action de grâce, selon le voeu de MM. les électeurs de 1789, par A.-R.-C. Bertolio, l'un des électeurs de 1789, et représentant de la commune de Paris.* Paris: Buisson, 1790.

A8 Jean-André Michel. *Discours prononcé le 14 juillet, jour de la Fédération, dans la principale église du Département de la Manche, en présence de la Garde Nationale, par J.-A. M., Licencié ès Loix de la Faculté de Paris, Vicaire épiscopal, Électeur et Président de la Société des Amis de la Constitution séante à Coutances.* Coutances: Agnès, 1791.

A9 "Discours prononcé par J.-L. [Jean-Lambert] Tallien, Fondateur et Président de la Société Fraternelle des Patriotes de l'un et l'autre sexe, séante aux Minimes, Place-Royale"/"Discours prononcé sur les Ruines de la Bastille le 14 juillet 1791, par M. [Jean-François] Letellier, auteur des Transparens qui y ont été placés le 18 juillet 1790." *Fête civique sur les Ruines de la Bastille, le 14 juillet, l'an troisième de la Liberté.* N.p., 1791. 3–16.

A10 Henri-Baptiste Grégoire. *Discours sur la Fédération du 14 juillet 1792 . . . , dont la Société des Amis de la Constitution de Blois a voté l'Impression.* Orleans, 1792. (Included in Henri-Baptiste Grégoire, *Oeuvres,* ed. Albert Soboul, 12 vols. [Nendeln and Paris: KTO Press, 1977], 211–21.)

A11 "Discours prononcé le 25 Messidor an II, dans la Convention, par l'orateur

d'une députation de la Société des Jacobins admise à la barre." *Moniteur* 297
(15 July 1794), reprinted in *Moniteur universel,* 21:212–13.

A12   Lazare-Nicolas Carnot. "Discours du président du Directoire prononcé devant ce corps le 13 thermidor an IV." *Moniteur* 313 (31 July 1796), reprinted in
Moniteur universel, 28:368–69.

A13   Jean Debry (Corps législatif, Conseil des Cinq-cents). *Motion d'Ordre sur l'anniversaire du 14 juillet.* Séance du 26 Messidor an V. Paris: Imprimerie Nationale,
an V.

A14   Jean Debry. "Discours prononcé le 27 Messidor, an V, devant le Directoire."
Moniteur 298 (16 July 1797), reprinted in *Moniteur universel,* 28:742–43.

A15   Napoléon Bonaparte. "Proclamation à l'occasion du 14 juillet." *L'Historien* 612
(25 July 1797): 84–85.

A16   "Discours du citoyen Desbarreaux, président de l'administration municipale."
*Procès-Verbal de la Fête du 14 Juillet, Célébrée dans la commune de Toulouse, le 26 Messi-
dor, an 5.* Toulouse: Besian et Tislet, 1797. 4–8.

A17   Gustave Langlois. *Discours prononcé par le citoyen Langlois, Président de l'Administration Centrale de l'Eure, à la Fête du 14 Juillet, le 26 Messidor, an VI.* Evreux: Imprimerie Ancelle, 1798.

A18   Antoine-Christophe Merlin de Thionville. "Discours du Président du Directoire, prononcé au Champ-de-Mars." *Moniteur* 299 (17 July 1798), reprinted in
Moniteur universel, 29:316.

A19   Marie-Joseph Chénier. "Discours du Président des Cinq-cents devant ce corps,
le 26 Messidor an VI." *Moniteur* 298 (16 July 1798), reprinted in *Moniteur universel,*
29:313–14.

A20   Jacob-Augustin-Antoine Moreau. "Discours du Président des Anciens prononcé devant ce corps le 26 Messidor an VI." *Moniteur* 298 (16 July 1798), reprinted in *Moniteur universel,* 29:314–15.

A21   Félix Faucon. *Discours de Félix Faucon, Député de la Vienne, sur le Quatorze Juillet.*
N.p.: Baudoin, 1798.

A22   Jean-Antoine Marbot. *Discours prononcé par Marbot (de la Corrèze), président du
Conseil des Anciens, à l'occasion de la fête du 14 juillet. Séance du 26 Messidor, an VI.*
Paris: Imprimerie Nationale, 1798.

A23   *Discours prononcé au Temple des Lois, en la Commune de Mons, par le Citoyen Volcke-
rick, Administrateur du Département de Jemappes, pour la célébration de l'anniversaire du
14 Juillet 1789.* Mons: A. J. Lelong, 1798.

A24   *Adresse aux Français sur le Quatorze Juillet.* N.p., [1800]. Bibliothèque Nationale,
Lb⁴³.100.

A25   *Corps Législatif. Conseil des Anciens. Discours prononcé par C. L. Baudin (des Ar-
dennes), Président du Conseil des Anciens, pour l'anniversaire du 14 juillet. Séance du
26 Messidor an VII (1799).* Paris: Imprimerie Nationale, an VII.

A26   *Discours prononcé à Nancy le 25 Messidor an VIII, à la célébration des Fêtes réunies de la
Concorde, et de l'Anniversaire du 14 Juillet, par le Citoyen Mongin, Professeur à l'Ecole centrale du Département de la Meurthe.* Nancy: Guivard, Imprimeur du Préfet, 1800.

A27   Lucien Bonaparte. *Discours prononcé dans le Temple de Mars, par L. Bonaparte, Mi-
nistre de l'Intérieur, le 25 Messidor an VIII, pour la Fête du 14 Juillet et de la Concorde.*
Paris: Imprimerie de la République, 1800.

A28   Gabriel Mollevaut. *Discours prononcé par Gabriel Mollevaut, Professeur à l'Ecole Centrale de la Meurthe, en présence des Autorités civiles et militaires, et des Citoyens de Nancy, assemblés pour célébrer la fête du 14 Juillet.* Nancy: Guivard, Imprimeur du Préfet, [1802].

APPENDIX B: SOURCES FOR THE SEIZURE OF THE MARSEILLE BASTILLE

B1   "Lettre de M. Doinet, Mécanicier, Sergeant de la Garde-Nationale, attaché au Bataillon du District du Manège, à M. Beaugeard, Rédacteur du Journal de Provence." *Journal de Provence* 10, no. 1 (Tuesday, 4 May 1790): XXVIII 4–7. (Excerpts reprinted in *Moniteur* 133 [13 May 1790]: IV 43 of the reprint.)

B2   *Marseille sauvée, ou Détail exact du Siège et de la Prise du fort S. Jean de cette Ville, par la Garde Nationale et le Peuple. Avec récit de la trahison de M. de Calvet, commandant de la place, qui a été pendu sur la brèche, et sa tête promenée au bout d'une pique.* Marseille: Imprimerie du Dilligent, [1790]. (Other edition, [Paris]: De l'Imprimerie de Voland, n.d.)

B3   *Marseille sauvée, ou Les trois journées à jamais mémorables. Extrait du Courrier de Marseille, No. 4.* Marseille: De l'Imprimerie de F. Brebion, Imprimeur du Roi et de la Ville, [1790]. (Other edition, N.p., n.d.)

B4   *L'Oraison funèbre du fort Saint-Nicolas.* N.p., [1790].

B5   *La Mort de la Bête à cent Têtes, ou l'Enterrement de l'Aristocratie et des Aristocrates. Le 30 Avril 1790.* N.p., [1790].

B6   *État et Recette générale des Dons faits à l'Assemblée patriotique par divers Corps Ecclésiastiques, Séculiers et Religieux, Religieuses, Députés, Syndics, Prieurs, et par divers Particuliers, pour la démolition des Citadelles et Forts.* Marseille: De l'Imprimerie de Jean Mossy, Père et Fils, [1790].

B7   Letter to the minister of the interior, Saint-Priest, concerning the razing of the Marseille fort. Neither dated nor signed. Archives Nationales F⁷ 3659, 1.

B8   *Discussion de l'Affaire de Marseille, entre MM. d'André, la Fayette, Castellanet et le Comte de Mirabeau. Extrait du Journal de Paris, No. 134.* Marseille: Chez F. Brebion, Imprimeur du Roi et de la Ville, [1790].

B9   *Discours de MM. Mirabeau, La Fayette, Castellane et Lamet, concernant la prise des Forts de Marseille.* Marseille: Imprimerie de P. Ant. Favet, Imprimeur du Roi et de la Ville, [1790].

B10   *L'Ecritoire patriotique. Requête à Desmoulins, Procureur-Général de la Lanterne.* N.p., [1790]. Archives Nationales F⁷ 3659, [1].

B11   [Article summing up the Marseille affair, giving the *Gazette de Beaucaire* as source]. *Révolutions de France et de Brabant* 25 (17 May 1790): 560–68.

B12   "Prise des citadelles de Marseille et de Montpellier." *Révolutions de France et de Brabant* 27 (31 May 1790): 17–26. (Includes the engraving *Démolition du Fort St. Jean près Marseille.*)

B13   *Délibération du Corps Municipal de la Ville de Marseille, sur un Décret de l'Assemblée Nationale, sanctionné par le Roi qui ordonne d'arrêter la démolition de la Forteresse St. Nicolas.* Marseille: J. Mossy, Père et Fils, 1790.

B14   *Adresse du Conseil-Général de la Commune de Marseille, à l'Assemblée Nationale, sur la démolition des Forts, et portant une nouvelle dénonciation du Sr. de Saint-Priest.* Marseille: Imprimerie de J. Mossy, Père et Fils, Imprimeurs de la Nation, du Roi et de la Ville, 20 May 1790.

B15   *Adresse du Conseil-Général de la Commune de Marseille au Roi.* Marseille: J. Mossy, Père et Fils, 20 May 1790.

B16   *Discours de M. Brémond-Julien, prononcé à l'Assemblée Nationale, concernant la démolition du Fort St. Nicolas; avec celui de M. le Comte de Mirabeau, qui a défendu les intérêts de Marseille, du 30 Mai 1790.* Marseille: Imprimerie P. Ant. Favet, [1790].

B17   [Speeches of the special delegates of the city of Marseille before the National Convention, ed. Brémond-Julien]. *L'Observateur Marseillais* 17 (13 June 1790): 65–68.

B18   Barthélemy-Joseph, Comte de Villeneuve-Bargemont. *Première et seconde opinions . . . au sujet des dernières dénonciations faites à l'Assemblée Nationale contre la ville de Marseille.* N.p., [1790]. Here quoted from the reprint in *Archives parlementaires,* 1st ser., 15:721–23.

B19   *Adresse à l'auguste Assemblée Nationale par les 50 Citoyens qui se sont emparés, le 30 avril, du Fort Notre-Dame de la Garde.* Marseille: F. Brebion, 2 June 1790. (Reprinted in *Révolutions de France et de Brabant* 34 [19 July 1790]: 500 and 35 [26 July 1790]: 541–48.)

B20   *Lettre de M. Mirabeau l'aîné aux braves Marseillais, en réponse à celle de la prise des trois Forts.* Marseille: F. Brebion, [1790]. (Includes *Lettre des Citoyens . . . d'Arles; Lettre . . . des Cordeliers à Paris; Lettre aux Volontaires . . . de la prise de la Bastille . . . ,* among others.

B21   "Lettre du Club des Amis des Droits de l'Homme, à la municipalité de Marseille. Réponse de la municipalité de Marseille. . . ." *L'Observateur Marseillais* 12 (5 June 1790): 47–98.

B22   Etienne Chompré. *Aux Marseillais.* Marseille: Chez F. Brebion, 28 August 1790.

B23   *Victoire glorieuse adressée aux Citoyens de Marseille sur les révolutions françaises. Discours prononcé dans l'Assemblée Patriotique par M. Blanc-Gilly, Administrateur du Département des Bouches du Rhône.* N.p., [November 1790].

B24   *Club des Cordeliers. Extrait du registre de la Société des Amis des Droits de l'Homme et du Citoyen, du 15 mai 1791.* Paris: Imprimerie de Momoro, [1791].

APPENDIX C: SELECTION OF GERMAN NEWSPAPERS AND PERIODICALS

C1   *Altonaischer Mercurius* 119 (27 July 1789)-130 (14 August 1789): 1515–1698.

C2   *Augspurgische Ordinari Post-Zeitung* 176 (24 July 1789)-186 (5 August 1789): no pagination.

C3   *Allgemeine politische Statenzeitung* (Göttingen) 16 (28 July 1789): 141–47.

C4   *Bayreuther Zeitung* 89 (27 July 1789)-107 (22 August 1789): 651–725.

C5   *Berlinische Nachrichten von Staats- und gelehrten Sachen* 89 (25 July 1789)-94 (6 August 1789): 674–706.

C6   *Königl. privilegierte Berlinische Zeitung von Staats- und gelehrten Sachen* 90 (28 July 1789)-96 (11 August 1789): no pagination.

C7   *Erlanger Real-Zeitung auf das Jahr 1789* 58 (28 July 1789)-67 (28 August 1789): 517–609.

C8   *Friedens- und Kriegs-Courier* (Nuremberg) 178 (25 July 1789)-217 (9 September 1789): no pagination.

C9   *Frankfurter Staats-Ristretto, oder kurzgefasste Erzählung der neuesten und merkwürdigsten Begebenheiten der europäischen Staaten* 115 (24 July 1789)-165 (19 October 1789): 493–720.

C10   *Hanauer Neue Europäische Zeitung* 115 (24 July 1789)-121 (3 August 1789): no pagination.

C11   *Staats- und Gelehrten Zeitung des Hamburgischen unpartheyischen Correspondenten* 118 (25 July 1789)-175 (3 September 1789): separate pagination.

C12   *Leipziger Zeitung* 144 (27 July 1789)-169 (27 August 1789): 857–971.

C13   *Mancherlei zur angenehmen und nützlichen Unterhaltung,* ed. Cleve Nicolaus Hüther, printed and published by Johann Wilhelm Müller, no. 1 (July 1789): 57–63 and no. 2 (August 1789): 110–16.

C14   *Privilegirte Mainzer Zeitung* 87 (22 July 1789)-92 (3 August 1789): no pagination.

C15   *Neueste Weltbegebenheiten von einem Weltbürger* (Kempten) 89 (27 July 1989)-92 (3 August 1789): 737–66.

C16   *Politische Gespräche der Todten* (Neuwied): 30 (25 July 1789): 258. See also "Geheimer Brief-Wechsel zwischen Lebendigen und Todten," in 29 (23 July 1789): 235–40 and supp. 7 of 24 July 1789: 25–27.

C17   *Politisches Journal* (Hamburg), issues of July and August 1789: 890–94, 904–14.

C18   *Schwäbischer Merkur* (Stuttgart) 88 (24 July 1789)-93 (5 August 1789): 295–313.

C19   *Wiener Zeitung* 60 (29 July 1789)-63 (8 August 1789): 1923–2021.

C20   *Frankfurter Kaiserliche Reichs-Ober-Post-Amts-Zeitung* (Frankfurt: Thurn und Taxis, 1789) 113 (17 July 1789): 3.

4. BASTILLE SYMBOLISM IN MODERN FRANCE

The Republican Legacy of the French Revolution

S UPERFICIALLY, IT MAY SEEM THAT NAPOLÉON'S SYSTEMATIC
attempt to suppress the political culture of the French Revolution—or redirect it toward his own person—and with it Bastille symbolism, was successful. From the Bourbon restoration under
King Charles X through the empire of Napoléon III there were
neither state commemorations of 14 July nor public Bastille celebrations. Instead, the increasingly crumbling imperatorial colossus of an
elephant stood on the Place de la Bastille. But if the more covert sec-
tors of social communication are taken into account, it becomes clear
that Bastille symbolism continued to live on subliminally. From 1815
until 1870, the Bastille once again functioned—as it had before 1789—
as a distinctive symbol and as an ideological guidepost for the domestic opposition and critics of the system, although in a more nuanced
and conscious way than before. For after the revolutionary experiences
of the storming and razing of the Bastille and after Palloy's nationwide popularization of the Bastille myth, a few allusions sufficed, and
the mere mention of the Bastille constituted a political act.

Heroic Martyrs of Freedom in History and Literature

If one first of all inquires into the general image of the Bastille in
nineteenth-century France[1] and looks for a sufficient number of similar, comparable sources in which this image can be discerned, one
encounters a series of forgotten histories of the Bastille. Since we are
interested in the history of a symbol and an ideology, we will disregard
the mere collection of facts as well as literary-critical representations[2]
in order to concentrate on a few specific texts. Almost without ex-

		Texts						
	1. Dufey 1833	2. Fougeret 1834	3. Fougeret 1840	4. Arnould 1844	5. *Histoire* 1878	6. Coeuret 1889	7. Coeuret 1889
General assessment of the B.	pp. v–xiv, 35, 135, 140, 142, 162–63, 190	vol. 1: 64–70	pp. 5, 6, 8	vol. 1: 3–12; vol. 6: 170–89, 198, 22, 245	pp. 1–2, 183–84, 249, 319, 335, 352–56	pp. 45–61	pp. 59–60
Iron mask	pp. 74–114	vol. 1: 310–33	pp. 11–15	vol. 5: 185–88	pp. 177–82		
Leprévôt de Beaumont	pp. 168–77, 328–66	vol. 2 278–304	pp. 22–30, 49–71	vol. 6: 86–107	pp. 278–94		
Latude	pp. 156–61, 367–68	pp. 108–206	pp. 15–22	vol. 5: 276–327	pp. 197–224	pp. 14–19	
Count de Lorges	pp. 140, 369–77			vol. 6: 276, 336			
Storming of the B.	pp. 369–77	vol. 2: 321–90	pp. 35–46	vol. 6: 198–333	pp. 366–96	pp. 63, 70–93	p. 61

Note: Full bibliographic documentation on these histories is given in appendix A at the end of this chapter.

Main Focuses of Content (vertical label left of rows)

Table 8. Main Thematic Focus of the Histories of the Bastille, 1833–1889

ception, they are produced by authors and publishers oriented toward the interests and tastes of a broad audience (table 8).[3] They belong to phases of French domestic politics in which the repressed revolutionary heritage broke through again, and with it its symbolism: after the July Revolution of 1830, during the Paris Commune of 1871, and on the centennial of the Revolution. These writings draw a dark and terrifying picture of the Bastille of the ancien régime.

The liberal lawyer and journalist Pierre Dufey turned to writing after three years of deportation in Paris in 1821. In 1833, he portrayed the Bastille as foreign to the French tradition of freedom, as an inquisitorial instrument of the despotic arbitrary rule of ministers influenced by Jesuits, and as a place of martyrdom for members of the Enlightenment, who were increasingly persecuted in the late eighteenth century. "How the dungeons of the Bastille were overflowing with victims! How many of them were destroyed by the excess of their sufferings or put an end to their pain by suicide!" (A1:35). Similarly, W.-A. Fougeret, a former employee of Mirabeau's, sees a "dismal monument of feudalism" in the Bastille, whose victims "shed rivers of tears" (A3: 5–6). Drawing in parts word for word on Linguet's chronicle of scandal from 1783, he describes the uniqueness of the Paris Bastille, "the tortures of the mind," "the impenetrable mystery," the "oubliettes," and the illegality that was the order of the day there (A2: vol. 1:69–70).

The monumental *Histoire de la Bastille* was directed by the drama writer Auguste Arnould, presented like a novel, illustrated with many engravings, and was also distributed by street traders in the form of affordable installments.[4] It is full of negative qualifications of this "monument which expresses despotism like no other" (A4: vol. 5: 198): "enslavement of the nation by the rulers . . . , pointless torture, arbitrary arrests instead of proper justice—that, in a few words, is the history of the old Bastille" (A4: vol. 1:12). Engravings render such notions visible by transforming the external form of the fortress into a threatening emblem (figure 41) or by showing how a prisoner with chains around his neck, hands, and feet languishes with bread and water in an underground dungeon.[5] The latter picture, which combines romantic horror and political pathos, was also widely sold by Arnould's employee Camille Leynadier in illustrated tabloids.[6]

An anonymous popular depiction of 1878 did concede a certain improvement in prison conditions in the late eighteenth century (A5:319) but was still characterized by a tone of political and romantic horror, emphatically expressed in the following opening sentences opposite an engraving of Latude's escape:

> The Bastille! That was nothing but tyranny. Its thick walls, its high towers, its stagnating dungeons that stared at passersby with their dark, small openings bore witness for the workers day by day, for centuries, to the victims buried there, to the undeserved punishments and eternal desperation, the work of despotism and the whims of rulers. The dark monument is shrouded in legendary terror. Its humid walls sweat tears; the dreadful sounds that it emitted consisted of moanings, sighs, and sobs; when in between there rose a burst of laughter, it was the laughter of madness. (A5:1–2)

Auguste Coeuret's richly illustrated anniversary publication (A6) avoided such obvious mystifications but did follow the scandalous histories of the eighteenth century, especially Linguet's. Only the ultra-Catholic Count Alphonse Couret, a contentious lawyer from Grenoble, dared to present an account from the conservative point of view at the same journalistic level. He calls Latude an "inventor of imaginary conspiracies," Linguet an "advocate excluded from the bar," and the Bastille under Louis XVI a "prison in disuse" in which

Figure 41. Louis Jean Désiré Schroeder after Dauzats, The Bastille. Steel engraving, 150 by 99 mm, in Arnould et al., *Histoire* (A4), vol. 2, before p. 1.

only a few crooks, counterfeiters, and one or two "madmen from noble houses" had been kept.

> When it fell, the Bastille had been nothing more than a bad memory for several years. No, the people, apart from infrequent exceptions, never had any reason to complain about the Bastille. . . . It was rather the authors, the writers, journalists, poetasters, and novelists, the composers of pamphlets and tabloids . . . who denounced the Bastille and exploited the unthinking and unconscious anger of the poor French people against the Bastille. (A7: 39–40)

It is characteristic of the deep social roots of the old Bastille myth that this factually correct but antirepublican critique remained isolated among the popular histories of the Bastille.

The individual histories substantially drew on the stories of suffering of prominent prisoners of the Bastille in the ancien régime from La Porte and Bucquoy to Voltaire and Cagliostro. Even the invented Count de Lorges and his supposed treatise of 1789 appeared, although Arnould admits that he searched in vain for authentic documents concerning him (table 8). In many works, Linguet's "memoirs," which along with other texts were reprinted uncritically several times,[7] served as the main evidence of existing prison conditions. But the most extensive and passionate passages—apart from Couret's oppositional text, which is silent on the matter (A7)—were devoted to three especially adventurous and compelling prisoners' stories that were suited to literary adaptation with fictive dialogues.

It is therefore no coincidence that the symbolically significant protagonists of these three stories became the "heroes" of their own historical novels. The first one is the legendary man in the iron mask, the supposed victim of a death sentence pronounced by Louis XIV himself and of the principle of secrecy of the old Bastille. The literature on the "Homme au masque de fer" includes a four-volume novel of 1804 that was immediately translated into German[8] and a dime novel of the popularizer Camille Leynadier around the middle of the century.[9] In between, there were a number of speculative attempts to uncover the mysterious identity of the masked man.[10]

The second symbolic figure of the Bastille seized by the literature of the nineteenth century was the "martyr of freedom" Latude. While Réne-Charles Guilbert de Pixérécourt, a successful vaudeville author, brought him onstage at the Paris Gaîté Theater on 15 November 1834 with music by Niccolò Piccini,[11] the popular writer Alexandre Ducourneau[12] turned the material into a dime novel. The novelist Clémence Robert took the greatest liberties, however. In a "cloak-and-dagger novel," which she "historically" supports with references, Robert describes the Paris Bastille as a "terrible colossus" and a "mass of rock."[13] The arrest of Latude and his fellow escapee Alègre proves the accusation to be true: "Coverups and darkness ruled in these arbitrary incarcerations . . . ; cowardly, banditlike despotism had its arrests executed during the night by disguised agents, because it feared the opposition of the people."[14] Exposed to the provocative sight of the clock in the inner courtyard of the Bastille,[15] helplessly at the mercy of the governor of the prison, the "Grand embastilleur,"[16] the "escape heroes" Latude and Alègre[17] are not spared the underground dungeon: "Heavy rusty chains taken from the corpses of those who had died in the dungeons and carefully kept in a separate room opened their rings and closed again around the arms and legs of the prisoners."[18] But the desired counterviolence of the people is not far away. Liberated from the *cachot* with the assistance of a guard and loving women, Latude and Alègre join the rebelling workers who are gathering at an inn in the forest of Vincennes outside the capital. Their leader is none other than the famous Linguet.

> "Well then," Linguet said and arose, "so we can soon hope to begin the attack on the ancien régime. And . . . the first breach we will cut in it will cleave the old walls of the Bastille, this most visible and tangible embodiment of despotism." "That is right," the followers called in unison. "Down with the Bastille!" [19]

The third popular Bastille martyr of the nineteenth century is Jean Claude Guillaume Leprévôt de Beaumont, who was cast in prison in 1768 for spreading seditious rumors. He was released in September 1789 from the Bicêtre prison and only after lengthy efforts gained a lifelong annuity in 1792. During the French Revolution, Latude had upstaged him. But after 1830 literature fashioned him into a patriotic pioneering champion of the suffering people who was thrown into prison by the government and the corn traders because he had exposed and denounced their shady dealings in basic foods, and the profits they were making from the impoverishment of the ordinary people. Even though the 1765 contract between Inspector General Clément Charles François L'Averdy and the miller Malisset that Leprévot unearthed actually served to regulate state stocks,[20] the Bastille literature not only appropriated this "documented" legend of the "famine plot" [21] but expanded it as well. Elie Berthet, one of the most assiduous writers of historicizing trivial literature of the time, marketed a novel on the subject, which was printed at least three times,[22] and also a drama, which premiered on 17 June 1839 in the Paris theater Porte Saint-Martin. The final act of the piece took place in the Bastille on 14 June 1789. The corn speculator Malisset flees from the hungry rebels into the Bastille, but the people, led by Leprévôt's son Jules, storm the fortress, killing the prison guards and the governor, whose secret papers lead to the liberation of the old Leprévôt from a hidden prison cell. Like a second Count de Lorges, he greets daylight with the exclamation "My life's dream has become reality! The people have bread! Praised be God, who has liberated a great nation along with me!" [23]

As in the case of Latude, literature, here too, expresses subliminal collective ideas by drawing direct personal and causal connections between the "martyrs of freedom" of the ancien régime and 14 July 1789, connections that the histories of the Bastille could not offer for reasons of historical accuracy. In other words, literature voiced the subliminal desire of the authors of these histories, superimposing on past historical facts the firm conviction of republican France that a factually based and necessary development led from the old "Bastille despotism" to 14 July.

This thesis is confirmed by other fictions that treat the historical material of the Bastille even more freely. Eugène Sue's popular family history *Les Mystères du peuple*,[24] one of the first serial novels (1842–43) and at the same time one of the most successful works of popular literature (after 1848), could not do without a victor of the Bastille: the blacksmith Jean Lebrenn. After the fall of the fortress, he leads Leprévôt de Beaumont and an old man with a long beard (the imaginary Count de Lorges) through the streets of Paris in triumph. In his victory speech, he declares the aristocratic conspiracy to be proven and cries out to the cheers of the people:

> Yes, the victory over the Bastille is without a flaw, and that is why it has such a large, such an immense importance . . . : The revolution begun in the name of the sacred rights of humankind must be completed! . . . The conquest of the Bastille also means that the people have understood that no freedom is possible as long as a fortress, the symbol of military and despotic power, threatens the disarmed city with its cannons! This great day of 14 July also represents an act of brotherliness among the people, who feel compassion for all victims of tyranny. . . . The storming of the Bastille, this sublime victory, will gloriously have immeasurable consequences; it will give our enemies a salutary fright . . . ; the French Revolution will reaffirm its immortal principle, which is summarized in the divine words: liberty, fraternity, equality![25]

It is hardly surprising that the bishop of Annecy threatened the Catholics in his diocese with excommunication if they read this anticlerical as well as revolutionary novel, or that a high court confiscated the work in 1857 and imposed harsh fines and prison sentences on its publishers.[26]

The extent to which Eugène Sue's version of the Bastille myth corresponded with the ideas of the republican-minded French can be seen in the success of the almost simultaneous serial novel *Ange Pitou* by Alexandre Dumas Père, which the newspaper *La Presse* published from 17 December 1850 to 26 June 1851.[27] Once again, the historical symbolic figures were concentrated into "collective" ideal types. The Bastille martyrs are represented by Doctor Gilbert, a gardener's assistant keen on education who studies with Cagliostro, takes part in the American Revolutionary War against England, writes antiabsolutist pamphlets, and for that reason is imprisoned in the Bastille. The entire storming of the Bastille culminates in the liberation of this spokesman of the Revolution. It is led by the eloquent proletarian Ange Pitou, an archetypal victor of the Bastille. Louis XVI impotently watches the Revolution, conscious of atoning for the crimes committed by the mistress of his predecessor against Latude.[28] More than ever, the ancien régime and Revolution, despotism and freedom appear as complementary sides of the highly charged but indissoluble symbol "Bastille."

The Storming of the Bastille: A National Act of Faith

The histories of the Bastille stress the *despotic* significance of the Bastille, as portrayed in the descriptions of 14 July 1789, rather than its significance as a symbol of freedom. What did the general image of the storming of the Bastille consist of in the nineteenth century? In order to provide a preliminary answer, as representative as possible, we have put together a textual corpus of nineteen accounts of the storming of the Bastille. This corpus is made up of schoolbooks on the history of France that were published over the course of the entire century, were successful, and represented the main domestic political tendencies of their time.[29]

With seven texts to their credit, the authors oriented toward republicanism and affirming the French Revolution form the largest group. They go from Lettelier in Napoleonic times (B1) through Duruy around the middle of the century (B9) to influential schoolbook authors in the 1880s such as the moderate Blanchot and Ducoudray (B11, B13), the anticlerical Zévort (B12), the well-known Professor Lavisse (B15), and the especially successful coauthors Augé and Petit (B18). Six textbooks by Catholic authors hostile to the Revolution make up a rather substantial opposing faction: the schoolbooks of the legitimizer Lefranc (B4) and the ultramontane Gabourd's work (B6) from the time of the July Revolution; Magin's book (B8), which was much used in the Second Empire; and the antirepublican textbooks of the Catholic school order (B10), Abbé Melin (B14), and the cleric Choublier (B17) from the late nineteenth century. Between these two irreconcilable camps, the liberal stance held its own with the histories of Saint-Ouen (B2), Bonnechose (B3), Belèze (B5), Chausolles (B7), Bertrand (B16), and Segond (B19), a Catholic who had been converted to the Republic.

None of these history books can completely conceal the importance of 14 July for world history. But *how* this epochal event is presented varies widely according to a work's political point of view. In general, a text's perspective can be determined simply by observing how much space is allotted to the storming of the Bastille. Accounts hostile to the Revolution—with one exception (B4)—spend only a few lines on it; and while some of the liberal schoolbooks treat the topic rather briefly as well (B2, B5, B16), others go into more detail (B3, B7, B19). With one exception—Blanchot's elementary book (B11)—the republican histories devote one or more pages to the Bastille. The same holds true for illustrations, which begin appearing in 1881. Conservative accounts avoid providing a picture, showing only the undamaged Bastille in one instance (B17); the liberal schoolbooks alternate between that same illustration (B16) and a picture of the attack on the Bastille (B19). The republican textbooks, by contrast, all use illustrations—two of the undamaged Bastille (B11, B15), three of the assault (B12, B13, B18), with two of them using also portraits of Mirabeau (B11) and Desmoulins (B18). So merely going into detail concerning the storming of the Bastille, and making it visually accessible in the schoolbooks, can be understood as an acknowledgment of a revolutionary tradition that the conservatives tried to repress through as much concealment as possible.

On an individual basis, the descriptions of 14 July 1789 that are given in "right" and "left" schoolbooks could hardly be any more different. The Catholic-Royalist depictions concentrate mostly on two points. First, they pronounce the storming of the Bastille illegal and superfluous. The badly advised king (B8) amassed "his own troops" (B4, B8, B14) around Paris only in order to maintain law and order. Not he, but political clubs had prepared a coup d'état, and a group of conspirators led by the Duc d'Orléans (B4) had used the concentration of royal troops and rumors of a plot to incite the population (B10). The governor of the Bastille did not commit any treason but faintheartedly "opened the gates" to the "rebels" (B4). Second, the texts denounce the rebellious "mob from the suburbs" (B4), the "crimes of the bloodthirsty crowd" (B14), and the "horrible massacre" (B6, B10) of de Launay and Flesselles, with which the mob "besmirched" and "dishonored" (B6, B17) its victory.

The liberal and republican depictions are quite different from this one, and so similar to each other that they can be discussed together here. They take the people's anxieties concerning a conspiracy before 14 July seriously (B1), mention the "hostile attitude of the court" toward the National Assembly (B3, B15), report the plan of an attack on Paris (B17) and other "violent plans" (B9; see also B11), describe the threatening cannons of the Bastille (B7, B12), and stress that the numerous royal regiments surrounding Paris consisted mainly of foreigners, especially Germans (B9, B12, B13). They also emphasize the mobilizing effect of the old horrible image of the Bastille, that "so often cursed dark castle" (B9) "which recalled all the perversions of despotism" (B12; see also B13), "the symbol . . . of despotism, arbitrary rule, and arrest warrants" (B18; see also B7). Thus provoked, and entreated by Camille Desmoulins at the Palais-Royal (B9, B13, B18, B19), "the people" arise in just rebellion. As a matter of course, the battle cry "To the Bastille!" becomes the "cry of the entire population" (B3; see also B9, B18), which overruns the Bastille "like a raging sea" (B13). In the attack, Vainqueurs such as Elie and Hulin distinguish themselves (B9, B12). The acts of revenge against de Launay and Flesselles are certainly regrettable, but they are presented as the bloody deeds of "bandits," as the acts of a "mob" that the victors of the Bastille are no longer able to keep under control (B12, B13) and after which "everything returns to order" (B1). Even though the liberation of the prisoners of the Bastille is seldom mentioned, the legendary Count de Lorges does make one appearance (B18). Finally, the summary assessment appears in the guise of the famous, but not documented, exchange between Louis XVI and the Duc de La Rochefoucauld-Liancourt that is said to have occurred when this gentleman brought the news of the storming of the Bastille to the king late in the evening of 14 July: " 'This is a rebellion,' the king says. 'No, sire, this is a revolution,' the great citizen answers" (B3; see also B11, B12, B19)—a legitimizing quotation repressed by all of the textbooks hostile to the Revolution. That it only appears in schoolbooks after 1834 will soon be explained.

As the analysis of schoolbooks shows, the Bastille myth was handed down to an entire generation of students at primary and secondary schools in remarkable breadth and unity, first in latent opposition to monarchist governments, then—after 1871—more openly in ideological accord with the young Third Republic. If the descriptions of 14 July 1789 given in schoolbooks are compared to those given in the histories of the Bastille examined above (table 8), it can be seen that the republican and liberal textbooks to a large extent repeat the discourse of the popular histories, if only in a much-simplified version. Except for Dufey, who in 1833 repeats the fictive account of the alleged Count de Lorges, and the conservative Couret, who in 1889 openly spurns recounting the "unnecessary capitulation of the Bastille,"[30] all our histories of the Bastille extensively relate 14 July, and do it in the tradition of the revolutionaries of 1789–90. The Arnouldian compilation of 1844 goes even further by interpreting the old frightening vision of the Bastille as the actual motive for the attack with new absoluteness:

> For the people . . . had understood the double tyranny of the Bastille as state prison and as fortress. They had been told of the sufferings of the prisoners, of their enslavement and their tortures, and those tortures were also recalled in this moment [before the storming of the Bastille]. They had been told the story of the kings and the great with their cruelty, their whims, their miserliness, and their arbitrariness, which found their outlet in this prison. These high towers from which rifles and cannons could be fired to shoot down houses and humans and set the city on fire were shown to the people. —Towers that alone would rise over a sea of ruins and slaves. The people were told that the storming of the Bastille would not only conquer a fortress and a state prison but also secure a principle . . . , the principle of freedom. And now they were shown the grave of freedom behind the walls of the Bastille.[31]

This heroic stylization and mystification of the storming of the Bastille was not, however, restricted to the historiographically lowly spheres of schoolbooks and popular nonfiction. It was also repeated at the more demanding level of the "critical" histories of the Revolution written by Adolphe Thiers (1823–27) and Louis Blanc (1847–62), and mirrored by Hippolyte Taine's conservative account (1875–93). Another example of such stylization is Jules Michelet's *Histoire de la Révolution* (1847–53), probably the most famous and for a long time the most widely read history of the Revolution of all. Michelet wrote his thirteenth chapter, which is devoted to the storming of the Bastille, under the influence of republican opposition to the July Monarchy (which temporarily cost him his professorship), the death of his father (a sansculottic witness to the Revolution), and Bastille journalism from Linguet's *Memoirs* to *La Bastille dévoilée,* which he quotes in his notes.[32] Even though in the description of events he admits that "the Bastille was not taken; it surrendered," that its governor had "lost his senses and could give no orders,"[33] he nevertheless entitles the chapter "Storming of the Bastille" and interprets 14 July according to the republican-nationalist "myth." The goal of 14 July 1789 is predetermined; it is introduced almost biblically as a quasi-divine mission:

> With daylight, one idea dawned upon Paris, and all were illumined with the same ray of hope. A light broke upon every mind, and the same voice thrilled through every heart: "Go! and thou shalt take the Bastille!" . . . The attack on the Bastille was by no means reasonable. It was an act of faith.[34]

The recipient of the charge and the executor of the religious act is not, however, a prophet, not a divinely gifted individual, but the people ("le peuple"), a political community of faith following the example of Madame Legros, who stood up for the martyr of freedom Latude, in a way not unlike what Eugène Sue had described five years earlier:

> What was the Bastille to them? The lower orders seldom or never entered it. Justice spoke to them, and, a voice that speaks still louder to the heart, the voice of humanity and mercy; that still small voice which seems so weak but that overthrows towers, had, for ten years, been shaking the very foundations of the doomed Bastille.[35]

Michelet identifies the actual motive for the crowd's march to the Bastille only after this introduction. Of course, it consists of the well-known terrifying image, which once again is taken for historical truth:

> There were many other prisons, but this one was the abode of capricious arbitrariness, wanton despotism, and ecclesiastical and bureaucratic inquisition. The court, so devoid of religion in that age, had made the Bastille a dungeon for free minds,—the prison of thought. Less crowded during the reign of Louis XVI, it had become more cruel. . . . The Bastille was known and de-

tested by the whole world. Bastille and tyranny were, in every language, synonymous terms. Every nation, at the news of its destruction, believed it had recovered its liberty.[36]

Michelet's subsequent description follows the accounts of the conquerors of the Bastille of 1789, describes the courtyard of the Bastille as a "monstrous well," and repeats the thesis of de Launay's treason, calling him "that greedy, sordid soul" and an "infamous and barbarous" henchman.[37] Like the republican schoolbooks, it neutralizes the crowd's violent execution of de Launay and Flesselles by portraying the killings as the momentary bursts of passion of the angry masses ("la multitude"), which even the herculean victor of the Bastille Hulin was unable to control. Michelet also gives the episode a conciliatory ending by describing how the victors succeeded in obtaining an amnesty for the imprisoned invalides, how the French Guards returned to their barracks, and how the patriotic donations for the victims of 14 July were distributed. Thus idealistically sanitized and limited in its violence, the storming of the Bastille attains an almost religious consecration. Michelet achieves this effect not only through his writerly artistry and eloquence but also through the use of popular myths surrounding the Revolution, which he makes the guideline for his interpretation. Thus Bastille symbolism fashions the representation of historical "reality," and in turn receives the consecration of "critical" history.

How close historiography came to literature, which is generally more open to myths—especially in Michelet's case—can be seen in comparisons not only with the above-mentioned writings of Eugène Sue and Alexandre Dumas but also with a drama by Louis Combet that premiered on 30 June 1886 in Lyon.[38] Both scenes of this drama are set in 1789 in one of the underground dungeons of the Bastille called oubliettes; humidity is running down the walls, and the thunder of cannons as well as the faraway sounds of *Ça ira* and the *Marseillaise,* the most popular revolutionary songs of 1790 and 1792, can occasionally be heard. The first scene consists of the monologue of an anonymous prisoner chained to the wall since 1743. A despot and "royal Minotaur" had had him thrown into this "grave" in order to satisfy his lust with the victim's fiancée, and to silence the man's protests concerning the judicial murder of his father.[39] As the prisoner cries for "justice and freedom" in the last throes of desperation, the flaming inscription

"14 July 1789!!!" appears on the dark wall of the dungeon. At the same time, the figure of "Liberté," armed with a sword, enters the vault to the thunder of cannons and opens the second scene. It is explained that she is completing the work of the Enlightenment figures Rousseau, Diderot, and Voltaire by asking the "martyr"—a second Lazarus—to rise, touching him with the sword and speaking the words "Away with the past!" The chains burst all at once, and the aged prisoner with his long beard is transformed into a youthful hero who enthusiastically greets the beginning of the new era of virtue, humanity, and freedom that is dawning after fourteen centuries of slavery. And to the strains of the *Marseillaise,* the crowd of conquerors of the Bastille in the background strikes up the final cry of victory, "Long live freedom!"

Without equaling Michelet's dramatic art, Combet's piece works with similar pathos and similar borrowings from biblical images and formulas. Like Michelet, only more unabashedly, it paints ideal scenes in which historical phenomena from different contexts are combined to form a condensed artistic picture. In both cases, the myth of Bastille despotism practiced by the ancien régime gives 14 July legitimacy and luster. Against this background, the attack on the Bastille becomes a political resurrection, the beginning of a liberal history of salvation—in a process more explicit and conscious than what was experienced by the revolutionaries of 1789.

Michelet and Combet were no exceptions. Their poetic transfiguration of the storming of the Bastille was continued by Romain Rolland's drama *Le 14 Juillet,* the opening piece of an "Iliad" about the Revolution conceived to have ten parts and with which the young author wanted to found a French "popular theater." [40] After 21 March 1902, the drama was initially performed twenty-nine times at the Renaissance-Gémier theater in Paris, with conspicuous crowd scenes, and was much noticed by the republican and socialist press. [41] In fact, the "people"—in Michelet's sense—represented by an unusually large number of actors (thirty-five), were the collective hero of the drama. The characters consisted of anonymous archetypes—the worker, the craftsman, the citizen, and the student—all of whom are under the spell of an impending conspiracy, along with the figures of the actual conquerors of the Bastille Hoche and Hulin as well as the spokesmen Marat and Camille Desmoulins, that is, "friends of the people" who did not actually participate in the attack. As this group represents the energy and the new political consciousness of the "peuple," the nine-year-old Julie, daughter of a washerwoman from the Rue Saint-Antoine, represents its human sensitivity. The Bastille, which towers as a threatening silhouette in the background, is present throughout the entire action as "a cancer" in the body of the workers' district Saint-Antoine, a "great bulk . . . engulfed in the black night" that "catches in [the] throat" of anyone who sees it.[42] The actual stimulus for its storming comes, however, not from the popular speaker Desmoulins but from Julie, who from the window of her apartment, full of compassion, has watched the nocturnal conveyance of prisoners to the Bastille. When Marat on 14 July 1789 half-jokingly asks her what she wants, she demands "Liberty" for "the poor people who are in prison" and points down the Rue Saint-Antoine to "the big prison."[43] Julie says the same thing to Hoche and Hulin. As soon as the people hear the slogan, the old terrifying image of the Bastille reveals its entire range of meaning and its mobilizing power. This image breaks forth in the crowd's obsessive screams:

> The Bastille! The Bastille! Break the yoke! At last! Down with that stupid mass! Monument of our defeat and degradation! The tomb of those who dare speak the truth! —Voltaire's prison! —Mirabeau's prison! —The prison of Liberty! Let's breathe! —Monster, you will fall! We'll pull down every stone of you! Down with the murderer! Coward! —Cut-throat![44]

Driven by this collective memory, the crowd conquers the Bastille in no time at all. The execution of de Launay is neither staged nor mentioned. Instead, Julie, who has taken part in the assault riding on Hulin's shoulders, becomes the hero of the day. She obtains amnesty for the imprisoned invalides and in the festive final scene set in the inner courtyard of the conquered fortress appears as a young goddess of freedom. With a girl from the people who personifies the Bastille myth and celebrates its storming as a humane, unbloody act—the republican interpretation of 14 July could hardly have been staged more sublimely. And as Rolland wrote to Firmin Gémier, the drama's director, in 1902, he manipulated historical materials quite consciously:

> I know the history. I make use of it and try to convey a true impression of the great dramatic events that actually happened. But I have not slavishly subjected myself to the constraints of truth. I am less interested in a sterile reconstruction of the past than in

bringing out in past events what corresponds with our present-day issues and battles.[45]

Instead of a history of events, Romain Rolland offers the history of a symbol, one influenced by a myriad of associations—just as the other poetic versions of the Bastille's storming we have mentioned have been.

Utilizations in Domestic Politics:
From the July Revolution to the Resistance

The Bastille, reinterpreted as a symbol of political freedom and national identity during the French Revolution, did not live on only in the collective consciousness of the French expressed by historiographers and poets. In the nineteenth century and beyond, it also served as a powerful instrument for shaping public opinion and argument in the realm of domestic politics. In the early years it was used mostly as a weapon of the republican movement; then—beginning in the 1880s—it became more and more an almost magical way to appeal to the unanimity and enthusiasm of the French citizenry. Pushed aside by Napoléon and the Bourbons returning in 1815, Bastille symbolism initially remained present in the political underground. In 1829, for instance, the popular protest singer Pierre-Jean de Béranger, who was held at the La Force state prison, on the anniversary of 14 Juillet composed a song of the same name in which he complained about being imprisoned as an "Apostle of Freedom" forty years after 1789. But the memory of his—imagined—youth comforts him and fills him with hope for the present as well:

> I was very young; people cried, "Revenge! / To the Bastille! to arms! quickly, to arms!" / Shopkeepers, citizens / Craftsmen— they all raced off. / . . . Victory to the people! They have conquered the Bastille! / A bright sun glorified this great day.[46]

And indeed, a year later the July Revolution led to the abdication of the last Bourbon king and the founding of a constitutional monarchy under the Citizen King Louis-Philippe. This revolution, and especially the fights that were waged from 27 to 29 July 1830 on the Paris barricades between workers and citizens on the one side and royal troops on the other, was widely interpreted as a new storming of the Bastille. A certain Pierre Colan, for instance, who signed himself "Patriote de '89," praised the people's soldiers of 1830 as the heirs of the victors of the Bastille: "Their sons wished to die for freedom or win; so that their arms could not again be placed in chains, they went to war once more."[47] An anonymous pamphlet begins with an emblematic title woodcut of the attack on the Bastille and then goes on to draw a parallel between the "glorious" days of July 1830 and 14 July 1789 — taking up the metaphor of the sun in the process:

> Greetings, 14 July! Greetings to you, beautiful day, dawn of freedom; . . . may your hot sun light again in our hearts the fire that the despotism of a family outlawed by our fathers tried to extinguish in vain. This day on which an insecure government is about to be displaced is unforgettable because of the conquest of the Bastille and the national festival of an entire free people. Patriots, the July sun still shines over the children of freedom.[48]

The same image is used in a victory poem by Casimir Delavigne,[49] and as early as 31 August 1830 the Paris Théâtre du Cirque Olympique produced a hurriedly rehearsed drama on the storming of the Bastille. In this piece, Mirabeau calls for a fight on the barricades against the impending coup ("Block your streets, unpave them!"), a citizen declares resistance to be an obligation ("Resistance is a duty!"), and La Fayette congratulates the rebels on the conquest of the Bastille: "Citizens, you have overthrown the bulwark of tyranny."[50] Actually, La Fayette, the commander of the National Guard in 1789, was still politically active in 1830; though no longer a member of the military, he was still a leader of the opposition against Charles X. By establishing a symbolic and personal link between the July Revolution and the taking of the Bastille, the opposition gained additional legitimacy and a historical consecration.

The citizens' monarchy also had to pay its dues to this image, even though it was not comfortable with the revolution to which it owed its existence. On 30 August 1830, it took on the legal obligation to build a monument for those who died in the July Revolution. Immediately, one A.-S.-M. Bonneville, a member of the National Guard from Faubourg Saint-Antoine, presented a design for this monument to Louis-Philippe in an audience on 7 September. Bonneville thought the monument belonged nowhere else but on the still-vacant site of the former Bastille, "in the place where the hated towers stood," and spoke of "this Bastille which for too long hid the crimes of tyranny behind its walls until those walls finally collapsed under the outrage of the people, who had become conscious of their rights. . . . This former breeding ground of destroyed despotism must become a pleasant place in victorious freedom."[51] Bonneville did not suggest a funeral monument but a victory pillar, an "Obélisque National" with an enormous inscription drawing a parallel between 14 July 1789 and 27–29 July 1830 as the first and second epochs of freedom, along with two bas-reliefs, one showing the storming of the Bastille, the other the storming of city hall in 1830.[52]

For the time being, neither monarch nor parliament took up these suggestions. In 1831, however, on the official anniversary of the July Revolution and on the occasion of laying the foundation for a later column, a quite similar monument was erected on the Place de la Bastille and represented in popular pamphlets (figure 42). One illustrated paper depicts Pierre Colan singing about "seventeen eighty-nine" as the "model for eighteen thirty."[53] But the eventual July Column, which was set up in the same place and finally dedicated on 28 July 1840, avoided such parallels with revolutionary history. The genius of freedom topping it holds a torch in her right hand and broken links of a chain in her left, without explicitly taking up the earlier designs for Bastille monuments.[54] Nevertheless, the symbolic connection between the July Column and the Bastille was present in the social consciousness, as a jubilee poem by Théophile Gautier clearly indicates when it interprets the monument as a new "Panthéon" on the "sacred ground" of 14 July.[55]

The Bastille symbolism reemerging from the underground in 1830 put pressure on the politicians of the July Monarchy to legitimize themselves. The extent of this pressure can be seen in the parliamentary debate over the request of the surviving conquerors of the Bastille to finally receive a state pension—which they had been promised for a long time—as compensation for their service on 14 July 1789. This debate went on with interruptions from October 1831 until April 1833. The reactionary representatives strongly rejected the proposition, because "the crimes" of the Revolution had begun on 14 July 1789,[56] because "the principle of disorder" had invaded French history with the attack on the Bastille, and because no "revolt against the constitution and the laws" could be officially sanctioned.[57] The majority, by contrast, followed the opinion of the minister of the interior, Apollinaire

Figure 42. Provisional monument for the victims of the July Revolution on the Place de la Bastille. Etching, 238 by 161 mm, published by Dopter, Paris, 1831 (Bibliothèque Nationale, Estampes, Qb1, M 111803).

Maurice Antoine Argout, that the storming of the Bastille and the revolution of 1789 could not be "taken to court,"[58] since "the revolution of 1830 was indissolubly connected with the revolution of 1789,"[59] and since "the July Revolution could not refuse the revolution of 1789 a sign of sympathy."[60] In this context, the Duc de La Rochefoucauld-Liancourt's famous exchange with the king was recalled—an exchange not confirmed in the immediate sources on the storming of the Bastille but instantly recorded in schoolbooks. La Fayette was the first to refer to it,[61] followed by Count Pentécoulant;[62] then Gaëtan de La Rochefoucauld looked it up in his father's handwritten diary and on 22 April 1833 quoted the "authentic" version in parliament: "'What a revolt!' he also said. I answered him, 'O sire, say revolution!'"[63] Achieving exactly the opposite of what he had intended, the conservative son of La Rochefoucauld-Liancourt thus made it clear to the still-hesitant representatives that they had to acknowledge the storming of the Bastille for their own legitimation. As a "tribute from the revolution of 1830 to the revolution of 1789,"[64] they therefore passed a bill awarding an annual pension of 250 francs to the surviving 401 Vainqueurs de la Bastille—more a symbolic act than an adequate social support.

While the July Monarchy thus obtained historical and political legitimacy from its concessions to supporters of the liberal-revolutionary agenda, the reactualization of the terrifying image put domestic pressure on it at the same time. For the obstinate plans of the government to establish a belt of fortresses around the capital were opposed in the liberal press, and in early underground socialist journalism, with the accusation that Paris was to be encircled by "Bastilles." Whether these plans actually took up Bourbon projects to prevent popular rebellions[65] or were motivated by real fear of war, they provoked a fierce public discussion of the "embastillement de Paris."[66] A central committee of the "patriotic press" appealed to the suburbs against this first attempt by the government to increase the number of fortresses surrounding Paris to fourteen: This "vaste plan d'embastillement" was not only a "slaughter of liberty" (liberticide) but also part of an effort to impose entrance taxes on basic foods for the workers of the suburbs.[67] The liberal newspaper the *National* added that the planned "fourteen Bastilles" were also intended to prevent the fraternization of soldiers and citizens. In general, they were a body foreign to "the politically most important city in the world . . . , the capital of the revolutionary principle and of national sovereignty."[68] Such disparagements, supported by the well-known negative image of the Bastille, contributed to the government's decision to drop the proposal for the time being.

But seven years later, the monarchy resuscitated its plan, now envisaging seventeen to twenty fortresses connected by a wall. The proposal gave rise to an entire "war" of pamphlets; in the public sphere a few champions [69] supported it, but critics outnumbered them by far.[70] Liberal authors and military specialists called a fortification of the Paris conurbation against possible German invaders hopeless; therefore, the planned fortresses could be directed only at the "enemy within" and hence served the function of "Bastilles."[71] The former editor-in-chief of the newspaper *Intelligence* called the minister of the interior who was running the project, Louis Adolphe Thiers, a "modern Richelieu." He accused Thiers of falling back on the time-honored instrument of "tyranny" against "this cursed people" and, if he had a chance, of wanting to cover all of France with a net of Bastilles: "Our fathers destroy them, and we rebuild them; that is logic and progress!"[72] A poem about 14 July used the memory of the storming of the Bastille as a means of opposing the planned fortifications by repeating the appeal "A bas les bastilles!"[73] (Down with the Bastilles!) eight times. A communist group warned that "a tyrannical faction" was using "the twenty Bastilles" to reestablish "hated despotism,"[74] and in 1841 formed a "Société de la Bastille"[75] consisting of forty-odd battle-ready workers.

The planned "Bastilles" were probably criticized most violently by the early communist Etienne Cabet on his return from exile in England. He entitled the second of his *Lettres sur la crise actuelle* "No Bastilles!" since they "would be the ruin of Paris, of freedom and independence." In 1830, he claimed, the new regime had pretended to be close to the people, had let them sing the *Marseillaise,* had called the workers "comrades," and had insisted it "never would need Bastilles"; but now it was linking its continued existence to exactly such Bastilles, which it disguised as "fortifications." These bastions could serve to isolate the government from the people and to bombard and starve the capital. If Louis XVI had had such an instrument of power at his disposal in 1789, the entire French Revolution would have been impossible. And now?

Paris encircled by Bastilles! What an idea! Never mind that the conquest of the Bastille in '89 was the reason for the Revolution, for the overthrow of the aristocracy and despotism. Without 14 July . . . citizens and the people would still groan under the burden of the entire ancien régime, of feudalism, of the court, of clerics, of the privileged, of monopolies, of the most humiliating servitude: all cities that had Bastilles (Marseille, Toulon, Montpellier, Valence, etc.) followed the example of Paris; the storming of the Bastille was celebrated by the entire nation, by all nations, by all following generations; it is our fathers' glory, it is France's glory.[76]

From the perspective of the revolutionary tradition of the symbol, this plan of fortresses certainly did seem like treason against the legitimizing foundation of the July Monarchy. Going even further, Cabet had Minister of the Interior Thiers voice an almost Machiavellian plan in a fictive dialogue with a prisoner: "Now I have to solve the great problem of the Bastille. . . . What a plan! It will be more than a construction, it will be the construction of absolute monarchy in France, in Europe, in the world. . . . These Bastilles will decide all questions, they will dictate all laws."[77]

But this time, the appeal of the symbol "Bastille" was not strong enough to prevent the representatives from finally approving the project of building the fortresses in April 1841.[78] Though the forts, which were built or remodeled for 140 million francs, did not prove to be Bastilles, they did turn out to be the most expensive bad investments made by the French state in the nineteenth century. They did not have any recognizable military effect either in 1848 or in 1870–71, and were razed between 1920 and 1924.

Nonetheless, the Bastille achieved its long-term effect on domestic politics not as a terrifying image of impending dictatorship but rather as a symbol of freedom in the tradition of the Revolution of 1789. After all, it was the most popular and significant emotional sign for the self-identification of the republican movement, and its gathering point. This fact remained hidden for a long time, expressing itself only in more or less secret anniversary celebrations of 14 July, for instance, in the "proletarian and democratic banquet" with 120 participants in Rouen on which Cabet's underground newspaper *Journal du Peuple* reported on 19 and 26 July 1840.[79] Even during the Paris revolution of 1848, which ended Louis-Philippe's reign, Bastille symbolism was reactivated incidentally when the rebels marched to the July Column on 24 February to burn the throne there, and when the temporary government solemnly proclaimed the republic three days later in the same significant location.[80]

The reference to 14 July did not become a fixed component of public political discourse until after the fall of Napoléon III, when monarchists, upper-middle-class notables, and republicans entered into free competition for the majority in the new National Assembly. Especially the radical republican Léon Gambetta based most of his systematic work at the grass roots in the provinces and his fiery campaigns of the 1870s on Bastille symbolism. On 14 July 1872, for instance, Gambetta organized a festive banquet framed by tricolors and revolutionary songs in the small town of La Ferté-sous-Jouarre in the département of Seine-et-Marne. On this occasion, he gave a sensational speech in front of one thousand eight hundred guests and then published it in his newspaper, the *Républicain,* as well as on posters and in cheap brochures. In this speech, he invoked the "moral, social, and political unity" of France on 14 July 1789 and the enthusiasm over the storming of the Bastille at the time: "Wherever there were magnanimous souls, tears of joy were shed when it was learned that the Bastille had been taken, and that none less than the people of Paris had destroyed this fortress of tyranny, this dark and threatening symbol of the moral and physical oppression of the French." And he called on the republicans to draw together around the maligned message of freedom of 1789: "The fourteenth of July was the Revolution that emancipated everyone."[81]

While conservatives had watched legends form around the attack on the Bastille in 1789 almost without uttering a word, they now launched a journalistic counteroffensive. Newspaper supplements called the victors of the Bastille, "of whom Gambetta speaks with admiration," "a group of murderers"[82] and gleefully described the bloody scene of de Launay's decapitation.[83] The historian and popularizer Marius Sepet specially published a series of paperbacks called *Brochures populaires sur la Révolution française* (thirty-six pages per issue at a price of twenty centimes) in order to counteract the formation of myths.[84] The first issue was devoted to the "legend" of the storming of the Bastille and "exposed" it as the "first day of the Terror."[85] But the idealistic image of 14 July, consolidated by schoolbooks and popular histories of the Bastille, could not be demystified by these later attempts—especially since at the same time those attempts were opposed by republican responses expressly supporting interpretations such as Gambetta's and claiming that the contemporary joy over the fall of the Bastille proved in and of itself that it had been necessary, legal, and glorious.[86]

The celebrations for the hundredth anniversary of Rousseau's death were consciously scheduled for 14 July so that the republicans could gather under the sign of the Bastille. In the Myers arena, in front of six thousand guests, among them many politicians and intellectuals, Deputy Jacques Hilaire Théophile Marcou gave an emphatic speech celebrating Rousseau as the spiritual father of the storming of the Bastille:[87]

> How can we celebrate this destroyer of monarchy, this demolisher of all servitude, this theoretician of democracy better than with the cannon thunder of the Bastille and the cheers of the four hundred thousand confederates on the Champ de Mars who swore unity, protection, and brotherhood to each other? Let me express this desire: I wish Rousseau's statue would be set up on the July Column arising above the ruins of the Bastille. The Bastille, this symbol of the tyranny of kings, this quintessence of the cruelties of the ancien régime! Its name arouses the most hateful memories and sends a cold shudder of terror down one's spine; but immediately our courage arises again full of pride, and we remember the heroism of the victors of the Bastille, who triumphed over this monument of barbarism, this monstrous prison where the victims of royal whims, princely vengeance, or the hate of their favorites and mistresses languished as if in their grave.

And the orator invoked all the well-known stories of scandal, including Latude's, in order to derive the attack of the "people" from them—as had Sue and Michelet:

> In the night of 13 to 14 [July] [1789], they had a frightening vision and inspiration. The past appeared and showed them the victims of tyranny; their moaning penetrated the centuries and stirred the people to the core. They looked deep into this hell of the Bastille and, shuddering, swore to avenge the former generations and save the following generations. They considered themselves the executors of these martyrs' testaments. The very next morn-

ing, they arose with the firm resolution of conquering the Bastille and, if necessary, dying in the process.

At the following banquet, attended by eight hundred participants, Clovis Hugues recited his poem *Rousseau et la Bastille,* in which he praised the members of the Enlightenment as the true "démolisseurs" of the Bastille. Such July rallies were simultaneously symptoms and means of the republican movement, which was growing stronger. In 1879, Jules Grévy beat the monarchist Marshal Mac-Mahon to become the first certified republican state president of the Third Republic.

Consequently, the Bastille was now transformed from an opposition symbol to an emblem of the state, and 14 July from a subversive day of commemoration to a national holiday.[88] The corresponding bill was brought into the Chamber of Deputies by sixty-four representatives led by the democrat Benjamin Raspail on 21 May 1880, captured a clear majority of parliament, and was officially introduced on 6 July. In the decisive session of the Chamber of Deputies on 8 June, the radical representative Antoine Achard justified the proposal on behalf of the relevant committee with reference to the double memorability of 14 July:

> The holiday will commemorate the storming of the Bastille of 14 July 1789 and at the same time the Festival of the Federation of 14 July 1790. The storming of the Bastille was the glorious prelude and the first act of the Revolution; it brought the old world to an end and opened a new world. . . . The Festival of the Federation created the modern world [and] founded the indestructible basis of the unity of the fatherland. (On the left side: Very good, very good!) —The people . . . have always celebrated 14 July more than any other memorial day; it is their festival, because it was the festival of freedom and the fatherland. —So in a certain sense, we suggest it as a confirmation of a popular festival.[89]

So the violent character, as it were, of the storming of the Bastille was covered over by the ideal image of the national celebration of its first anniversary. Hence, 14 July was also commemorated enthusiastically in 1880 with decorative garlands and tricolors, a military parade, and dances of light in the evening. "What we are celebrating today," the radical representative Camille Pelletan said in Paris, "is the resurrection of France, the human miracle of the storming of the Bastille,

Figure 43. 14 July 1880–14 July 1789. Color lithography, 160 by 200 mm, published by H. Laas, Paris, 1880 (Bibliothèque Nationale, Estampes, Qb1, M 120653).

which is like a festival. On 14 July, France rose from the monarchist grave, and the walls of the royal castle fell like the walls of Jericho."[90] Souvenir broadsheets that were sold in the streets for a few centimes represented the same idea in depicting the parade in honor of the incipient "Republic," the soldierly oath of allegiance to the "Republic," the fraternization of the rebellious citizens and soldiers, or the scattering of the upper middle class before the advance of the victorious "Republic"—all of this against the background of the Bastille.[91] Another broadsheet (figure 43) again shows, on one side—under the sign of the fallen crown and the Bourbon lilies—torturers and martyrs in the dungeons of the Bastilles, and above them the prison's fall. On the other side—under the guardianship of a Mary-like hovering "Republic"—the July Column is presented as a symbol of a new time of political progress and economic and social prosperity. This pictorial diptych thus succinctly depicts the Bastille's double legacy and the perception of 14 July 1789 as an epochal break.

The July celebrations of 1880 opened a decade of veritable *Kultur-kampf* over the significance of 14 July, one that ended in favor of the republicans with the celebrations of the centennial of the French Revolution held on 14 July 1889. The Catholic and monarchist areas of France resisted having a date forced on them as a national holiday that for conservatives symbolized all the terrors of the French Revolution:

> The fourteenth of July 1789 in itself and in its consequences was a day of disorder, of rebellion and mass drunkenness, a day of vileness and lies, a day of broken oaths, a day of military disobedience, desertion, and treason, a day of plundering, bestial barbarity, and cannibalism. . . . In short, it signified the amnesty of all crimes and the actual beginning of a revolutionary epoch that was correctly called the Terror.[92]

Conservatives tried to ridicule the Bastille myth.[93] Parts of the country, especially large segments of the population in midwestern France in the area of the former Vendée, secretly or openly boycotted the July celebrations. In some places, the magistrates refused the necessary funds to hold public festivities, a handful of civil servants and some teachers and proprietors celebrated privately, the public celebrations were postponed until the following Sunday and priests loudly denounced the "massacres" of the Revolution from the pulpits.[94] In Angers on 16 July a government commissioner confiscated eighty copies of a poster[95] that recombined revolutionary images to create a counterrevolutionary indictment of the national holiday (figure 44). "The Republic" appears as a murdering and fire-setting Fury, trampling the insignia of all traditional royal, church, and religious authority and, as the background shows, leaving guillotines and pillaged churches behind.

But such gloominess could neither enduringly cloud the ideal image of 14 July, which was deeply anchored in the collective consciousness, nor diminish the growing popularity of the national holiday.[96] For one thing, this day gave socialists the opportunity to get their supporters together, win young activists, and mobilize their followers. Emile Digeon, for example, deduced the lesson from the storming of the Bastille that the "people" should take matters into their own hands, should not let themselves be disarmed by the "bourgeoisie," and should tear down new Bastilles.[97] Jean Bernard Passerieu pro-

ANNIVERSAIRE DU 14 JUILLET

LA PRISE DE LA BASTILLE

a été le premier acte de la Révolution, et son anniversaire
a été choisi pour devenir la fête de la République. — L'image
ci-dessous contemporaine de la première République, donne
en traits frappants une idée de notre histoire à cette époque.

LA RÉPUBLIQUE

d'après une gravure conservée à la Bibliothèque Nationale

La torche d'une main, le poignard de l'aute, la tête couronnée de serpents, vêtue d'une robe
illustrée de têtes de morts, la République marche entre l'incendie et la guillotine, foulant aux pieds
la Croix et l'Évangile, la tiare et la couronne royale.

Figure 44. Anniversary of 14 July. Anonymous transfer etching, 1883 (Archives Départementales Isère, 54 M 3). Cf. as model picture the anonymous etching *La République* of 1797 (Musée Carnavalet, Est., PC. Hist. 25 C), reprinted in the exhibition catalog *La Guillotine dans la Révolution* (Florence and Vizille, 1987), no. 172.

ceeded similarly in his series of newspaper articles in the *République radicale* addressed "to the youth of France":

14 July!

What a glorious anniversary!

A giant of flesh and blood throws himself on the colossus of granite; the people attack the very stones that support the entire edifice of feudalism. With the destruction of the Bastille, Paris gives the entire world an enormous inspiration . . . ; it breaks the chains, it elevates France, which had been enslaved for centuries, wins independence, clears the way for freedom. . . . You, the young people of today, are entrusted with the task of battle![98]

In spite of individual dissenting voices,[99] the celebrations of the centennial of the French Revolution became a triumph for the supporters of the national holiday. The many faces of the Bastille myth were depicted once again in a flood of jubilee writings, among them poems celebrating the taking of the Bastille as a victory of the people over a man-eating monster.[100] An enterprising businessman had the old Bastille rebuilt in plaster on a smaller scale in the Paris Rue Suffren and invited the curious to empathize with the tortures of Latude and the other martyrs of freedom in the dungeons—for a small entrance fee.[101] While the Paris World Exhibition was intentionally opened on a less revolutionary date, the hundredth anniversary of the first deliberations of the States General of 1789 (6 May), the socialists just as intentionally began their Second International on 14 July 1889. Paul Lafargue's opening speech in the red-lined Petrelle Hall updated the day in the context of the proletarian class struggle:

The bourgeoisie celebrated the *hundredth year of its Revolution,* a revolution that proclaimed it would set up justice, freedom, and equality among men and that ended in nothing less than the cruelest and most unrestrained exploitation of the workers. Not only has the bourgeoisie shattered the aristocracy in order to seize control of society themselves, they have razed the *feudal Bastille* in order to set up capitalist *Work Bastilles* in the entire country in which they condemn the children, women, and men of the proletariat to the tortures of overwork.[102]

Altogether, the decade of militant national festivities from 1880 until 1889 considerably contributed to the diffusion and establishment of republican values, along with 14 July, throughout the country. And it did so on the basis of a generally familiar Bastille symbolism that once again proved to be a vehicle for national political culture.

How much the national holiday had become a matter of course can be seen, for instance, in this circular for city officials that the prefect of the southwestern département of Corrèze published in the regional press in July 1901:

> As every year, you are again called to celebrate the national festival, the festival of the republic, this year. You will give the anniversary of the storming of the Bastille all the more luster as it has become the festival of the government. . . . You will decorate public buildings with the three colors that the Revolution has bequeathed to France. You will make sure that students, women, and men come together for banquets, for dances and games. You will especially ensure that old age and childhood are honored. May the emotional community of freedom and peace animate your meeting, and may one cry ring out from the hearts of all citizens: "Long live the Republic!" [103]

A much-used handbook of model speeches for mayors, school principals, and all representatives of public life conveys a typical impression of the obligatory speeches given on these occasions. The average speech is built on the emotionalizing double symbol of the Bastille. On the one hand, reference to the old terrifying image was supposed to reinforce the republican detestation of the ancien régime: "A fortress, a prison, a grave where guilty and innocent rotted alive as it pleased the mighty. In a sense, the Bastille was the symbol, the visible sign of royal despotism. . . . Its mere name terrified the most courageous." On the other hand, the invocation of the storming of the Bastille was intended to appeal to patriotic enthusiasm and national pride:

> But in 1789, a magnanimous anger at the injustice and oppression of kings gave the people of Paris unsuspected powers; they took this mysterious fortress, which was considered impregnable, by force. And they gave once again to the prisoners, the victims of royal autocracy, which the people could no longer bear, their freedom. . . . With the taking of the Bastille . . . the age of progress and freedom began. [104]

In contrast to the widespread acceptance of this republican credo, the reactionary attempts to present the assault on the Bastille as a bloody deed planned by German and English conspirators,[105] or even to employ the negative image of the Bastille against Jews and Free-masons,[106] were a peripheral phenomenon. Nevertheless, the professional zeal of the July celebrations waned after 1890. They continued to provide an opportunity to demonstrate proletarian solidarity,[107] but the more the bourgeois right took control of the popular national holiday, the more the left distanced itself from what was seen as the festival of the "bourgeoisie."[108]

Since then, the Bastille myth, which had just about been declared state ideology, has lost much of its virulence. Subliminally, it is still an ingrained element of French political culture that can easily be reactivated in times of crisis, or when drastic decisions in domestic politics must be taken, in order to invoke national unity or support the struggle for more social justice. Two examples shall illustrate these two main functions of Bastille symbolism.

During the crisis of the 1930s, the left recalled the patriotic and emancipatory appeal of the Bastille and tried to utilize the July celebrations for their movement. Victor Basch, chairman of the Ligue des droits de l'homme, declared in Paris in 1935:

> As on 14 July 1789, when the people of Paris tore down the royal dungeon stone by stone, the people today are committed to start the attack on our own Bastilles—the Bastille of fascism, the Bastille of despicable laws, the Bastille of misery, the Bastille of economic and financial conglomerates, the Bastille of war: Bastilles that 150 years of violent battles and four revolutions have not succeeded in tearing down.[109]

Around the same time, the communists, who had been converted to nationalism—since it was more effective with the voters—tried to rally their supporters round the model of the conquerors of the Bastille of 1789: "The workers of the suburbs, the authentic proletarians of the time, created 14 July."[110] The official account of the party newspaper rejoiced: "An entire nation stands up for freedom."[111] When communists, socialists, and radical socialists formed the Popular Front the following year, they declared their alliance on 14 July 1936 while a mass rally was being held on the Place de la Bastille around the July Column, which was decorated with flags and pictures of Enlightenment figures and revolutionaries.[112] Even an intellectual such as Romain Rolland made a contribution by recalling the old Bastille, that "dun-

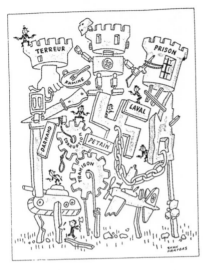

Figure 45. Stan Frayoas, The Bastille of Vichy and Germany. Pen-and-ink drawing, reprinted in Paul Trouillas, *Le Complexe de Marianne* (Paris: Seuil, 1988), 187.

geon of freedom," and calling for the storming of "other Bastilles"[113] and by bringing his drama *Le 14 Juillet* of 1902 back onstage with new music by politically committed new composers.[114]

If the Popular Front had above all updated the social and emancipatory significance of 14 July, the Resistance reactivated more of its patriotic and nationalist potential.[115] Full of allusions, one Resistance caricature (figure 45) depicted Hitler's occupational régime in France as a cleverly devised mechanism of informers, denunciation, arrests, and tortures that made the principle of the Bastille its system. After the new prime minister of the Vichy government Pierre Laval had announced in his speech of 22 June 1942 that he would collaborate with the German occupation even more loyally than his predecessor, Pétain, the Resistance issued a call to celebrate the upcoming 14 July as a day of national resistance against Hitler and Laval. In the early morning hours of 14 July 1942, airplanes dropped leaflets over the entire country containing the text of an appeal that had been previously broadcast on London radio:

> People of France, 14 July gives you all the opportunity to demonstrate your feelings and prove that your will can still be accomplished. It is the festival of the *fatherland,* the festival of *freedom.* In this hour in which the fatherland has been sold and freedom is trampled on, you shall celebrate it with more enthusiasm than ever. May the French people rise to their full power on this anni-

versary of their first victory. . . . All of you, demonstrate on 14 July. That is your national duty. Long live France![116]

Other leaflets, put out by the "Secours Populaire de France," called on the citizens of France to storm the prisons of the "slaughterers": "Hitler and Laval are preparing a Saint Bartholomew's massacre of patriots. *As in 1789,* let us all enter the modern prisons and break the chains of all those who are imprisoned because they thought and acted *French!*"[117] A poster entitled *14 Juillet 1942,* printed on both sides, was especially explicit. Under the title it called it "France's mission" to emulate the pioneers of freedom of 1789:

> On 14 July at 6 P.M., march in great numbers to the city hall of your town, or even better, if circumstances allow, to the prison where the courageous French who have fought for freedom are incarcerated. . . . In honor of the executed hostages and the political prisoners that the police of Vichy can hand over to Hitler's police whenever they please, lay down flowers in front of the gates of the jails or the parish halls. . . . Patriots, let us raise our heads! Let us shake off the dictatorship of the traitors. Let us work for the liberation of the country! Let us remember the spirit of eternal France. All to work with faith! All to work so that a storm of freedom breaks loose in our country on 14 July 1942.[118]

It is hardly surprising that the actual liberation of France in 1945 was triumphally celebrated with three days of July festivities.

More recently, Bastille symbolism seems to be losing its political and social importance. Every year, the banalization of 14 July, becomes a day for outings, grows more firmly established[119] and demands are made to free the holiday of state planning and once more turn it into a political festival:

> The anniversary of the storming of the Bastille must no longer be a festival of ritual rhetorical exercises, of grrreat [grrrande] military parades, of farandole dances. The fourteenth of July is the festival of the people. It is the people who must march on 14 July and have a procession.[120]

The old argument over the significance of the storming of the Bastille[121] has finally given way so universally to a positive assessment of the deed of liberation of 1789 that in 1986 even the arch-Gaullist

Figure 46. Moi San, The co-habitation of 14 July. Pen-and-ink drawing, 127 by 152 mm, *Le Canard enchaîné* 3429 (16 July 1986): 8.

prime minister (the president elected in 1995) Jacques Chirac had no choice but to join the socialist president of the Republic, François Mitterrand, in publicly paying tribute to the Bastille as a national symbol on 14 July. A caricature in the satirical weekly the *Canard enchaîné* (figure 46) represents both leaders as victors of the Bastille, Mitterrand in a Jacobin cap and in the clothing of the sansculottes, while Chirac wears a nobleman's outfit with a picture of the crown on his breast and is whistling a rather forced *Ça ira*. They are deeply hostile to each other, each carrying the head of the other on a pike. But they are united by the Bastille, the symbol of the political identity of modern France.

So even though the polemical and militant features of Bastille symbolism are increasingly covered, much as they were at the 1790 Festival of the Federation, by stagings of patriotic harmony on the national holiday, a few sparks can be relit to activate the emancipatory, combative potential of the Bastille. The examples already adduced serve as proof, as do the 1989 bicentennial celebrations, in which our symbol was omnipresent in faiences and jewelry, postcards and stamps, T-shirts and paper napkins. On the one hand, republican unity was invoked in the small town of Gérardmer in the Vosges by the transformation of the market fountain into a small Bastille, and in Amiens by art students burning a two-and-a-half-meter clay Bastille on 24 June 1989.[122] On the other hand, all groups of the left were at the same time mobilizing against the imminent official celebrations among western heads of state on the Champs-Elysées in a mass rally on the Place de la Bastille: "The Revolution has not ended. The Revolution is the Third Estate, it is the oppressed peoples of the Third World and all who are exploited. It has nothing to do with the pageantry of the summit meeting that Mitterrand is holding."[123]

APPENDIX A: HISTORIES OF THE BASTILLE, 1789–1889

A1   Pierre Joseph Spiridon Dufey. *La Bastille: Mémoires pour servir à l'histoire secrète du gouvernement français, depuis le 14e siècle jusqu'en 1789.* Paris: Krabbe, 1833.

A2   W.-A. Fougeret. *Histoire générale de la Bastille, depuis sa fondation, 1369, jusqu'à sa destruction, 1789.* 2 vols. Paris: Gauvain, 1834.

A3   W.-A. Fougeret. *Histoire de la prise de la Bastille et de ses plus célèbres prisonniers. Suivie de la description de la Colonne de Juillet.* Paris: Gauvain, 1840.

A4   Auguste Arnould, Jules Edouard Alboise Du Pujol, and Auguste Maquet. *Histoire de la Bastille depuis sa fondation en 1374 jusqu'à sa destruction 1789; ses prisonniers, ses gouverneurs, ses archives; détails des tortures et des supplices usités envers les prisonniers; révélations sur le régime intérieur de la Bastille; aventures dramatiques, lugubres, scandaleuses; évasions; archives de police.* Deluxe ed. 6 vols. Paris: Administration de la Librairie, 1844.

A5   *Histoire de la Bastille,* par un ancien publiciste. Paris: Fayard, 1878.

A6   Auguste Coeuret. *La Bastille: Histoire — Description — Attaque et Prise.* Paris: J. Rothschild, 1889.

A7   Alphonse Couret. *La Bastille depuis ses origines jusqu'à sa chûte (1369–1789).* Orléans: Herbuison, 1889. (Also published in *Revue du monde Latin* 16 [December 1888]: 449–67 and 17 [1889]: 44–62.)

APPENDIX B: TEXTBOOKS ON THE HISTORY OF FRANCE

B1   Charles-Constantin Letellier. *Instructions sur l'histoire de France. . . .* 4th ed. Paris: Prieur, 1811. 266.

B2   Laure de Saint-Ouen. *Histoire de France depuis l'établissement de la monarchie jusqu'à nos jours.* Paris: Colas, 1827. 154.

B3   Emile de Bonnechose. *Histoire de France. . . .* 2 vols. Paris: Firmin-Didot/Hachette, 1834. 2:156–57.

B4   Emile Lefranc. *Histoire de France depuis la Gaule primitive jusqu'en 1830, revue, corrigée et annotée.* Lyon and Paris: Périsse, 1835. 457–59.

B5   Guillaume-Louis Belèze. *L'Histoire de France mise à la portée des enfants.* Paris: Delalin, 1841. 42.

B6   Amédée Gabourd. *Abrégé élémentaire de l'histoire de France depuis les origines gauloises jusqu'à nos jours.* Paris: Périsse, 1844. 222.

B7   P. Chausolles. *Précis de l'histoire de France . . . à l'usage des collèges.* Paris: Pradel et Goujon, 1844. 259–60.

B8   Alfred Magin. *Histoire de France abrégée depuis les temps les plus anciens jusqu'à nos jours.* Paris: Delagrave, 1852. 223.

B9   Victor Duruy. *Abrégé de l'histoire de France.* Cours de quatrième. New ed. 3 vols. Paris: Hachette, 1854: 3:463–67.

B10   F.P.B./F.I.C. (Frères des écoles chrétiennes). *Histoire de France (Cours moyen).* Tours and Paris, 1880. 309.

B11   Désiré Blanchot. *Nouvelles leçons élémentaires d'histoire de France à l'usage des enfants du premier âge.* Paris: Belin, 1881. 109–10.

B12   Edgar Zévort. *Histoire de France (Cours moyen).* Paris: Picard-Bernheim, 1882. 145–47.

B13   Gustave Ducoudray. *Cours d'histoire. Cours moyen. Histoire élémentaire de la France.* Paris: Hachette, 1884. 90.

B14   Jean-Baptiste Melin. *Petite Histoire de la France depuis les origines jusqu'en 1884 (Cours moyen).* 7th ed. Paris: A. Moulins, 1885. 182.

B15   Ernest Lavisse. *La Première Année de l'histoire de France (programme de 1882).* 14th ed. Paris: Colin, 1887. 160–61.

B16   V. Bertrand. *Histoire de France à l'usage du cours moyen. Ouvrage conforme au programme d'histoire développé pour les écoles du département du Nord.* 2d ed. Lille: Lenoir, 1889. 82.

B17   A. Choublier. *Histoire sommaire de la France.* Vol. 2. Paris: Delalain, 1890. 123.

B18   Claude Augé and Maxime Petit. *Deuxième Livre d'histoire de France.* Paris: Larousse, 1893. 188.

B19   Emile Segond. *Histoire de France depuis la guerre de cent ans jusqu'à nos jours (Cours moyen).* Paris: Hatier, 1894. 22.

FINAL REMARKS

On the Origin and Function of a Historical Symbol

FOR CONTEMPORARY FRANCE, THE STORMING OF THE BAS-
tille represents "l'événement no. 1" of the Revolution—the
most important *event* of the French Revolution, according to
the results of a poll taken by the French weekly *Nouvel Observateur* in
January 1989.[1] At the same time, the Bastille, the former state prison
taken on 14 July 1789, is one of the four great *symbols* of the French
Revolution to the French—together with the Declaration of Rights,
the slogan "Liberté—Egalité—Fraternité," and the French national
anthem, the *Marseillaise*, which was composed in 1792. And finally,
the attack on the Bastille constitutes the only prominent event of the
French Revolution that is *not* associated with one of the great *names* of
the Revolution. Neither Robespierre nor Danton, neither Mirabeau
nor Marat nor La Fayette participated in the storming of the Bastille
or was connected with it. In the consciousness of the French—and
this idea prevailed quite early outside France as well, especially in Germany—14 July 1789 is a genuinely *national*, collective event. Its authors
are the people, "le peuple," "la Nation" as a whole.

How can the unparalleled "career" of the collective symbol "storming of the Bastille" be explained? On the one hand, it can certainly
be explained by the historical fact that the fall and destruction of the
infamous state prison was a prophesied, "expected" event. Philoso-
phers and writers such as Linguet and Mercier had predicted it and
viewed it as a precondition for a new era of freedom. The Bastille
was thus almost ideally suited as a *symbol of the break* between the ancien régime and the Revolution, between despotism and freedom. As
a two-dimensional, bipolar symbol it embodied on the one hand the

"terrors" of the ancien régime, which were darkly painted the stories of prisoners, and it symbolized on the other hand the accomplishments of the Revolution, which led to the "Epoque de la Liberté," the beginning of a new era of freedom, equality, and fraternity. This awareness of a radical break, which was part of the self-understanding of the revolutionaries of 1789, and which forms the basis for legitimation of the modern French republic, could be represented by the symbol of the Bastille in various ways:

graphically, through a pictorial representation, for instance, of the assault or through a visual juxtaposition of the towering, proud fortress and the mere ruins that remained as early as 1790;

argumentatively, through the use of the term "Bastille" as a sociopolitical catchword in pamphlets, political speeches, and chansons and on posters;

narratively, through the huge number of stories about the Bastille that had circulated during the eighteenth century and have done so increasingly since the Revolution—from voluminous novels and historiographical representations to popular literature and street ballads;

theatrically, through the dramatization of the successful assault in plays as well as popular reenactments of the storming of the Bastille, especially at the Revolution festivals of the years 1789 to 1799; and

plastically, through monuments, sculptures, tobacco boxes, and dominoes in the form of the Bastille, but especially through the patriotic cult, initiated by Pierre-François Palloy, around the Bastille stones as "votive images of freedom."

This history of the forms of the collective symbol "Bastille" directs perception toward the forgotten, the buried, the unfamiliar— and most of all toward the incredibly intense political popular culture of the revolutionary era, which found identification figures in the victors of the Bastille and expression in the belief in the magical powers of sacred objects (relics) such as Palloy's Bastille stones and Latude's ladder.

For two hundred years, the terms "Bastille" and "14 July" have been not only slogans in France's political language but also symbolic weapons in arguments in domestic politics and in national self-presentation. As a weapon of the domestic opposition, the symbol "Bastille" was much employed above all in the last decades of the ancien régime, in the years 1815–70, and during the Vichy government. Here, the two sides of the collective symbol "Bastille"—the former state prison as a symbol of despotism and 14 July as emblematic of the new freedom—became signs of recognition and vehicles of legitimation for political groups and movements that appealed to the radical democratic and revolutionary tradition of the Revolution. The use of the collective symbol "Bastille" as a weapon in domestic political arguments clearly emphasized its activist, militant dimension. Transferable to just about any "bastion of corruption and tyranny," the storming of the Bastille represented an almost archetypal symbolic action in domestic politics, which justified political action in the widest sense— including the use of violence—and fulfills this function up to the present day. In its militant domestic form, the Bastille symbol played an important role, for example, in Marseille in 1790, when the patriots of the city called for the storming of the local "Bastilles" of Saint-Jean and Saint-Nicolas, and also in 1943–44, during the occupation of France by German troops, when the French Resistance called for the violent destruction of the Gestapo's concentration camps, which were called new Bastilles.

The utilization of the Bastille symbol as a core around which national identity could crystallize worked differently. Together with the national hymn, the Panthéon as the national tomb of France's great men, and a national history newly written after 1789, the day of the fall of the Bastille became a symbol of the greatness and unity of revolutionary France, the Grande Nation, after 1790. On the officially celebrated national holiday of 14 July the French government does not call for dynamic political action or for militant activism but invokes the revolutionary tradition of 14 July as a basis for modern France in vague terms—today as much as during the Revolution. On 14 July, which in France is traditionally commemorated with a turbulent popular festival as well as grand military parades, the unity of the nation is demonstrated, social harmony is celebrated, and the positive side of the legacy of 1789 resting on broad social consensus is invoked. As an *official* national symbol, the storming of the Bastille had already ossified into a "cold event" during the Revolution, had already become the kind of occasion that is celebrated and cited, reactivated and recalled in the collective memory again and again but that, as such, definitely belongs to the past.

Why this political "domestication" of the Bastille as a collective symbol, its "sidelining" and "taming" could not succeed—during the Revolution or in the two hundred years since—becomes clear in the importance, virulence, and vitality of French domestic political arguments since 1789. Even the Bicentenaire, the festivities for the two-hundredth anniversary of the French Revolution that France celebrated in 1989, was characterized by very different, antagonistic "readings" of the collective symbol "storming of the Bastille." While Mitterrand's socialist government—in this respect completely in the tradition of the Grande Nation—had a magnificent, media-friendly, and mostly depoliticized spectacle entitled *La Marseillaise* staged on the Champs-Elysées on 14 July and invited the heads of government of the seven leading Western industrial nations to the event, a militant counterevent took place the same day on the Place de la Bastille. This alternative festival, organized by the extraparliamentary opposition, student groups, and the PCF, understood itself as a protest against the summit meeting of the rich ("Le sommet des riches") and the 14 July of cash ("Le 14 juillet du fric").[2] The speakers at this rally, among others, the former student leader and participant in the revolution of 1968 Alain Krivine, called on their audience to storm today's Bastilles—poverty in the Third World, unemployment, racism, the violation of human rights—instead of indulging in national self-adulation and pompous stagings of power in the manner of Mitterrand and his prime minister Rocard.[3] But the contradictions between the official use of the symbol "Bastille" and the political demands, hopes, and dreams connected with it broke through most clearly and radically in the French colonies.[4] Just as revolutionary France had introduced 14 July as a national holiday in the annexed departemental capital Nice after 1793, and in occupied Mainz after 1794, and had thereby expressed the Grande Nation's missionary urge to expand, so too was it exported to the French colonies outside France. During the revolutionary period 14 July was celebrated in the French Antilles and Senegal; since 1880 it has also been observed in Indochina and Algeria, and since the mid-1880s on Madagascar and in the French colonies in western and central Africa. French colonial administrators consciously emphasized the military character of the event, stressed the superiority of French civilization, underlined above all the unity of the nation, and in speeches compared the colonial conquests to the act of liberating the Bastille, the precolonial kingdoms and tribal principalities to the "despotic" ancien régime.[5]

In contrast to this official discourse, intellectuals from Africa and the Maghreb in the 1920s began to stress the emancipatory significance of the collective symbol "Bastille," which could not be completely suppressed in the official speeches on 14 July. In 1939, on the 150th anniversary of the storming of the Bastille, the Senegalese representative Lamine Guèye published an article with the programmatic title "L'Esprit de la Révolution" in a west-African newspaper. Similarly, intellectuals such as the author and journalist Bernard Dadié from the Ivory Coast pointed out the flagrant contradictions between the reality of colonialism and the liberal ideology the French Third Republic invoked every 14 July in its colonies with pomp and circumstance. Bernard Dadié, born in 1915, was later to become the minister of culture of the Ivory Coast, which gained its independence in 1960. He was sentenced to several years in prison by a French court in Grand-Bassam (Gulf of Guinea) in 1949 for publishing "anti-French newspaper articles," and for being a member of the democratic umbrella organization RDA (Rassemblement Démocratique Africain). While still in prison, he wrote a poem entitled "Ce que m'a donné la France" (What France has given me). This poem illustrates the long-distance effect and continuing relevance of the collective symbol "Bastille," which became a catalyst in processes of forming political consciousness, and a vehicle for political demands not only in France and Germany but also in the Third World:

France has given me neither the rifles nor the gunpowder nor
   the bullets that forever shoot down black or white brothers.
France has given me neither my handcuffs nor my years in
   prison nor the misery that presses down on me.
It has given me neither the dirty hole in which I am lying nor
   the unjust justice nor again the mass grave. . . .
My France has given me VERCINGÉTORIX, who full of anger
   disputed CAESAR's right to Gaul, as a role model. . . .
My France has shown me PASTEUR and that array of selfless
   scientists who forgot themselves in order to save their
   brothers and give the world a better destiny.
And above all, it has shown me, with imperious index finger,
   the people of France, who ran toward the Bastille, where a
   mere warrant put human beings in chains and threw them
   into dungeons full of vermin.[6]

Finally, a 1987 poem by the South African writer Dennis Brutus, who after several stays in prison in his home country emigrated to the

United States and lives there in exile, demonstrates that the collective symbol "Bastille" has retained a certain fascination even outside the French-speaking world up to the present day. In his poem "For the Prisoners in South Africa," Brutus compares South Africa's apartheid policy to a huge Bastille, likening it to the prison the citizens of Paris stormed, tore down, and destroyed in a violent act of liberation on 14 July 1789:

> What squats its vast bulk
> at the end of my mind's
> shadowy recesses
> dominating my thinking like a
> legendary bastion, Bastille.[7]

APPENDIX

Reports on the Storming of the Bastille, 1789

---

1   Gorsas, *Le Courrier de Versailles à Paris et de Paris à Versailles* 1, nos. 8–13 (13–20 July 1789).

2   *Journée du 14, Paris, le 15 Juillet 1789.* N.p., n.d. Bibliothèque Nationale 8° Z; Le Senne 8810 (18).

3   *Relation exacte de ce qui s'est passé dans la Députation en parlementaire à la Bastille, & de tout ce qui l'a précédé. Ce 15 Juillet, par un Citoyen Electeur & témoin oculaire.* N.p., n.d. Bibliothèque Nationale Lb³⁹.7373.

4   Pierre-Benjamin Boucheron. *Récit de ce qui s'est passé sous mes yeux le Mardi 14 Juillet 1789, à onze heures du matin.* Paris: Lacloye, 1789.

5   *Journal de Paris* 197 (16 July 1789): 837–40.

6   *Il étoit temps, ou La semaine aux événements.* N.p., n.d. Bibliothèque Nationale Lb³⁹.7413.

7   *La Semaine mémorable. Discours prononcé après un Te Deum en musique, dans une Assemblée d'Artistes de tous les genres, sous le nom de Société d'Apollon.* Paris: Prault, 1789. Bibliothèque Nationale Lb³⁹.2090.

8   [Pierre-Jean de Béranger]. *Supplément au Point du Jour.* Paris: Lagrange, n.d. Bibliothèque Nationale Lc².143.

9   Louis-Abel Beffroy de Reigny. *Précis exact de la Prise de la Bastille, rédigé sous les yeux des principaux Acteurs qui ont joué un rôle dans cette expédition, & lu le même jour à l'Hôtel-de-Ville.* N.p., 1789. (Reprinted in *Le Courrier des Planètes* 2, no. 67 [1 August 1789]: 31–46 and continued in the *Supplément nécessaire au Précis exact de la Prise de la Bastille, avec des Anecdotes curieuses sur le même sujet.* N.p., n.d.)

10 [Louis-Antoine de Caraccioli]. *La Capitale délivrée par elle-même.* N.p., n.d.

11 *Les Lauriers du fauxbourg Saint-Antoine, ou Le Prix de la Bastille renversée. Du lundi 20 juillet 1789.* N.p., n.d. Bibliothèque Nationale 8° Z; Le Senne 8810 (20).

12 *Relation de ce qui s'est passé à Paris depuis le 11 du présent mois, jusqu'au 15.* N.p., n.d. Bibliothèque Historique de la Ville de Paris 958.954.

13 *L'Ouvrage des six jours, ou Lettre d'un Membre du District des Feuillans, à son Ami, sur la révolution de Paris, 20 Juillet 1789.* Paris: Volland, n.d. Bibliothèque Historique de la Ville de Paris 580, no. 66.

14 *Journal général de l'Europe* 87 (21 July 1789).

15 *Révolutions de Paris, dédiées à la Nation* 1 (12–17 July 1789): 1–27. Unless otherwise specified, English versions are taken from the contemporary translation, *The Paris Revolution Magazine* (London: Dilly, 1790). (Excerpts from *Révolutions de Paris* are also translated in Godechot, *Taking*, 321–26.)

16 *Le Grenadier patriote, ou Le despotisme détruit en France, avec les détails les plus exacts sur la Révolution présente.* N.p., n.d. Bibliothèque Historique de la Ville de Paris 951.721.

17 *Révolutions de Paris, ou Récit exact de ce qui s'est passé dans la Capitale, & particulièrement de la prise de la Bastille, depuis le 11 Juillet 1789, jusqu'au 23 du même mois.* N.p., n.d. Bibliothèque Nationale Lb^{39}.2049.A.

18 *Extrait d'une lettre de Paris, du 15 Juillet 1789.* N.p., n.d. Bibliothèque Historique de la Ville de Paris 19.879.

19 [Honoré-Gabriel de Riquetti, Count Mirabeau]. *Dix-neuvième Lettre du comte de Mirabeau à ses commettans, du 9 Juillet jusqu'au 24 du même Mois. Le Courrier de Provence, commencé le 2 Mai 1789* 1, no. 19 (Paris, 1789).

20 *Le Siège de la Bastille prise par la Bourgeoisie. . . .* Broadsheet, Figure 9 in the present volume.

21 [François-Guillaume Ducray-Duminil]. *La Semaine mémorable, ou Récit exact de ce qui s'est passé à Paris depuis le 12 jusqu'au 17 Juillet.* Nantes: Louis, 1789.

22 *Journal politique national* 8 (28 July 1789). Reprinted in Antoine Rivarol, *Journal politique national et autres textes*, ed. Willy de Spens (Paris: Union Générale d'Editions, 1964), 50–54.

23 *La Victoire des Parisiens, ou La Liberté Françoise, par G.T., Citoyen.* Paris, 1789 Bibliothèque Nationale Lb^{39}.5715.

24 Louis de Flue. *Relation de la Prise de la Bastille le 14 Juillet 1789, par un de ses défenseurs. Revue rétrospective ou Bibliothèque historique*, 1st ser., 4 (Paris, 1834): 284–98. Quotations from the English translation can be found in Godechot, *Taking*, 292–307.

25 *Attaque, défense et reddition de la Bastille, du 14 Juillet 1789.* Paris: Brunet, Desenne, 1789. Bibliothèque Nationale Lb^{39}.7374.

26 P.-B. Ridet de Saint-Chéron-Les-Chartres. *Récit des événemens remarquables qui ont opéré la Liberté des Français, du Samedi premier Août 1789.* Paris: Cailleau, 1789.

27 *Les Fers brisés, pour servir de supplément aux Vitres cassées, par le véritable Père Duchesne.* N.p., n.d. Bibliothèque Historique de la Ville de Paris 964.987.

28 Jean-Baptiste Humbert. *Journée de Jean-Baptiste Humbert, horloger, qui, le premier, a monté sur les tours de la Bastille.* Paris: Volland, 1789. (Reprinted in Godechot, *Taking*, 277–86.)

29 *Le Parisien fêté, ou Tribut aux Parisiens, sur la Liberté qu'ils ont rendue à la France par leur valeur, Paris ce 15 Août 1789.* Paris: Cailleau, 1789. Bibliothèque Nationale Lb^{39}.7697.

30 Jean-Baptiste-Marie-Louis La Reynie de la Bruyère. *A mes concitoyens et à mes camarades.* N.p., n.d.

31 Jacques-Alexis Thuriot de la Rozière. *Récit relatif à la prise de la Bastille.* Paris: Cailleau, 16 July 1789.

32 Louis-Abel Beffroy de Reigny. *Histoire de France pendant trois mois; ou Relation exacte, impartiale & suivie des événements qui ont eu lieu à Paris, à Versailles & dans les Provinces, depuis le 15 Mai, jusqu'au Août 1789. . . .* Paris: Belin, 1789.

33 *Remarques et Anecdotes sur le château de la Bastille, suivies d'un détail historique du siège, de la prise et de la démolition de cette forteresse.* Paris: Goujon, 1789. 53–110.

34 *Journal de la Compagnie des citoyens arquebusiers royaux de la Ville de Paris, sur la révolution actuelle.* Paris: Ricart, 1789. Bibliothèque Nationale Lb³⁹.2303.

35 Claude Fournier-L'Héritier. *Extrait d'un Mémoire contenant les services de la Compagnie de M. Fournier, l'un des Commandans du District de Saint Eustache, depuis le 13 Juillet 1789, époque de la Révolution.* N.p., n.d.

36 *La Bastille dévoilée, ou Recueil de pièces authentiques pour servir à son histoire.* 2d ed. Paris: Desenne, 1789.

37 Claude Cholat. *Service fait à l'attaque et prise de la Bastille.* Paris: Brunet, Desenne, 1789.

38 *Etrennes mignonnes curieuses et utiles pour l'année 1790.* Paris: Masson, 1789. 62–72.

39 *Etrennes nationales, curieuses et instructives, enrichies de figures, d'anecdotes historiques, et augmentées de la Révolution de Paris, pour l'année 1790.* Paris: Cailleau, 1789. 33–42.

40 *Le Petit Théâtre de l'Univers. Etrennes naturelles, précieuses, instructives et amusantes.* Paris: Langlois, 1789.

41 *Relation véritable de la Prise de la Bastille, le quatorze Juillet 1789, par J. Rouel, Cultivateur.* Paris: Hérault, 1790.

42 *Gravures historiques des principaux événemens depuis l'ouverture des Etats-Généraux de 1789.* Paris: Janinet, Cussac, 1790. Each series of plates is paginated separately:
   - 11. Evénement du 14 Juillet 1789
   - 12. Evénement du 14 Juillet 1789
   - 13. Evénement du 14 Juillet 1789
   - 14. Evénement du 14 Juillet 1789
   - 15. Evénement du 14 Juillet 1789
   - 16. Evénement du 14 Juillet 1789
   - 17. Historique de la grande journée du 14 Juillet 1789

43 *Précis des événemens depuis le 5 mai 1789 jusqu'à ce jour Ier Juillet.* Paris: de l'imprimerie d'un royaliste, 1790. Bibliothèque Nationale Lb³⁹.3672.

44 Louis-Guillaume Pitra. *Mémoires.* In Flammermont, *La Journée*, 1–56. English translation of some excerpts can be found in Godechot, *Taking*, 308–20.

45 Jean-Joseph Dusaulx. *De l'Insurrection parisienne et de la prise de la Bastille.* Paris: Debure, 1790. Reprinted in Hippolyte Monin, ed., *Mémoires de la Bastille. Linguet et Dusaulx* (Paris: Librairie des Bibliophiles, 1889).

46 *La Bastille au Diable.* Paris: Laurens, 1790. Bibliothèque Nationale Lk⁷.7695.

47 [François-Marie de Kerverseau et al.]. *Histoire de la Révolution de 1789, et de l'établissement d'une constitution en France; précédée de l'exposé rapide des administrations successives qui ont déterminé cette Révolution mémorable.* 19 vols. Paris: Clavelin, 1790. 1: 305–43, 2:1–102.

48 [Félix-Louis-Christophe Ventre de La Touloubre, called Galart de Montjoye]. *L'Ami du Roi, des Français, de l'ordre et sur-tout de la vérité, ou Histoire de la Révolution de France, et de l'Assemblée Nationale.* 4 vols. Paris: Gattey, 1791.

49 Jean-Paul Rabaut Saint-Etienne. *Almanach historique de la Révolution françoise, pour l'année 1792.* Paris and Strasbourg: Onfroy/Treuttel, 1791.

50 C. André. *Almanach Historique et révolutionnaire, ou Précis de toute la Révolution*

Française et des opérations armées jusqu'à la chute du tyran Robespierre. Paris: Barba et Aubert, an III. 15–20.

51   [Louis-Ange Pitou]. *La Révolution en Vaudevilles, ou Précis exact et circonstancié de ses principaux événemens* . . . Paris: Champion, an III.

52   *Journées mémorables de la Révolution française, par demandes et par réponses, à l'usage de la jeunesse, républicaine, par un citoyen de la section du Mont-Blanc.* Paris: Barba, an III. Bibliothèque Nationale La^{32}.597. 24–50.

NOTES

INTRODUCTION

1 Jean-Marie Le Guévellou, *A la Bastille! 14 juillet 1789* (Paris: Nathan, 1983).

2 Exhibition catalog of the Galerie Artom, *Bastille 89, 89 artistes prennent la Bastille* (Paris: Editions de l'Eclat, 1985).

3 One hundred eighty parts of the mural were supposed to be set in a steel construction, making up a wall four meters high and twenty meters long. In the fall of 1987, the firm Saint-Gobain Vitrage (Ateliers du vitrail et de la mosaïque, 5 Avenue P. Gaudin, F-83690 Salernes) looked in vain for sponsors at the exhibition of ideas in Paris's La Valette Park.

4 Results of a nationwide representative poll taken between 15 and 21 November 1984 from one thousand individuals; published and analyzed in the *Nouvel Observateur,* 7 December 1984, 36–39. These results are confirmed by the representative polls of the SOFRES institute, which were published in *Le Monde* of 4 January 1989 and in the *Nouvel Observateur* of 5–11 January, 34–36.

5 Jean-Paul Sartre, *Critique of Dialectical Reason,* vol. 1, *Theory of Practical Ensembles* (London: NLB, 1976), 351–444. See also Lawrence D. Kritzman, "The Myth of the Bastille and Sartre's French Revolution," *Esprit créateur* 29 (1989): 84–91.

6 Reported in *Le Monde* 11284 (12 May 1981): 9.

7 See the texts and reports in *Humanité* 13562 (28 March 1988): 1–17. During the rally, corresponding leaflets were given out. The political pamphlet by Ariel Kyrou and André-Jean Gattolin, *Reprenons la Bastille: Manifeste des nouveaux sans-culottes* (Paris: Balland, 1988), argues similarly.

8 Bloch, *Principle*: 1:162–63.

9 Eckhart Kauntz, "Im Schatten Cattenoms," *Frankfurter Allgemeine Zeitung,* 12 July 1986, Saturday Supplement, illustrated.

10 Although he falls behind Flammermont, *Journée* in parts, Godechot, *Taking* is considered the standard work as far as historical events are concerned. However, it completely misses the symbolic tradition. Mistler, *Juillet,* a popular, well-illustrated book, has wrongly been neglected. Cottret, *Bastille* pays attention to symbolism but often investigates it only superficially and at second hand. Chaussinand-Nogaret, *Bastille* remains mostly a history of events. Quétel,

Bastille lists an impressive range of material but interprets it only impressionistically and without giving individual sources.

11 See, after Biré, *Légendes,* 55–107, especially the numerous books and articles by the librarian of long standing at the Bastille archive of the Paris Arsenal Library, Funck-Brentano (e.g., *Legends, La Bastille, Les Lettres,* "Documents," "La Bastille," etc.), with whom Kircheisen, *Grim Bastille* tacitly concurs; more recently, among others, Quétel, *Essai.*

12 See, for instance, Percy Ernst Schramm, *Herrschaftszeichen und Staatssymbolik,* 3 vols. (Stuttgart and Munich: Hiersemann/Monumenta, 1954–78).

13 Here, the sociology of facts and the history of mentality meet. See Peter L. Berger and Thomas Luckmann, *The Social Construction of Reality* (Harmondsworth: Penguin, 1966), and Rolf Reichardt, "Histoire des Mentalités," *Internationales Archiv für Sozialgeschichte der deutschen Literatur* 3 (1978): 130–66.

14 Link's numerous works on this subject have contributed to the comprehensive cooperative effort by Axel Drews, Ute Gerhard, and Jürgen Link, "Moderne Kollektivsymbolik: Eine diskurstheoretisch orientierte Einführung mit Auswahlbibliographie," *Internationales Archiv für Sozialgeschichte der deutschen Literatur* special issue 1 (Tübingen: Niemeyer, 1985): 256–365, esp. 256–73.

15 Concerning this concept see Bronislaw Baczko, *Les Imaginaires sociaux: Mémoires et espoirs collectifs* (Paris: Payot, 1984), esp. 10–55.

16 See Karl Loewenstein, "Betrachtungen über politischen Symbolismus," in *Gegenwartsprobleme des internationalen Rechts und der Rechtsphilosophie,* Festschrift für Rudolf Laun, ed. Demetrious S. Konstantopoulos and Hans Wehberg (Hamburg: Giratdet, 1953), 559–77.

17 The authors are preparing a comprehensive bibliography and iconography on this subject.

18 See the discussion begun by Jacques Godechot, "Revue de Presse," *Annales historiques de la Révolution française* 56 (1984): 301–2, answered by Hans Ulrich Gumbrecht, Rolf Reichardt, and Hans-Jürgen Lüsebrink, "Tribune et débats," *Annales historiques de la Révolution française* 58 (1986): 103–5.

19 See the preparatory essays by the authors of this volume, Lüsebrink, "Die 'Vainqueurs de la Bastille'" and Lüsebrink and Reichardt, "La Bastille," "La Prise," and "Les Récits."

20 See Reinhart Koselleck and Rolf Reichardt, eds., *Die Französische Revolution als Bruch des gesellschaftlichen Bewusstseins: Vorlagen und Diskussionen der internationalen Arbeitstagung am Zentrum für interdisziplinäre Forschung der Universität Bielefeld* (Munich: Oldenbourg, 1988).

1. GENESIS OF A POLITICAL SYMBOL

1 See Bournon, *Bastille,* 1–35.
2 Ibid., 47–103.
3 See Paul Morand, *Fouquet, ou le Soleil offusqué* (Paris: Gallimard, 1985), and Cottret, *Bastille,* 78–85.
4 See Quétel, *Essai,* 64–68. See also below.
5 See Le Petit, *Oeuvres:* 151–52.
6 *Les Soupirs,* 33, reprinted as *Les Voeux,* 123. Concerning the presumable authorship of Michel Le Varron, see Gotthold Riemann, *Der Verfasser der Soupirs de la*

France esclave qui aspire après la liberté (1689–90) (Berlin: Ebeling, 1938). Concerning the background see Lionel Rothkrug, *Opposition to Louis XIV: The Political and Social Origins of the French Enlightenment* (Princeton: Princeton University Press, 1965).

7   See also Voltaire's poem of 1715 and below, pp. 26–27.

8   See Reichardt, "Bastille," 12–22. The sources evaluated in the following are Renneville, *L'Inquisition; Evénement des plus rares; Anecdotes; Remarques historiques;* Linguet, *Mémoires;* [Latude], *Histoire;* and *Le Comte de Lorges.*

9   Cf. the story—otherwise insignificant for our inquiry—of the middle-class Robert, comte de Paradès in his *Mémoires,* 167–84, and the English translation, *Secret Memoirs,* 137–46.

10   See the biographical note in Albert Savine, ed., *La Vie à la Bastille: Souvenirs d'un prisonnier d'après les documents d'archives et les mémoires* (Paris: Michaud, 1908), 9–16.

11   The original German text of the first four lines can be found in fig. 2. The second four lines are from Renneville, *Entlarvte Französische Inquisition,* 1:125.

12   This translation is from the German excerpt in *Beschreibung,* 229–95, here 235–36. [A contemporary English translation, *The French Inquisition; or, The History of the Bastille in Paris* (London: Bell, 1715), 65–67, was not available before this book went to press.]

13   *Beschreibung,* 261–62, 289. This passage is not included in the English version of Renneville's text. Its inclusion in *Beschreibung* demonstrates which passages in Renneville received most attention during the eighteenth century, at least in Germany.

14   Renneville, *L'Inquisition françoise, ou l'Histoire de la Bastille,* 4 vols. (Amsterdam and Leiden, 1719–24), and the German translation, *Historie der Bastille zu Paris* (Nuremberg: Felssecker, 1758).

15   *Die so genannte Hölle,* vi.

16   Letter of 31 January 1714 in Leibniz, *Correspondenz,* 3:476. See also p. 421, for Sophie's letter of 4 January 1714.

17   *Die so genannte Hölle,* 16, and *Evénement des plus rares,* preface, respectively.

18   *Evénement des plus rares,* 133, 107–9, 111, 205–7.

19   *Die so genannte Hölle,* vii. The German version of the engraving is an even more obvious denunciation of the Bastille than the otherwise identical French original.

20   Ibid., viii–xi.

21   *A un ami, à l'occasion du Mémoire de M. Mazers de la Tude, ou Histoire de l'abbé Bucquoit* (Paris: Buisson, 1788).

22   See Quétel, *Essai,* 49–52, and Cottret, *Bastille,* 135–45. Other titles from the voluminous literature on this subject are Jules Loiseleur, *Trois énigmes historiques: La Saint-Barthélemy, l'affaire des prisons . . . , le masque de fer . . .* (Paris: Plon, 1882); Jean-Christian Petitfils, *L'Homme au masque de fer, le plus mystérieux des prisonniers de l'histoire* (Paris: Perrin, 1970); and Harry Thompson, *The Man in the Iron Mask: A Historical Detective Investigation* (London: Weidenfeld and Nicolson, 1987).

23   See the memoirs attributed to Mme de Vieux-Maisons, *Mémoires secrets pour servir à l'Histoire de Perse* (Amsterdam: Aux Dépens de la Compagnie, 1745), 20–22.

24   Voltaire, *Age,* 2:8–9.

25   See Pierre Paul Clement, *Les Cinq Années littéraires, ou Nouvelles littéraires . . . ,*

4 vols. (The Hague: De Groot, 1754), 4:48–58 (letter of 1 May 1752); Louis Chaudon, "Le Masque de Fer," in *Nouveau Dictionnaire historique portatif* (1766), 5th ed., 8 vols. (Caen: G. Le Roy, 1783), 5:7–9; Germain-François Poullain de Saint-Foix, "Lettre à l'auteur de ces Feuilles sur l'Homme au Masque de Fer," *Année littéraire* 6, no. 6 (10 October 1768): 128–32; *Lettre de Saint-Foix au sujet de l'Homme au masque de fer* (Amsterdam and Paris, 1768); Henri Griffet, *Traité des différentes sortes de preuves qui établissent la vérité de l'histoire* (Liège: Bassompierre, 1769); and Germain-François Poullain de Saint-Foix, *Réponse au R. P. Griffet et Recueil de tout ce qui a été écrit sur le prisonnier masqué* (London and Paris: Ventes, 1770).

26   Charles de Fieux, chevalier de Mouhy, *Le Masque de Fer, ou les Aventures du père et du fils*, 6 vols. (The Hague: Hondt, 1750).

27   [Mercier], *Entretiens*, 38.

28   Pierre de La Porte, *Mémoires* (Geneva, 1756), 122–201.

29   Marguerite-Jeanne Cordier de Launay, the Baroness Mme de Staël, *Mémoires*, 4 vols. (London, 1755; two more editions by 1767). See also the English translation, *Memoirs*, 2 vols. (New York: Dodd Mead and Co., 1892).

30   See Catherine-Laurence Maire, *Les Convulsionnaires de Saint-Médard: Miracles, convulsions et prophéties à Paris au XVIIIe siècle* (Paris: Gallimard, 1985).

31   See the song "Les Gémissements de la France" of 1730 in *Chansonnier historique du XVIIIe Siècle*, ed. Emile Raunié, 10 vols. (Paris: Quantin, 1879), 5:234–37. See also Maire, *Les Convulsionnaires* (note 30), and fig. 4.

32   See Robert Kreiser, *Miracles, Convulsions, and Ecclesiastical Politics in Early Eighteenth-Century Paris* (Princeton: Princeton University Press, 1978), 294, 336–37.

33   *Anecdotes . . . touchant la conduite tyrannique & barbare qu'on a exercée sur Denyse Regné à la Bastille* (n.p., 1760), 20–24, 52, 57, 117, 135.

34   *Mémoires secrets* of 19 and 23 March 1775 (7:311, 313).

35   John Howard, *The State of Prisons in England and Wales*, 2 vols. (Warrington: Eyres, 1777), 1:129–31. See also the French translation, *Etat des prisons, des hôpitaux et des maisons de force*, 2 vols. (n.p.: La Grange, 1788), 1:380–86, and the German translation, *Ueber Gefängnisse und Zuchthäuser* (Leipzig: Weygand, 1780).

36   *Historical Remarks*, preface. See also the French original *Remarques historiques*, preface, and one German translation in *Beschreibung*, 4–6.

37   *Historical Remarks*, 5–6. See also *Remarques historiques*, 8–10, and another German translation, *Ausführliche Beschreibung der Bastille . . .* (Berlin: Spener, 1789), 5–6.

38   *Historical Remarks*, 7. See ibid. also on Renneville (22–23) and on the man in the iron mask (27–29). The pages in the original *Remarques historiques* are 11–12, 34–35, and 39–43 respectively. Concerning the oubliettes see also *Beschreibung*, 16–17, 50.

39   *Ausführliche Beschreibung* (note 37), 12. See also *Remarques historiques*, 21, 23.

40   See Hans-Jürgen Lüsebrink, *Kriminalität und Literatur im Frankreich des 18. Jahrhunderts* (Munich: Oldenbourg, 1983), 173–240, and Wolfgang Schmale, *Entchristianisierung, Revolution und Verfassung: Zur Mentalitätsgeschichte der Verfassung in Frankreich, 1715–1794* (Berlin: Duncker und Humblot, 1988).

41   Mirabeau, *Enquiries*, 216, 91, 211. For the French original, see Mirabeau, *Des lettres de cachet*, 1:254, 105, and 249.

42   Mirabeau, *Enquiries*, 325, see also 211, 343; cf. Mirabeau, *Des lettres de cachet*, 2:25, 1:249, 2:45.

43   Mirabeau, *Enquiries,* 340; see also 353–56, 365; cf. Mirabeau, *Des lettres de cachet,* 2:42, 57, 73–74.

44   Mirabeau, *Enquiries,* 215–19, 326, 341, 373; see also Mirabeau, *Des lettres de cachet,* 1:254–56; 2:26, 43, 82.

45   See Mirabeau, *Enquiries,* 225 and 359 respectively; cf. Mirabeau, *Des lettres de cachet,* 1:262, 2:61.

46   Mirabeau, *Enquiries,* 91, 211–12, 226, 314, 374, among others; see also Mirabeau, *Des lettres de cachet,* 1:105, 249, 264; 2:10, 84.

47   Michel de Cubières, *Voyage à la Bastille, fait le 16 juillet 1789* (Paris: Garnery et Volland, 1789), 11–12.

48   Mirabeau quoted by Pierre Manuel in his preface to *Lettres originales de Mirabeau, écrites au donjon de Vincennes, pendant les années 1777, 78, 79 et 80,* 4 vols. (Paris: Garnery, 1792), 1:2. Mirabeau pretended to have written his pamphlet of 1782 in a *cachot* (*Enquiries,* 314; *Des lettres de cachet,* 2:11).

49   The *Mémoires secrets* report his case on 17 October and 21 November 1780, between 5 December 1780 and 23 April 1782, and on 16–20 May and 4 November 1782 (16:26, 65, 82; 20:198–99, 254, 257–60; 21:169). See also Darline Gay Levy, *The Ideas and Careers of Simon-Nicolas-Henri Linguet* (Urbana: University of Illinois Press, 1980), 200–210.

50   *Annales politiques, civiles et littéraires du dix-huitième siècle* 10, nos. 73–75 (January 1783): 1–160.

51   Linguet, *Memoirs,* 2:11, 39; 1:18; 2:44, 21 respectively. See also Linguet, *Denkwürdigkeiten,* 58, 83, 16, 88, and 109 respectively.

52   Linguet, *Memoirs,* 2:47, 53, 51; and Linguet, *Denkwürdigkeiten,* 91, 96, 94. Concerning this clock, see Maxime Vuillaume, *L'Horloge et les cloches de la Bastille* (Tours: Deslis, 1896).

53   See Linguet, *Memoirs,* 4:13, 1:45–46, 2:37—there is no reference to Mirabeau in Goldsmid's edition—and Linguet, *Denkwürdigkeiten,* 122–23, 43–44, 81–82, 154.

54   Linguet, *Memoirs,* 3:29; see also 2:48 and Linguet, *Denkwürdigkeiten,* 117, 93.

55   Linguet, *Memoirs,* 1:30, 2:13, respectively; see also 1:29; 2:11–12, 41; and Linguet, *Denkwürdigkeiten,* 29, 60, 27, 59, 85.

56   Linguet, *Memoirs,* 1:33; see also 1:52, 4:28–29, and Linguet, *Denkwürdigkeiten,* 31, 50, 132.

57   Linguet, *Memoirs,* 3:23, 1:9, and Linguet, *Denkwürdigkeiten,* 112, 8.

58   Linguet, *Memoirs,* 2:39, and Linguet, *Denkwürdigkeiten,* 83–84.

59   Linguet, *Memoirs,* 1:8, and Linguet, *Denkwürdigkeiten,* 6–7.

60   Linguet, *Memoirs,* 2:6; on the *lettres de cachet* see also 1:19, 21, 44–46, 48; 3:27–29; and Linguet, *Denkwürdigkeiten,* 54, 17, 20, 42–43, 46, 117.

61   For some reason, this passage is left out in Goldsmid's edition. It is translated in *Memoirs of the Bastille* (180) and in Linguet, *Denkwürdigkeiten* (136).

62   Linguet, *Memoirs,* 1:10; see also 1:7, 32; 4:29–30; and Linguet, *Denkwürdigkeiten,* 9, 6, 30, 133.

63   Linguet, *Memoirs,* 1:28; 2:12, 47–48; and Linguet, *Denkwürdigkeiten:* 26, 60, 92.

64   See Linguet, *Memoirs,* 2:15, and Linguet, *Denkwürdigkeiten,* 62.

65   See *Courrier du Bas-Rhin* 1 (1 January 1783): 3 (published in Cleves).

66   Bachaumont, *Mémoires secrets* of 6 April 1783 (22:190–92). The caption is from Voltaire's drama *Alzire* of 1736, act 2, scene 2. The complete preamble to the

edict can be found in *Recueil général des anciennes lois françaises de 420–1789*, ed. François-André Isambert et al. (Paris: Belin-Le-Prieur, 1821), 26:378. For the German translation (*Denkwürdigkeiten*), a new engraving was cut.

67   See our investigation of the semantic field in Lüsebrink and Reichardt, "La Bastille," 198–214.

68   Jeremy Popkin, "Umbruch und Kontinuität der französischen Presse im Revolutionszeitalter," in *Die Französische Revolution als Bruch des gesellschaftlichen Bewusstseins*, ed. Reinhart Koselleck and Rolf Reichardt (Munich: Oldenbourg, 1988), 167–74.

69   See the *Correspondance secrète, politique et littéraire* of 10 September 1783 (n.p., 1783) (15:104–8) ascribed to Louis-François Mettra.

70   See Jean Dusaulx, *Observations sur l'Histoire de la Bastille de Monsieur Linguet . . .* (London: by the author, 1783), as well as Thomas Evans, *A Refutation of the Memoirs of the Bastille* (London: Cox, 1783), and the French version, *Réfutation des Mémoires de la Bastille . . .* (London: Cox, 1783).

71   [Servan], *Apologie*, 16.

72   See Frantz Funck-Brentano, *The Diamond Necklace* (Philadelphia: Lippincott, 1901).

73   *Lettre*, 3. Bachaumont's *Mémoires secrets*, for instance, reported on the prisoners continuously, esp. between 30 May and 27 June 1786 (32:75–81, 107–8, 116–17, 134–44).

74   Dumas, *Cagliostro*, 207–36.

75   Thilorier, *Mémoire*, 1–3, 29–30. A ten-page summary of this memorandum with all the passages quoted was published under the same title in Berg by Fauche in 1786. See also the version in the English translation, *The Life of the Count Cagliostro* (London: Hookham, 1787).

76   See Hans-Jürgen Lüsebrink, "L'Affaire Cléreaux (Rouen, 1785–1790): Affrontements idéologiques et tensions institutionnelles sur la scène judiciaire à la fin du XVIIIe siècle," *Studies on Voltaire and the 18th Century* 119 (1984): 892–900; Sarah Maza, "Le Tribunal de la nation: Les Mémoires judiciaires et l'opinion publique à la fin de l'Ancien Régime," *Annales E.S.C.* 42 (1987): 73–90; and Hans-Jürgen Lüsebrink, "Die verfolgte Unschuld und ihre Advokaten—Zur Rhetorik und öffentlichen Wirkung empfindsamer Rede im Frankreich des 18. Jahrhunderts," in *Empfindsamkeiten: Akten des 2. Passauer Interdisziplinären Literaturwissenschaftlichen Kolloquiums*, ed. Klaus P. Hansen (Passau: Rothe, 1990), 121–35.

77   Cagliostro quoted from the translation in Dumas, *Cagliostro*, 210–13. There seems to be no contemporary translation of the letter. The French original is the *Traduction d'une lettre écrite par M. le Comte de Cagliostro, à M.***, trouvée dans les décombres de la Bastille* (n.p.: Imprimerie de P. de Lornel, 1786), 2–6. See also *Lettre du comte de Cagliostro au peuple anglois, pour servir de suite à ses Mémoires* (n.p., 1786). Long excerpts from the letter appear in Bachaumont's *Mémoires secrets* of 10 August 1786 (32:230–33).

78   Bachaumont, *Mémoires secrets*, 22 December 1781 (18:224). See also [Jean-Baptiste Brissot], *Lettres sur la liberté politique* (Liège, 1783), 58.

79   Hans-Egon Holthusen, *Sartre in Stammheim* (Stuttgart: Klett-Cotta, 1982). Our comparison is limited to the resonance of the trials in the public sphere; of course Baader was not a Bastille prisoner at Stammheim.

80 In the following, see Funck-Brentano, *La Bastille,* 153–57, and René Pomeau, ed., *Voltaire et son temps* (Oxford: Voltaire Foundation, 1985), 1:94–114, 203–9.

81 "J'ai vu . . . ," in Voltaire, *Œuvres,* 1:294–95. The early circulation of the poem is attested to by its transcript in the "Chansonnier Maurepas," where it appears under the title "Les Maux de la fin du règne de Louis XIV" in Raunié, *Chansonnier* (note 31), 1:1–2. According to Theodore Besterman, *Voltaire* (Chicago: University of Chicago Press, 1969), 54, this poem is not actually by Voltaire but probably by Antoine Louis Lebrun.

82 This poem was first copied by hand in Grimm's *Correspondance littéraire* of 15 April 1761; see the critical edition of the first half of 1761, ed. Ulla Kölving (Uppsala and Stockholm: Almquist and Wiksell, 1978), 73–75. It was also reprinted in Voltaire, *Oeuvres,* 9:353–56, and in Raunié, *Chansonnier* (note 31), 2:216–21.

83 "The Huron," Voltaire, *Works,* 3:107; see also "L'Ingénu," Voltaire, *Oeuvres* 21: 271.

84 Letter from Phélypeaux to Jourdan de Launay of 21 April 1726 (= Besterman [*Voltaire,* note 81] D 272, 288).

85 André-Michel Rousseau, *L'Angleterre et Voltaire* (Oxford: Voltaire Foundation, 1976), 132.

86 "The Henriade," Voltaire, *Works,* 38:68–69; see also "La Henriade," Voltaire, *Oeuvres,* 8:125.

87 See the letters of Voltaire to Thieriot of February 1733 (Best. D 570, 292), from Chevalier probably to d'Hémery of 26 December 1753 (Best. D 5603, 342), and from Voltaire to Palissot of 16 March 1767 (Best. D 14048, 444). Diderot actually served his sentence at Vincennes.

88 Quétel, *Essai,* 11–16, 123–69; Brian E. Strayer, "'Lettres de Cachet' and Social Control in the 'Ancien Régime,' 1659–1789" (Ph.D. diss., University of Iowa, 1987); Arlette Lebigre, *La Justice du Roi: La Vie judiciaire dans l'ancienne France* (Paris: Michel, 1988), 53–57. See also the documentation by Michel Foucault and Arlette Farge concerning the early eighteenth century, *Le Désordre des familles: Lettres de Cachet des Archives de la Bastille au XVIIIe siècle* (Paris: Gallimard, 1982).

89 Reprinted in Lebigre, *La Justice* (note 88), 295–96.

90 René de Castries, *Mirabeau, ou l'Echec du destin* (Paris: Fayard, 1986), 125, 150, 157, 182–83, 215, 219, 252.

91 Pierre Grosclaude, *Malesherbes, témoin et interprète de son temps* (Paris: Fischbacher, 1961), 330–35. See also the circular from Minister of the Interior Louis-Auguste le Tonnelier, Baron de Breteuil to the inspectors of 25 October 1784; reprinted in Bachaumont's *Mémoires secrets* of 31 December 1784 (27:102–11).

92 Fundamentals in Funck-Brentano, *Les Lettres;* supplements in Bégis, "Registre," and Bord, "Prisonniers."

93 François Xavier Emmanuelli, "'Ordres du Roi' et lettres de cachet en Provence à la fin de l'Ancien Régime," *Revue Historique* 252 (1974): 357–92, here 381–83.

94 See in general Vladimir S. Lublinski, *La Guerre des Farines* (Grenoble: Presses Universitaires de Grenoble, 1979), 179–213.

95 See "A Spy in Grub Street" in Robert Darnton, *The Literary Underground of the Old Regime* (Cambridge: Harvard University Press, 1982), 41–70, 223–29. We would also like to thank Mr. Darnton for information provided in letters on the writers in the Bastille.

96   This information was kindly supplied by Gudrun Gersmann from her disserta-
      tion recently finished in Bochum on the social history of the "écrivains obscurs"
      in prerevolutionary France: *Im Schatten der Bastille: Die Welt der Schriftsteller, Kol-
      porteure und Buchhändler am Vorabend der Franmösischen Revolution* (Stuttgart: Klett-
      Cotta, 1993). The manuscript by M.-C. Jou, "Les Gens de livre embastillés,
      1750–1789" (thèse de 3e cycle, Université de Paris I), was not available to us.
97   Handwritten list of 371 books and 64 almanacs and brochures, Bibliothèque de
      l'Arsenal, mss. 6495, fols. 1–44.
98   Some diaries then unpublished recognized this fact, e.g., that of the financier
      La Joncière, who was imprisoned in 1724. See Albert Babeau, "Un Financier à
      la Bastille sous Louis XV," *Mémoires de la Société de l'histoire de Paris et de l'Ile-de-
      France* 25 (1898): 1–46.
99   Biré, *Légendes,* 65–68; Funck-Brentano, "La Bastille," 56, and *La Bastille,* 193.
100   Biré, *Légendes,* 71–77; Funck-Brentano, "La Bastille," 65–68, and *La Bastille,* 114–
      17.
101   Biré, *Légendes,* 77–78; Funck-Brentano, "La Bastille," 68–69.
102   Biré, *Légendes,* 81–83; Funck-Brentano, "La Bastille," 278–80. See also the articles
      and book by Paul Sérieux and Lucien Libert, "Les Anormaux constitutionnels
      à la Bastille," *Chronique Médicale* 18 (1911): 609–19, 641–48; *Le Régime des aliénés en
      France au XVIIIe siècle* (Paris: Masson, 1914); and "Le Service médical de la Bas-
      tille," *Bulletin de la Société française d'histoire de la médecine* 20 (1926): 117–34, 218–23.
103   Funck-Brentano, *La Bastille,* 108. Letter of the police lieutenant Nicolas-René
      Berryer to the director, Chevalier, of 24 January 1757. In Ravaisson-Mollien,
      Archives, 12:441.
104   Biré, *Légendes,* 78–80; Bégis, "Registre," 533–35, 537, and 541–42.
105   Letter of Bernard-René-Jourdan de Launay to state minister Villedeuil of 2 July
      1789, quoted in Lély, *Marquis de Sade,* 272. The French original can be found
      in Donatien-Alphonse-François de Sade, *Lettres et mélanges littéraires écrits à Vin-
      cennes et à la Bastille,* ed. Gilbert Lély (Paris: Editions Borderie, 1980), 39–40. See
      also ibid. 86–88, 123, 133, 440, 444; Biré, *Légendes,* 74–75; and Bégis, "Registre,"
      532–34.
106   We would like to thank Werner Jost for interpretive assistance. Man Ray initially
      outlined the Sade portrait as a pen-and-ink sketch and used it for his illustra-
      tions of Eluard's poems. See *Les Mains libres: Dessins de Man Ray, illustrés par les
      poèmes de Paul Eluard* (Paris: Bucher, 1937), 127.
107   See primarily Sven Stelling-Michaud, "Le Mythe du despotisme oriental,"
      Schweizerische Beiträge zur Allgemeinen Geschichte 18–19 (1960–61): 328–46; Franco
      Venturi, "Oriental Despotism" *Journal of the History of Ideas* 24 (1963): 133–42;
      and Robert Shackleton, "Le Mot 'despote' et 'despotisme,' " in *Les Lumières en
      Hongrie, en Europe centrale et en Europe orientale: Actes du 3e colloque de Matrafüred*
      (Budapest: Akademiai Kiado, 1977), 51–96.
108   Mercier, *Memoirs,* 1:43. See also the French original, *L'An 2440, rêve s'il en fut
      jamais,* ed. Raymond Trousson (Bordeaux: Ducros, 1971), 112.
109   Louis-Sébastien Mercier, *La Destruction de la Ligue, ou la Réduction de Paris* (Am-
      sterdam, 1782). Also in Mercier, *Théâtre complet,* 4 vols. (Amsterdam and Leiden:
      Vlam and Murray, 1778–84), 4:111–49.

110 Louis-Sébastien Mercier, *Tableau de Paris,* rev. ed., 12 vols. (Amsterdam, 1783–88), here 3:275–78 (chapter entitled "Bastille"); see also 8:214–15 (chapter entitled "Lettres de cachet") and 11:290. There are several English translations of Mercier's *Tableau,* but while only one contains the chapter on the Bastille, none includes the chapter on the lettres de cachet.

111 Dulaure, *Nouvelle Description,* 1:69–70.

112 Charles Théveneau de Morande, *Le Gazetier cuirassé, ou Anecdotes scandaleuses de la Cour de France* . . . (London: Imprimé à cent lieues de la Bastille, à l'enseigne de la liberté, 1771), v note a, 18–19 (new editions 1777 and 1785). See also his *Mélanges confus sur matières fort claires, par l'auteur du Gazetier cuirassé* (London: Imprimés sous le Soleil, [1771]), 5–6.

113 Charles Théveneau de Morande, *La Gazette noire, par un homme qui n'est pas blanc, ou Oeuvres posthumes du Gazetier cuirassé* (London: Imprimé à cent lieues de la Bastille . . . , 1784), 7–9. See also Paul Robiquet, *Théveneau de Morande: Etude sur le XVIIIe siècle* (Paris: Quantin, 1882).

114 See "A Clandestine Bookseller in the Province" in Darnton, *Literary Underground* (note 95), 122–47, here 139.

115 Beaumarchais, *Théâtre,* 793. On the greater context, see Claude Petitfrère, *1784 — Le Scandale du Mariage de Figaro, prélude de la Révolution française* (Paris: Complexe, 1989).

116 Campan, *Memoirs,* 2:12. The French original is in the *Mémoires de Madame Campan, première femme de chambre de Marie-Antoinette,* ed. Jean Chalon (Paris: Ramsay, 1979), 139.

117 Beaumarchais, *Barber,* 346.

118 See *Mémoire présenté au Roi par Sgr. le duc d'Orléans et signé par M. le Mis.* [Charles-Louis] *du Crest, son chancelier, le 20 août 1787* (n.p., 1787). See also Bachaumont, *Mémoires secrets,* 3 November 1787 (36:136–37).

119 Reprinted in Bournon, *Bastille,* 303–6, here 305.

120 *Dialogue,* 4–11.

121 [Carra], *L'Orateur,* 5–6. Quoted from the contemporary German translation, *Der Redner der Reichsstände,* in *Französische Staatsanzeigen, gesammelt und hg. zur Geschichte der grossen Revolution,* no. 1 (Leipzig: Kummer, 1791), no. 1, 13.

122 *Archives parlementaires,* 5:149 (cahier of the district Les Froux near Chevreuse, electoral district of Paris).

123 See the grievance registers of the Third Estate in Charles-Louis Chassin, ed., *Les Elections et les cahiers de Paris en 1789,* 4 vols. (Paris: Jouaust et Signaux, 1888–89); of Paris intra muros (3:364); and of the city districts Les Mathurins (2:427), Eglise des Théâtins (2:437), and Louis-de-la-Culture (2:469–70).

124 Ibid., 3:324.

125 Reprinted in *Archives parlementaires,* 4:40. See also the *cahiers* of the Third Estate of the barony of Boulainvilliers (*Archives parlementaires,* 1st ser., 4:337), the rural district Grand et Petit Charonne (ibid., 410), and the Provençal city Martigues (*Archives parlementaires,* 1st ser., 6:343).

2. THE STORMING OF THE BASTILLE

1   For accounts of the storming of the Bastille see, as standard works, Flammermont, *Journée;* Rudé, *The Crowd;* Godechot, *Taking;* Chaussinand-Nogaret, *Bastille;* and Schulze, *Der 14. Juli 1789.* The following sketch of events does not intend to compete with these detailed descriptions, which are in part supported by documentary evidence. Instead, it is limited to a selection of facts that are important for the upcoming interpretation of the history of the symbol.

2   See Chaussinand-Nogaret, *Bastille,* 92: "They said, they repeated, that fifteen thousand men were marching into Paris under orders to burn, kill, destroy; some of them had already been seen in Rue Saint-Antoine, marching resolutely toward the Place de la Grève to break into the Hôtel de Ville." On the problem of the unprovable thesis of an "aristocratic plot," see the still fundamentally important Pierre Caron, "La Tentative de contre-révolution de juin-juillet 1789," *Revue d'histoire moderne et contemporaine,* 1st ser., 8 (1906–7): 5–34, 649–78.

3   See Chaussinand-Nogaret, *Bastille,* 96.

4   Ibid.

5   Babeuf, *Pages,* 73.

6   See the handwritten report of an eyewitness: "13 July (from Paris). Arriving in Paris, witnessed the terrible riot that just took place; there was fire, five barriers were burned, and at the time when the crowd was excited, one had reason to fear that the fire was not far away." See also the engravings in *Révolutions de Paris* 1 (12–17 July 1789): before p. 6.

7   Ms. in the Bibliothèque Nationale, nouvelles acquisitions françaises (n.a.f.) 2670, fol. 55.

8   Godechot, *Taking,* 227–32.

9   See *Relation de ce qui s'est passé à l'Abbaye Saint-Germain, le 30 Juin au Soir* (n.p., 1789).

10 See the contemporary reports in Godechot, *Taking,* 243–44. "When de Launey [*sic*] was dead, the people said: 'The Nation requires that his head be shown to the public, so that it may know his guilt'" (244).

11 Guiffrey, "Documents," 505 (testimony of the cook Dénot, who had cut off de Launay's head, on 14 July 1789).

12 Ibid.

13 See, e.g., Campe, "Briefe," 56–57.

14 Ducray-Duminil, *La semaine,* 15: "It is good to teach people from the country the marvelous result here of the day of 14 July, which is also called the day of miracles." See also Louis-Abel Beffroy de Reigny, *Histoire de France pendant trois mois . . . , depuis le 15 Mai, jusqu'au 15 Août 1789* (Paris: Belin, 1789), 69–70; ibid., 19, 23, 70, 159, references to Providence.

15 Concerning the peasants' revolution that began on 16 July, see primarily Georges Lefebre, *La Grande Peur de 1789* (Paris: Colin, 1932). Concerning Rouen, see Claude Mazauric, "Bordier et Jourdain: La Fête jacobine et le discours politique à Rouen en l'an II," in *Jacobinisme et Révolution: Autour du Bicentenaire de Quatre-vingt-neuf* (Paris: Editions Sociales, 1984), 155–93.

16 Chaussinand-Nogaret, *Bastille,* 99. "On the thirteenth, very excited, he wanted to act; meeting Madame de Staël, Necker's daughter, he became elated again:

'I want,' he said to her, 'to take revenge for your father on these bastards, who want to butcher us.'"

17 See Siméon-Prosper Hardy, "Mes Loisirs," Bibliothèque Nationale, ms. fr. 6687 ("15 Juillet 1789").

18 On this matter, see Rolf Reichardt, "Bastillen in Deutschland? Gesellschaftliche Aussenwirkungen der Französischen Revolution am Beispiel des Pariser Bastillesturms," in *Deutschland und Europa in der Neuzeit: Festschrift für Karl Otmar Freiherr von Aretin zum 65. Geburtstag,* ed. Ralph Melville et al., 2 vols. (Stuttgart: Steiner, 1988), 1:419–67, here 451.

19 Quoted from Chaussinand-Nogaret, *Bastille,* 105.

20 See ibid.

21 This understanding is demonstrated in exemplary fashion in Pierre Rétat, ed., *L'Attentat de Damiens: Discours sur l'événement au XVIIIe siècle* (Paris: CNRS, 1979).

22 An unsurpassed listing of original sources is offered by Flammermont, *Journée;* see also Frantz Funck-Brentano, "Bibliographie critique de la prise de la Bastille," *Revue des études historiques* 65 (1899): 284–91. The list of sources in the appendix of reports (back of this volume) intentionally omits handwritten reports (letters, recollections, etc.), i.e., those not published at the time. Hereafter text references to sources in this appendix are by number (e.g., no. 28).

23 A number of lyrical accounts of the storming of the Bastille, which were addressed to educated readers and often designated the events of the time only in code, were not taken into account in the analysis: Charlet, *Triomphe de la France, Poème* (n.p., 1789); *La Parisiade, poème héroï-tragicomique dédié au comité d'inquisition. Par un Hottentot* (Cape of Good Hope, 1789), 16–21; *Pot-pourri sur les événemens arrivez dans Paris, les 13, 14, et 17 Juillet 1789. Par un patriote, ce 20 Juillet 1789* [Paris, 1789]; *Révolutions lyriques, ou le Triomphe de la liberté française* (Paris: Frère, 1790); *La Prise de la Bastille, ou le Despotisme vaincu. Poëme en trois chants, dédié à M. le marquis de La Fayette* (Paris: Volland/Petit, 1790); *Récit historique de ce qui s'est passé dans la ville de Paris . . . ,* in *Chansonnier national ou recueil de chansons . . .* (Paris: Valleyre, 1790), 7–12.

24 See Pierre Rétat, "Forme et discours d'un journal révolutionnaire: Les 'Révolutions de Paris' en 1789," in *L'Instrument périodique: La Fonction de la presse au XVIIIe siècle,* ed. Claude Labrosse and Rétat (Lyon: Presses Universitaires, 1985), 140–78.

25 More in Jeremy Popkin, *Revolutionary News: The Press in France, 1789–1799* (Durham: Duke University Press, 1990).

26 See Hans-Jürgen Lüsebrink and Rolf Reichardt, "Oralität and Textfiliation in rezeptionspragmatischer Perspektive: Sozio-kulturelle Fallstudien zur Konstitution populärer Druckschriften und zur Rezeption der 'Mémoires' von Latude in den Jahren 1787–1793," in *Zur Geschichte von Buch und Leser im Frankreich des Ancien Régime: Beiträge zu einer empirischen Rezeptionsforschung,* ed. Günter Berger (Rheinfelden: Schäuble, 1986), 111–44.

27 Louis-Abel Beffroy de Reigny, *Testament d'un électeur de Paris* (Paris: Mayeur, Desenne, etc., an IV [1796], 124–25.

28 *Dictionnaire,* no. 1, 420 (art. "Bastille").

29 See also no. 17:3, Barnave's letter of 15 July 1789 from Versailles: "Lettres inédites sur la prise de la Bastille," ed. J. de Beylié, *Bulletin de l'Académie delphinale* 19 (1905): 288; and the letter of the Marquis de Ferrières to his wife from Ver-

sailles of 17 July 1789: "The events . . . followed with such speed that one week took up the space of one year" (Ferrières *Correspondance inédite* . . . , ed. Henri Carré [Paris: Alcan, 1932], 90).

30 *Almanach des douze ministres,* 63. The frontispiece of the brochure is reprinted in the Ploetz volume *Die Französische Revolution,* ed. Rolf Reichardt (Freiburg: Ploetz, 1988), 220.

31 Illustration and interpretation in Herding and Reichardt, *Bildpublizistik,* 84–85.

32 Villencour, *Harangue,* 2. See also no. 33:60–64 and no. 38:64.

33 See the anonymous colored etching *Fédération Anti Patriotique des ci-devant Aristocrates,* Bibliothèque Nationale, Collection Histoire de France, M 99861. Shown and interpreted in *Die Bastille,* 30.

34 See also no. 15:7–8 and the etching accompanying the French original (for the title of the English translation) *Motions du Palais Royal le 12 yet* [juillet] *1789,* reprinted in the exhibition catalog *Revolution in Print: The Press in France, 1775–1800,* ed. Robert Darnton and Daniel Roche (Berkeley: University of California Press, 1989), 153.

35 Desmoulins, *Oeuvres,* 2:21–28. René Farge demythologizes in "Un Episode de la journée du 12 juillet 1789: Camille Desmoulins au jardin du Palais-Royal," *Annales révolutionnaires* 7 (1914): 646–74.

36 This song is printed in Letourmi's pictorial newspaper on the storming of the Bastille and reprinted in Lüsebrink and Reichardt, "Oralität" (note 26), 137.

37 *Réflexions,* 4–5.

38 *Exploits,* 8.

39 "Tableau du commencement du siège et de la prise de la Bastille par une patrouille commandée par Jean-Armand Pannetier, citoyen du faubourg St. Antoine," Archives Nationales, undated ms., C35, no. 298², fol. 1ᵛ).

40 Guilbert, *Almanach,* 24.

41 See no. 18:2, among others. In contrast, Beffroy de Reigny stresses that de Launay had wanted to flee and had worn civilian clothes without his cross of Saint Louis (no. 10:9–10; no. 32:87).

42 See *Testament de Charles de Launay, Gouverneur de la Bastille, trouvé à la Bastille, le jour de l'assaut* (n.p., 1789), 2–7.

43 See *Adresse de remerciement à Monsieur Belzébuth, Prince souverain des Enfers, au Peuple Parisien, sur l'envoi des cinq traîtres exterminés les 14 et 22 juillet* (n.p., 1789), 3.

44 *Les Quatre Traîtres,* 7, and *Les Enragés,* 10–12, respectively.

45 See, e.g., *Récit des malheurs, peines et souffrances qu'éprouvoient les prisonniers enfermés à la Bastille, par l'un d'eux détenu pendant 50 ans dans cette Prison* (Paris: Cailleau, [1789]) or *Epître d'un prisonnier délivré de la Bastille* (n.p., 1789).

46 No. 18:2–3. No. 6:10–11 reports very similarly on the same "Count d'Estrade," who had languished in the *cachot* for twenty-five years. Probably both accounts actually refer to the Count de Solages, who had been in the Bastille at the instigation of his family only since 1784. In no. 17:17 the same figure is called "comte de Straze."

47 *La Bastille,* 6–7. See also Villencour, *Harangue,* 5.

48 *Le Comte de Lorges,* 16, reprinted in *Mémoires historiques,* 2:357–73, and in extracts in no. 46:19–30.

49 See *La Bastille dévoilée*, no. 5, 132–33.

50 Feydel, *Particularités*, 5–6. See also *Elégie sur la démolition de la Bastille de Paris, le 22 juillet 1789* (n.p., n.d.), British Museum, R. 63(13).

51 See *Le Sourd du Palais-Royal, ou Anecdote Singulière arrivée dans les derniers troubles de Paris* (n.p., [1789]).

52 A suggestion to keep the ruins of the Bastille as a memorial did not meet with much approval; see *Idées* and below.

53 See also no. 15 (French original) and the anonymous pamphlet *La Liberté sur le trône et l'esclavage sous les pieds* (Paris: Cressonnier, [1789]), 6.

54 E.g., Pierre-Jean-Georges Callières de l'Estang, *Chanson sur la prise des Invalides et de la Bastille* (Paris: Nyon le Jeune, n.d.).

55 See also *Aux Français, sur le 14 Juillet* (n.p., [1789]), 5–6.

56 Desloges, *Almanach*, 25.

57 *Observations*, 2–3. See also no. 16:44.

58 *La Bastille dévoilée*, no. 2, 22–23.

59 See *Die Bastille*, 33–34 (figs. 22, 25).

60 *Monseigneur le duc de Chartres visitant la Bastille, le jeudi 13 Août 1789* (Paris: Laporte, [1789]) and *La Journée parisienne, ou Triomphe de la France* (Paris: Volland [1789]).

61 Cubières-Palmézeaux, *Voyage*, 21.

62 Mauclerc, *Le Langage*, 1–2.

63 *Le Voile*, 2–3. See also *Les Crimes dévoilés: Ordre de l'attaque de la ville de Paris, projettée par la nuit du 14 au 15 Juillet 1789* (n.p., [1789]) and *Découverte de la Conjuration* (n.p., [1789]).

64 [Brizard], *Adresse*, 6. See also *Copie de quelques pièces intéressantes, trouvées à la Bastille, où l'on voit la manière dont M. Delaunay se défaisoit des mauvais sujets* (n.p., [1789]); *Copie des lettres originales manuscrites trouvées dans les ruines de la Bastille le 15 juillet 1789* (Paris: Lormel, 1789); *Recueil fidèle de plusieurs manuscrits trouvés à la Bastille* (Paris: Girardin, 1789); *Notice des services d'Alexandre de Baran, chargé par MM. de l'Hôtel-de-Ville, & par le District de Saint-Louis de la Culture, de l'enlevement des archives & des effets de la Bastille . . .* (n.p., [1789]); as well as a poster on the city hall of 24 July 1789 calling on the citizens to hand in any papers from the Bastille, Bibliothèque Nationale, fol. Lb[40] .3271, no. 2.

65 See also Cubières-Palmézeaux, *Voyage*, 25–26, as well as *Les Oubliettes retrouvées dans les souterrains de la Bastille* (Paris: Grangé, [1789]).

66 Cf. no. 50:18n.

3. REVOLUTIONARY SYMBOLISM UNDER THE SIGN OF THE BASTILLE

1 There was a Bastille showcase, for instance, in the fall of 1789 in Bolbec; see also Mona Ozouf, "Le Simulacre et la fête," in *Les Fêtes de la Révolution*, ed. Jean Ehrard and Paul Viallaneix (Paris: Clavreuil, 1977), 323–53, here 341–42.

2 Answer of the attorney Bernadau at the end of December 1790 to the survey of Abbé Grégoire concerning speech and reading habits in the provinces, *Lettre*, 143.

3 Falloux, *Madame Swetchine*, 1:18.

4   *Anecdotes curieuses et plaisantes relatives à la Révolution de France* (Paris, 1791), 11–12.

5   *Chronique de Paris* 102 (12 April 1790): 407.

6   *Le Rôdeur français* 4 (3 December 1789): 62.

7   See the chapter "La Bastille et les faïences" in Georges Lecocq, *La Prise de la Bastille et ses anniversaires* (Paris: Charavay, 1881), 153–63. Color illustrations in Michel Vovelle, *La Révolution française—Images et récit*, 5 vols. (Paris: Messidor, 1986), 1:176, 276–77. See also Edith Mannoni, *Les Faïences révolutionnaires* (Paris: Massin, 1989), 20–21, 62.

8   A certain Lethien advertised a "Couteau National" that had the Bastille as its handle; depending on model, the price was between twelve and seventy-two livres. See *Mercure de France*, 31 October 1789, 119.

9   Two examples are in the permanent exhibition of the Paris Musée Carnavalet, room 71, inv. no. MB 599 and MB 603; illustration in Michel Beurdeley, *La France à l'encan, 1789–1799: Exode des objects d'art sous la Révolution* (Paris: Tallandier, 1981), 22.

10   These are mostly relatively cheap colored engravings on sticks of jacaranda wood. See, for instance, the exhibition catalog *Actualités—Vie parisienne* (Paris: Musée Carnavalet, 1973), 137; also the exhibition catalog *Freiheit, Gleichheit, Brüderlichkeit, 200 Jahre Französische Revolution in Deutschland* (Nuremberg: Germanisches Nationalmuseum, 1989), no. 111 and color plate on p. 294.

11   Toile de Jouy of 1791, red print on white calico; it shows, among other things, musicians and dancing citizens on the ruins of the half-razed Bastille. See plate 57 in Robert Forrer, *Die Kunst des Zeugdrucks vom Mittelalter bis zur Empirezeit* (Strasbourg: Schlesier, 1898).

12   Report from a correspondant in the Gotha *Journal des Luxus und der Moden* 4 (October and November 1789): 453, 489. The *Gazette d'Amsterdam* had already printed a similar report on 1 September 1789, 20. *Rôdeur français* 3 (29 November 1789): 43 reports a depiction of the storming of the Bastille on the outside paneling of a cabriolet. The Paris Magasin des Modes Nouvelles writes of "shoe buckles à la Bastille" on 11 November 1789 and of hairstyles "à la Bastille" on 21 September and 1 December 1789. Annemarie Kleinert examines this phenomenon and documents it with contemporary illustrations in "La Révolution et le premier journal illustré paru en France," *Dix-huitième Siècle* 21 (1989): 285–309, and also "La Mode—Miroir de la Révolution française," *Francia* 16, no. 2 (1989): 75–99.

13   Schulin, *Die französische Revolution*, 228.

14   Two dozen French coins taking up the subject of the Bastille and medals of the time of the Revolution are cataloged in Michel Hennin, *Histoire numismatique de la Révolution française* (Paris: Merlin, 1826), nos. 22, 24–30, 35, 36, 71–75, 90, 156, 160, 186, 187, 349–53, 362. See also Guy Beneut, "La Bastille," in *Collectionneurs et collections numismatiques: Monnaies, médailles et jetons* (Paris: Hôtel de la Monnaie, 1968), 303–7.

15   Printed and personally signed circular from Palloy of 31 December 1789; supposedly this circular was presented to the twelve hundred delegates along with the pictured medal. Bibliothèque Nationale 4°Lb^{39}.10468.

16 *Beiträge*, 3–5. The two other translations are *Die enthüllte Bastille, oder Sammlung ächter Beiträge zur Geschichte derselben*, 7 vols. (Lübeck: Donatius, 1789–91), and *Die entlarvte Bastille oder Sammlung authentischer Nachrichten zum Behuf ihrer Geschichte*, 4 booklets (Bayreuth: Zeitungsdruckerei, 1789–91). There appears to be no contemporary English translation.

17 *Mémoires historiques*, 1:ix.

18 *Courrier de Paris dans les Provinces et des Provinces à Paris* 12, no. 13 (17 May 1790): 193.

19 *Extrait des Registres du comité de Saint-Louis-de-la-Culture* (Paris: Hérault, 1790). See also *Particularités sur la découverte de plusieurs cadavres trouvés dans les souterrains de la Bastille* (n.p., [1790]), signed "La Vérité, ouvrier de la Bastille."

20 Article by Audouin in the *Journal universel, ou Révolutions des Royaumes* 104 (6 March 1790): 1246.

21 *Moniteur* 123 (30 April 1790), reprinted in *Moniteur universel*, 4:267–68.

22 Concerning these celebrations and the speeches given on the occasion, see *Hommage à l'Assemblée nationale du modèle de la Bastille. . . . Délibérations et différentes pièces relatives aux cadavres trouvés dans la Bastille . . .* (Paris: Hérault, 1790), 18–31. See also *Chronique de Paris* 155 (8 June 1790): 635.

23 *Almanach du Père Duchesne*, 55.

24 *La Journée*, 1–2.

25 Herding and Reichardt, *Bildpublizistik*, 30–31, 141–48.

26 Pierre Prillard, "La Glorification des Vainqueurs de la Bastille," *Actes du Congrès national des sociétés savantes: Section d'histoire moderne et contemporaine* 100 (1977): 461–76, here 469. See also André Souyris-Rolland, "Les Vainqueurs de la Bastille et leurs décorations," *Revue des Amis du Musée de l'armée* 88 (1983): 59–80.

27 Prillard, "La Glorification" (note 26), 469.

28 Parein and Estienne, *Appel*, 1 note 1.

29 Lacroix and Farge, *Actes*, 1st ser., 3:19; see also *La Gazette nationale, ou le Moniteur universel* 22 (22 January 1790): 177.

30 *Archives parlementaires*, 1st ser., 16:371 (session of 19 June 1790).

31 Ibid. The honorary diploma presented in 1790 (Brevet de Vainqueur de la Bastille) can be seen in the collection of copperplate engravings of the Bibliothèque Nationale (Collection de Vinck, no. 1643) and is reproduced in Vovelle, *La Révolution française* (note 7), 1:170–71.

32 *Archives parlementaires*, 1st ser., 8:248 (session of 18 July 1789).

33 See Rudé, *The Crowd;* also George Rudé, "La Composition sociale des insurrections parisiennes de 1789 à 1791," *Annales historiques de la Révolution française* 24 (1952): 256–88.

34 *Les Lauriers*, 6.

35 Pont-Cale [pseud.], "Projet de statue à l'horloger Humbert: Le Premier Vainqueur de la Bastille," *Intermédiaire des chercheurs et curieux* 595 (30 September 1892): cols. 325–26.

36 Prillard, "La Glorification" (note 26), 469–70.

37 Léonard Bourdon, *Recueil des actions héroïques et civiques des Républicains français*, 5 vols. (Paris, an II [1794]), 1:1: "This work, intended to be read, according to your decree, in the popular assemblies on the days of the Decade, and in the

public schools, should merit inclusion in elementary books, popularly called classics; it should present a good model of narration." The biographical sketch concerning Humbert can be found in Bourdon, 4–5.

38   Lacroix and Farge, *Actes,* 1st ser., 6:244–45.

39   "Fermentation occasionée par le décret relatif aux 'Vainqueurs de la Bastille,'" *Courrier des LXXXIII Départements* 13, no. 23 (27 June 1790): 346–51, here 349–50.

40   *Ami du Peuple* 155 (7 June 1790), 169 (30 June 1790): 387, 388.

41   Lacroix and Farge, *Actes,* 2d ser., 2:41–43.

42   Fournel, *Les hommes,* 310.

43   Joseph Durieux, *Les Vainqueurs de la Bastille* (Paris: Champion, 1911), 9.

44   Fournel, *Les hommes,* 325–32; see also Pierre d'Hugues, "Les Derniers Vainqueurs de la Bastille," *Revue hebdomadaire* 7, no. 7 (July 1911): 381–408, here 384–86.

45   H. G. Aulard, ed., *Recueil des actes du Comité de salut public* (Paris: Imprimerie Nationale, 1889–1932), 6:58–60.

46   Jacques Guilhaumou, "Zeitgenössische politische Lebensgeschichten aus der Französischen Revolution (1793–1794)," in *Die Französische Revolution als Bruch des gesellschaftlichen Bewusstseins,* ed. Reinhart Koselleck and Rolf Reichardt (Munich: Oldenbourg, 1988), 358–78.

47   See also Hans-Jürgen Lüsebrink, "Die Vainqueurs de la Bastille: Kollektiver Diskurs und individuelle 'Wortergreifungen,'" in Koselleck and Reichardt, *Die Französische Revolution* (note 46): 231–357.

48   Parein, *La Prise,* 64.

49   Ibid.

50   Concerning this drama, see Lüsebrink, "Evénement."

51   Parein, *Les Crimes,* 1, 2, 4, 49–50.

52   Ibid., 50–51.

53   The German translation is "Protokollirte Aussage des J. B. Humbert, welcher der erste war, so auf den Thurm der Bastille stieg," *Bayreuther Zeitung* 109 (10 September 1789): 795–97, and 110 (12 September 1789): 802.

54   Rossignol, *La Vie,* 65.

55   Guiffrey, "Documents," 503–4 (interrogation of François-Félix Dénot by the Châtelet court).

56   Jean-Joseph Dusaulx, *De mes rapports avec J.-J. Rousseau, et de notre correspondance* (Paris: Didot le Jeune, 1789).

57   *Aux Fils aînés de la Révolution Française, Enfants de 1789; Hommes de 1809* (Paris: Imprimerie de Pelletier, 1809).

58   *Bayreuther Zeitung* 91 (30 July 1789): 664.

59   Rigby, *Letters,* 69–70. The engraving *L'Heure première de la Liberté* (1789) is reproduced in *Die Bastille,* 41.

60   *Le Comte de Lorges,* 9.

61   *Délivrance de Mr le Conte* [sic] *de Lorges par la Nation, le 14 Juillet 1789* (Paris, 1789); here *Complainte de Mr le Conte* [sic] *de Lorges* (see fig. 23).

62   Ibid., third stanza: "Que je vous rends de grâves / ô braves Citoyens / votre valeur surpasse / Les Scipions les Romains."

63   *Le Comte de Lorges,* 13.

64 See ibid., 4: "He had asked the nation for a retirement where he could peacefully end his career, and . . . his request had been granted."

65 Ibid.: "I obtained permission to go and see him again, and took advantage of that; he told me the story of his imprisonment and promised to tell me the details of the other circumstances of his life."

66 *Révolutions de Paris* 1 (12–17 July 1789): 14.

67 *Chronique de Paris* 145 (13 August 1793), article on p. 4 entitled "Voici les diverses inscriptions gravées sur des pierres de la Bastille, et qui étoient imposées sur l'emplacement où étoit autrefois cet antre de douleur" (Here are the various inscriptions engraved on the stones of the Bastille, which were placed where that cave of suffering was).

68 For this reason, they were called "oubliettes."

69 Trenck, *Geschichte*, 132 and 138.

70 Ibid., 135.

71 See Hans-Jürgen Lüsebrink, "La Bastille, château gothique," *Europe* 62 (1984): 104–12.

72 *Remarques et Anecdotes sur le château de la Bastille* (Paris: Goujon, 1789). This volume is subtitled "Suivies d'un détail historique du siège, de la prise et de la démolition de cette forteresse" (Followed by a historical account of the siege, the capture, and the demolition of this fortress). The Count de Lorges is mentioned on 81–82.

73 *La Bastille dévoilée*, no. 5, 132–33.

74 Ibid., 133.

75 Concerning Latude's biography, see Funck-Brentano, *Legends;* Armand Praviel, *Les Evasions de Latude* (Paris: Editions de France, 1934); and Quétel, *Escape.*

76 Quoted from Quétel, *Escape,* 133.

77 Henri Masers de Latude, *Mémoires de M. De Latude, ingénieur* (Paris 1789).

78 See Henri Masers de Latude, *Lettre à Milord Grosvenor* (n.p., [1789–90]), Bibliothèque Historique de la Ville de Paris, 776, fol. 63. Lord Grosvenor offered Latude six thousand guineas for the exhibition of his ladder.

79 Sorel, "Envoi," 67.

80 *Chronique de Paris* 204 (23 July 1790): 814: "Mr. la Tude, known all over Europe for having spent thirty-five years in the Bastille, a victim of Madame de Pompadour, was presented at the Society of the Friends of the Constitution in Paris, and was accepted as a member by acclamation."

81 Latude and Linguet, *Memoirs,* 53. The title of the original French edition, *Le Despotisme dévoilé, ou Mémoires de Henri Masers de Latude, détenu pendant trente-cinq ans dans diverses prisons d'Etat; rédigés sur les pièces originales par M. Thiery,* 2 vols. (Paris: Lejay fils, 1790; new ed., 1793), is translated as " *'Despotism Unmasked'; or, Memoirs of Henri Masers de Latude, Imprisoned during Thirty-Five Years in Various State Prisons"* (ibid., 49).

82 *Mercure de France,* June 1790, 129–51, and July 1790, 33–46, 56–81 (review by La Harpe), here 129: "This book, which anyone who knows how to read should read, is without question the most precious monument in all respects, for it portrays all the extremes of which humanity is capable."

83 Ibid., 230.

84 See *Moniteur* 129 (9 May 1790): 314; 59 (28 February 1791): 491; 73 (14 March 1791): 611.

85 See Representative Jean-Georges-Charles Voidel in *Moniteur* 73 (14 March 1791): 611: "But should a generous nation encourage cowardice such as that of which Mr. Latude was guilty?"

86 *Moniteur* 28 (28 January 1792): 228: "When tyranny brought down the weight of its hand on that unfortunate man, he traced in his own blood a plan to increase national strength, a plan conceived in his dungeon." See also *Moniteur* 58 (27 February 1792): 484.

87 *Moniteur* 196 (15 July 1793): 119.

88 Edmond and Jules Goncourt, *Histoire de la Société française pendant la Révolution* (1854; new ed., Paris, 1864), 271.

89 See Robert, *Mémoires*. See also the following reports and petitions by Jean Claude Guillaume Leprévôt de Beaumont: *Dénonciation d'un pacte de famine générale au roi Louis XV, ouvrage manuscrit trouvé à la Bastille, le 14 juillet dernier* (n.p., [1789]); *Le Prisonnier d'Etat, ou Tableau historique de la captivité de J. C. G. Le Prévôt de Beaumont* (Paris, 1791); *Dénonciation, pétition et rogation . . . aux représentants de l'Assemblée nationale* (n.p., 1791), reprinted in *Ami du Peuple* 416 (1 April 1791): 143–48; *Dénonciation et pétition . . . aux représentants de l'Assemblée de la seconde législature* (n.p., [1 November 1791]). See also *Rapport de la commission des lettres-de-cachet sur la pétition de J. C. G. Leprévôt* (Paris: Imprimerie Nationale, 1792). Further records on this case can be found in the Archives Nationales, DV. 1–8.

90 Palloy, *Adresse à la Convention*, 3.

91 Pierre-François Palloy, "Lettre au Conseil général du Calvados," 26 October 1790, quoted in T. Raulin, "Le Pseudo-Patriote Palloy et les administrateurs du Calvados de 1790 à 1794," *Bulletin de la Société des antiquaires de Normandie*, 1900–1901:307–76, here 316.

92 See *Moniteur* 112 (22 April 1790), reprinted in *Moniteur universel*, 4:176 (report of the Academy of Sciences' committee of inquiry).

93 See Palloy's 5 November 1790 letter to the administrative committee of the département of Puy-de-Dôme, quoted in C. Jaloustre, "Une Pierre mémorable, souvenir de la Bastille (Clermont)," *Revue d'Auvergne* 14 (1897): 224–25.

94 Many accounts of the dedications of the Bastille stones in the provinces give an exact list of these items; see, for example, Pierre-François Palloy, "Mes Frères," a speech delivered at the Jacobin club, Paris, 1792, Archives Départementales Seine 4 AZ 719, 13: "I swore to use all my courage to propagate the fruits of our budding constitution. France is a new world, and in order to conserve this victory, it was necessary to scatter the debris of our former slavery like the Levite who in revenge scattered the limbs of his wife."

95 Palloy, "Mes Frères," 13.

96 The terms used here are present in all of Palloy's writings; see "gage de la liberté" and "emblême de la liberté," among others, in Palloy's letter to the Département de la Marne of 4 November 1790, Archives Départementales Marne 1 L 282.

97 Pierre-François Palloy, letter to the Société populaire de Nantes, 28 Brumaire an II, Bibliothèque Nationale, ms. n.a.f.3241, fol. 178, 1.

98 Palloy, *Eloge*, 7.

99 See *Extrait du Procès-Verbal du Dép. du Loiret (Orléans)*, 10 September 1793, 2.

100 Guillaume, *Procès-Verbaux*, 311 (session of 11 March 1792).

101 Palloy's *Dépense faite pour la fête champêtre sur le ruines de la Bastille le jour de la Commémoration du 14 juillet 1791* (Bibliothèque Historique de la Ville de Paris, ms. C.P. 5252-61, reg. no. 14, fols. 4147-48) lists the expenses for the festival of 14 July 1791 as 608 livres for the payment of the orchestra as well as for balustrades, garlands, and for the purchase of Phrygian caps. On top of this, Palloy had to pay the workers ordered off the Bastille to set up the site for the festival.

102 Thérèse Pila, "Les Fêtes sous la Révolution: Sceaux-l'Unité," *Histoire du Bal de Sceaux*, exhibition 11–28 June 1981 (Sceaux: Amis de Sceaux, 1981), 7–8.

103 A colored etching of this scene by André Basset is reproduced and interpreted in Herding and Reichardt, *Bildpublizistik*, 102–3 (fig. 132), and in *Die Bastille*, 62.

104 *Journal des Hommes du 14 Juillet* 14 (28 July 1796): 1.

105 Palloy, *Adresse aux Représentants*, 11.

106 *Archives parlementaires*, 1st ser., 86:560 (letter from Palloy to the National Convention, 29 Ventôse an II).

107 Palloy, *Discours*, 3. On this issue, see also Hans-Jürgen Lüsebrink, "Votivbilder der Freiheit—Der 'Patriote Palloy' und die populäre Bildmagie der Bastille," in *Die Bastille*, 71–80.

108 The copy of the *Hymne des Marseillais* in the Bibliothèque Nationale with the call number 4°Ye. 840 carries the handwritten addition "Imprimé aux frais du patriote Palloy."

109 [Pierre-François Palloy], *Hymne dédié aux Citoyens Français, chanté le jour de la fête de la République, à la gloire des braves guerriers, le 1er vendémiaire an IX,* Bibliothèque Historique de la Ville de Paris 104.142 (no. 32). At the bottom, the song has the following addition: "This hymn was composed at the commune and district of Sceaux-l'Unité, département Seine, and then addressed to the armies, By P.F.P., *Patriot for Life*."

110 Palloy, *Les XVI Commandements*, 1.

111 Ibid.

112 Pierre-François Palloy, *Exposition des faits relatifs à la démolition de la Bastille, le 12 mars 1791, au club électoral* ([Paris:] Imprimerie de Renaudière, 1791), 18: "To instill more character in the hearts of our citizens, I therefore had the fortunate idea of spreading the picture of this abominable monument to all parts of the French empire, and to every good citizen."

113 See *Notes pour les frais d'impression*, Bibliothèque Nationale, ms. n.a.f. 3241, fol. 266; Palloy, *Discours*, 4; *Procès-Verbal de la célébration des fêtes de la liberté aux 9 et 10 Thermidor* . . . (Brussels, [1795]), Bibliothèque Nationale, Gr.Z. Le Senne 718 (12); and Combet, *La Révolution*, 146 respectively.

114 Pierre-François Palloy, Lettre to Collot d'Herbois (1793), Bibliothèque Historique de la Ville de Paris, ms. C.P. 5249, carton 1): "I am sending you The XVI Patriotic Commandments, by a True Republican, the book about my progres-

sion, which is much lighter in comparison with yours; but it is prompted by the emotions of a free man and a true republican who closely follows the progress of our triumphant Revolution. I am in the habit of having all the speeches that I give in public assemblies printed, along with the responses of the presidents."

115   Pierre-François Palloy, "Mémoire d'impression et fourniture de papiers faits au Citoyen Palloy, par le Citoyen Testu, Imprimeur-Libraire Rue Hautefeuille no. 14 [pour] Discours prononcé en présence des Bataillons de Volontaires et Citoyens d'Epernay, de neuf feuilles un quart à 42 liv. la feuille," in *Notes* (note 113).

116   See, e.g., Palloy's ballad *Aux fils aînés de la Révolution Française: Enfants de 1789, Hommes de 1809; ou la Conscription du plus heureux présage,* to the tune of "Au pas redoublé" (Paris: Pelletier, 1809).

117   Alexandre Dumas père, *Louis XVI et la Révolution* (Paris: Michel Levy, 1892); Jules Michelet, *Histoire de la Révolution Française,* ed. Gérard Walter, 2 vols. (Paris: Gallimard, 1952), 1:1232. The passage on Palloy is not included in the English translation of Michelet's history.

118   On this subject, see Hans-Jürgen Lüsebrink, "Sprache und Literatur," in *Die Französische Revolution,* ed. Rolf Reichardt (Freiburg and Würzburg: Ploetz, 1988), 241–62.

119   *Journal de Louis XVI et de son Peuple, ou le Défenseur . . .* 99 (March 1791): 3: "The King accepted this portrait, they say, with much sensitivity, and said (or rather they report that he said), 'I am *infinitely* flattered by this portrait of myself engraved on one of the Bastille's stones: while reminding me of the *strength* of the French people, it will also remind me that gratitude demands that I do anything in my power for their prosperity.' Then, returning to the counsel room where his ministers awaited him, His Majesty said, 'Messieurs, here is my portrait on a stone from the Bastille; it will be a great lesson to all of us and teach us what we owe to the people.'"

120   Advertisement in the *Journal de Versailles, des départements de Paris, de Seine et de l'Oise* 42 (12 July 1790): 172.

121   This is what Palloy calls the Bastille stones, e.g., in a letter of November 1790. See Palloy's letter to the [Département de la Marne, 4 November 1790, Archives Départementales Marne, 1 L 282.

122   Palloy, "Discourse," 5.

123   See, e.g., the circular received by the département of the Nord, which like the letter to officials in Calvados, already cited above, reads: "It did not suffice for me to have participated in the destruction of this fortress's walls, I had the desire to immortalize the memory of its terror"; Archives Départementales Nord, ser. 50, doc. 790, Lettre de Palloy, 29 October 1790.

124   Ibid.

125   *Tableau nominativ des citoyens qui composent l'association des Apôtres de la Liberté. Dressé et arrêté le 14 Juillet 1792,* Bibliothèque Nationale, ms. n.a.f. 3241, fols. 140–42, here fol. 142.

126   Bord, "Journal," 173.

127   Ibid.: "Nothing is more characteristic of a département like Diez than that they begged me to take their case into consideration. I told them they should write

to Mr. Mirabeau or Mr. Barnave to that end, since it was they who made the machine run. They told me that it would please them if I myself wrote telling them I had seen the situation; I wrote immediately to Messieurs Mirabeau and Barnave regarding what I had seen."

128 Ibid., 175: "I announced myself as Mr. Palloy's deputy and went to the other départements in order to have the dedication festivities of the Bastille carried out; they found me much disposed to that. . . . At Aix the département did not receive me well, and I owe it to the inn that I got out of that misery."

129 Ibid., 176: "I played the role of Orosmane in *Zaïre*. I had loud applause only for this one line: 'I hate the entire world, I despise myself.' "

130 Titon-Bergeras, letter addressed to Mr. Palloy, 2 June 1791, Bibliothèque Historique de la Ville de Paris, ms. C.P. 5252: "The one from Poitiers was the least brilliant[,] which is not my fault[:] after having waited three days[,] the département decided that it was not fitting to give so much importance to this dreaded ceremony[!], and that the priests were not numerous enough to cause a riot."

131 In 1792, his name is no longer on the list of the Apostles of Freedom. See Bibliothèque Nationale, ms. n.a.f. 3241, fol. 140 (list of sixty names).

132 Other Apostles of Freedom were named Requies, Jacquemot, and Jourmery. See Palloy's letter to Titon-Bergeras, 20 May 1791, Bibliothèque Historique de la Ville de Paris, ms., 3.

133 Most of these accounts are in Palloy's papers in the Bibliothèque Historique de la Ville de Paris, ms. C.P. 5249-62.

134 Titon-Bergeras, letter to Mr. Palloy, 10 January 1791, Bibliothèque Historique de la Ville de Paris, ms. 5, 1.

135 Archives Départementales Vienne, ser. 50, Procès-Verbaux des Séances du Département, 20 October 1790, fol. 30.

136 Bord, "Journal," 170.

137 See Titon-Bergeras, letter to Mr. Palloy (note 134). See also the Archives Municipales Bordeaux, *Délibérations du Corps municipal*, 1:25 (29 June 1790, letter from Palloy), 146 (26 December 1790, arrival of Titon-Bergeras), and 4:545 (28 December 1790, deliberations of the département concerning the speeches given on the occasion of the model of the Bastille sent by Palloy, architect of Paris). A printed version is the *Extrait des Registres de Délibérations du Directoire du Département de la Gironde* (Bordeaux, 1790).

138 Titon-Bergeras, letter to Palloy, 17 October 1790, Bibliothèque Historique de la Ville de Paris, ms.

139 See Justin Ledeuil, *La Révolution à Dijon, 1789–1795* (Paris: Dumoulin, 1872), and Louis Hugueney, *Les Clubs Dijonnais sous la Révolution: Leur rôle politique et économique* (Dijon: Nourry, 1905), 41–86.

140 Daniel Ligou, "Population, citoyens actifs et électeurs à Dijon aux débuts de la Révolution Française (1790-1791)," *Actes du Congrès national des sociétés savantes, section d'histoire moderne* 88 (1964): 243–75.

141 In this context, *Welches* means "barbarian" or "ignorant, coarse person" in the Voltairean sense.

142 Landes, *Discours*, 57–58.

143 Ibid., 57.

144   Archives Municipales Dijon, ser. 1 d ½ (24 February 1790–2 January 1792), Registre des Délibérations de la Municipalité de Dijon, fol. 236 (Tuesday, 9 November 1790).

145   Ibid., fol. 277 (Tuesday, 7 December 1790). A more extensive investigation of the reception of Voltaire's drama *Brutus* during the French Revolution and its catalytic function is Hans-Jürgen Lüsebrink, "Réécritures et formes de réception du 'Brutus' de Voltaire au XVIIIe siècle," *Studies on Voltaire and the Eighteenth Century* 305 (1993): 1871–74.

146   Navier, "Discours," 13.

147   *Journal Patriotique du Département de la Côte d'Or* 92 (23 November 1790): 401–3.

148   *Ephémérides d'Administration du Département de la Côte d'Or* 25 (20 January 1791): "Séance du 23 novembre 1790."

149   See, e.g., the Archives Départementales Côte d'Or, ser. 50, 545, carton 1 (1793).

150   Pierre-François Palloy, letter to Mr. Bergeras, 20 January 1791, Bibliothèque Historique de la Ville de Paris, ms. C.P. 5252, 2–3: "You give me a lot of hope concerning the reception that is being prepared for the effigy of the Bastille; it will be glorious, . . . you will be in a position also to conduct an oral lawsuit, perhaps better than the one conducted by the département of the Côte d'Or. If things are as one hopes, we will have to get it done by Gorsas and Prudhomme."

151   See, e.g., Pierre-François Palloy, *Citoyens Président et Administrateurs* [circular letter] (Paris: 25 July 1793), Bibliothèque Nationale, Le Senne 718 (46): "Citizens, while you pay tribute to the Declaration of Rights, I give you information concerning one stone from the Bastille that I beg you to accept: this slab will replace the one bearing the portrait of the traitor Louis."

152   Pierre-François Palloy, *Serment républicain, délivré avec une médaille de fer provenant des chaînes de la Bastille, signé par lui* (Paris: 2 mars an II), Bibliothèque Historique de la Ville de Paris, ms. C.P. 6392, pièce 18.

153   See *Extrait des Registres du Département Mont-Blanc, séant à Chambéry* (Chambéry: Lullin, 1793); Pierre-François Palloy, *Adresse aux Brabançons* (Paris: Guilhemat, 1792); and Jacques-Joseph Chapel/Delecroix, *Procès-Verbal de la célébration des fêtes de la Liberté aux 9 et 10 Thermidor, et de l'inauguration d'un modèle en relief de la Bastille, envoyé par le patriote Palloy au département de la Dyle, à Bruxelles* (Brussels: Tutot, 1795). See also Hans-Jürgen Lüsebrink, "L'Exportation de la 'flamme nationale': Rhétorique et lectures du 14 Juillet aux frontières de la République," in *La Révolution française — L'espace et le temps recontruits: Actes du colloque de Marseille (février 1989),* ed. Monique Cubells and Philippe Joutard (Aix-en-Provence: Publications de l'Université de Provence, 1990), 85–96.

154   Archives Départementales Alpes-Maritimes, Registre des Procès-Verbaux des Séances du Directoire du District de Nice, session of 28 May 1793, fols. 11–13, here fol. 12 ("Discours de M. Woillez").

155   Bastille inscription quoted in Combet, "Les Fêtes," 15.

156   Combet, *La Révolution,* 294.

157   "Extrait des Délibérations de la Société populaire de la ville de Nice, séance du 13 may 1793, l'an 2e de la République une et indivisible," Bibliothèque Historique de la Ville de Paris, ms. fol. 229–30, here fol. 229, 1: "The Society sang with passion and enthusiasm, 'Allons Enfans de la patrie,' and a brother in arms added a chorus here."

158 Ibid., 2.

159 See, e.g., M. Roques, soldier in the National Guard, in November 1790 in the southwestern town of Cahors, when the crates with Bastille objects delivered by Palloy's Apostles of Freedom were opened: "From that very moment the citizen became soldier, and the Citizen-Soldier walked toward that huge and terrible dungeon with intrepid step." See *Discours prononcé le 28 novembre 1790, à l'ouverture des caisses contenant les débris de la Bastille, imprimé d'après le vœu de tous les bons Citoyens, par M. Roques fils, soldat de la garde nationale, membre de la société des Amis de la Constitution et Docteur en Médecine* (Cahors, 1790), 2.

160 On the Citoyen-Soldat, see the excellent article by Pierre Rétat, "Aux armes, citoyens! 1789 ou l'apprentissage de la guerre," *Commentaire* 11, no. 42 (summer 1988): 526–33, which, however, touches on the Bastille only in passing.

161 On this central issue of medieval and early modern popular culture, see Roger Chartier and Dominique Julia, "Le Monde à l'envers," *L'Arc* 65 (1976): 43–53, which includes a secondary bibliography.

162 *Le Comte de Lorges*, 11.

163 Siméon-Prosper Hardy, "Mes Loisirs," Bibliothèque Nationale, ms. ffr. 6687, fol. 475: "Du lundi quatorze septembre)."

164 See, e.g., *Courrier de Versailles à Paris* 71 (16 September 1789): 259–60; *Révolutions Nationales*, 14 September 1789, 171–73.

165 *Courrier de Versailles à Paris* 71 (16 September 1789): 259–60: "Two things in particular aroused everyone's curiosity: they carried an effigy of the Bastille on the shaft of a cart: the soldiers, the cannons, the dead, the dying, the flames, nothing was left out, not even the traitor de Launay's little white flag."

166 Ibid., 260: "The rest of the day was like a popular festival. . . . we sang and enjoyed ourselves almost until the next morning."

167 *Courrier de Versailles à Paris* 35 (11 August 1789): 223, 226. The sermon also exists as a monograph (see app., no. 1) and was reprinted in the *Journal Encyclopédique* 6 (1789): 434–47 and 8 (1789): 251–60.

168 Bachaumont, *Mémoires secrets*, 20 March 1776 (9:115).

169 Ibid., 9:223.

170 On early commemorations of 14 July 1789, see Bord, *La Prise*.

171 *Chronique de Paris* 102 (12 April 1790): 407.

172 *Bouche de Fer* 79 (1 July 1791): 5–6.

173 See pp. 79–85 above as well as app., no. 20, 315: "Swift as an electric spark, it [14 July] suddenly sent the sacred fire of liberty through the hearts of all."

174 Gonchon, *Projet*, 16. The printing permit for Gonchon's text is dated 9 December 1789.

175 See Victor Fournel, "L'Orateur du Peuple Gonchon," in *Le Patriote Palloy. L'Orateur du Peuple Gonchon* (Paris: Honoré Champion, 1892), 259–363. Fournel assumes that Gonchon also took part in the storming of the Bastille, even though he is absent from the official list of Vainqueurs de la Bastille.

176 Gonchon, *Projet*, 5.

177 *Enterrement*, 1–6. A pictorial version of the symbolic funeral procession suggested here is given in the etching *L'Enterrement de l'Aristocratie*, reprinted in *Die Bastille*, 51.

178 See Pierre-François Palloy, *Détails des fêtes données au Champ-de-Mars, sur les ruines*

de la Bastille, aux Champs-Elisées, à la Halle neuve et sur la Seine, le 18 juillet 1790 (Paris: Imprimerie du Rédacteur, 1790), 2, 7. See also Gaston Maugras, *Journal d'un étudiant (Edmond Géraud) pendant la Révolution, 1789–1793,* new ed. (Paris: Plon, 1790), 73.

179   Pierre-François Palloy, *Depense faite pour la fête champêtre donnée sur les ruines de la Bastille* (Paris, 1791), Bibliothèque Historique de la Ville de Paris, ms. C.P. 5252-61, reg. no. 14, fol. 4148).

180   Marc-Antoine Désaugiers, *La prise de la Bastille: hiérodrame tiré des livres saints, suivi du cantique en action de grâces "Te Deum laudamus"* (Paris: Cailleau, 1790), 35, and *Séance relative à la cérémonie du Te Deum, tenue à l'Auleoîcle le 25 juin 1790* (Paris: Cailleau, 1910), 65 (letter of 17 July 1790).

181   Trénard, "Les Fêtes," 197.

182   *Courrier de Paris dans les Provinces* 28 (31 July 1790): 436–37.

183   Ibid., 442: "The patriotic club held a celebratory mass for the peace of the patriots who died in the siege of the Bastille, and who succumbed in Nismes and Montauban fighting to defend the fatherland."

184   Archives Municipales Grenoble LL 217 (10).

185   Lacroix, "Fêtes," 366–67.

186   Ibid., 368.

187   Detailed sources of speeches are listed by number in appendix A.

188   See, e.g., the allegory of the oath of federation of 1790 on the etching *Cupidon, tambour national,* reprinted in Herding and Reichardt, *Bildpublizistik,* 81.

189   See also table 6, A25–28.

190   A17:28: "Malta, the Bastille of the Mediterranean, the cherished refuge of the aristocracy, fell to the blows of our Argonauts, the tricolored flag has already crossed a stunned Egypt, and the Red Sea, always following the voice of God, protector of free men, will provide an easy passage to the French republicans who will console the Indians for the evils they have suffered at the hands of Europe's tyrants."

191   Archives Départementales Côte d'Or, ser. 50545, fol. 47.

192   Lucien Bonaparte formulates similar ideas in his speech in 1800, e.g.: "today, we find ourselves at a moment we have been waiting to reach for ten years" (A24:12).

193   *Idées,* 2. See also the same suggestion made to the National Convention by Representative Barère de Vieuzac on 14 July 1790, *Motion de M. Barère de Vieuzac, 14 juillet 1790* (Paris 1790). See also the *Archives parlementaires,* 1st ser., 17:69–70.

194   See, e.g., François Antoine Davy de Chavigné, *Projet d'un monument sur l'emplacement de la Bastille, à décerner par les Etats-Généraux, à Louis XVI, Restaurateur de la liberté publique, et à consacrer à la Patrie, à la liberté, à la Concorde et à la Loi* (Paris, 1789); *Projet d'un Monument pour consacrer la Révolution* (Paris: Didot le Jeune, 1790); plan of an unknown stonemason presented to parliament on 3 November 1791, in *Archives parlementaires,* 1st ser., 34:619–20; and *Récit exact de la fête nationale qui a eu lieu hier; et description fidèle de celle qui doit se célébrer aujourd'hui sur l'emplacement de la Bastille* (Paris, 1791). Contemporary engravings of the designs by Davy de Chavigné (1790), Sellier (1790), and Prieur (1791) and of allegorical Bastille monuments are reprinted and explained in *Die Bastille,* 56–59.

195   Concerning these projects, see Pierre-François Palloy, *Adresse et Projet général, dédié à la Nation, présenté à l'Assemblée Nationale et au Roi des Français, par Palloi, Architecte-Entrepreneur* ([Paris]: 11 March 1792 [an IV]), 12.

196   Decree of 16 June 1792, arts. 1 and 2, *Archives parlementaires,* 1st ser., 45:279.

197   See Palloy, *Adresse* (note 195).

198   *Révolutions de Paris* 145 (14–21 April 1792): 100–107.

199   See the notes and illustrations in *Die Bastille,* 64–65.

200   [Frege], *Genrebilder,* 123. See also the popular woodcut of 1831, reprinted in *Die Bastille,* 66.

201   *Manifeste,* 1.

202   *Le Moine qui n'est pas bête* (n.p., [fall 1792]), 3.

203   *Père Duchesne* 89 (October 1791): 3.

204   *Père Duchesne* 172 (end of September 1792): 2–3; see also the club speech of M. Anthoine of 12 August 1792, reprinted in François-Alphonse Aulard, *La Société des Jacobins,* 6 vols. (Paris: Librairie Jouaust, 1889), 4:195; as well as *Grand Détail de l'exécution de tous les conspirateurs et brigands* (n.p., [1792]), 2.

205   *Père Duchesne* 102 (end of December 1791): 7–8.

206   Palloy, *Pétition,* 1, 3.

207   [Bias-Parent], *Catéchisme,* 50–51. Dorfeuille reused the phrase in a speech to the citizens of Chambéry on 20 February 1794, published in *Journal Républicain des deux départmens Rhône et Loire* 37 (24 March 1794): 256, as did Palloy in his poster *Morale et devoirs des Français* (n.p., [spring 1794]).

208   *Grand Détail,* 2.

209   *Journal de la Municipalité et du département de Paris,* 6 March 1791; quoted in Lacroix and Farge, *Actes,* 1st ser., 2:776.

210   *Révolutions de Paris* 88 (12–19 March 1791): 497, and 108 (30 July–6 August 1791): 178. See also *Révolutions de France* 82 (27 June 1791): 175. More quotations from the press appear in Lacroix and Farge, *Actes,* 2d ser., 2:786–95 and 3:13–18.

211   *Orateur du peuple* 19 (end of August 1790): 147–48. See also *Révolutions de Paris* 55 (24–31 July 1790): 137.

212   *Révolutions de Paris* 6 (6–22 August 1789): 43.

213   See Bord, *La Prise;* Daniel Ligou, "A propos de la révolution municipale," *Revue d'histoire économique et sociale* 38 (1960): 146–77; and Lynn A. Hunt, "Committees and Communes: Local Politics and National Revolution in 1789," *Comparative Studies in Society and History* 18 (1976): 321–46.

214   See Georges Lefebvre, *La Grande Peur de 1789* (Paris: Colin, 1932), 65, 95, 98, 103–4, 148.

215   *Révolution authentique et remarquable arrivée à Brest en Bretagne, avec la prise du fort de l'Amiral, de Recouvrance et du fort Gonête* (Paris: Letelier, [1789]), 1–3. Similar events are reported in the pamphlet *Révolutions de Caen, capitale de la Basse-Normandie* (n.p., [1789]), 3–7.

216   See Bord, *La Prise,* 40–41.

217   See ibid., 100–104, and Michel Lhéritier, *Les Débuts de la Révolution à Bordeaux d'après les Tablettes manuscrites de Pierre Bernadau* (Paris: Rieder, 1919), 75–80.

218   Ernest Cuaz, *Le Château de Pierre-Scize et ses prisonniers* (Lyon: Rey, 1907).

219   Albert Champdor, *Lyon pendant la Révolution, 1789–1793* (Lyon: Guillot, 1983), 15.

220 *La Résurrection du marquis de Brunoy* (Lyon, 1789). Concerning this matter, the Paris *Nouvelliste universel* 8 (29 August 1789), edited by Houet, wrote: "We often heard people shout about this paper, which is an extract of what is supposed to be a letter from Lyon, in which—after the details concerning the capture of Pierre-Scize by the bourgeoisie—they add that the governor had the Marquis de Brunoy, who had been dead for almost fifteen years, brought out of a dungeon. Nobody believed this anecdote, which was patently false; let us also mention it, less in order to dissuade our readers than to record here our surprise about the ease with which any old story is made public" (7).

221 Albert Metzger and Joseph Frédéric Louis Vaêsen, eds., *Lyon en 1792* (Lyon: Georg, 1883), 124–48.

222 *Calendrier,* 8.

223 *Procès verbal,* 3–4. See also Edouard Herriot, *Lyon n'est plus,* 4 vols. (Paris: Hachette, 1939), 3:49–51.

224 See Paul Gaffarel, "La Prise des bastilles Marseillaises (avril–mai 1790)," *La Révolution française* 72 (1919): 314–25, and more extensively, Reichardt, "Prise et démolition," 53–61. (Publications relating to the capture of the Marseille bastilles are listed in appendix B at the end of this chapter.)

225 Bord, *La Prise,* 216. On the local and regional background, see Claude Badet Lourde, *Histoire de la Révolution à Marseille et en Provence depuis 1789 jusqu'au Consulat,* 2 vols. (Marseille: Senés, 1838); Georges Guibal, *Mirabeau et la Provence en 1789,* 2 vols. (Paris: Thorin, 1891), 2:233–75; Séverin Vialla, *Marseille révolutionnaire. L'armée-nation (1789–1793)* (Paris: Chapelot, 1910); and Dominique Radiguet, "Foules et journées révolutionnaires à Marseille (août 1789–25 août 1793)" (Diplôme d'études supérieures, Université d'Aix, 1968), 74–84.

226 *Révolutions de Paris* 44 (8–15 May 1790): 302. Sources for the seizure of the Marseille bastilles are listed by number in appendix B.

227 René Pillorget, *Les Mouvements insurrectionnels de Provence entre 1596 et 1715* (Paris: Pedone, 1975), 822–23.

228 Camille Desmoulins considered this "strongly exaggerated" (B11:560), and in the National Convention it was even called a "fable" (*Archives parlementaires,* 1st ser., 15:442).

229 See the report of the Marseille city council as presented to the National Assembly on 28 May by Minister of the Interior Saint-Priest, *Archives parlementaires,* 1st ser., 15:705.

230 Report in the city council meeting of 18 May 1790; see the handwritten minutes of the meeting in the city archive of Marseille, D1 D8, fols. 39–40.

231 See the exact list of donors and their donations in B6.

232 Guibal, *Mirabeau* (note 225), 2:268.

233 See the minutes of city council meetings (note 230) as well as the minutes of the meetings of the general council of Marseille of 1–18 May 1790 (city archive of Marseille, D1 D1, fols. 60–84). Some of these protocols were published in B13, B16, and B17.

234 This was most of all due to Count Mirabeau, the idol of the citizens of Marseille; some of his steps are documented in B9 and B20.

235 *Ami du Peuple* 118 (30 May 1790): 7–8.

236 In July 1792, for instance, the citizens of Paris look forward to embracing "the

conquerors of Fort Saint-Nicolas" in the confederates sent from Marseille. See *Journal des sansculottes* 2 (6 July 1792): 6.

237   See Lüsebrink and Reichardt, "La Prise."

238   *Journal d'Etat et du Citoyen* 8 (1 October 1789): 162: "the crowd of spectators that had come there made the hall resound with repeated applause." On 24 August 1789, a French correspondent reported from London, "They presented the Storming of the Bastille in London, and this play was surprisingly successful"; Bibliothèque Historique de la Ville de Paris, ms. 736, "Nouvelles à la main," fol. 38.

239   Marian-Hannah Winter, "La Prise de la Bastille, pantomime de cirque de 1789," *Bulletin de la Société archéologique, historique et artistique le vieux Papier* 74, no. 247 (January 1973): 13–14. On p. 12, there is a reprint of the etching *A Grand View of the Attack and Taking of the Bastille at Paris.*

240   *Annales patriotiques et littéraires de la France, et affaires politiques de l'Europe* 19 (21 October 1789): 3. "The Covent Garden theater was ordered not to present the *Prise de la Bastille.*"

241   Stewart, "The Fall," 83.

242   *Hibernian Journal* quoted in ibid.

243   *Chronique de Paris* 206 (25 July 1790): 966.

244   *Vedette, ou Précis de toutes les nouvelles du jour,* 7 June 1791, 2–3.

245   See, e.g., the report in *Courrier du Bas-Rhin* 63 (6 August 1791): 643.

246   See, e.g., the account in *Journal des Clubs ou Sociétés Patriotiques* 37 (27 July 1791): 565–66, as well as *Courrier du Bas-Rhin* 65 (13 August 1791): 658–59.

247   French newspapers such as the *Feuille hebdomadaire de la Généralité de Limoges* 28 (13 July 1791) speak of "more than fifty cities in England" (112).

248   Ibid.

249   *Chronique de Paris* 204 (23 July 1790): 815. Concerning Amsterdam, see also the account in *Journal de la Société de 1789* 9 (29 July 1790): 39.

250   See the extensive account of the celebrations in Lausanne on 14 July 1791 in *Courrier du Bas-Rhin* 62 (3 August 1791): 637–38.

251   Ibid., 638; see, e.g., the toast "à la nation helvétique."

252   *Gazetier* 51 (23–26 November 1790): 212.

253   On the dissemination of news about the Revolution in German, see Erich Pelzer, "Die französische Revolutionspropaganda am Oberrhein (1789–1799)," in *Die französische Revolution und der deutsche Südwesten,* ed. Hans-Otto Mühleisen (Munich and Zurich: Schnell und Steiner, 1989), 165–67.

254   Campe, "Briefe," 33 (9 August 1789).

255   Ibid., 30.

256   See Karl Hammer, "Deutsche Revolutionsreisende in Paris," in *Deutschland und die Französische Revolution,* ed. Jürgen Voss (Munich: Artemis, 1983), 26–42, and Thomas Grosser, *Reiseziel Frankreich: Deutsche Reiseliteratur vom Barock bis zur Französischen Revolution* (Opladen: Westdeutscher Verlag, 1989), 183–220.

257   These twenty publications are listed by number in appendix C at the end of this chapter.

258   *Staats- und gelehrte Zeitung des Hamburgischen unpartheyischen Correspondenten* 118 (25 July 1789): n.p.

259   *Kurzgefasste Geschichte,* 34–54.

260   Buri, *Sammlung*, 1:11–12.

261   [Ludwig Ysenburg Buri], *Die Bastille, ein Trauerspiel in vier Aufzügen. Nach franzö-sischen Originalen bearbeitet* (Breslau and Brieg: Christian Friedrich Gutsch, 1790). See also Lüsebrink, "Evénement."

262   Buri, *Sammlung*, 1:11–12.

263   On Menzel, see Georg Wolfgang Augustin Fikenscher, *Gelehrtes Fürstentum Bai-reuth*, 12 vols. (Nuremberg: Lechner'sche Buchhandlung, 1803), 6:43–45.

264   *Die entlarvte Bastille*, 187–88. After the quotation, the text goes on, "S[ee] *Bair[euther] Zeit[ung]*, no. 89 this year, p. 649. Translator's note."

265   Buri, *Sammlung*, 2:4.

266   See Lüsebrink, "Evénement."

267   See Robert Darnton, *The Literary Underground of the Old Regime* (Cambridge: Harvard University Press, 1982).

268   Reichard, "Bauernunruhen," 59 and 68–69.

269   Christine and Gerd van den Heuvel, "Begrenzte Politisierung während der Französischen Revolution: Der 'Gesmolder Bauerntumult' von 1794 im Hoch-stift Osnabrück," in *Soziale Unruhen in Deutschland während der Französischen Revolu-tion*, ed. Helmut Berding (Göttingen: Vandenhoeck und Ruprecht, 1989), 111–29.

270   Reichardt, "Bastillen in Deutschland?" 455–67.

271   *Obscuranten-Almanach*, cover pages. The German original reads, "Pfeiffenge-quick, Paucken- und Trommelgeroll, / Der Ketten und Peitschengetös / Und das Brüllen der Gepeitschten / Ist diesem Landesvater allein Musik."

272   Knigge, *Kiste*, 220–21.

273   *Mainzer Zeitung* 120 (28 Messidor an VI = 16 July 1798): 1, cols. 1–2.

274   *Mainzer Zeitung* 119 (26 Messidor an VI = 14 July 1798): 4, cols. 1–2.

275   Lembert, *Rede*, 3–4.

276   Ibid., 6.

277   See Goethe, *Goethe's Theory*, xxii and xxiv respectively. For the German original, see Johann Wolfgang von Goethe, *Werke*, Hamburg ed., 14 vols. (Hamburg: Wegner, 1948), 13:314–19.

278   Jean Paul, *"Komet,"* 253 (vol. 2, chap. 12).

279   See Claire Lüsebrink, "Un Défi à la politique de la langue nationale: La Lutte autour de la langue allemande en Alsace sous la Révolution Française," *LINX* 15 (1987; special issue, "Langue et Révolution"): 146–68.

280   *Rot un Wiss: Monatsschrift der Elsass-Lothringer* 10 (July 1976): n.p.

4. BASTILLE SYMBOLISM IN MODERN FRANCE

1   See Jean-Albert Bédé, "Le Quatorze Juillet et sa fortune littéraire, 1789–1802," in *Essays on Diderot and the Enlightenment in Honor of Otis Fellows*, ed. John Pappas (Geneva: Droz, 1974), 36–56.

2   See Pierre Joigneux, *Histoire générale de la Bastille*, 3 vols. (Paris: by the author, 1838); Henri Gourdon de Genouillac, *Histoire nationale de la Bastille, 1370–1789 . . .* , illustrated ed. (Paris: Roy, 1880); Bord, *La Prise* and "Prisonniers"; Bournon, *Bastille;* as well as Funck-Brentano's numerous works.

3   Texts expressing the legacy of the Bastille are listed by number in appendix A at the end of this chapter.

4   In 1853, the police confiscated forty-one installments of this *Histoire de la Bastille* and four volumes of Eugène Sue's *Mystères de Paris* in the house of the illegal peddler Jacques Barbaras, a former butcher from Strasbourg. Barbaras was sentenced to a fine of sixteen francs and to eight days in prison. See Rudolf Schenda, *Volk ohne Buch: Zur Sozialgeschichte der populären Lesestoffe, 1770–1910* (Munich: Deutscher Taschenbuch Verlag, 1977), 129–30.

5   Steel engraving by Louis Marckl and Philibert Langlois, "*Prisonnier dans son Cachot.* Dessiné d'après nature par l'architecte Palloy le jour de la prise de la Bastille, extrait du cabinet du Colonel Marin," A6:title page.

6   *Histoire de la Bastille* (Paris: Boisard, 1852) (= Illustrations littéraires, no. 3); reprints in 1863 and 1882. See also Claude Wittkowski, *Monographie des éditions populaires: Les Romans à quatre sous, les publications illustrées à centimes, 1848–1870* (Paris: Pauvert, 1981), 5–32.

7   Saint-Albin Berville and François Barrière, eds., *Mémoires de Linguet sur la Bastille et de Dusaulx sur le 14 Juillet* (Paris: Baudoin, 1821); François Barrière, ed., *Mémoires de Linguet et de Latude, suivis de documents divers sur la Bastille* (Paris: Didot, 1866); Hippolyte Monin, ed., *Mémoires sur la Bastille: Linguet, Dusaulx* (Paris: Librairie des Bibliophiles, 1889). A mosaiclike documentation is given by Joseph Delort, *Histoire de la détention des philosophes et des gens de lettres à la Bastille et à Vincennes,* 3 vols. (Paris: Didot, 1829).

8   Jean-Baptiste Regnault-Warin, *L'Homme au masque de fer,* 4 vols. (Paris: Frechet 1804). The German translation by Absalon Friedrich Marx is *Der Mann mit der eisernen Maske,* 4 vols. (Leipzig: Fleischer, 1804–5).

9   Claude Leynadier, *Le Masque de fer* (Paris: Boiseard, 1851) (= Illustrations littéraires, no. 2). At least five reprints of this volume were published in the 1870s.

10 Joseph Delort, *Histoire de l'Homme au masque de fer, accompagnée de pièces authentiques* (Paris: Delaforest, 1825); Pierre de Taulès, *L'Homme au masque de fer, mémoire historique . . . où l'on démontre que ce prisonnier fut une victime des Jésuites* (Paris: Peytieux, 1825); Paul Lacroix, *L'Homme au masque de fer* (Paris: Magen, 1837; reprint, 1840); Louis Louvet, *L'Homme au masque de fer* (Paris: Treuttel et Würtz, 1842); Paul Lecointe, *Les Mensonges politiques, ou Révélation des mystères du Masque de fer et de Louis XVII* (Paris: Frey, 1847); L. Letourneur, *Histoire de l'homme au masque de fer* (Plancy: Société de Saint-Victor, 1849).

11 René-Charles Guilbert de Pixérécourt and Anicet Bourgeois, *Latude, ou 35 ans de captivité: Mélodrame historique en 3 actes et 5 tableaux* (Clermont-Ferrand: Vaussière et Perol, 1835). Reprinted at least nine times the same year.

12 Alexandre Ducourneau, *Latude* (Paris: Harvard, 1851) (= Romans, contes et nouvelles illustrés 5, no. 41).

13 Robert refers to the writings of Linguet, Latude, and Leynadier and to *La Bastille dévoilée.*

14 Clémence Robert, *Latude, ou les Mystères de la Bastille: Roman de cape et d'epée* (Paris: Librairie Illustrée, 1875). All quotations are from the second edition of 1878 entitled *Les Mystères de la Bastille.* Here Robert, *Les Mystères,* 29.

15 Ibid., 30 and 43.

16 Ibid., 110.

17 Ibid., 121.

18 Ibid., 125.

19   Ibid., 252.
20   Steven L. Kaplan, *The Famine Plot Persuasion in Eighteenth-Century France* (Phila-
     delphia: American Philosophical Society, 1982) (= *Transactions of the American
     Philosophical Society* 72, no. 3, 52–57.
21   See the etching *Le Prisonnier d'Etat* of 1789, reprinted in *Die Bastille*, 41. This
     legend is followed even by Edmond Le Mercier, *Le Prévôt, dit de Beaumont, pri-
     sonnier d'Etat pendant vingt-deux ans et deux mois à la Bastille et différentes prisons pour
     avoir dénoncé le pacte de famine* (Paris: Miaulle-Duval, 1888).
22   Elie Berthet, *Le Pacte de Famine*, 2 vols. (Paris: Roux et Cassanet, 1847).
23   Foucher and Berthet, *Pacte*, 5.
24   First published in installments in the *Journal des Débats* from June 1842 to Octo-
     ber 1843. See René Guisse, Marcel Graner, and Lilane Durand-Dessert, "Des
     'Mystères de Paris' aux 'Mystères du Peuple,'" *Europe* 55 (1977): 152–68, and
     Volker Klotz, " 'Les Mystères de Paris.' Offentlichkeit und Eröffnung des mo-
     dernen Abenteuerromans," *Romanistische Zeitschrift für Literaturgeschichte* 2 (1978):
     175–96. On the confiscation of this novel, see note 4 above.
25   Sue, *Mystères*, 221–29. Although there is an English translation of this novel,
     The Sword of Honor; or, The Foundation of the French Republic, trans. Solon de Leon
     (New York: New York Labor News Company, 1910), John Lebrenn (as he is
     called) here makes no speech after the liberation of the prisoners of the Bastille.
26   See Nora Atkinson, *Eugène Sue et le roman-feuilleton* (Paris: Nizet, 1929), 110, 113–15.
27   See Anne Léoni, Geneviève Mouillaud, and Roger Ripoll, "Feuilleton et
     Révolution: 'Ange Pitou,'" *Europe* 52 (1974): 101–18, and Anne Léoni and Roger
     Ripoll, "Quelques Aspects de la Révolution française dans le roman-feuilleton,"
     Revue d'histoire littéraire de la France 75 (1975): 389–414.
28   Alexandre Dumas, *Ange Pitou* (Boston: Little, Brown, and Co., 1894), esp.
     chaps. 14–28 of the first volume and 2–6 of the second. Dumas also wrote a
     drama about Finance Minister Fouquet, who was imprisoned under Louis XIV:
     Le Prisonnier de la Bastille: Fin des Mousquetaires . . . (Paris: M. Lévy, 1861).
29   We would like to thank Christian Amalvi for invaluable help in selecting and
     obtaining these texts. Sources for these texts are listed by number in appen-
     dix B. On republican schoolbooks, see Dominique Maingueneau, *Les Livres
     d'école de la République, 1870–1914* (Paris: Le Sycomore, 1979), as well as Pierre
     Nora, "Lavisse, instituteur national," in *Les Lieux de Mémoire*, ed. Pierre Nora,
     4 vols. (Paris: Gallimard, 1986), 1:247–89. An English translation of this work
     is in preparation at Columbia University Press, *Realms of Memory: Rethinking the
     French Past*. On the significance of illustrations in schoolbooks see Ségolène Le
     Men, *Les Abécédaires français illustrés du XIXe siècle* (Paris: Promodis, 1984); Yves
     Gaulupeau, "L'Histoire en images à l'école primaire, un exemple: La Révolu-
     tion française dans les manuels élémentaires (1870–1970)," *Histoire de l'Education*
     30 (1986): 29–52; as well as the exhibition catalog *La Révolution française racontée
     aux Enfants* (Rouen: Musée National de l'Education, 1987).
30   See A1, A7.
31   See A4: vol. 6:245; cf. 6:199.
32   See most recently Ann Rigney, "Du récit historique: La Prise de la Bastille
     selon Michelet (1847)," *Poétique* 75 (September 1988): 267–78.

33 Jules Michelet, *Histoire de la Révolution,* ed. Gérard Walter, 2 vols. (Paris: Gallimard, 1952), 1:146–62. Quotations in the text are taken from the English translation, here Michelet, *History,* 142–43.

34 Michelet, *History,* 161–62.

35 Ibid., 163–64.

36 Ibid., 162.

37 Ibid., 168–69.

38 Louis Combet, *1789, ou Sous la Bastille: Drame en 2 scènes en vers* (Lyon: Georg, 1886).

39 The Chevalier de la Barre, who was beheaded in 1766 for an alleged act of sacrilege, and for whose rehabilitation Voltaire fought, is chosen as the fictive father figure.

40 See David James Fisher's essays "Romain Rolland and the French People's Theatre," *Drama Review* 21 (1977): 75–90, and "Rolland and the Ideology and Aesthetics of French People's Theater," *Theatre Quarterly* 9 (1979): 83–103.

41 See, e.g., the review by Paul Flat, "Le 14 Juillet," *Revue politique et littéraire: Revue bleue,* 4th ser., 17 (1902): 439–41.

42 See Rolland, "The Fourteenth," 27, 61, and 63 respectively.

43 Ibid., 37.

44 Ibid., 88–89.

45 Unedited letter quoted in Erika Demenet, "Die Französische Revolution als Gegenstand des Theaters, 1890–1979 (Diss., Freiburg, 1982), 84–85.

46 Béranger, *Oeuvres,* 3:259. The original text is "J'étais bien jeune; on criait: Vengeons-nous! / A la Bastille! aux armes! vite, aux armes! / Marchands, bourgeois, artisans couraient tous. / . . . Victoire au peuple! il a pris la Bastille! Un beau soleil a fêté ce grand jour." The text was sung to the popular melody "A soixante ans il ne faut pas remettre."

47 Colan, *Réveil,* 13.

48 *14 Juillet,* 1. See also the anonymous brochure *Au Peuple de 1830. 14 Juillet 1789. Prise de la Bastille,* 1831, Bibliothèque Historique de la Ville de Paris, 29720.

49 The poem "Une semaine à Paris. Aux Français" of 1830 reads in part: "Ce soleil de juillet qu'enfin nous revoyons, / Il a brillé sur la Bastille, / Oui, le voilà, c'est lui! La Liberté, sa fille, / Vient de renaître, à ses rayons. / Luis pour nous, accomplis l'oeuvre de délivrance; / Avance, mois sauveur, presse ta course, avance: Il faut trois jours à ces héros" (This sun of July which we see again at last, / It shone on the Bastille, / Yes, here it is, it is the same one! Liberty, her daughter, / Has just been reborn in her rays. / Complete for us the work of delivrance; / Advance, savior month, speed your way, advance: There heroes need three days) (Delavigne, *Oeuvres,* 517).

50 N., *La Prise,* 8–9, 18.

51 Bonneville, *Essai,* 3.

52 See A.-S.-M. Bonneville, *Lettre à MM. les députés des Départements, sur le projet de Monument national commémoratif des journées de Juillet 1789 et 1830, à élever sur la Place de la Bastille* (Paris: Belin, 1832), 6 and 27.

53 See Colan's song "Les Vainqueurs du Louvre au monument de la Bastille" on the melody of "De l'Orphelin des trois jours." See Chassaignon's poster *Le Tombeau des Braves de Juillet* (Paris: Dupont, 1830), Bibliothèque Nationale fol.

Lb^{49}.1655, which includes a woodcut of the conquest of the Louvre. See also the two pictorial broadsheets *Hommage rendu par Philippe 1er aux cendres des citoyens morts pour la liberté* . . . (Paris: Codoni, 1831), Bibliothèque Nationale, Estampes Qb1, M 111807, and *Monument élevé à la mémoire des citoyens morts pour la liberté,* anonymous engraving of 1831, ibid., M 111804.

54 See the official description of the monument and the ceremony, *Inauguration de la Colonne de Juillet 1830: Programme de la Cérémonie Funèbre du 28 Juillet 1840 et Description du Char funèbre* (Paris: H. Fournier, 1840), Bibliothèque Nationale, Estampes, Collection de Vinck, nos. 12.431–33, as well as the festival program of Remusat, the minister of the interior, *4ome Anniversaire des Journées de Juillet* (Paris: Chassaignon, 1840), Bibliothèque Nationale, 4°Lb^{51}.3118.

55 See Gautier's poem "Le 28 Juillet 1840," which takes up two-thirds of a folio page in the *Moniteur Universel,* 28 July 1840, 1763.

56 *Archives parlementaires,* 2d ser., 79:121 (statement of Gaëtan de la Rochefoucauld in parliament on 23 January 1833).

57 Ibid., 80:763, 761 (speech of the Marquis de Deux-Brézé in the Chamber of Peers on 9 March 1833).

58 Ibid., 79:121 (remarks in parliament on 23 January 1833) and 81:226 (in the Chamber of Peers on 15 March 1833). See also 83:51 (La Fayette in parliament on 22 April 1833).

59 Ibid., 84:223 (committee report of Count Mathieu Dumas in parliament on 15 March 1833).

60 Ibid., 80:339 (Argout in the Chamber of Peers on 25 February 1833).

61 Ibid., 79:120 (to applause in parliament on 23 January 1833).

62 Ibid., 81:227 (in the Chamber of Peers on 15 March 1833).

63 Ibid., 83:84. Since the diary is missing, this later record cannot be verified.

64 Ibid., 80:769 (Argout in the Chamber of Peers on 9 March 1833).

65 Report of the minister of the interior Aimé-Marie-Gaspard Clermont-Tonnerre to Charles X of 7 May 1826; reprinted in *Associations nationales en faveur de la presse patriote . . . les projets du gouvernement actuel ne sont que la continuation des projets des Bourbons de la branche aînée* (Paris: Auffray, 1833), 1–5.

66 See Patricia O'Brien, "'L'Embastillement de Paris': The Fortifications of Paris during the July Monarchy," *French Historical Studies* 9 (1975): 63–82.

67 "L'Embastillement de Paris ne menace pas seulement les libertés publiques," *Associations* (note 65), 5–8.

68 See the articles "Les Bastilles ne sont pas une absurdité dans le système du 7 août, du 13 mars et du 11 octobre" and "Aux Parisiens," *National,* 11 and 13 July 1833. Quoted from the separate printing in *Associations* (note 65), 1 and 6.

69 One of these was Representative Louis from the département of Aude, *Paris doit-il être fortifié? Examen historique de cette question* (Paris: Krabbe, 1840).

70 See, e.g., A. Delhomme, *Du projet des fortifications de Paris* (Paris: Mansut Fils, 1840); Alexandre Lenoble, *Aux Français: Une pensée sur les fortifications de Paris* (Paris: Dondey-Dupré, 1840); as well as the anonymous *Lettres sur les fortifications de Paris: A Messieurs les Rédacteurs en chef de journaux* (Paris: L. Lévy, 1840).

71 See Auguste Luchet, *Justes Frayeurs d'un habitant de la banlieue à propos des Fortifica-*

tions de Paris (Paris: Pagnerre, 1840), and François Arago, *Etudes sur les fortifications de Paris considérées politiquement et militairement* (Paris: Agnerre, 1843).

72   Lahautière, *Deux Sous,* 3–8.

73   Hodde, "La Prise."

74   Dézamy, *Conséquences,* 7.

75   See Abgar Rubenovič Ioannisjan, *Revoljucionno kommunističeskoe dviženie vo Francii v 1840-1841 gg* (Moscow: Nauka, 1983), 13–20. Claus Scharf kindly gave us access to this study.

76   Cabet, *Lettres,* 4–22.

77   Cabet, *Dialogue,* 6. On the role of the minister, see John P. T. Bury and Robert P. Tombs, *Thiers (1797–1877): A Political Life* (London: Allen and Unwin, 1986), 71, 82–83, 182, 196, 201, 204, 232, 283.

78   See Douglas Johnson, *Guizot, or Aspects of French History, 1787–1874* (London: Routledge and Kegan Paul, 1963), 183–87.

79   See Rosemonde Sanson, *Le 14 Juillet: Fête et conscience nationale, 1789–1965* (Paris: Flammarion, 1976), 21.

80   See Maurice Agulhon, *Marianne into Battle: Republican Imagery and Symbolism in France, 1789–1880* (Cambridge: Cambridge University Press, 1981), 64–67.

81   Gambetta, *Discours,* 2:365–93, here 371–72, 391.

82   Guillaumot, *Exploits.*

83   See Auguste Vitu, *Le Contre-Poison* (Paris: Imprimerie de Roussel, 1878) (supplement to the *Figaro,* 21 May 1878).

84   See Charles-Olivier Charbonnel, *Histoire et historiens: Une Mutation idéologique des historiens français, 1865–1885* (Toulouse: Privat, 1976), 377.

85   Poncins and Montaigne, *La Prise,* 35. By 1882, this volume had seen four editions.

86   See Jacques Malacamp, *Vous en avez menti! Réponse péremptoirement prouvée adressée aux détracteurs systématiques de ce fait à la fois légitime et glorieux: La Prise de la Bastille* (Paris and Brussels: Chez Tous les Librairies, 1874), esp. 37, 41, 45; and Louis Combes, "Le Dernier Jour de la Bastille," in *Episodes et curiosités révolutionnaires* (Paris: Madre, 1872), 37–72.

87   The following quotations come from *Le Centenaire,* 19, 23, 81, 84. See also Jean-Marie Goulemot and Eric Walter, "Les centenaires de Voltaire et Rousseau," in Nora *Les Lieux* (note 29), 1:381–420.

88   See Christian Amalvi, "Le 14-Juillet: Du 'Dies irae' à 'Jour de fête,'" in Nora, *Les Lieux* (note 29), 1:421–72, and Sanson, *14 Juillet* (note 79), 31–38.

89   *Journal officiel de la République française,* 8 June 1880, 6267.

90   Article in the newspaper *La Justice,* 16 July 1880, reprinted in Sanson, *14 Juillet* (note 79), 208. See also, e.g., Frédéric Bataille, *La Fête Nationale: Deux Poésies patriotiques* (Montbéliard: Petermann, 1881), as well as Paul Berne, *Souvenir du 14 Juillet 1880. Trois dates: Fête nationale du 14 Juillet 1880 — le 14 Juillet 1789 — le 14 Juillet 1790* (Lyon, 1880).

91   See, respectively, the broadsheets of 1880: *La République triomphante préside à la grande fête nationale du 14 Juillet 1880; 14 Juillet 1880, Anniversaire de la Prise de la Bastille; 14 Juillet 1789 — 14 Juillet 1880; Dédié aux Vainqueurs de la Bastille. 14 Juillet 1789 —*

14 Juillet 1880, Bibliothèque Nationale, Estampes, Qb.1, M 120646, M 120683, M 120655, M 120661.

92   *Une Leçon,* 9.

93   See, e.g., the interview of Hugues Le Roux with Frantz Funck-Brentano in the *Temps,* 12 July 1888, section "La Vie à Paris."

94   Jean-Clément Martin, "Quatorze Juillet 1880 — Quatorze Juillet 1889, l'instauration de la fête nationale dans l'Ouest," *Annales de Bretagne et des pays de l'Ouest* 91 (1984): 201–47. See also Eugène Roulleaux, *La Prise de la Bastille et la fête du 14 juillet* (Fontenay-le-Comte: Imprimerie Vendéenne, 1882).

95   See Martin, "Quatorze" (note 94), 211.

96   See ibid., 218–31; Sanson, *14 Juillet* (note 79), 80–106; and Amalvi, "Le 14-Juillet" (note 88), 430–45.

97   Digeon, *Le 14 Juillet,* 1–8.

98   "Le 14 Juillet," *République radicale,* 13 July 1888. This article is reprinted with the other pieces in the series in Passerieu, *Lundis,* 115–40, here 114, 120–21. See also the text by a victor of the Bastille's son, Eugène Bonnemère, *1789: La Prise de la Bastille, 14 juillet — 14 août,* Education morale et civique: Bibliothèque de la jeunesse française (Paris: Martin, Librairie Centrale des Publications Populaires, 1881).

99   The pamphlet *La Journée du 14 Juillet 1789: Prise de la Bastille (Documents historiques)* (Paris: Pillet et Dumoulin, [1889]) describes the storming of the Bastille as a day of murder instigated by the Freemasons.

100 See esp. Auguste Blémont, *La Prise de la Bastille* (Paris: Quantin, 1889). See also Stéphane Arnoulin, *Prise de la Bastille: 14 Juillet 1789 — 14 Juillet 1889* (Paris: Goupy et Jourdan, [1889]) and an anonymous *La Prise de la Bastille — 14 Juillet 1789* (Toulouse: Baylac, [1889]).

101 Pictured in Perrusson and Colibert, *La Bastille & la rue St. Antoine en 1789,* color lithography (Paris: Mercadier, 1880). (See Jean Garrigues, *Images de la Révolution: L'Imagerie républicaine de 1789 à nos jours* [Paris: Editions du May, 1988], 94.) With it, a guide was published, by G. Rémy, entitled *Histoire de la Bastille et de la Rue Saint-Antoine avant 1789: Reconstitution Historique* (Paris: Librairie de la Bastille, à la Bastille, 1888).

102 *Protokoll,* 1–2.

103 Monteil, "Le 14 Juillet."

104 Doriac and Dujarric, *Toasts,* 206–8.

105 P. Hylaire [Etienne-Marie Boulé Hilaire de Barenton, pseud.], *Le 14 Juillet: La Prise de la Bastille!* (Paris: by the author, [1914]), poster with an illustration of the storming of the Bastille (= Le Tract populaire illustré 209).

106 See the illustrated weekly newspaper *Bastille, journal antimaçonnique,* Paris 1901–14, as well as Amalvi, "Le 14-Juillet" (note 88), 452–53, and the poster *Détruisons la Bastille!!!* reprinted in ibid., 451.

107 On 14 July 1906, for instance, the trade unions around Grenoble organized a festival to celebrate a strike victory. See the anonymous article "La Fête prolétarienne de Voiron," *Droit du Peuple* 12–13 July 1906, Archives Départementales Isère, 54 M 33.

108 In addition to the above-mentioned works by Sanson and Amalvi, see esp. the

regional study by Pierre Vallin, "Fête, mémoire et politique: Le 14 Juillet au Limousin (1880–1914)," *Revue française de science politique* 32 (1992): 949–72.

109 Basch text published in *Les Cahiers des droits de l'homme: Bulletin de la Ligue des droits de l'homme,* 31 July 1935, 517.

110 See the party newspaper *Humanité,* 2 July 1935.

111 *Humanité,* 15 July 1935. See also Georges Guy-Grand, "Quatorze Juillet 1935," *Grande Revue* 3 (1935): 148–53.

112 Picture in Amalvi, "Le 14-Juillet" (note 88), 456.

113 Rolland, "Quatorze Juillet."

114 See the handwritten production material in the Bibliothèque Nationale, Dépt. de Musique, ms. 15012 (1–7). The music, composed for a wind orchestra and a choir, consisted of an overture by Jacques Ibert, a prelude to the second act by Albert Roussel, incidental music by Georges Auric, Darius Milhaud, Charles Koechlin, and Daniel Lazarus, as well as a "Marche sur la Bastille" by Arthur Honegger.

115 See in general Jean-Marie Guillon, "150 ans après, la commémoration de la Révolution, 1939 ou 1944?" in *Var, Terre des Républiques: 1789–1989,* ed. Fédération des oeuvres laïques et SNIP (La Garde: Var Matin/République, 1988), 235–44.

116 Leaflet entitled *14 Juillet 1942,* signed "Les Mouvements de Résistance," Archives Départementales Isère, 54 M 34/2. On this matter, see Sanson, *14 juillet* (note 79), 133–34.

117 Leaflet starting "Français, Français of 1942, Archives Départementales Isère, 54 M 34/2. See also ibid., further leaflets of the Secours Populaire de France, beginning, respectively, with the words "Femmes de France!" "Citoyens, Citoyennes!" "Français et Françaises!" An example of Resistance poetry under the sign of the Bastille is the only subsequently published poem, "La Nuit de Juillet," by Louis Aragon, in *La Diane française* (Paris: Seghers, 1950), 59–63.

118 Poster signed "Le Front National de Lutte pour l'Indépendence de la France," Archives Départementales Isère, 54 M 34/2. This file also contains a leaflet of the PCF with the address "Patriotes!"

119 See, e.g., Mona Ozouf, ". . . Notre 14-Juillet," *Nouvel Observateur,* 12 July 1980, 14–18.

120 Bacoi, "La Bastille," 59.

121 See the contributions in the special issue "Bastille—révolte ou révolution?" *Le Point Révolution* 2 (1988): 39–46.

122 On this occasion, the magistrate of Amiens had posters and invitations printed; information kindly supplied by Eric Walter.

123 Leaflet of the "Ligue communiste révolutionnaire" handed out at a rally entitled "8 Juillet: Vive la Révolution." An appeal given out earlier by the groups of the left is entitled *A la Bastille!*

FINAL REMARKS

1 See also the report in the daily newspaper *Libération,* 9 July 1989, 1–3, under the title "La Bastille prise en verlan: Manifestation-concert contre le 'sommet des riches.'"

2   The leftist/socialist weekly *Nouvel Observateur* struck the same note with an extensive file in its issue of 13–19 July 1989, 12–17, titled "Ces Bastilles qui restent à prendre. Justice, police, administration, éducation, immigration, droit des femmes . . ." (These Bastilles which still need to be taken. Justice, police, administration, education, immigration, women's rights . . .).

3   See François Furet, "1789, si c'était à refaire . . . Un Sondage SOFRES," *Nouvel Observateur* 5–11 January 1989, 42–44.

4   In the following, see also Hans-Jürgen Lüsebrink's essays, "Freiheitsmythos und 'Export der Guillotine': Zur Wahrnehmung der Französischen Revolution in den afrikanischen und karibischen Literaturen des 20. Jahrhunderts," *Romanistische Zeitschrift für Literaturgeschichte* 3–4 (1988): 363–77, and "Les 14 Juillet coloniaux—La Révolution Française et sa mémoire dans l'Empire colonial français," *Französisch heute* 3 (September 1989): 307–19.

5   See the two works cited in n. 4 as well as Yves-Georges Paillard, "Marianne et l'indigène: Les Premiers 14 Juillet coloniaux à Madagascar," *Information historique* 45 (1983): 107–20.

6   Dadié, "Ce que m'a donné."

7   Brutus, "Prisoners," 3. We would like to thank Dennis Brutus for his willingness to discuss this matter during a lecture at Cornell University.

WORKS CITED
AND FURTHER REFERENCES

PRIMARY SOURCES

Almanach des douze ministres, pour l'année 1790. Paris, 1790.

Almanach du Père Duchesne, ou le Calendrier des bons citoyens. Paris, [1791].

Anecdotes aussi sûres que curieuses touchant la conduite tyrannique et barbare qu'on a exercée sur Denyse Regné à la Bastille. N.p., 1760.

Associations nationales en faveur de la presse patriote: Comité central et Comité parisien. Paris: Auffray, [1833].

La Bastille. Paris, 1789.

La Bastille dévoilée. Paris: Desenne, 1789–90.

Beiträge zur Geschichte der Bastille in Auszügen und Abschriften einiger merkwürdiger und authentischer Papiere, die bei der Eroberung derselben gefunden wurden. Vol. 1. Frankfurt and Leipzig: Varrentrapp und Wenner, 1789.

Beschreibung und Geschichte der Bastille während der Regierungen Ludwig des Vierzehnten, Fünfzehnten und Sechzehnten. Berlin: Unger, 1784.

Calendrier républicain, tel qu'il a été décrété par la Convention nationale . . . Avec les décrets relatifs à Ville-Affranchie. . . . Commune-Affranchie: Imprimerie Républicaine, an II (1794).

[Carra, Jean-Louis]. *L'Orateur des Etats-généraux.* N.p., n.d.

Dialogue entre le donjon de Vincennes et la Bastille. N.p., [1787–88].

Les Enragés aux enfers, ou Nouveau dialogue des morts. N.p., 1789.

Enterrement du despotisme, ou funérailles de l'aristocratie. Paris: Favet, 1790.

Die entlarvte Bastille, oder Sammlung authentischer Nachrichten zum Behuf ihrer Geschichte. Bayreuth: Zeitungsdruckerei, 1789.

Erzählung der beyden Revolutionen vom 12ten [sic] Julius und 5ten October 1789, welche Paris und Frankreich in Freyheit gesetzt haben. Frankfurt: n.p., 1789.

Evénement des plus rares, ou l'Histoire du sieur abbé comte de Bucquoy, singulièrement son évasion du Fort-l'Evêque et de la Bastille. N.p., 1719.

Exploits glorieux du célèbre Cavanagh: Cause première de la Liberté Françoise. Paris: Cressonier, [1789].

Grand Détail et Relation de tout ce qui s'est passé à Vincennes, et aux Tuileries. N.p., [1791].

Historical Remarks and Anecdotes on the Castle of the Bastille. 2d ed. London: Cadell and Johnson, 1784.

Idées d'un Citoyen au sujet de la Bastille, à l'occasion d'un concours affiché au Palais-Royal. [Paris, 1790].

La Journée Parisienne, ou Triomphe de la France. Paris: Volland, n.d. [July 1789].

Kurzgefasste Geschichte der Bastille aus den besten und neuesten Berichten gezogen, mit einer summarischen Uebersicht der eigentlichen Veranlassung ihrer Zerstörung. Frankfurt and Leipzig, 1789.

Les Lauriers du Fauxbourg Saint-Antoine, ou le Prix de la Bastille renversée. Paris, Monday, 20 July 1789.

Une Leçon d'histoire, ou le 14 Juillet 1789 avec ses antécédents et ses conséquences. Grenoble, 1880.

Lettre à l'occasion de la détention de S.E.M. le Cardinal de Rohan à la Bastille. N.p., 1785.

Manifeste au peuple français. N.p., [1792].

Mémoires historiques et authentiques sur la Bastille, dans une suite de près de trois cens Emprisonnemens. 3 vols. London and Paris: Buisson, 1789.

Moniteur universel: Réimpression de l'ancien Moniteur, seule histoire authentique et inaltérée de la Révolution française depuis la réunion des Etats-Généraux jusqu'au Consulat (mai 1789–nov. 1799) avec des notes explicatives. 32 vols. Paris: Plon frères, 1847–54.

Obscuranten-Almanach auf das Jahr 1798. Altona, 1798.

Observations patriotiques sur la prise de la Bastille, du 14 Juillet 1789, et sur les suites de cet événement. Paris: Debray, 1789.

Procès verbal des premiers démolitions qui eu lieu dans Ville-Affranchie ci-devant Lyon. . . . Ville-Affranchie: Le Roy, [1794].

14 Juillet, ou Prise de la Bastille. Paris: Chaigneau, 1830.

Les Quatre Traîtres aux enfers: Dialogue. Paris: Volland, 1789.

Rebmann, Andreas Georg Friedrich. *Obscuranten-Almanach auf das Jahr 1798.* Paris: G. Fuchs, 1798.

Réflexions d'un Citoyen adressées aux Gardes-Françoises, au sujet de la belle action qu'ils ont faite. N.p., [1789].

Remarques historiques et anecdotes sur le château de la Bastille. N.p., 1774.

Die so genannte Hölle der Lebendigen, das ist die Welt-beruffene Bastille zu Paris, woraus sich der bekannte Abt, Graf von Bucquoy durch seine kluge und hertzhafften Anschläge glücklich mit der Flucht befreyet und errettet. . . . N.p., 1719.

Les Soupirs de la France esclave, qui aspire après la liberté. Amsterdam, 1689.

Les Voeux d'un Patriote. Amsterdam, 1788.

Le Voile déchiré, ou les Projets des conjurés mis au jour. N.p., [1789].

SECONDARY WORKS

Agulhon, Maurice. *Marianne au combat: L'Imagerie et la symbolique républicaines de 1789 à 1880.* Paris: Flammarion, 1979.

Archives parlementaires de 1787 à 1860: Recueil complet des débats législatifs et politiques des chambres françaises. . . . 209 vols. Under the direction of Jerome Madival. 1st ser.: 1787–99. 82 vols. 2d ser.: 1800–1860. 127 vols. Paris: Dupont, 1862–1913.

Babeuf, Pierre-Noël. *Pages choisies.* Paris: Maurice Dommanget, 1935.

Bachaumont, Louis-Petit de, et al. *Mémoires secrets pour servir à l'histoire de la république des lettres en France depuis 1762 jusqu'à nos jours, ou Journal d'un observateur.* 36 vols. London: J. Adamson, 1772–82.

Bacoi, Roland. "La Bastille est toujours debout." *Le Crapouillot: Magazine libre trimestriel* 67 (July 1965): 59.

Die Bastille: Symbolik und Mythos in der Revolutionsgraphik. Catalog of the exhibition of the Landesmuseum and the Universitätsbibliothek of Mainz. Mainz: Schmidt, 1989.

Beaumarchais, Pierre-Augustin Caron de. *The Barber of Seville and The Marriage of Figaro.* Great Neck, N.Y.: Barron's, 1964.

———. *Théâtre.* Edited by Maurice Allem and Paul Courant. Paris: Gallimard, 1957.

Bédé, Jean-Albert. "Le Quatorze Juillet et sa fortune littéraire, 1789–1902." In *Essays on Diderot and the Enlightenment in Honor of Otis Fellows,* edited by John Pappas. Geneva: Droz, 1974. 36–56.

Bégis, Alfred. "Le Registre d'écrou de la Bastille de 1789 à 1792." *Nouvelle Revue* 2, no. 7 (1880): 522–47.

Béranger, Pierre-Jean de. *Oeuvres complètes.* 4 vols. Paris: Perrotin, 1830.

[Bias-Parent]. *Catéchisme français républicain.* Paris: Debarle, an II (1793–94).

Biré, Edmond. *Légendes révolutionnaires.* Paris: Champion, 1893.

Bloch, Ernst. *The Principle of Hope.* 3 vols. Cambridge: MIT Press, 1986.

Bonneville, A.-S.-M. *Essai sur quelques monuments nationaux et d'utilité publique.* Paris: David, 1830.

Bord, Gustave. "Journal de route d'un vainqueur de la Bastille envoyé en mission par le Patriote Palloy." *Revue de la Révolution* 7 (1886): 163–77.

———. *La Prise de la Bastille et les conséquences de cet événement dans les provinces jusqu'aux journées des 5 et 6 octobre 1789.* Paris: Champion, 1882.

———. "Les Prisonniers enfermés à la Bastille sous Louis XVI." *Revue de la Révolution* 1 (1883): 61–64, 92–96, 123–28, 156–60, 190–92 and 2 (1883): 31–32, 60–64, 90–96, 123–28, 151–59.

Bournon, Fernand. *La Bastille.* Paris: Imprimerie Nationale, 1893.

[Brizard, Gabriel]. *Adresse à tous les districts, au sujet des papiers de la Bastille.* Paris: Volland, 1789.

Brutus, Dennis. "For the Prisoners in South Africa." In Brutus, *Airs and Tributes,* edited by Gil Ott. Camden, N.J.: Whirlwind Press, 1990. 3.

Buri, Ludwig Ysenburg. *Sammlung der zuverlässigsten Nachrichten, die neueste Revolution in Frankreich betreffend.* 2 vols. Neuwied: Gehra, 1789–90.

[Cabet, Étienne]. *Dialogue sur les Bastilles entre M. Thiers et un courtisan.* Paris: Bajat, 1841.

Cabet, Étienne. *Lettres sur la crise actuelle: 2e lettre. . . .* Paris: Rouannet, 1840.

Campan, Jeanne Louise Henriette. *Memoirs of the Private Life of Marie Antoinette.* 2 vols. New York: Tudor, 1934.

Campe, Joachim Heinrich. "Briefe aus Paris, zur Zeit der Revolution geschrieben (1790)." In *Die Französische Revolution: Berichte und Deutungen deutscher Schriftsteller und Historiker,* edited by Horst Günther. Frankfurt: Deutscher Klassiker Verlag, 1985. 9–102.

Le Centenaire de Jean-Jacques Rousseau célébré à Paris sous la présidence de Louis Blanc. Paris: Derveaux, 1878.

Chaussinand-Nogaret, Guy. *La Bastille est prise: La Révolution commence.* Paris: Editions Complexe, 1988.

Colan, Pierre. *Le Réveil du lion, ou Paris dans les immortelles journées du 27, 28 et 29 juillet 1830.* Paris: Lerosey, 1830.

Combet, Joseph. "Les Fêtes révolutionnaires à Nice (1792–1794)." *Annales de la Société des lettres, sciences et arts des Alpes-Maritimes* 21 (1909): 1–42.

———. *La Révolution dans le Comté de Nice et la Principauté de Monaco (1792–1800).* Paris: Alcan, 1925.

Le Comte de Lorges, Prisonnier à la Bastille pendant trente-deux ans; enfermé en 1757, du temps de Damien, et mis en liberté le 14 Juillet 1789. Paris: Poinçot, Septembre 1789.

Cottret, Monique. *La Bastille à prendre: Histoire et mythe de la forteresse royale.* Paris: Presses Universitaires de France, 1986.

Cubières-Palmézeaux, Michel de. *Voyage à la Bastille, fait le 16 juillet 1789, et adressé à Mme de G.* Paris: Garnery et Volland, 1789.

Dadié, Bernard B. "Ce que m'a donné la France." *Le Démocrate: Organe quotidien du Parti Démocratique de la Côte d'Ivoire* 148 (2 September 1950): 2 and 149 (3–4 May 1950): 2.

Delavigne, Casimir. *Oeuvres complètes.* Paris: Didier, 1855.

Desloges, E. *Almanach de la Raison.* N.p., an II (1793–94).

Desmoulins, Camille. *Oeuvres.* 10 vols. Paris: Ebrard, 1838.

Dézamy, Théodor. *Conséquences de l'embastillement et de paix à tout prix: Dépopulation de la capitale, trahison du pouvoir.* Paris: by the author, 1840.

Dictionnaire néologique des hommes et des choses. Paris: Moutardier, an VIII (1800).

Digeon, Emile. *Le 14 Juillet 1789: Aperçu historique du vrai rôle du peuple dans la prise de la Bastille.* Imprimerie de Décembre, 1884.

Doriac, André, and Gaston Dujarric. *Toasts, Allocutions et Discours modèles pour toutes les circonstances de la vie privée et publique.* New ed. Paris: A. Michel, 1931.

Ducray-Duminil, François-Guillaume. *La Semaine mémorable, ou Récit exact de ce qui s'est passé à Paris, depuis le 12 jusqu'au 17 juillet.* Paris, 1789.

Dulaure, Jacques-Antoine. *Nouvelle description des curiosités de Paris.* 2d ed. 2 vols. Paris: Lejay, 1787.

Dumas, François Ribadeau. *Cagliostro.* New York: Orion, 1966.

Durieux, Joseph. *Les Vainqueurs de la Bastille.* Paris: Champion, 1911.

Falloux, Alfred-Frédéric-Pierre de, ed. *Madame Swetchine, sa vie et ses oeuvres.* 2 vols. Paris: Vaton, 1860.

Feydel, Gabriel. *Particularités concernant la Bastille.* Paris: Volland, 2 August 1789.

Flammermont, Jules, ed. *La Journée du 14 juillet 1789. Fragments des mémoires inédits de L. G. Pitra, électeur de Paris en 1789.* Paris: Société de l'Histoire de la Révolution Française, 1892.

Foucher, Paul, and Elie Berthet. *Le Pacte de Famine: Drame historique en 5 actes.* Paris: Dubuisson, 1857.

Fournel, Victor. *Les Hommes du 14 juillet: Gardes-Françaises et vainqueurs de la Bastille.* Paris: Calmann-Lévy, 1890.

———. *Le Patriote Palloy et l'exploitation de la Bastille.* Paris, 1872.

[Frege, C. G.]. *Genrebilder aus Paris im Sommer 1844.* Leipzig: Hirschfeld, 1845.

Funck-Brentano, Frantz. "Documents sur la Bastille." *Revue rétrospective* n.s. (1 July 1889): 28–48.

———. "La Bastille d'après ses archives." *Revue historique* 42 (1890): 38–73, 278–316.

———. *La Bastille et ses secrets.* Paris: Tallandier, 1979.

———. Les Dernières Années de la Bastille d'après de nouveaux documents. *Revue des questions historiques* 32 (1898): 89–118.

———. *Legends of the Bastille.* New York: Scribner's, 1899.

———. *Les Lettres de Cachet à Paris: Etude suivie d'une liste des prisonniers de la Bastille, 1659–1789.* Paris: Imprimerie Nationale, 1903.

———. *Les Secrets de la Bastille, tirés de ses archives.* 1932. Reprint, Paris: Gallimard, 1965.

Gambetta, Léon. *Discours et plaidoyers.* Edited by Joseph Reinach. 11 vols. Paris: Charpentier, 1881.

Godechot, Jacques. *The Taking of the Bastille, July 14th, 1789.* New York: Scribner's, 1970.

Goethe, Johann Wolfgang von. *Goethe's Theory of Colours.* Translated by Charles Lock Eastlake. London: Murray, 1840.

Gonchon, Clément. *Projet d'une fête nationale pour être exécuté le 14 juillet 1790, Anniversaire de la Prise de la Bastille.* Paris: V. Hérissant, 1790.

Grégoire, Henri-Baptiste. *Lettres à Grégoire sur le patois de France, 1790–1794.* Paris: Durand et Pedone-Lauriel, 1880.

Guiffrey, Jules Joseph. "Documents inédits du 14 juillet 1789." *Revue Historique* 1 (1876): 499–507.

Guilbert, Philippe-Jacques-Etienne. *Almanach des Gens du Goût, pour l'an V de la République.* Rouen: Veuve Guilbert et Homent, [1796].

Guillaume, James, ed. *Procès-Verbaux du Comité d'instruction publique de l'Assemblée Législative.* Paris: Imprimerie Nationale, 1899.

Guillaumot, Henri. *Exploits des Révolutionnaires pendant le mois de juillet.* Reims: Imprimerie Coopérative, [1875]. Special issue of the series Causerie du dimanche.

Herding, Klaus, and Rolf Reichardt. *Die Bildpublizistik der Französischen Revolution.* Frankfurt: Suhrkamp, 1989.

Hodde, Lucien de la. "La Prise de la Bastille." In *Strophes et chansons politiques.* Paris: Wiart, 1845. 425–27.

Jean Paul. *Der Komet. Sämtliche Werke.* 1st ser., vol. 15. Weimar: Böhlau, 1937.

Jeanvrot, Victor. *Le 14 Juillet: Histoire de la fête nationale et de la prise de la Bastille.* Paris: Charavay, 1886.

Kircheisen, Friedrich Max. *The Grim Bastille.* London: Hutchinson, 1930.

Knigge, Adolph Freiherr von. *Aus einer alten Kiste: Originalbriefe, Handschriften and Dokumente aus dem Nachlass eines bekannten Mannes.* Ed. Hermann Klencke. Leipzig: Kollmann, 1853.

Lacroix, Jean Bernard. "Fêtes révolutionnaires." *Annales de Haute Provence* 307 (first trimester 1989): 351–68.

Lacroix, Sigismond, and René Farge, eds. *Actes de la Commune de Paris pendant la Révolution.* 1st ser., 6 vols., 2d ser., 8 vols., index. Paris: Cerf, 1894–1942.

Lahautière, Richard. *Deux Sous pour les Bastilles, s'il vous plaît.* Paris: Fiquet, 1840.

Landes, Pierre. *Discours aux Welches* [Dijon, 1790]. Reprinted in "L'Avocat Landes et le *Discours aux Welches:* Contribution à l'étude du parti aristocrate à Dijon au début de la Révolution," by Jean Dagey. *Annales de Bourgogne* 4 (1932): 55–68.

[Latude, Henri Masers de]. *Histoire d'une détention de trente-neuf ans dans les prisons d'Etat, écrite par le prisonnier lui-même.* Amsterdam, 1787.

Latude, Henri Masers de, and Simon-Nicolas-Henri Linguet. *Memoirs of the Bastille.* Translated by J. Whitham and S. F. Mills Whitham. London: Routledge, 1927.

Leibniz, Gottfried Wilhelm. *Correspondenz von Leibniz und Prinzessin Sophie*. Edited by Onno Klopp. 3 vols. Hannover: Klindworth, 1873.

Lély, Gilbert. *The Marquis de Sade: A Biography*. New York: Grove Press, 1961.

Lembert, A. *Rede für die Feier des 14. Juli, gehalten zu Mainz am 26. Messidor, Jahr VI.* [Mainz, 1798].

Lemoine, Henri. *Le Démolisseur de la Bastille* [Palloy]: *La Place de la Bastille, son histoire de 1789 à nos jours*. 2d ed. Paris, 1930.

Le Petit, Claude. *Oeuvres libertines*. Edited by Frédéric Lachèvre. Paris: Capiomont, 1918.

Linguet, Simon-Nicolas-Henri. *Denkwürdigkeiten der Bastille.* . . . Berlin: Unger, 1783.

—————. *Mémoires sur la Bastille et sur la détention de M. Linguet, écrits par lui-même*. London: Spilsbury, 1783.

—————. *Memoirs of the Bastille*. Edited by Edmund Goldsmid. 4 vols. Edinburgh: Private, 1884.

Lüsebrink, Hans-Jürgen. "La Bastille, château gothique." *Europe* 62 (1984): 104–12.

—————. "Evénement dramatique et dramatisation théâtrale: La Prise de la Bastille sur les tréteaux français et étrangers (1789–1799)." *Annales historiques de la Révolution française* 275 (January–March 1989): 337–55.

—————. "Oralität und Textfiliation in rezeptionspragmatischer Perspektive: Soziokulturelle Fallstudien zur Konstitution populärer Druckschriften und zur Rezeption der 'Mémoires' von Latude in den Jahren 1787–93." In *Zur Geschichte von Buch und Leser im Frankreich des Ancien Régime: Beiträge zu einer empirischen Rezeptionsforschung*, edited by Günter Berger. Rheinfelden: Schäuble-Verlag, 1986. 111–43.

—————. "Die 'Vainqueurs de la Bastille': Kollektiver Diskurs und individuelle 'Wortergreifungen.' " In *Die Französische Revolution als Bruch des gesellschaftlichen Bewusstseins*, edited by Reinhart Koselleck and Rolf Reichardt. Munich: Oldenbourg, 1988. 321–57.

—————. "Votivbilder der Freiheit—der 'Patriote Palloy' und die populäre Bildmagie der Bastille." In *Die Bastille* 77–102.

—————. "Die zweifach enthüllte Bastille: Zur sozialen Funktion der Medien Text und Bild in der deutschen und französischen 'Bastille'-Literatur des 18. Jahrhunderts." *Francia* 13 (1985, published in 1987): 311–31.

Lüsebrink, Hans-Jürgen, and Rolf Reichardt. "La Bastille dans l'imaginaire social de la France à la fin du XVIIIe siècle (1774–1799)." *Revue d'histoire moderne et contemporaine* 30 (1983): 196–234.

—————. "La Prise de la Bastille comme événement total: Jalons pour une théorie historique de l'événement à l époque moderne." In *L'Evénement: Actes du Colloque organisé à Aix-en-Provence par le Centre méridional d'histoire sociale, les 16, 17 et 18 septembre 1983*. Aix-en-Provence: Publications de L'Université de Provence-Marseille: Jeanne Lafitte, 1986. 77–102.

—————. "Les Récits du 14 juillet en France et en Allemagne." In *L'Image de la Révolution Française*. 4 vols. Paris: Pergamon Press, 1989. 1:315–24.

Mauclerc. *Le Langage des murs, ou les Cachots de la Bastille dévoilant leurs secrets*. Paris: Lefèbre, 1789.

[Mercier, Louis-Sébastien]. *Entretiens sur le Palais-Royal*. Utrecht: Buisson, 1786.

Mercier, Louis-Sébastien. *Memoirs of the Year Two Thousand Five Hundred.* 2 vols. London: Robinson, 1772.

Michelet, Jules. *History of the French Revolution.* Translated by Charles Cook. Edited by Gordon Wright. Chicago: University of Chicago Press, 1967.

Mirabeau, Honoré-Gabriel de Riquetti, Count. *Des lettres de cachet et des prisons d'Etat.* 2 vols. [Supposedly] Hamburg, 1782.

———. *Enquiries Concerning Lettres de Cachet: The Consequences of Arbitrary Imprisonment.* Dublin: Whitestone, Byrne, Cash, Moore, and Jones, 1787.

Mistler, Jean. *Le 14 Juillet.* Paris: Hachette, 1963.

Monteil, Edgar. "Le 14 Juillet." *Le Bonhomme limousin,* 11 July 1901.

N., Henri, and Théodore N. *La Prise de la Bastille: Gloire populaire.* . . . Directed by Adolphe Franconi. Music by M. Sergent. Paris: P. J. Hardy, 1830.

Navier, Claude-Bernard. "Discours de M. Navier." In *Procès-Verbal de ce qui s'est passé à la séance du 13 novembre 1790, de l'Assemblée Administrative du Département de la Côte d'Or: À l'occasion de l'ouverture des caisses renfermant le modèle de la Bastille.* . . . Dijon: Capel, 1790. 12–16.

Palloy, Pierre-François. *Adresse à la Convention nationale, le 26 Vendémiaire, l'an II.* Paris: Imprimerie Renaudière Jeune, 1794.

———. *Adresse aux Représentants du Peuple, le 15 Messidor, l'an II.* Paris, 1794.

———. "Discours prononcé à l'Assemblée Nationale Législative, le Vendredi 7 octobre, troisième année de la Liberté." In *Adresse à l'Assemblée Nationale Législative.* [Paris, 1791]. 3–8.

———. *Discours prononcé à la société de Sceaux-l'Unité, le 10 Frimaire, l'an II.* [Paris]: Imprimerie Renaudière, [30 October] 1793.

———. *Eloge, Discours, Lettres et vers, adressés à la section du Théâtre-Français.* Paris, 1793.

———. "Mes Frères, mes amis, mes Concitoyens." N.p., [1792].

———. *Pétition faite à la barre de la Convention nationale, le août 1793.* Paris, 1793.

———. *Les XVI Commandements Patriotiques, par un vrai Républicain.* [Paris, 1794].

Parein, Pierre-Mathieu. *Les Crimes des Parlements, ou les Horreurs des prisons judiciaires dévoilées.* Paris, 1791.

———. *La Prise de la Bastille, fait historique en three actes en prose, et mêlé d'ariettes.* Paris: Girardin, 1791.

Parein, Pierre-Mathieu, and Antoine Estienne. *Appel à l'Assemblée Nationale, à celle de la Commune, et aux Districts de Paris, Pour et aux nom des Volontaires Nationaux de la Bastille.* Paris: Imprimerie Momoro, 1789.

Passerieu, Jean Bernard. *Les Lundis révolutionnaires: Historique anecdotique de la Révolution française, 1789.* 3d ed. Paris: Librairie Française, 1884.

Petitfils, Jean-Christian. *La Vie quotidienne à la Bastille du moyen-âge à nos jours.* Paris: Hachette, 1975.

Poncins, Léon de, and Gabriel Léon de Montaigne. *La Prise de la Bastille.* Paris: Librairie de la Société Bibliographique, 1876.

Protokoll des internationalen Arbeiter-Congresses zu Paris, abgehalten vom 14. bis 20. Juli 1889. Nuremberg: Wörlein und Co., 1890.

Quétel, Claude. *La Bastille: Histoire vraie d'une prison légendaire.* Paris: Laffont, 1989.

———. *De Par le Roy: Essai sur les lettres de cachet.* Toulouse: Privat, 1981.

———. *Escape from the Bastille: The Life and Legend of Latude.* New York: St. Martin's Press, 1990.

Ravaisson-Mollien, François, ed. *Archives de la Bastille.* 19 vols. Paris: Durand and Pedone-Lauriel, 1866–1904.

Reichard, Heinrich Ottokar. "Die sächsischen Bauernunruhen, 1790." Anonymous essay partly copied from Liebenroth. In *Revolutions-Almanach von 1793.* Göttingen, 1792. 58–80.

Reichardt, Rolf. "Bastille." In *Handbuch politisch-sozialer Grundbegriffe in Frankreich, 1680–1820.* Edited by Reichardt and Eberhard Schmitt. Munich: Oldenbourg, 1988. No. 9, 7–74.

———. "Bastillen in Deutschland? Gesellschaftliche Aussenwirkungen der Französischen Revolution am Beispiel des Pariser Bastillesturms." In *Deutschland und Europa in der Neuzeit: Festschrift für Karl Otmar Freiherr von Aretin zum 65. Geb.,* edited by Ralph Melville et al. 2 vols. Stuttgart: Steiner, 1988. 419–67.

———. "Die Bildpublizistik zur 'Bastille,' 1715 bis 1880." In *Die Bastille* 23–70.

———. "Politische Druckgraphik in der Französischen Revolution: Die Bildwelt der 'Bastille' als Beispiel." *Marxistische Studien: Jahrbuch des IMSF* 14 (1988): 243–72.

———. "Prints: Images of the Bastille." In *Revolution in Print: The Press in France 1775–1800,* edited by Robert Darnton and Daniel Roche. Berkeley: University of California Press, 1989. 223–51.

———. "Prise et démolition des 'bastilles marseillaises'—Evénement symbole révolutionnaire." In *Marseille en Révolution,* edited by Claude Badet. Marseille: Editions Rivages/Musées de Marseille, 1989. 53–67.

Renneville, Constantin de. *Entlarvte Französische Inquisition oder Geschichte der Bastille.* 4 vols. Nuremberg: Felssecker, 1715–26.

———. *L'Inquisition françoise, ou l'Histoire de la Bastille.* Amsterdam: Roger, 1715. English trans.: *The French Inquisition; or, The History of the Bastille in Paris, the State Prison in France.* London: Bell, 1715.

Rigby, Edward. *Dr. Rigby's Letters from France &c in 1789.* Edited by Lady Eastlake. London: Longman, Green, and Co., 1880.

Robert, Clémence. *Les Mystères de la Bastille.* Paris: Calmann-Lévy, 1878.

Robert, comte de Paradès. *Mémoires secrets de Robert, comte de Paradès, écrits par lui au sortir de la Bastille.* N.p., [spring] 1789.

———. *Secret Memoirs of Robert, Count de Paradès.* London: Baldwin, 1791.

Rolland, Romain. "The Fourteenth of July." In *The Fourteenth of July and Danton.* Authorized translation by Barret H. Clark. New York: Henry Holt and Co., 1918. 13–132.

———. "Quatorze Juillet 1789 et 1936." *Europe* 163 (15 July 1936): 293–97.

Rossignol, Jean. *La Vie véritable du citoyen Jean Rossignol vainqueur de la Bastille et général en chef des armées de la République dans la guerre de Vendée (1759–1802), publiée sur les écritures originales, par Victor Barrucaud.* Paris: Plon, 1896.

Rudé, George. *The Crowd in the French Revolution.* Oxford: Clarendon Press, 1959.

Schulin, Ernst. *Die französische Revolution.* Munich: Beck, 1988.

Schulze, Winfried. *Der 14. Juli 1789. Biographie eines Tages.* Stuttgart: Klett-Cotta, 1989.

[Servan, Antoine-Joseph-Michel de]. *Apologie de la Bastille, pour servir de réponse aux Mémoires de M. Linguet sur la Bastille.* Kehl and Lausanne: Lacombe, 1784.

Sorel, Alexandre. Envoi d'une pierre de la Bastille à la ville de Compiègne. *Bulletin de la Société historique de Compiègne* 6 (1884): 64–77.

Stewart, John Hall. "The Fall of the Bastille on the Dublin Stage." *Journal of the Royal Society of Antiquaries of Ireland* 84 (1954): 78–89.

Sue, Eugène. *Les Mystères du peuple, ou Histoire d'une famille de prolétaires à travers les âges.* Vol. 13, *Le Sabre d'Honneur, ou Fondation de la République française, 1715–1851.* Paris: Administration de la Librairie, [1857].

Thilorier, Jean-Charles. *Mémoire pour le comte de Cagliostro, accusé, contre M. le Procureur Général, accusateur, en présence de M. le Cardinal de Rohan, de la Comtesse de la Motte, & autres Co-Accusés.* N.p.: Lattin, 1786.

Trénard, Louis. "Les Fêtes révolutionnaires dans une région-frontière: Nord-Pas-de-Calais." In *Les Fêtes de la Révolution,* edited by Jean Erhard and Paul Viallaneix. Paris: Société des Etudes Robespierristes, 1977. 191–221.

Trenck, Friedrich Freiherr von. *Geschichte der französischen Revolution.* In *Sämtliche Schriften.* Strasbourg, 1791. 9:25–236.

Villencour. *Harangue aux Héros parisiens.* Paris, 1789.

Voltaire, François-Marie Arouet. *The Age of Louis XIV.* 2 vols. London: Dodsley, 1753.

———. *Oeuvres complètes.* Edited by Louis Moland. 52 vols. Paris: Garnier, 1883–85.

———. *The Works of Voltaire.* 43 vols. Paris: Dumont, 1901.

INDEX OF PERSONS, PLACES, AND TERMS

absolutism, 19
Achard, 229
Aix-en-Provence, 136–37
Alègre, 113, 209
Alpes-Maritimes, 122, 144–45, 197
Alsace, 144, 199
Amiens, 239
Angers, 231
Angoulême, 103
Anna of Austria, 15
Annecy, 211
Argençon, de, 13
Argout, 224
aristocracy, 159, 166. See also conspiracy: aristocratic
Arné, 87–88, 90–93, 159
Arnould, 207f., 215
Arsenal, 42
Artois, Count de, 46, 150, 187
Aubespry, 115
Augé, 212
August 10, 1792, 129, 162

Babeuf, 40
Bailly, 46, 87, 95, 120, 187
barbarism, 20, 64, 66
Barnave, 136
Basch, 235
Bassenge, 23
Basses-Alpes, 136
Bastille: combative potential of, 238–39; as emblem, 25, 206–7; as hell, 12, 21, 64, 110, 144; march to, 57–61; medical care in, 31; as place of inquisition, 9, 34; replicas of, 133, 148, 151, 155; site of, 123, 128, 165, 221; as social knowledge, 47; stones of, 120–23, 126, 131–39; victors of (see Vainqueurs). See also Bastille as symbol; Place de la Bastille
Bastille as symbol, 4–5, 146, 180, 184, 241; ambiguity of, 4, 73; of despotism, 4, 19–23; double symbolism of, 73; emotional appeal of, 5, 23–24, 37, 235; of freedom, 4, 123; graphic versions of, 242; iconicity of, 4, 13, 33; mobilizing effect of, 169–70; motivatedness of, 4, 7, 32; power of, 25, 37; semantic secondary of, 4, 7
Bayreuth, 189
Beaumarchais, 35
Beaupoil de Saint-Aulaire, 113
Beausset, 177
Beffroy de Reigny, 48–49, 52–53, 58, 60, 67, 72, 77, 101, 110
Belèze, 213
Belle-Isle, Count of, 31
Belliard, 101
Béranger, 48, 220
Berkeley, 26
Bernaville, 9, 43
Berthet, 210

Bertrand, 213
Bessin, 89–90
Bezenval, 59
Bicêtre, 106, 112, 210
Birmingham, 182
Blanc, 215
Blanchot, 212–13
Bloch, 2
Blois, 137
Böhmer, 23
Bonaparte, Lucien, 157, 162
Bonaparte, Napoléon. *See* Napoléon
Bonnechose, 213
Bonneville, 221–22
Bordeaux, 79, 137, 139, 172
Boucheron, 58, 102
Bourdon, 92, 94
Bourdon des Planches, 92
Brest, 171
Breteuil, Baron de, 25, 39
Brissot, 30
Brittany, 155, 172
Brizard, 101
Broglie, Marshal de, 55, 76
Brunoy, 172
Brussels, 129, 144
Brutus, 123, 149
Brutus, D., 245–46
Bucquoy (de Manican), 12, 208
Burgundy, 12, 142
Buri, 185, 188–89

Cabet, 225–26
cachot, 8, 11, 30, 209
Caen, 105
cages de fer, 18
Cagliostro, 24–25, 208, 212
Calvados, 118
Calvet, 177
Campan, 35
Campe, 110, 183
Canu, 114
Caraman, 175
Carra, 36, 82–83, 108–9, 190
Cattenom, 2
celebrations/festivals commemorating

July 14, 1, 89, 105, 123, 147–69, 182,
  194, 197, 226–39, 243; in 1790 (Festival
  of the Federation), 153–54, 156, 238;
  in 1798, 195; in 1800, 156; in 1880, 231;
  centennial, 206, 231–32; bicentennial,
  244
Cercle Social, 83
Chaillot, 46
Châlons, 111
Chambéry, 144
Chamillard, 15
Champ de Mars, 39, 123, 154
Champs-Elysées, 154, 244
Charenton, 32, 43, 112, 115
Charles X, 205, 221
Chausolles, 213
Chirac, 238
Cholat, 58, 102f.
Choublier, 212
citizens' crown, 68, 87, 114
Citoyens-Soldats, 94, 96, 99, 104–5, 146,
  156, 188
cockade, 46–47, 56, 172, 191
Coeuret, 207
Colan, 221–22
Collot d'Herbois, 129
Combet, 217–18
Comeyras, 113
Conciergerie, 41
Condé, Prince of, 76, 104
conspiracy, 142, 150, 176, 213–14; aris-
  tocratic, 76–77, 157, 171, 175; fear of,
  44, 56, 159, 171, 213–14; plans for, 54,
  77–78; rumors of, 150, 213
Constituent Assembly, 46, 116, 123, 132
Conti, 93
convulsionnaires, 16–17
Corbet, 35
Corday, 122
Corrèze, 254
Cosson, 196
Côte d'Or, 140, 142f.
Couret, 207, 215
Crébillon (fils), 27
Cretaine, 87
crime de lèze-majesté, 46, 104

critique of the system, 19
Crosne, 35
Cross of St. Louis, 64, 68
crown prince, 131
Cubières-Palmézeaux, 73, 101, 110
culture: popular, 127, 131; elite, 131;
   political, 205
Curtius, 40, 57, 68, 111

Dadié, 245
Damiens, 107
Danton, 241
Daveau, 155
Davy de Chavigné, 168
Déduit, 57
Delavigne, 221
Dénot, 44, 102f.
Désaugiers, 155
Desbarreaux, 163
Desenne, 81
Desmond, 87
Desmoulins, 40, 45, 56, 83, 190, 213–14,
   218–19
despotism, 19–23, 25, 27, 33, 53–54, 57,
   63–66, 69, 72, 74, 77, 81–84, 100, 121,
   123, 134, 143–44, 146, 150, 152–53, 157,
   159, 165–66, 175, 180, 183f., 195, 206–7,
   209, 214, 222, 225, 234, 241, 243
diamond necklace, affair of, 23, 28
Diderot, 27, 101, 104, 218
Digeon, 231
Digne, 136
Dijon, 139–43
Doinet, 178
Dôle, 93
Douai, 155
drama, 178, 188, 242; political, 92, 156.
   See also Combet; Désaugiers; Parein;
   Rolland
Dreux, 36
Dublin, 181–82
Dubois, 86, 89
Ducoudray, 212
Ducourneau, 209
Dufey, 206, 215
Dumas, 130, 217

Dumas (père), 211
Du Puget, 35
Duruy, 212
Dusaulx, 48, 75, 87, 94, 98, 104–5, 115,
   120, 133
Dyle, 144

1830, 169, 206
Elie, 43–44, 92, 96, 214
Epernay, 129
Erlangen, 187
Estrade, Count de, 67
Eure, 163
Evreux, 163

family honor, 27
family interests, 31
Faubourg Saint-Antoine, 6, 35, 40, 59,
   90, 95, 106, 126, 132, 148–49, 151–52,
   164, 171, 219, 221
Fauchet, 94, 149–50, 159–60, 164
Fausset, 98
fear. See conspiracy
Festival of Freedom, 129
Festival of Reason, 126
Festival of the Supreme Being, 126
flag: with the Bastille motif, 148, 151,
   170; of the nation, 177. See also tricolor
Flesselles, 41–42, 61, 189, 214, 217
Fleurus, 16
Fleury, 16
Forcalquier, 156
formation of meaning, 53, 77–78, 131
Fougeret, 206
Fouquet, 6
Frankfurt, 185, 188, 194
freedom, 72, 74, 80, 100, 123, 127, 144,
   146, 162, 166, 217–18, 221–22, 229,
   241–42; Apostles of Freedom, 120,
   134, 136–40, 144, 146, 220; Festival
   of Freedom, 129; Freedom Square
   (Place de la Liberté), 166; guarantor
   of, 122; martyrs of, 178, 205, 210, 233;
   monument of, 122; principle of, 215;
   relics of, 120
Frege, 168

French Revolution, 5, 30, 205, 225
Fréret, 27
Fréron, 83

Gabourd, 212
Gambetta, 227–28
Gautier, 49, 52–53
Gautier, T., 222
Gémier, 219
George I, 9
Geradmer, 239
Gesmold, 191
Gilbert, 212
Goethe, 198
Gonchon, 152
Gorsas, 48, 83–84, 93, 139, 143, 189
Gotha, 191
Göttingen, 194
governor of the Bastille, 103, 186, 213. *See also* Launay
Grande Peur, 44
Grégoire, 145
Grenoble, 155, 157, 207
Grévy, 229
Grosvenor, Lord, 114
Guadeloupe, 122
Guèye, 245
Guyton de Morveau, 142

The Hague, 12, 48
Halem, von, 110, 185
Hamburg, 185, 191–95, 198
Hanau, 185
Hardy, 46, 148, 150
Harny, 99, 190
Haschka, 191
Hébert, 169; Hébertists, 126
Helvétius, 103–4
Henri IV, 26
Hercules, 86
heroes/victors of the Bastille. *See* Vainqueurs
heroic action, 190, 209
heroes' monument, 221–22
Hirschtal, 3

Hitler, 236f.
Hoche, 219
Holbach, 30
Holland, 9, 182
Howard, 18
Hugues, 229
Hulin, 43–44, 58, 87, 92, 159, 214, 217, 219
Humbert, 90–93, 101–4

Invalides, 41, 57, 61
Isis, 168

Jacob, 139
Jagot, 145
Janinet, 49, 53
Jansenism, 16
Jean Paul, 198
Jemmapes, 144, 164
Jesuits, 16
July 14, 89, 126, 139; anniversaries of, 83; day of liberation, 108; great day of, 72, 129, 211; in 1790, 123, 125, 147, 229; speeches for, 144–45, 158; symbolism of, 134, 143–44, 159. *See also* celebrations
July Column, 1, 168–69, 222, 235
July Revolution, 206, 220–21, 224
Jungk, 2
Juvenal, 104

Kassel, 194; state prison, 191
Klopstock, 194–95
Knigge, 194–95
Krivine, 244

La Beaumelle, 20, 27, 31
Lacroix, 113
La Crosnière, 87
Lafargue, 233
La Fayette, 46, 86–87, 95, 120, 154, 187, 221, 224, 241
La-Ferté-sous-Jouarre, 227
La Force, 41
La Grey, 87

La Harpe, 116
Lajoinie, 2
Lally, 20
Lambesc, 41, 56, 76
Lamoignon, 54
Lamothe-Valois, 23
Landes, 140
Langlois, 163
Langres, 90, 101
Languedoc, 106
La Porte, 15, 208
La Reynie (de la Bruyère), 58, 94, 103
La Rochefoucauld, G., 224
La Rochefoucauld-Liancourt, 214, 224
Lasource, 116
Latude, 7, 13, 25, 31, 77, 112–18, 120, 133, 168, 170, 183, 190, 206–7, 209–10, 212, 216, 228, 233, 242
Launay, Marquis de, 40, 42–45, 59–67, 86, 103, 149–50, 157, 188–89, 196, 214, 217, 219, 227
Lausanne, 182
Laval, 236–37
L'Averdy, 210
Lavisse, 212
Lebrenn, 211
Lefevre, 41
Lefranc, 212
Le Gros, 134–40, 144
Legros, Mme., 112, 114, 216
Leibniz, 12
Leipzig, 194
Lembert, 196–97
Le Noir, 64, 115
Lepelletier, 123
Le Petit, 6
Leprévôt de Beaumont, 117, 210–11
Letellier, 212
Letourmi, 49
lettres de cachet, 7, 17, 19, 21, 25–26, 28, 35–36, 112–13, 141
Leviticus, 122
Leynadier, 207, 209
liberty. See freedom
Liège, 48, 182–83

lily banner, 155
Linguet, 7–8, 20–23, 25, 34, 70, 77, 206–7, 210, 216, 241
Loire, 137
London, 9, 20, 25, 181
Lorges, Count de, 7, 67–68, 107–12, 147–48, 172, 184, 208, 210–11, 214–15
Louis XI, 6
Louis XIV, 7, 13, 15, 26, 106, 110, 175, 209
Louis XV, 107–8, 116
Louis XVI, 21, 25, 30, 34, 36, 39–40, 46, 70–71, 120, 126, 131–32, 143, 152, 162, 165, 169, 185, 187–88, 208, 212, 214, 216, 225
Louis-Philippe, 95, 130, 220–21
Loustalot, 83
Louvre, 114
lynch law, 44, 63–64, 177, 180
Lyon, 139, 172–73, 217

MacMahon, 229
Magin, 212
Maillard, 92
Mainz, 144, 195–98, 244; Church of St. Peter, 196
Malisset, 210
Mallingre, 196
Malta, 163
man in the iron mask, 13, 15, 34, 77, 110–11, 209
Man Ray, 32–33
·Manuel, 30, 110
Marat, 83, 94, 122, 180, 190, 218–19, 241
Marbot, 157, 161
Marburg, 194
Marcou, 228
Marie-Antoinette, 24, 55, 126
Marseillaise, 127–28, 145, 225, 244
Marseille, 173–81, 226, 243
Martin, 92
martyrs, 27, 31f., 85, 106, 178, 205, 210, 218, 228, 233
Mauclerc, 111
Melin, 212

Menzel, 189

Mercier, 15, 33, 241

Michelet, 130, 215–16

Mirabeau, 19, 30, 34, 48, 55, 74, 95, 136, 170, 206, 213, 219, 221

Mitterrand, 238

Mons, 144

Montauban, 155

Mont-Blanc, 122, 144

Montjoye, 63

Mont-Tonnerre (Donnersberg), 122, 144, 197

monuments, 21, 36, 69–70, 129, 165, 169, 221–22; of heroes, 221–22; of July 14 anniversary, 147; national, 128; plaster elephant, 168, 205

motivation for action, 169

Nantes, 122, 172

Napoléon I, 95, 104, 130, 156–57, 162–63, 168–69, 205, 220

Napoléon III, 205, 227

national holiday. See July 14

National Assembly, 39, 45, 48, 73, 76, 89, 93, 126, 136, 141, 159, 168–69, 180

National Guard, 46, 85, 87, 89, 93, 106, 134–35, 148, 152, 154, 170–71, 173, 221

nature, 166

Navier, 142

Necker, 39–40, 45, 56, 76, 152

Netherlands. See Holland

Neuchâtel, 19, 34

Neuwied, 185, 188

Nevers, 80

Nice, 122, 129, 144–47, 197, 244

Nîmes, 136

Noailles, Count de, 48

Notre-Dame, 47, 155

Notre-Dame de la Garde, 175–76, 178

Oberkampf, 80

Oelsner, 185

Orléans, 123, 137, 139

Orléans, Duc de, 35, 40, 56, 213; house of, 45

Osnabrück, 191

oubliettes, 18, 20, 31, 217

Oudart, 87

Palais-Royal, 40, 45, 55–56, 58, 63, 67, 81, 111, 165, 214

Palloy, 73, 81–82, 84, 102, 105, 110, 113, 115, 117–47, 151–52, 165–68, 170, 180, 190, 205, 242

Pannetier, 102

Panthéon, 96, 125, 148, 222, 243

Paradès, Count de, 117

Parein, 94, 98–99, 104–5, 111

Paris, 12, 33, 48, 54–55, 72, 76, 118, 123, 126, 171, 178, 211, 224–25; city council, 171, 173; city hall, 41, 44, 46, 60–61, 106, 148, 189; fights on the barricades, 220; sansculotte movement, 152

Pâris, 16

Parlement, 100

Parlement de Bourgogne, 140

Passerieu, 231

Pau, 137

Pelletan, 229

Pellissance, 136

Pentécoulant, 224

people, the, 86, 94, 99, 102, 104, 144, 161, 216, 218–19, 225–26, 228, 236–37, 241; sovereignty of, 45, 47, 166

Pétain, 236

Peters, 70–71

Petit, 212

Petits-Augustins, 87

physiocrat, 27

Piccini, 209

Pierre-Scize, 172–73

Pirithous, 86

Pitou, 49, 56, 211–12

Pitra, 59, 66

Pixérécourt, 209

Place de la Bastille, 35, 71–72, 148, 165–69, 205, 222, 235, 239

Place de la Grève, 41, 57, 63, 189

Place de la Liberté, 166

Place Vendôme, 168–69

Poitiers, 137

Polignac, 64, 93

Pommay, 132
Pompadour, Marquise de, 108, 111–12, 115–16
Pope, 103
popular art, 127–28
popular culture, 127, 131
Popular Front, 235–36
popular justice, 63
Priestley, 182
prisoners of the Bastille, 43, 106, 110, 147, 150, 217; liberation of, 64–65, 178, 214
Protestants, 6, 9; emancipation of, 30
Provence, 173, 180
Prudhomme, 48, 83–84, 143

Quatre-Vingts church, 87
Quimper, 137
Quimperlé, 155

Rabaut Saint-Etienne, 30, 49
Raspail, 229
Raynal, 103–4, 121, 190
razing: of the Bastille, 21, 35–36, 69–70, 74–75, 120, 129, 132, 165, 235; of Fort Saint-Nicolas, 178; of the Marseille bastilles, 178
Rebmann, 192–93
Regné, 16
Reichard, 191
Rennes, 137
Renneville, 9–12, 16, 18, 20, 34, 108, 183
Republic, 231–32
Resistance, 236–37, 243
Richelieu, 6, 15, 54, 225
Riez, 136
Rigby, 106
right, divine, 27
Rivarol, 48
Robert, 209
Robespierre, 241
Rocard, 244
Rohan, Cardinal de, 24, 26, 64
Rolland, 218–20, 235–36
Rossignol, 98, 102–5
Rouen, 226; rebellion, 44

Rousseau, 103–4, 121, 123, 176, 218, 228
Rousselet, 102
rumors, 44

Sade, Marquis de, 31–33, 43, 66
Saint-André-des-Arts, 79, 101
St. Bartholomew's massacre, 55, 76, 237
Saint-Brieuc, 137
Saint-Domingue, 122
Saint-Etienne-du-Mont, 90
Saint-Geneviève, 79, 148, 151
Saint-Huruge, Marquis de, 45
Saint-Jacques, 149
Saint-Jean, 175–179, 243
Saint-Lazare, 41
Saint-Louis-de-la-Culture, 42, 83
Saint-Marcel, 16, 40, 170
Saint-Méry, 90
Saint-Nicolas Fort, 175, 178–80, 243; razing, 178
Saint-Ouen, 213
Saint-Paul, 120
Saint-Priest, 176
Saint-Quentin, 40
sansculottes, 152, 169, 216, 238
Santerre, 102
Sartine, 108, 113, 115, 117
Sartre, 1, 25
Savoy, 144, 199
Saxony, peasants' revolt in, 190
scandal lawsuits, 24
Sceaux, 125–26, 128–29
Schickele, 199
Schulz, 184
Segond, 213
Seine-et-Marne, 227
Sepet, 227
sequences, narrative, 48, 53
Seurre, 163
Sieveking, 194–95
Solages, Count of, 44, 106–8
Sombreuil, Marquis de, 41
songs, 72, 147, 154, 194, 220; revolutionary, 163, 217, 227
Sophie, electress, 12
sovereignty. See people

speeches, 161–62, 165; funeral orations, 149, 180; on July 14, 157–58
Staël, Madame de, 15, 45
Stanhope, 182
States General, 36, 38
Strasbourg, 128, 183
Straze, Count, 67
Sue, 211, 216–17
Suffren, Rue, 233
Sun King. *See* Louis XIV
Supreme Being, 126, 155
Switzerland, 182
symbol, 125, 142; collective, 5, 32, 36, 78, 81, 241–44, 246; stylization of, 60, 171, 215. *See also* Bastille as symbol
symbolic action, 25, 37, 69, 78, 157, 170–71, 243
symbolic figures, 32, 66, 112, 170, 209, 211–12

Taine, 215
Tavernier, 44, 108
theater: company, 137; Covent Garden Theater, 181; Drury Lane Theater, 181; Théâtre de l'Ambigu, 92; Théâtre des Italiens, 99; Théâtre du Cirque Olympique, 221; Théâtre Français, 122; Théâtre Gaîté, 209; Théâtre Porte-Saint-Martin, 210; Théâtre Renaissance-Gémier, 218
Thévenau de Morande, 34, 190
Thiers, 215, 225f.
Thiery, 116
Thilorier, 24
Thuriot de la Rozière, 42, 49, 87, 97
Titon-Bergeras, 134–40, 144
torture, 20, 30, 230
Toulon, 226
Toulouse, 163

Tours, 137
Trajan, 166
translation: of French newspaper accounts, 189; of Renneville, 9; of revolutionary almanac, 49
treason, 42, 217
Trenck, Baron von, 110
tricolor, 46, 155, 227, 234
Troyes, 34
Tussat, Club, 140–41, 146
tyranny, 127

utopia, 160, 195

Vainqueurs, 68–69, 86–98, 100–104, 149–50, 163–64, 178, 191, 195, 214, 224, 238
Valence, 226
Varenne, 170
Vendée, 231
Versailles, court of, 38–40, 46, 55, 112–13
Vestier, 113–14
Vichy, 236–37, 242
Vienne, 138
Villeneuve, 80
Villette, Marquis de la, 113
Vincennes, 16, 19, 26, 32, 35, 112, 115, 170, 210
Volontaires de la Bastille, 87, 94–95, 104
Voltaire, 13, 26–27, 31, 44–45, 72, 77, 96, 113, 121, 125, 137, 141, 189, 208, 218–19

Walloon, 144
Whyte, 44
Wissembourg, 164
Woillez, 144–45
writers, imprisoned, 29–30

Zévort, 212

.

Hans-Jürgen Lüsebrink is chair of French Cultural Studies and
Intercultural Communication at the Universität des Saarlandes,
Germany. Rolf Reichardt is head of the scholarly reference
department, Universität Mainz, Germany. Norbert Schürer is
a graduate student in the Graduate Program in Literature at
Duke University.

Library of Congress Cataloging-in-Publication Data
Lüsebrink, Hans-Jürgen.
[Bastille. English]
The Bastille : A history of a symbol of despotism and freedom /
Hans-Jürgen Lüsebrink and Rolf Reichardt ; translated by
Norbert Schürer.
p.   cm. — (Bicentennial reflections on the French Revolution)
Includes bibliographical references and index.
ISBN (invalid) 0-8223-1902-0 (cloth : alk. paper).
ISBN 0-8223-1894-6 (pbk. : alk. paper)
1. Bastille. 2. France—History—Revolution, 1789–1799—
Influence. 3. Liberty—History. 4. Symbolism in politics—France.
I. Reichardt, Rolf. II. Title. III. Series.
DC167.5.L8713 1997
944.04—dc21   96-51990   CIP